POSTCARDS
FROM SCOTLAND

Dedicated to my father-in-law,
Graham Whiteley (1959-2024)

POSTCARDS FROM SCOTLAND

Scottish Independent Music 1983-1995

Grant McPhee

OMNIBUS PRESS
London / New York / Paris / Sydney / Copenhagen / Berlin / Madrid / Tokyo

Copyright © 2024 Omnibus Press
(A Division of Wise Music Limited)

Cover designed by Amazing15
Picture research by the author

HB ISBN: 978-1-9131-7247-3

Grant McPhee hereby asserts his right to be identified as the author of this work in accordance with Sections 77 to 78 of the Copyright, Designs and Patents Act 1988.

All rights reserved. No part of this book may be reproduced in any form or by any electronic or mechanical means, including information storage or retrieval systems, without permission in writing from the publisher, except by a reviewer who may quote brief passages.

Every effort has been made to trace the copyright holders of the photographs in this book but one or two were unreachable. We would be grateful if the photographers concerned would contact us.

A catalogue record for this book is available from the British Library.

Typeset by Palimpsest Book Production Ltd, Falkirk, Stirlingshire

Printed in the Czech Republic

www.omnibuspress.com

Contents

Contributors	ii
Preface	xi
Introduction	1
1 The new sound of young Scotland	11
2 Edinburgh: a new dawn	29
3 Creation: the swinging sixties in the eighties	50
4 Rote Kapelle and the Shop Assistants	70
5 Back to Creation: the ascent of The Jesus and Mary Chain	79
6 Meanwhile, elsewhere in the east	97
7 As good as Ramones Records: 53rd & 3rd Records	125
8 A new era for indie music	130
9 Scotland is bigger than you think	178
10 The landscape is changing	267

11 Endings and new beginnings	284
12 Splits and ends	318
13 A new guitar sound for Glasgow	344
14 Further adventures of The Orchids, Garage and a new golden age of indie	372
15 New blood and old success	408
16 The sound of young Scotland: the beat goes on	452
Thanks to	455
Bibliography and Sources	457
Picture Credits	463
Index	465

Contributors

Gerard 'Caesar' McInulty (The Wake)
Duglas T. Stewart (BMX Bandits)
Gerard Love (Teenage Fanclub)
Norman Blake (Teenage Fanclub)
Raymond McGinley (Teenage Fanclub)
Jim McCulloch (The Soup Dragons, BMX Bandits)
Ross Sinclair (The Soup Dragons)
Frances McKee (The Vaselines)
Eugene Kelly (The Vaselines, Captain America)
Charles Kelly (The Vaselines)
Roy Lawrence (Captain America)
Gordon Keen (BMX Bandits, Captain America)
James Hackett (The Orchids)
Chris Quinn (The Orchids)
John Scally (The Orchids)
Martin Hayward (The Pastels)
Bernice Simpson (The Pastels)
Brian Taylor (The Pastels)

Sandy McLean (Fast Forward distribution)
Richard Scott (Rough Trade's the Cartel)
Alan McGee (Creation Records)
Angus McPake (Jesse Garon and the Desperadoes, The Thanes)
Jowe Head (Swell Maps)
Lenny Helsing (The Thanes)
Alan McLean (The Thanes)
Mal Kergan (Rote Kapelle)
Ian Bins (Rote Kapelle)
Andrew Tully (Rote Kapelle, Jesse Garon and the Desperadoes)
Chris Henman (Rote Kapelle)
Joe Foster (Creation Records)
Jim Shepherd (Jasmine Minks)
David Keegan (Shop Assistants)
John McCorkindale (Villa 21 Records)
Douglas Hart (The Jesus and Mary Chain)
Murray Dalglish (The Jesus and Mary Chain)
Michael Kerr (Meat Whiplash, The Motorcycle Boy)
Paul McDermott (Meat Whiplash, The Motorcycle Boy)
Stephen McLean (Meat Whiplash)
John 'Joogs' Martin (Primal Scream)
Jonathan Muir (Rote Kapelle)
Margarita Vazquez Ponte (Rote Kapelle, Jesse Garon and the Desperadoes)
David Miller (Finitribe)
John Vick (Finitribe)
Laura McPhail (Shop Assistants)
Ann Donald (Shop Assistants)
Johnny Smillie (Thrum)
Dave Gormley (Thrum, a.c. acoustics)

CONTRIBUTORS

Ian Hoey (The Dragsters)
Sean Dickson (The Soup Dragons)
Hugh Mclachlan (The Pretty Flowers)
Grant MacDougall (Splash One promoter)
Ian Boffey (The Dragsters)
Andy Crone (The Big Gun)
Andrew O'Hagan (The Big Gun)
Allan Carruthers (The Big Gun)
Francis Macdonald (BMX Bandits, Teenage Fanclub)
Grant McLean (Sunday Drivers)
Craig McAllister (Sunday Drivers)
Ian White (The Wendys)
Joe McAlinden (BMX Bandits, Superstar)
Dave Barker (Glass Records)
Katy Lironi (The Fizzbombs)
Stuart Cant (The Onion Cellar)
David Scott (The Motorcycle Boy)
David Scott (The Pearlfishers)
Janie Nicoll (The Vultures)
David Douglas McCarthur (The Hardy Boys)
Graham MacDonald (Baby Lemonade)
Chris Davidson (Greenock promoter)
Derek Moir (This Poison!)
Jimmy Jamieson (The Dragsters)
John Hogarty (BMX Bandits, Clouds)
Douglas MacIntyre (Creeping Bent Records)
Jim Barr (photographer)
Neville Street (Stella Five Records)
John Niven (author, The Wishing Stones)
Paul Campion (a.c. acoustics)

POSTCARDS FROM SCOTLAND

Caz Riley (a.c. acoustics)
Andrew 'McD' McDermid (Whiteout)
Monica Queen (Thrum)
Nick Kennedy (The Pterodactyls)
Steve Mason (The Beta Band)
Martin Parry (Napalm Stars)
Chris Connelly (Finitribe, Ministry, The Revolting Cocks)
Paul Livingston (Trashcan Sinatras)
John Douglas (Trashcan Sinatras)
James MacDonald (Ege Bam Yasi)

Preface

'This is like a crime scene reconstruction.' Frances McKee, The Vaselines, on being interviewed for *Teenage Superstars*, the film on which this book is partly based.

Frances makes an interesting observation. While not a crime scene, we are attempting the reconstruction of an era – Scotland's eighties and nineties independent music scene – and there are considerations for us to take into account when telling this story. The cognitive interview technique developed by Edward Geiselman was to specifically address witness inconsistencies during police interviews. However, despite a few unkind record reviews during the eighties and nineties, this book is not about criminal records; it's about rock'n'roll. Well, a specifically Scottish version of it anyway.

The law deals primarily with strict facts and feelings rarely receive consideration. However, for human interactions (with musicians especially), feelings should be considered. With this in mind, it is important to note that the interviews that make up the main narrative of this book were not conducted with a view to providing evidence for a court case, but to capture the fun, drama and excitement of being in a band. It's easy to think that musicians are all gregarious and love nothing more than to talk about themselves, but, in my experience, that hasn't been the norm. I've come to understand that, while I may think it would have been fun to be in a band, that perception is often far removed from the reality. For many, being young and in a band is often an intense experience where the highs of having a 'record of the week' are often countered with the other experiences of being in an independent band: disappointment, arguments, frustration . . . For some, it is remembered as an unpleasant time in their lives. Musicians invest a lot in their art.

I conducted the interviews with a sensitivity to the ups and downs of the creative process and trying to balance the truth. One of the four stages in Geiselman's cognitive technique is to 'report everything they can remember'. I think we've definitely achieved this. My approach is to chat to everyone like we were having a chat in the pub: simply put, asking everyone to tell me their story, because everyone has a story to tell.

It should be noted that this book is not intended to be a fast-paced series of snappy soundbites. I've purposely let interviewees speak at length where it felt appropriate or allowed somebody to repeat a section of story previously recalled by someone else. While this sometimes interrupts the narrative and may be frustrating for some, I think it is important to report. I also made the decision to limit our allocated time in order to focus less on things that have been told countless times before – there's little need to discuss *Screamadelica* more than has already been written, for example – and instead focus that time on lesser-told

PREFACE

tales. I've often found such stories and alternative viewpoints present a more interesting and fruitful understanding of a music scene. I have also limited descriptive text and allowed the musicians to tell their own stories.

This is primarily a story that deals with youthful dreams and there's something almost universal about small-town teenagers dreaming of success in the big city. Irvine teenage dreams could easily be those of anywhere in Wales, England or anywhere. Importantly, it's also a story about the potential of doing it yourself, perhaps the most forgotten and powerful realisation one can make. While it may seem a cliché (something I'm quite comfortable with), I think my previous description of what my earlier documentary films are about is applicable to this book: this isn't really about independent music. It's not even really about Scotland. It's about young people taking control and expressing themselves creatively, without seeking permission from anyone in authority first – it just happens that the young people in this book chose punk rock.

I hope you enjoy their story.

Introduction

The beginning and end of the first Scottish DIY wave, 1977–81

Punk's 'Year Zero' moment in 1976, as has been forensically documented over the ensuing fifty years, shook up people's worlds. It didn't matter whether you fully bought into the Sex Pistols' rallying cry for anarchy; by virtue of its mere existence, you became infected with the UK punk virus, either by your action or by your reaction to it. No one who was interested in music could escape its touch, and as punk slowly worked its way up the country, eventually Scotland was no different to anywhere else when it finally arrived.

As in all the towns and cities it passed through, punk's effect on all aspects of Scotland's pop culture was immediate, fast and confusing for many. Music and youth were the prime focus for the culture-bending effects it brought; some were already patiently awaiting punk's arrival, like UFO devotees preparing to be transported to a brave new world. Others were only too happy to have their old worldview shattered and rebuilt from the ground up. Just as importantly, a vast majority of Scotland's youth were often violently opposed to this new movement.

As teenage fists flew, Scottish groups would use this antagonism towards them, allowing themselves to be permeated by it. It developed into one of their defining characteristics, a common thread that runs through every development throughout this story, from the Postcard-era bands to The Jesus and Mary Chain, to Bellshill and beyond. It often created a rebellious desire to become bona fide pop stars, which was possibly already present, but, for some, the mixture of opportunity and the defiant attitude introduced by punk actually allowed this to happen. For others, it was simply the moment to create their fantastically uncompromising interpretations of pop music. 'We were just waiting for it,' exclaimed The Dirty Reds' Tam Dean Burn.

Outside London, the idea of punk often arrived before the records themselves. Despite John Peel's best efforts, this sometimes created confusion as to what 'punk rock' actually sounded like. In many respects, Scotland's 'Wild West' period – that brief moment between the weekly music press announcing this new form of music and the soon-to-be-established, somewhat formal rules of punk – helped inspire the exciting, diverse and fresh sounds that ensued. It was this recurring attitude of punk as a concept that would remain the overriding force driving the independent music of Scotland throughout the entire 1977–97 period. Soon, the opportunity to hear punk's stars in the flesh would be available to everyone in Scotland's major cities; in Edinburgh, perhaps as a cultural precursor to the capital's late summer arts festival, a tentative dipping of toes into the water, this opportunity took place in one of the city's grandest, most prestigious venues.

Scotland's counterpart to Manchester's Lesser Free Trade Hall moment was the White Riot tour, which arrived at the Edinburgh

INTRODUCTION

Playhouse on 7 May 1977. Unlike the more famous Manchester event, almost everyone who claims to have attended this gig was actually there. The huge venue was crowded with blank canvas youths awaiting their future. This was where Scotland's new music scene had its origins, and the attitude of and influence on the country's future bands were set by the audience reaction. Each band acted like a giant mirror, reflecting back fresh-faced teenage hopes primed for their new lives. The DIY look and sound of support acts Subway Sect, Buzzcocks and The Slits were arguably as influential to a large part of Scotland's music scene as headliners The Clash were to others. Fashion (or anti-fashion) would mix symbiotically with the attitude.

Before it fractured into a thousand tribes, punk in Scotland revelled in this brief but glorious 'anything goes' attitude. Previous musical tastes had a huge effect on a young band's outlook: rather than taking the Year Zero approach of tearing down their old posters, they would reinterpret these influences into their own idea of punk. While Scotland never had its Beatles or Stones, it did have Alex Harvey and The Bay City Rollers, whose influences were assimilated into Scotland's first wave punk potpourri. The first wave of this music is testament to the sheer variety of interpretations of punk, all based around a common thread of attitude. Scotland wanted to progress quickly and do its own thing, and as the dust of the Playhouse gig settled, this is exactly what happened.

Hilary Morrison from Fast Product described her early experiences as 'Glam Punk'. 'We weren't like London punks; we didn't have any money. There wasn't the bondage trousers . . . the look was very much making yourself look as cool as possible because we'd all been into Bowie.' This approach to fashion became

3

another defining characteristic of Scotland's independent music scene. The striped T-shirts and bowl-cut image of mideighties Glasgow can now be witnessed in the many hipster bars around Williamsburg, New York. While Fast Product is synonymous with Scotland's post-punk landscape, there was a year-long spate of frantic activity before its appearance.

Lenny Love and Bruce Findlay were two of the most pivotal characters in Scotland's early punk scene. As well as feeding teenage minds by importing hard-to-find early punk singles, Bruce realised that he could support and nourish the burgeoning local punk scene from his independent chain of Scottish record shops, Bruce's Records. Bruce had already been in the music business for years and was a highly experienced promoter, far removed from the spotty-faced punk teenagers appearing everywhere. He understood that independent record labels went back much further than the Buzzcocks' *Spiral Scratch*, which was released on the band's own label, and recognised that the pioneers behind 1960s imprints such as Immediate, Track and most especially Island possibly shared many of the same sensibilities as punk.

Bruce's simple suggestion was for every independent record shop throughout Scotland to start its own record label and release valuable cultural vinyl artefacts from local bands. This was how he established his own label, Zoom! Records, in Edinburgh. There were branches of Bruce's Records throughout Scotland, and this allowed him to encourage and self-distribute many local start-up labels – NRG Records in Dundee, Bored in Glasgow and No Bad in Fife. All before Rough Trade and Fast.

The Valves, The Exile, Drive, Johnny and the Self Abusers and The Skids released some of Scotland's earliest punk singles.

INTRODUCTION

There was one record, however, that was not only a leading light in its own right but also indicated what would come later. This was 'Can't Stand My Baby' by The Rezillos, arguably Scotland's first independent single, released on Lenny Love's Sensible Records in August 1977, just a few days before Zoom's first release, The Valves' 'Robot Love'. So much of Scotland's later musical heritage is contained within the Rezillos single, including the roots of Fast Product.

In contrast to Edinburgh's success at The Playhouse, Glasgow City Council dealt their city's rebellious youth an early crippling blow after there was a riot at a Stranglers concert. The judgement was for all future punk gigs to be banned in Glasgow. As a result of this draconian measure, the Glasgow scene faltered. It would later reconvene in the nearby town of Paisley but the damage had been done. Many Glasgow bands did, however, survive this attempt at curtailment: The Subs and Johnny and the Self Abusers eventually splintered to form Scotland's biggest musical export from the period, Simple Minds. Initially signed to Zoom and managed by Bruce Findlay, they would go on to lasting critical and stadium success around the world.

The initial 1977 wave was soon to receive its own scorched earth moment. Those first bands were destroyed as quickly as they themselves had destroyed what came before them, with the arrival of a new label in early 1978.

Bob Last had recently become The Rezillos' manager. On tour with them, Last, co-conspirator Hilary Morrison and The Rezillos' guitarist Jo Callis were able to spot potential support acts among the new, exciting bands emerging from the North of England. The Mekons, Gang of Four, The Human League and Joy Division seemingly strove not to adhere to any previously established rules of musicianship. Hilary had also given Bob a copy of Buzzcocks' *Spiral Scratch*. These were the elements that inspired the genesis of their new record label: Fast Product.

Sharp, clever, intellectual and contrary, the label was the antithesis of everything punk had quickly become by early 1978. Fast Product dared to do the unthinkable in the music industry, quickly establishing itself at the forefront of what would be labelled post-punk. Soon, the three chords and leather jackets of 1977 were as out of step as Emerson, Lake and Palmer, and Edinburgh's youth were eagerly primed to grasp this next change. 'Punk quickly turned into post-punk. The slate had been wiped clean,' announced Josef K's Malcolm Ross gleefully.

The intense media interest that rapidly surrounded Fast's new roster of bands led to a new sense of excitement within Scotland's music scene. This teenage fever was further compounded by the fact that the record label seemingly operated from a tenement flat in Edinburgh but still somehow managed to grace the front cover of *NME*. In contrast to the previous punk nihilism, this new development was nourished by influences such as postmodernism, the Situationists, Captain Beefheart, The Velvet Underground and Andy Warhol's Factory. The inner circle of locals surrounding Fast – members of Scars, Fire Engines and Flowers among them – would later be awarded important support slots on tour with the more recognised Fast acts. More importantly for posterity, they would get their own coveted place on vinyl. Scars' Fast Product double A-side single, 'Adult/ery' and 'Horrorshow', has been described by Douglas MacIntyre as 'Scotland's "Anarchy in the UK"'.

The regional intensity generated by 'Horrorshow' helped inspire many to form their own bands, venues and even labels.

INTRODUCTION

By 1980, Fast had evolved into Pop:Aural to capitalise further on this new breed of local talent that included Boots For Dancing, Restricted Code and, of course, Fire Engines. Bob took the role of impresario and manipulator even further when he became manager of The Human League, eventually helping them to achieve an international number one single and album.

Meanwhile, Glasgow's punk ban was lifted at the turn of the decade – a timely moment. It heralded the arrival of Scotland's most celebrated independent record label, Postcard Records, which, along with Factory and Rough Trade, arguably had one of the greatest impacts on independent music. Simon Reynolds suggests that 'indie music as we know it was invented in Scotland'. It's hard to disagree. Orange Juice carried the DNA of almost every indie-pop band in their first few singles: jangling guitars, a fey, foppish appearance, arch, literate lyrics, and the feeling that any song was constantly on the verge of collapse came to typify what would later be known as an entire style in itself – indie.

Postcard and Orange Juice were everything that Fast Product was not. Like the reactionaries before them, they took the concept of the punk attitude but cleverly combined it with the forbidden past of the 1960s to create something completely fresh and original. Cutting and camp, the man behind Postcard – Alan Horne – was every bit as dangerous as Sid Vicious. Postcard may have lasted for only two short years but its iconic sleeve designs and labels, and the assorted talent of Orange Juice, Josef K and Aztec Camera, have allowed it to gain legendary status.

Orange Juice and Aztec Camera would soon head for the charts and major label success, leaving Postcard to quietly implode back in Glasgow. Entry-ism and selling-in – fuelled by

Fast, Stevo, Zoo and Scritti Politti – were de rigueur now in independent music and London wanted a piece of Scotland's hit-making action. Journalists and A&R men (because they were almost exclusively men) were flown to Glasgow and ordered to sign anyone standing vaguely near a guitar, especially if they had a long fringe and checked shirt.

The lights that Fast and Postcard shone onto a new scene brought other new bands to the fore. The fantastic, fresh new pop of The Bluebells, The Associates, Altered Images and Strawberry Switchblade all had their roots in the earlier DIY ethos; the major labels smartened them up just enough to bring them genuine pop chart success. The Big Gold Dream could be achieved but mainstream audiences would only accept this if a little polish was applied first.

Before its demise, Postcard had been heading in a sophisti-pop direction with The Jazzateers and French Impressionists, albeit in their idiosyncratic, shambolic style that only added to the Postcard charm. A lot of great music appeared from this period that had strong links with both camps – Del Amitri, Hipsway and Bourgie Bourgie, which included one of Scotland's most mercurial singers, Paul Quinn. So great was Alan Horne's desire and belief that Paul Quinn should become a star that he rebuilt and rebranded Postcard as a vehicle to achieve this. In 1984, Postcard was brought to both London the city and London the major record label, under the guise of a new subsidiary, Swamplands.

Joined by friends from the past – Fire Engines (now reborn as Win), James King and Memphis – Horne oversaw some records with real promise that was sadly unmatched by equivalent sales. As a result, Swamplands soon evaporated, but it is remembered as a marvellous postscript to Postcard's history.

INTRODUCTION

Most of the white heat from Scotland's 1977–81 independent high point had burned out by 1982. The Falklands War had begun and Margaret Thatcher was soon to win her second election. In little more than a few years, most of the little brothers or sisters of that youth explosion were looking at a future that was similarly grim to the one that had faced their elder siblings in 1976.

If 1983 and 1984 have been talked of as a wasteland for Scottish independent music, that wasteland was to open up fresh possibilities for a new generation to emerge. The punk rock attitude would soon be grasped once more in Scotland and become the antithesis of the blue-eyed soul that was fast becoming associated with Scottish music. This was a new dawn for DIY records, fashion, fanzines and an entire alternative industry.

This is how it began . . .

CHAPTER 1
1981-82

The new sound of young Scotland

The second wave of the Scottish underground had its roots firmly in its immediate past. Out of the ashes of Postcard and Fast emerged an entirely new scene that coalesced and erupted to form the next part of the story. Fittingly, both of these strands were birthed from the tenement flats from which each label initially exploded.

This story starts as 1981 turns into 1982, with interconnecting new beginnings forming in the homes of Postcard in Glasgow and Fast in Edinburgh.

It's a tale that begins with Altered Images, specifically their former guitarist, Gerard McInulty, and his new band, The Wake, with their beautifully dark brand of post-punk.

The Wake

Gerard 'Caesar' McInulty (Vocals/Guitar): I started The Wake immediately upon leaving Altered Images in 1981. I was a guitarist and vocalist. I met the drummer and co-founder Steven Allen through a mutual friend (actually Tich from AI). We enlisted our first bass player, Joe Donnelly, shortly after. It was clear that Joe was only going to be with us for a brief time as we were a bit too punky for his tastes I reckon. We worked on our songs, rehearsed and played a few gigs.

At The Red Star Club, The Wake were supported by a group that had a member who would later have a significant impact on Glasgow's emerging new independent music scene.

Charlie Kelly (Secession, aka The Gift, and The Vaselines): Secession started out being called The Gift, after the Velvets song. I was the singer and we played one gig supporting The Wake at The Red Star Club in Glasgow . . . the band consisted of myself, Peter Thompson, Jim Ross and Carole Branston. We had a Joy Division/New Order type sound. Peter wanted to do a version of 'Hard Rain', the Bob Dylan song, but I think he had in mind the Bryan Ferry version . . . unfortunately the lyrics were an epic undertaking and I forgot them during the song, ha ha, so it wasn't a big surprise that I got sacked the next day mid-hangover!

While Gerard was perfecting the darker sounds of Scottish indie something he had previously explored on 'Dead Pop Stars', the first Altered Images single, another band were starting to take shape who would very much take on the direct mantle of Postcard: The Pastels.

The Pastels

The Pastels' origins stretch back to 1979, when Martin Hayward and John McCorkindale were playing in their Bearsden Academy school band, The Cheap Gods.

Martin Hayward (Bass, The Cheap Gods): John (Corky) and I (and Stephen Pastel) were in the same year at school. The Cheap Gods formed at school. Corky vocals, John and Gilmore on guitar and drums. John and Gilly were a year younger. I got asked to play bass. We didn't have any equipment or real instruments. We got interviewed by Robin Gibson for Paisley fanzine *It Ticked and Exploded* before we had played a gig. They then put us on in a community centre in Ferguslie Park, billed as The Flowers/Mentol Errors/Cheap Gods, but on the night it's just us. We play a fair few gigs here and there, get fanzine write-ups, make a demo (sadly lost). I meet Bernice at university in St Andrews in 1979. She was drumming in The Delmontes.

Bernice Simpson (Drums, The Delmontes): There was a few of us that were all into music and we all dressed a bit differently than was obvious. We met up at this student union so it was just obviously some common interests there. I was playing in a band at the time and I suppose we did look a bit offbeat in St Andrews. It was quite a straight university, quite a prestigious university, and we were probably the ones that were wearing drainpipes and kind of weird, dyed hair and so there was a group of us that just got together and we befriended each other and got to know each other. And that was how we got together.

Brian Taylor (aka Brian Pastel/Brian Superstar, Guitar): Alan (Horne) and I shared several flats in Glasgow over the years. And we eventually ended up in what became the Postcard Records place, 185 West Princes Street. We lived there for years.

Stephen McRobbie (aka Stephen Pastel, Vocals, The Pastels; Interview from *Teenage Superstars* film): I remember that there was a kind of rivalry between Alan and Brian that was probably good natured and funny, but Brian had gone in opposition to what he perceived as the slightly *Face* side of Postcard. Brian has gotten quite rock'n'roll so he would listen to Johnny Thunders and Richard Hell and the Voidoids and R&B records and soul music. It was quite antagonistic sometimes.

Brian Taylor: I was working in a record shop at that point. Stephen used to hang around. I think we got talking at some point; he wanted to start a band so I thought why not. I think it was originally myself, Stephen and the original drummer was a guy called Chris Gordon who played briefly in Orange Juice at one point and I think Martin came in and then Bernice joined. She'd also been in that group called The Delmontes who had been doing quite well.

Martin Hayward: The Delmontes had us (The Cheap Gods) as support at The Netherbow in Edinburgh in late 1980. We were drunk and horrible. The Pastels supported us for their first gig in May 1981 at Bearsden Burgh Hall. We played a few shows together and I got increasingly disengaged and when asked in June 1982 by Brian if I want to play bass for The Pastels I agreed.

Bernice Simpson: I think they (The Delmontes) were told they had to get rid of me as a female drummer, who's clearly incompetent on the grounds of being female and a drummer and my brother just said, 'Well, that's that, we'll just walk away' . . . I think The Pastels at that point had had a line-up and then that had kind of not worked . . . that was when Martin said that him and I could join The Pastels. So, we went down and kind of had a bit of a rehearsal together, and it kind of worked. And that was it really. It was just, turn up, and if it kind of gels, fine. And if it didn't gel, I don't think I would have known much different.

Martin Hayward: When I first met Brian that was the West Princes Street flat and we would go round there. It's remarkable to me, thinking back now, how little curiosity I had about the Postcard stuff which was happening then. That was when they were doing it and that wasn't why I was there. I was there to progress what we were doing . . . There was a lot of rhetoric around punk rock about three chords, you don't need to be able to play, but to me Paul Cook, Steve Jones, Mick Jones, Topper Headon . . . these are musicians. When I heard The Slits' session they obviously could not in any sense play their instruments but what they produced was still fantastic music and that combination is extremely powerful and something of a touchstone still, so yeah, I would say that was my lightbulb moment.

We knew that our ability was limited, but I think the important thing is that we didn't allow that to stop us.

Fast Product > Fast Forward: Edinburgh

Meanwhile, over in Edinburgh, although Fast Product had ceased activity as a record label, they were still active with publishing and management within the music industry. Bob Last's time was now firmly taken up by management duties and ensuring that The Human League released a sequel to the recent number one album, Dare. *This meant that additional staff were required to run the existing Fast Product business operations, including the distribution wing, the Cartel.*

By bringing one particular member of staff into the fold, a new impresario had the opportunity to emerge: Sandy McLean, a recent arrival from Canada.

Sandy McLean (Fast Forward distribution): Well, the reason I came to Scotland was I had a Scottish granny. She told me so much about the country and inspired me to want to come and visit. My plan was to come here for a gap year, for one year, and then go back to university. And within a few weeks of arriving, I got a job at Bruce's Record Shop on Rose Street in Edinburgh, and it was so much fun that I really didn't want to go back to university. I worked there until Bruce closed them down and went away. And I went and worked for Virgin for a couple of years, and I was the singles buyer there, buying from Fast Product and the companies that were around at the time, so I got to know Bob and I got to know Simon Best even better because Simon ran the Fast Product warehouse.

THE NEW SOUND OF YOUNG SCOTLAND

The Fast Product warehouse was Scotland's contribution to the Cartel, which had been running for a couple of years. The Cartel was possibly the most important cog in the independent music infrastructure. While Spiral Scratch *had demonstrated that a band could release a DIY EP, and Desperate Bicycles, TVPs, Scritti Politti and Swell Maps went one step further, providing step-by-step recording instructions for like-minded punks, there was still one huge stumbling block distancing the 'indies' from the 'majors': distribution. Until the formation of the Cartel distribution scheme, the best an artist could hope for with a self-released single was to sell it at gigs and through classified ads, or to hassle the Rough Trade record shop to stock it. In fact, Rough Trade is where this new operation had its genesis, with one of its employees, Richard Scott. Sandy explains the infrastructure that would eventually be responsible for the rebirth of Scotland's independent music scene:*

Sandy McLean: Every time John Peel played an indie record, people would go to Rough Trade (the shop) and try and buy it, and they just got so big that they just couldn't handle it any more. So basically, Richard had this idea that he could swap records with other shops – Red Rhino in York, Revolver in Bristol, Backs in Norwich, kind of like-minded individuals who were involved in their local scenes.

Richard Scott (Rough Trade): The demand became absolutely enormous. Space was extremely limited at the shop, and it made sense that we should approach the best shops that we dealt with around the country to actually help because, basically, we couldn't deal with it. We had dealt very closely with Bob Last. I mean, he started at the same time as us in '77 and I can remember going up there and asking him, saying, you know, can you do local distribution? That's how it came, just mutual trust.

Through the operation, named the Cartel, record shops stocked 7-inch records by local acts from other areas, which in theory meant that an act in Liverpool, for example, could have its record stocked and sold in London, Bristol and York. It was a simple yet revolutionary idea. And it was immediately effective.

From this simple idea an entire alternative record industry was born, one that allowed an artist such as Depeche Mode to have a genuine Top 10 single in the real charts in 1980 through the simple act of shops swapping records. Even the 1960s 'independent' labels such as Immediate or Track could not achieve this without high-level manufacturing and distribution aid from majors such as EMI or Polydor. For the first time in the UK there was a real threat to the mainstream music industry, and it was being spearheaded by a bunch of hippies and kids who only two years earlier had been lambasted as a danger to society. The irony was that the earlier front-page headlines warning the public of the dangers of punk actually did come to pass. The difference was in the semantics. Punk was beginning to overthrow the establishment by means of its independent record industry.

Sandy McLean: At the start (at Fast), it was just a two-man operation. It was basically Simon Best, who was the drummer in The Flowers. He was in charge of the operation. Simon was spending more time involved in other projects and we needed somebody else to come in and basically run things . . . Simon came along and just said, 'Do you want to come be the manager of Fast Product distribution?' So, I went to see my boss at Virgin and said, 'If this goes tits up, can I come back?' And he said, 'Yeah, no problem.'

Sandy's decision was to become the genesis of almost everything that later happened in the continuing story of Scotland's independent music scene. If Sandy had chosen to remain at Virgin it is entirely possible that we would not have seen releases from acts such as The Vaselines, BMX Bandits or Teenage Fanclub. The history of those three bands is intrinsically tied up with Edinburgh's Shop Assistants and Glasgow's The Pastels, and it would soon converge with Sandy's own story.

The way forward: Glasgow

The collapse of Postcard in 1982 had left a wasteland in Glasgow for all things indie. Much like when The Beatles left Liverpool for London in 1964, the departure of Orange Juice, the vanguard of scratchy jangle, for the Big Gold Dream in London would create a sense of betrayal, confusion and lack of direction for young Glaswegians. This was felt especially keenly as only two years earlier an entire generation had been awakened to the possibilities of music changing lives and had seen those changes manifest in the culture of their city for the first time.

A cynic may say that the reason for the weekly music press's interest in locations outside London was to sell more papers in a particular city, and this was Glasgow's turn. Regardless, the reality was that, for the first time, this coverage gave Glaswegian youth an image of people just like them being presented as pop stars in newspapers. Remarkable. This triumph of youth culture occurred merely by making strange but wonderful DIY records, which would eventually get them on national radio and television. Even more remarkable. By 1982, however, the press had moved on to somewhere new, along with the bands themselves, and Glasgow was once again left on its own.

The Pastels were not about to let the city's two glory years slip by, and they stepped up to take on the mantle of the outsider in their own, unique way. A way that would eventually help define indie as a genre beyond a means of existence. Theirs was a defiant stance that incorporated the sound and attitude of early Orange Juice but, importantly, was to do with acting in entirely their own way, without heed to compromise, commerciality or bowing to record company pressure to appear on Top of the Pops. *It's difficult to convey how extreme this stance was, especially as it came from four mild-mannered, polite youths, not the mohawk thugs portrayed in* Sun *headlines.*

Martin Hayward: It was more their (Stephen and Brian's) take on things which was interesting and I could identify with rather than anybody's individual ability . . . it was quite exciting what they were trying to do. I could understand what they were trying to do and I could see where I could fit in there.

Bernice Simpson: I never pretended to be a rock drummer. I just loved The Cramps' rhythm. For me that was, just keep it really simple. You don't need to have your drumsticks tied to your arms and held upside down to be a real drummer . . . I don't think we ever thought that we were going be on *Top of the Pops*. It was a genuinely, almost like an art movement, as opposed to a band. I think that would be a fair way to put it, and I think if you look at the photos, you just think, what a strange collection of people.

Stephen Pastel: You know, if there's something around that's really, really good, you'll always be slightly in their shadow in a way, and Orange Juice moving away, although it was a negative thing culturally for Glasgow, I think it did create space for other people to develop . . . We were outsiders to begin with, it felt like there was nothing really like us.

Brian Superstar: No one had a bloody clue, and all you wanted to do was make some records. It was never particularly serious, it was never a kind of, you know, let's form a band and have a career in rock. It just was we formed a band because we were friends and it seemed like a good idea at the time to do it. But the group . . . nothing much would happen from one month to the next. I was working through most of that time anyway. It would be 'suddenly got a couple of weeks holiday'. You thought, 'Let's go . . . let's do a tour.' It was never a kind of full-time preoccupation. I think Stephen was at college through most of that and I was working. Martin and Bernice were both at college.

The Wake release the first single in post-Postcard Glasgow

The Pastels were taking things at their own pace, so they were not the first new Scottish independent band to release a single. First off the block in Glasgow's post-Postcard landscape were The

Wake, who released 'On Our Honeymoon' in a significant step in the development of the new generation. The B-side of the single was significant for bringing another key player into the recording world: Bobby Gillespie.

Gerard McInulty: We recorded a couple of demos at The Hellfire Club, a rehearsal place in Glasgow with basic recording equipment. Next, we decided to make a single and put it out on our own one-off label, Scan 45, a defiantly independent label.

[Independence was] the whole point of leaving the previous group as far as I was concerned. I wanted to go down the independent route following a rather soulless experience on the major CBS-owned Epic label. We decided to do our single at Wilf's Planet in Edinburgh as the Fire Engines had worked there. Taking a huge risk, I wrote both songs the night before the session and taught the bass lines to Joe on the day. I'd say that was the final straw for him. Also, Steven improvised his drumming. I asked our friend Bobby Gillespie to hold down a few synth notes for the track on the flip side. The single ('On Our Honeymoon') was released in 1982. We used the Rough Trade DIY factsheet as a guide to manufacturing it. Eventually, Bobby took over from Joe on bass. I was still writing the parts. We soon added Steven's sister Carolyn Allen on keyboards and that's when we had a definitive line-up and the beginnings of an identifiable style.

The 1982 single would attract the attention of Factory Records, and The Wake became the first Scottish band to be signed to the label.

Whaam! and The Pastels' debut release

The Wake's single was soon followed in post-Postcard and post-Fast Scotland by 'Songs for Children' from The Pastels. It formed another important part of the web that was needed to move Scottish independent music forward again.

Stephen Pastel: We recorded a demo and we sent it off and we were really, really fortunate. Dan Treacy, who was doing Whaam! Records at the time, wanted to release the demo as a single. I was pretty excited by that.

Dan Treacy fronted Television Personalities, a London-based post-punk band that in many ways would become the blueprint for the next generation of indie bands. Rather than focusing on the funk and angularity of contemporaries such as Gang of Four, Dan broke the number one rule of punk music and dared to look back at the past. Specifically, back to the London pop culture of 1965–67 – Carnaby Street, The Who, Kinks and The Creation. It's difficult to convey how much of a taboo this broke in the late seventies and early eighties. Although The Jam had similarly investigated this period, Paul Weller had successfully navigated it, appeasing the angry punk masses by incorporating the danger of the Sex Pistols into their attitude. Television Personalities had done the opposite and incorporated a Syd Barrett-esque whimsy mixed with an incredibly lo-fi production sound that generated its own degree of filth and fury among the Punk Taliban.

The Pastels released their first single, 'Songs for Children', on Dan Treacy and Joe Foster's seminal Whaam! record label in 1982. While not a 'hit', it certainly became a further blueprint for much of what would happen in eighties indie-land.

Creation stories

Television Personalities would influence not only The Pastels but also another huge part of Scotland's future, perhaps the biggest mover and shaker of them all, Creation Records' Alan McGee.

Alan McGee (Creation Records): The thing that I was influenced by, you know apart from punk, was Whaam!, which was Dan Treacy and Joe Foster. So that was where I was coming from, so it was never Postcard. I mean, I loved Alan Horne's attitude to life, right. I loved that whole 'fuck you', so I liked that. And I like Bob Last's whole Pop: Aural thing or Restricted Code, I loved the plastic bags. I loved that. You opened it up and it was 'Candyskin'. I loved the arts side of that but I suppose Creation, if it was aping anybody, and it was initially, it was Whaam! And it was Dan Treacy and Joe Foster and Ed Ball, that's who.

Jowe Head (Swell Maps and Television Personalities): Dan was a kindred spirit, and he was often criticised for his low production values. There's a virtue in being primitive, I think.

The Pastels' association with Whaam! lasted for only one single but it set them firmly on a singular path. It was a path that many others from subsequent bands and scenes would follow too.

There was a noticeable shift in attitudes in this emerging generation's take on 'independence'. There was less of a desire to infiltrate the mainstream, as Fast had advocated doing, and there was certainly a growing distrust of the major label system. In some cases, the attitude towards the record industry was one of pure animosity.

Angus McPake (Various instruments, The Rubber Dolfinarium, The Beeville Hive 5 and Jesse Garon and the Desperadoes): I think The Pastels were very influential, not just through their music but also about their attitude and how uncompromising they were about this – 'This is what we do. And this is how we do it and if you don't like it, you can fuck off.'

And I think that very much people in the Scottish indie scene that I knew felt like that. 'We're not going to sell out, we're not going to try and become pop stars. Let's just do what we do and do it our way.' And, you know, sink or swim by that . . . I think that's very much what seems to come across. Their gigs were always very uncompromising. It just felt that seven times out of ten they were dreadful but the three times out of ten they would be absolutely fantastic. Just completely nail it and be an amazing band. They definitely seem to be Year Zero. As far as that entire industry in Scottish antecedents. They seem to be the people that kicked it off.

Another of the biggest catalysts within this early scene was Alan McGee's friend Bobby Gillespie, referenced earlier as the latest member of Gerard McInulty's new band The Wake.

Alan McGee: I think he joined The Wake in '82 maybe, and then he was Altered Images' roadie before he was in The Wake. So he was an Altered Images roadie '79/'80 and then '82 he joined The Wake and then he got the Scream together with Beattie – that was just him and Beattie and then it ended up becoming a band.

That band would become Primal Scream.

The Wake and Factory Records

Gerard McInulty: As I remember it, at the time of 'On Our Honeymoon's' release, early in 1982 . . . Pastels were emerging, which was a positive, and, personally, I felt they were sort of kindred spirits although it was hardly obvious as we were understandably perceived as a Joy Division style group . . . It was later in the year, when we became involved with Factory Records, that we drifted away from Glasgow to some extent. The only band we hung out with and played alongside in 1982 happened to be a prototype version of Primal Scream. It was just Bobby and guitarist Jim Beattie at that point, creating a very experimental, Metal Box-influenced sound . . . Bobby was never a roadie. It's a myth. It came from my time in Altered Images. Bobby was a mate and travelled with us to most gigs. We didn't have any roadies. Bobby helped us take our gear to and from venues as any friend would, but that wasn't his role or anything. We remained pals when I left. It was the same deal with The Wake: he supported us and mucked in but he wasn't our roadie. When Joe left after the first single, I asked Bobby to play bass as I could show him the parts, which were fairly straightforward at that point. So, yes, he was a full member during our first album *Harmony* and the 'Something Outside' single, two years in all, and, during that period, he developed Primal Scream with Jim . . . When we went to Factory, Joy Division's legend was growing, New Order were very much on the rise, A Certain Ratio and The Durutti Column were quite prominent, and a few newer groups like ourselves were just finding their feet. In terms of getting signed, the four of us went down to Manchester and cold-called the New Hormones office where we met Richard Boon, manager of Buzzcocks, but the label was pretty much on hold as the group were so busy. Then we took a fresh copy of 'On Our Honeymoon', and our second demo, to Rob Gretton, New Order's manager and Factory director. He contacted us about doing some support slots with New Order. After a few shows, and having spoken to Tony Wilson about us, Rob asked if we wanted to record something for Factory. It was the ideal context for us at the time. There was a good budget available for studios and we had complete creative freedom to do whatever we wanted in terms of sound and design. Looking back, I can't imagine it was possible to have any more control than we had at Factory. Once you were welcomed into that slightly dysfunctional family, they just trusted your judgement, paid for everything, excellent studios, nice hotels, travel, and, perhaps, offered a bit of advice if requested.

CHAPTER 2
1982–84

Edinburgh: a new dawn

The DIY distribution network was in full flow in the early 1980s, with Sandy McLean now managing the Scottish arm through Fast Product. Bob Last was still having to dedicate his time to management duties and did not have the resources to fully dedicate himself to the Cartel. Fast's resources were still focused on solving the problem of a follow-up to *Dare*, as well as extended management duties, which now included ABC.

Brian Guthrie (Nightshift Records): The Scottish end of the Cartel was fronted initially by Fast Product with Bob Last, but Bob went more into running his label and doing things like Human League. The distribution arm kind of fell into Sandy's hands. Sandy worked with Bob and took over the original warehouse. Fast Forward was a small component in the Cartel, which was a bunch of distributors all around the country, like Red Rhino in Leeds, Backs, Rough Trade in London, various ones around the country. They would take on localised labels and then make the product available mutually through the whole system. Initially, it was a great system.

Sandy McLean: Bob got us to do a stock check, and it turned out we had actually, technically, lost like three grand that quarter, or something like that, so technically, we were insolvent and he pulled the plug on the company.

Nick Haines (Fast Product distribution employee): Bob, I think, being an ideas man, thought, well, look, there's other projects I want to invest my money in, and I can hardly invest in this, which is making me nothing at best, and losing me money at worst. Or I can invest in something I believe in.

The Fast Product distribution arm ceased to be and Sandy was now left without a job but with a lot of ambition for what he thought was a success.

Sandy McLean: I told Richard at Rough Trade what was going on and I told Tony Kostrzewa at Red Rhino what was going on. They said, 'Well, what are your figures like?' I basically just copied down some sales figures, sent them down. The pair of them looked at them and said, 'Come down to York. We'll talk about this.' They looked at it and said, 'On paper, you've got a viable business. I think we'll give it a go.' The chap from Red Rhino set us up with a nice office on 21A Alva Street (Edinburgh) and put me on the payroll and said, 'I'll pay your wage. I'll pay the rent and the telephones. You phone up the record shops, get the records into the shops and in the afternoon you concentrate on creating some product for the distribution system . . . so think about what you'll call it.' Well, I thought, I was always 'Sandy from Fast' and when I called up the shops, I'd say, 'Hey, it's Sandy from Fast,' so I just thought, well, Fast . . . Fast Product . . . Fast Forward!

With no actual business or legal links to Fast Product, the Fast Forward distribution company was born. It would become one of the most important pieces of infrastructure in Scottish music. Its dual role of distributing records from UK regional areas throughout Scotland and releasing local 'product' seemed simple enough. Distribution would be easy as it was something Sandy had already been doing pretty well with Fast Product for some years. And as the original Fast and Postcard had earlier ignited a sea of DIY bands across Scotland, then surely releasing more home-grown product would be as straightforward?

Despite being able to handle distribution for the Cartel hubs, Edinburgh, like Glasgow, was itself now a city bereft of the vibrant independent and underground music scene that had been so celebrated a few years earlier. The children of that generation were well educated in their history, though, and were ready to start plugging their equipment in.

Angus McPake: Scotland was not a great place to be a musician then. We know who the exceptions are. We know Hue and Cry, all that stuff in Glasgow, and Simple Minds and Big Country and things like that, which were sort of the standard-bearers for Scottish music at the time, which, you know, I absolutely can't think of worse ambassadors for it . . . Everything that they were doing was about being popular and being successful. Simple Minds for me is interesting . . . I don't know if there's something in their music or something about them that is conservative with both the small and big C. There's something about the music that's impossible to detect in a record, but I think it's that 'we're only here for the money'. I think Simple Minds had that in spades, just in everything, everything about Simple Minds – their videos, the way they looked, and just even the hooks and the melody and the lyrics. To me that's completely abhorrent. And it was, that's what was so typical of that period in Scottish music, it's just everyone who was involved was just there for the money. And I still have issues with anyone (like that) now. I can just say . . . it's kind of a sixth sense of someone who's not here because they're interested in making an artistic statement. They're only here because they want to be career musicians.

Things would soon begin to change in Edinburgh. Much as Television Personalities' Dan Treacy had influenced The Pastels , a kindred spirit named Lenny Helsing had also been led down a path of 1960s psychedelia. Lenny would soon emerge to become the flagbearer of Scotland's 1960s revivalists.
 The past was to be the future.

The Green Telescope

Edinburgh's nascent new independent scene was not fired by Orange Juice or the west coast of Scotland jangle. Instead, it was in thrall to UK and European freakbeat and early psychedelia, Nuggets-esque US garage and a smattering of UK punk attitude. It would be kickstarted by Television Personalities' plunge into the past, too. The first band to explore this would be The Green Telescope.

EDINBURGH: A NEW DAWN

Lenny Helsing (Vocals, The Green Telescopes and The Thanes; Various instruments, The Rubber Dolfinarium and The Beeville Hive 5): From hearing 'Part-Time Punks' on John Peel's show, when I was still at school, it inspired me to kind of skip school the next day and go uptown and buy a copy of 'Part-Time Punks'. And then, a couple of years later, I'd been getting into the psychedelic kind of scene, and then the TVPs came out with 'I Know Where Syd Barrett Lives', and it was like, wow.

Angus McPake: I think the Television Personalities were a big influence on a lot of people. It certainly ticks lots of boxes in that kind of DIY sense and songwriting and sort of independent spirit . . . The punk rock ethos was to destroy everything in the past and it was all about breaking new ground and making new music. But it soon turned out that there were a lot of bands who seemed to be vaguely under that banner who were sneaking things from the past sort of through without you knowing about it. Certainly, The Cramps were one of the first bands I discovered who, to me, were just so different but they obviously had all the sort of punk attitude. But, at the same time, they were basically sneaking rock'n'roll through the back door. To me, that was suddenly like the past was much more interesting than what was happening in the present.

Lenny's musical roots in Edinburgh actually went a little further back to the glory days of 1977 and '78 and it is important to this story and later evolutions of his bands to explore them.

Lenny Helsing: I knew a guy down in Longniddry [a village on the outskirts of Edinburgh] and he was pals with these guys in a band and they called themselves The Belsen Horrors. I met up with them and hit it off really well and so joined them. We did a few gigs and a few practices, didn't really do all that much. But our first gig was at the Art College supporting the Dirty Reds, who became the Fire Engines. And then after a while we were hanging around with the Scars and our drummer joined The Visitors. And so, you know, there was that sort of association with the Scars – fans anyway, and Visitors fans. And Steve, our guitarist, ended up depping for John Mackie from the Scars for a Siouxsie and the Banshees tour in 1980. So I got to go along as roadie, which was fantastic. So you play gigs up here, and a couple of gigs down in London. So in the music machine . . . and then after that it was a couple of years went by before I sort of got involved in anything else, which was the formation of The Green Telescope.

The Green Telescope would form the template for many of the Edinburgh garage-influenced bands emerging onto this new scene.

EDINBURGH: A NEW DAWN

Lenny Helsing: The group started in December 1980 as The Great Green Telescopic View of the World, which was basically Bruce McConville and myself. We then roped in our ex-Hells Angel friend Steve Monaghan on guitar too. I was also on guitar and vocals, and would play drums too if we were in a practice room situation. Bruce would be on organ and sometimes electric piano and also vocals. But it was mainly just stoned jams up at our top-floor flat in Merchiston Place to begin with. A few months later Steve kinda dropped out, although we were still friends. It was around then that Colin Blakey joined us on bass and flute. He stayed around for a couple of years while we played our first few gigs.

Alan McLean (Bass, The Green Telescope): I think I got to know Lenny maybe around 1981 or 1982 probably through Colin Blakey, the then bass player (and later whistles etc. for The Waterboys). The GT were at that point a three-piece: Lenny, Bruce 'Lyall' McConville on Farfisa organ and Colin. I first saw them playing on the back of a float on Princes Street playing 'Astronomy Domine' and I thought they were pretty cool. Lenny at that point was totally into the whole Syd Barrett thing and had the look and mascara and everything. I'm sure there must have been a bit of overlap with Scars, Josef K, etc. I was certainly well into them early eighties and I think Lenny roadied with the Scars on the Banshees tour, as Steve Fraser who briefly replaced me in the GT was playing bass for the Scars, John having broken his hand or something.

Lenny Helsing: We shortened our name to just The Green Telescope in the early months of 1981, and our first gig took place in January 1982 at a mental health drop-in facility in York Place called Contact Point . . . We played there again a few months later. There weren't many groups in town we could relate to when we began, although after we'd been gigging for a while and switched the line-up around we found out . . . that a few other groups were also into sixties psychedelic and mod garage sounds. One in particular that we bonded with was The Prescription, who told us they'd been seeing our posters around town for a while. Through mutual friends we also met some future Thanes alumni, drummer Ian Binns and bass player Mal Kergan, who were in the group Rote Kapelle.

The Edinburgh garage scene

The Edinburgh garage scene was evolving sharply, in typical Edinburgh fashion, with multiple bands sharing members playing different instruments. The Green Telescope, The Stayrcuse, The Rubber Dolfinarium and The Beeville Hive 5 were all part of this new universe.

Angus McPake: I remember being at a nightclub which was on Blair Street, which was an amazing club. And they played The Cramps amongst other things. And The Velvet Underground as well as playing Iggy Pop amongst other contemporary things. I was speaking to somebody about The Cramps and they said had I heard any *Pebbles* albums and I'd never heard of *Pebbles* albums. And they said, 'Well, quite a lot of songs The Cramps do are originally by the sixties bands,' and that was kind of like huge. This was suddenly like, 'What – they're not their own songs?' I'd never bothered looking at the labels to see that. Half the songs on the first two Cramps albums were written by other people and immediately I had to go out and get these *Pebbles* albums. That was life-changing . . . this is punk rock made from before I was born, which, that's just exciting in itself. And God, how could punk rock have been happening? You know, so long ago?

Ian Binns (Keyboards, Rote Kapelle; Drums, The Thanes; Vocals, The Stayrcase): The Stayrcase were originally myself, Mal (drums), David Keegan (guitar) and Alan McLean (Green Telescope/Thanes) (bass). Went through a couple of changes but ended up with myself, Lenny (drums), Alan (guitar) and Dave Beards (bass). Dave Beards was also in a few other bands during the eighties, including Oi Polloi, Varicose Veins (with myself on drums) and Forkeye. I think the first gig was 1985 at the Calais Palais (Lothian Road) supporting The Rubber Dolfinarium.

Alan McLean: Later I switched to guitar when David left and Lenny came in on drums. There were a few other changes. The line-up that recorded was Ian, Lenny, myself and Dave Beards from Oi Polloi on bass. Stayrcase gigs were generally pretty anarchic events as I remember, involving a lot of noise, broken glass and being told not to come back by the management. Our set was mostly garage punk covers off of *Pebbles* LPs with a couple of seventies punk songs like 'Vertical Slum' or 'Boredom' and one or two originals. I think we really just played around Edinburgh pubs like the Waterloo Bar.

Edinburgh now had a small but fully formed garage scene consisting of The Green Telescope and The Rubber Dolfinarium, later to become The Beeville Hive 5 and The Stayrcase. And most of them would consist of members of the same bands swapping instruments, which would become complicated for future musical historians and readers. Say what you like about U2, at least they were consistent in their line-up.

Lenny Helsing: A little later we met more future Thanes members Angus McPake (organ and guitar) and bass player Denis Boyle. I would soon become the drummer for a new group Angus had formed with singer John Doc, guitarist Ross Gallanders and Denis, called The Rubber Dolfinarium. This was in 1984. They in turn morphed into The Beeville Hive 5. The Green Telescope played a few gigs together with both groups. Btoc were another group who were around the Blair Street/Niddry Street rehearsal complex who played alongside us.

Rote Kapelle, 1983–84

Alongside garage, the band that would define what would become the other half of Edinburgh's mid-eighties indie sound was Rote Kapelle, whose origins go back to 1982. In fact, Rote Kapelle would not just be responsible for reviving Edinburgh's music scene; they would be partly responsible for helping generate the sparks that would ignite much of Scotland's music for the next forty years. It's fair to say that their history and family tree are fairly complicated, but the branches certainly reach a long way. As with The Green Telescope, their story begins on the outskirts of Edinburgh, this time in Balerno.

EDINBURGH: A NEW DAWN

Ian Binns: Mal and I lived on the same street (I've known him now for well over fifty years!) but didn't go to the same school. Mal knew Andrew [Tully] from school (he lived on the other side of Balerno), who had a way with words and was a bit of a show-off, so we thought he'd be good for vocals.

Mal Kergan (Bass, Rote Kapelle): We started hanging out together and also started discovering lots of new music together such as Echo and the Bunnymen, Teardrop Explodes, Joy Division, The Stranglers, Cabaret Voltaire, The Residents and other similar bands. Then at some point during 1980 Ian suggested that I buy a guitar so that we could make some music together (Ian had already built and was building some homemade electronic instruments in his spare time – he was good at making electronic things). However, instead of buying a guitar, I decided to buy a bass as I had been really impressed by the sounds and style of J. J. Burnel from The Stranglers. I started to learn the bass, and Ian and I started to make some sounds together but nothing really concrete came of it.

Andrew Tully (Vocals, Rote Kapelle and Jesse Garon and the Desperadoes): I had a little Joy Division badge on my grey coat. And Malcolm, who was later the bass player in Rote Kapelle, came up to me and he says, 'Oh, I see you're into Joy Division.' And that was where Rote Kapelle started.

Mal Kergan: I got talking to Andrew and shortly after struck up a great friendship with him. We shared a lot of similar musical interests and we used to hang out a lot at each other's houses. It was during this time that we had the idea of forming a band, and with the inclusion of Ian we had the basis of what would be Rote Kapelle. Originally, it was myself on bass, Andrew on vocals and Ian on guitar.

Ian Binns: No drummer or keyboards at that point. We played a single gig in Wooler, which wasn't great and showed that I really, really, really wasn't a guitarist. So I was duly nudged (kicked) out. Mal and Andrew then brought in Chris (Henman), whom Mal and Andrew knew from school (though a year above them). I returned once I'd got a cheap synth (a Transcendent 2000). Still no drums.

Chris Henman (Guitar, Rote Kapelle): I was at Currie [an Edinburgh suburb near Balerno] High School . . . I think Malcolm heard I liked punk/new wave bands and had a guitar, or maybe I spoke to him at some gigs. Anyway, he asked me to come round to his parents' house to try out for the band. There I met Andrew and Ian Binns. I didn't really know how to play the guitar or any other instrument then. But I went along with the punk ethos that anyone can play an instrument and join a band . . . I tried to act like quite punk rock or something and they did too, so these guys asked me to try out for the band, you know. I don't think there were many other contenders. He showed me how to play some barre chords, and off we went. Apparently Rote Kapelle had already played a gig by then with just Andrew, Malcolm and Ian in the line-up. I don't think they were happy with Ian's guitar playing, so they got me in. Ian then moved to keyboards.

Rote Kapelle played their first proper gig on 4 June 1983, at Balerno village hall.

EDINBURGH: A NEW DAWN

Marigold Tully (Andrew's mum): I remember sitting in that hall hoping there was no one there who knew us.

Chris Henman: I was so nervous that I had a nosebleed just before we were due to play. Blood all over the place. Had to try and wipe my face just before playing. I like to think it looked punk rock . . . This was my first gig, 18 years old. A guy called Dave Cully who was at uni with Ian in Stirling played drums.

The support band, The Crispie Crunchies, were to play another important role in the history of Rote Kapelle and the overall development of Scotland's independent scene. The Crispie Crunchies were a proto Buba and the Shop Assistants, led by David Keegan, later of the more formally titled Shop Assistants.

David would also later play a crucial role in bringing Edinburgh's and Glasgow's scenes together.

Chris Henman: I had met David Keegan at Napier [College] by then. I'd been round to his flat and he played me some tunes on his guitar. He said he had a band. So I asked him to support us. Though it turned out they didn't have a name. So when I asked him what name to put on the poster, he had to make up a name on the spot, and he said, 'The Crispy Crunchies'. I don't know who else was in them, and to be honest I can't remember anything about them playing.

David Keegan (Guitar, Shop Assistants): The Crispie Crunchies was a name just made up on the spot for this gig – I don't think we could decide what we were called. Line-up would have been Karen (vocals), Hazel (backing vocals), me (guitar), John (bass), Moray (drums).

Chris Henman: I think the gig was actually quite busy, with people who were from Currie High School. Just sitting on seats and watching. There was probably not much else going on in Balerno or Currie on a Saturday night.

Andrew Tully: At this point we didn't really know any other bands or how you went about getting gigs or rehearsal spaces. For ages we just rehearsed in Malcolm's house, making a racket in the room out the back, annoying the neighbours and eventually his accommodating mum and dad! People went off to college but that didn't particularly stall the momentum because there wasn't any momentum. In a way it helped broaden our horizons; we realised that there was a world out there. We started meeting other people, going to college parties, gigs in Edinburgh and Stirling, meeting each other's friends at college. Ian had a radio show at Stirling Uni – I remember him showing us a radio promo of The Smiths 'Hand in Glove' before anyone had heard of them – he's been a huge Smiths fan ever since (ha!). I think we were just growing up finally and realising that there was a world out there, outside our heads and outside Balerno!

David Keegan: I had moved down to Edinburgh when I was 16 from up in the Highlands. And I just expected there'd be bands playing every night. And it would just be lots and lots happening . . . Josef K had just split up. Likewise, the Fire Engines. So I seemed to get to Edinburgh at exactly the wrong time . . . there was actually a pretty good scene in Edinburgh with bands like The Green Telescope and The Rubber **Dolfinarium**. Almost everyone who played in a band played in a sixties garage punk covers band and had the *Pebbles* retrospective albums, which are these fantastic sixties garage compilations. They were super-influential, actually. I think for a lot of the bands at that time this was really kind of a new sounding music even though it was kind of like all sort of cheaply recorded stuff, so that was a great scene.

Andrew Tully: In Rote Kapelle, I was singing by that point. We had me and Malcolm, Chris on guitar, Ian on keyboards and we had a drum machine for a bit . . . And then we were looking for a female singer.

Chris Henman: When Andrew was at Edinburgh University in 1983, he met Alex Victoria Taylor . . . she had been at Edinburgh University with Andrew. I'm not quite sure why we wanted another singer. Possibly she was only meant to be a backing singer at first, but I think it was because Andrew wanted perhaps not to be the only singer or front person. Anyway it worked out and she started to become more involved in the tracks and took lead vocals on some songs.

Andrew Tully: So, she joined Rote Kapelle. And we did a handful of gigs.

Rote Kapelle with Alex Taylor

Chris Henman: David Keegan used to sit in on our practices in our Niddry Street room and play the drums for us, as we didn't have a regular drummer at the time. He used our room for his own band, and also used some of our equipment, like the drum kit. Instead of paying for his share of the rent for the room, he offered to play the drums for us at the practices. Seemed like a good arrangement. Which we agreed to. However, he wasn't willing to play the drums at any of our gigs! I remember I asked him.

The beating heart of Edinburgh's music scene was the huge, cavernous, waterlogged and dilapidated catacombs of Niddry Street. Each practice space was an individual component of these catacombs. A perfect place for a new musical underground.

EDINBURGH: A NEW DAWN

Chris Henman: People would rent a room in Niddry Street monthly. It would be something like £25 per month. There was no music equipment in there, so you had to bring your own amps, speakers, drum kit, etc., and leave it there. The place was very basic. In fact, really damp, with water running down the walls and rats running around. Mould used to grow on your amp. Anyway, once you paid for the room you could kind of do what you wanted with it. So people would get together and share it and pay part of the rent. They would also use the equipment that was there, belonging to other bands. Usually friends of yours. So as David was playing drums for us in some of our practices he must have met and heard Alex.

Ian Binns: David Keegan played drums with us for a very short while. Subsequently Johnny joined. He was another Balerno lad, but a bit younger than the rest of us.

Jonathan Muir (Drums, Rote Kapelle): Andrew left school and went off to Edinburgh Uni – although I think he still stayed with his parents in Balerno. I met him one night on the bus back from town and was chatting to him and told him I played the drums. He said that RK was looking for a drummer and we must have stayed in touch about it. I remember doing an audition in Niddry Street and was asked to join the band after they had sent me out of the room to discuss! I was a few years younger than the others although we had a common point of reference being mainly from Balerno. I vividly remember Alex as being incredibly glamorous and sophisticated but with a really infectious laugh – I can still hear it now. Andrew used to crack jokes and make her laugh. I was younger than the others – still at school and quite gauche – very much from the suburbs. I once asked Alex what she was studying at university and she told me it was home economics – and she was writing a thesis on roasting and basting. I almost believed her.

Buba and the Shop Assistants

David Keegan: For me, the exciting thing was going into The Other Record Shop in the High Street and finding this fanzine [Annabel 'Aggi' Wright's] *Juniper Berri Berri*, which had articles about the bands I really liked at the time, like Swell Maps and TV Personalities. That was my kind of thing. 'Oh my gosh, yes, somebody else up here likes this.' And that led me to get in touch with The Pastels.

I suppose the first I heard of The Pastels would have been the 'Heavens Above' single, which I thought for some reason would be heavier but I really liked it. It was really honest and direct at a time when all the bands seemed to be doing something really artificial, (like) trying to be really funky and American. But The Pastels were just playing stripped-down music and they had lots of the good influences from punk, like, you know, Buzzcocks and Subway Sect and things like that . . . It was as much that as it was details. Like on the back of the sleeve, there was a picture of the band and on the wall there was a Swell Maps poster. And for me that was like, this is the kind of details that really mattered . . . that was quite important to me at the time.

I sent through to Stephen a tape of some songs I'd done with some friends who had tried to get a band together. And they really liked it and suggested we might do a record with it, which to me was the most exciting thing . . . that was like, you know, I moved to Edinburgh to make a record. And it seemed this may actually happen. It was brilliant. I went through to meet Stephen in Glasgow.

Stephen Pastel: We became friends with David Keegan – he was one of the first people to write to The Pastels and he sent a tape of some of his songs. And they were great. He was living in Edinburgh, didn't quite have his group together, but sort of had an idea.

John McCorkindale (aka Corky, Villa 21 Records): I was friends with Stephen since we were teenagers at secondary school and

I was in a band with Martin and Bernice called The Cheap Gods. The first few gigs were with The Pastels and when Martin and Bernice joined I started doing electronic music and decided to start my own label. I heard the Buba and the Shop Assistants tape that David sent to Stephen, which I liked very much. I knew Aggi from around '82 and thought it might be a good record to put out.

Stephen Pastel: I think he was looking for maybe someone to sing. He didn't really want to be the singer. And I think he asked Aggi [Annabel Wright, later of The Pastels] to sing on it.

David Keegan: So John and Moray ended up coming along playing bass and drums. And Aggi sang on the record. So it was really a sort of temporary thing. I knew we wanted to do 'Something To Do' but I hadn't thought about B-sides or anything. So we just did a kind of instrumental for it. Just like a prototype 'Somewhere in China'. And that was it really. And it was the first time I'd ever set foot in a recording studio. No idea what to expect.

The band released the 'Something To Do' single as Buba and the Shop Assistants on Villa 21 Records. Produced by Stephen and David, the group was Aggi, David Keegan, John Peutherer on bass and Moray Crawford on drums.

The newly christened Buba and the Shop Assistants played a series of gigs with their friends, Rote Kapelle, at the Waterloo Bar, a hub where much of the scene was able to play to a live audience.

EDINBURGH: A NEW DAWN

David Keegan: This was after we recorded 'Something To Do' and before Alex joined. We played three gigs as Buba and the Shop Assistants with both Alex and Karen singing, including the Waterloo Bar one. After that Alex and I parted company with Karen, John and Moray.

Stephen Pastel: It was a good experience. It was nice to record and it's good. Then he (David) went on to do the Shop Assistants.

David would change course at Edinburgh's Napier College, where he was to meet the seeds of an entire new Edinburgh scene.

CHAPTER 3
1983-85

Creation: the swinging sixties in the eighties

Like Lenny Helsing, Alan McGee had been moved to investigate the past since moving from Scotland to London in 1980. He had first-hand experience of Television Personalities and their associates, most especially with the band's former bass player, Joe Foster.

On his arrival in London, Alan had himself formed a 1960s-inspired band, The Laughing Apple, with future Primal Scream guitarist Andrew Innes.

London, on the coat-tails of the Television Personalities' sixties scene, was the exact opposite of Scotland and was buzzing with bands who based themselves on defunct pop culture mixed with a modern punk, DIY attitude. Bands such as The Loft and The Jazz Butcher. One of Alan's first moves, again inspired by Dan Treacy, was to bring this scene together in the form of a club. He teamed up with Joe Foster and The Living Room was born.

CREATION

Joe Foster (Creation Records): Alan McGee decided he was going to be a promoter for all the bands we loved, and it's like, whoa, let's do it. We were all obsessed with music and we could all see that we had the same delusion and we'd back each other up. Which is very important . . . it's important when you're kids, because if you're going on about something and no one's backing you up, then nothing happens in your life. You've got to seek out people who you feel are going to back you up. Even if someone's laughing at all of you, at least there's more than one of you. You've got a team, you know.

Alan McGee: It was in WC1, it was in a place called The Adam's Arms, and then it went on to be The Roebuck – these pubs have probably all got different names now but yeah, it was just . . . I came along at . . . timing in pop music's an incredible thing, it's just a moment that you have to get right and, you know, if I'd done that at any other point it wouldn't have worked but I came along in May 1983 and the world wanted the TV Personalities and The Nightingales and The Three Johns and The Mekons, and I don't know why but they wanted these bands because these bands were only pulling about a couple of hundred people, so they weren't big enough for anybody to promote them and give them like a grand to come and play. But they were like . . . they could still pull an audience so in comes Alan McGee and Joe Foster in The Living Room and suddenly there's a scene. And we weren't even trying to create a scene, we were just trying to put on gigs. We'd stack 150 people in and suddenly it's a scene. We weren't even trying to create a scene, we were just trying to put on gigs, you know.

Freshly arrived in London, a group of Aberdonians, The Jasmine Minks, were trying their luck in the music industry and The Living Room and Alan were one of their first connections.

Jim Shepherd (Guitar/vocals, The Jasmine Minks): Alan said to me recently that we were the first people to have trust in him and I said that it was exactly the same for us, him taking an interest in us when no one else was interested. We started off by playing at the first Living Room gigs . . . London was dead in the evenings, hardly anybody walking around. The room was tiny with a few wall lights. No stage, no monitors, no stage lighting. But what a venue. It quickly became a meeting place for the dispossessed pop aficionados. No disco music, no fake electro drums, just guitar music and a bit of attitude thrown in. TVPs, The Loft, June Brides, The Nightingales, Jowe Head, Nikki Sudden. A real humanity to the place too. Alan and Joe were great. It was like a cult punk movement all over again, but tiny and in a venue where forty people packed the place. Their fanzine was great and took the piss out of everyone, even Joe's scathing attack on Paul Weller as the 'Crapaccino Kid'. Cherry Red were the enemy; jazzy, laid-back Everything But The Girl and the student bands were hated by us.

Joe Foster: There was a lot more of a following for all these things than the mainstream seemed to realise. The reason we started a record label is because we made so much money putting these shows on. Either we're going to become alcoholics, or we should actually do something proper with this money.

CREATION

Jowe Head: Alan says, 'Jowe, I'm going to start doing a label.' Great, what are you going to call it? So, he said, 'There's this great band that I heard at one of Dan's nights, and it's called The Creation.'

Creation Records was to become one of the most influential record labels of all time, not just in independent terms but also by achieving the sort of success many major labels would have killed for. Culturally, it changed British youth and in the process would make – and lose – a huge amount of money. From the very outset it would do things differently.

Joe Foster: We weren't friends or managers of the bands, we were just like them, and they were just like us. The thing is, selling a lot of records is not the same as being a star. Ivor Cutler, a major, major important figure in literature, and we got him; we signed Felt because, to us, Lawrence is a star, that's what we're about. Our big thing was not money, our whole thing was to present our picture of the world, and that's probably irrational behaviour, but I don't really care.

Creation's first release was a lacklustre effort from Everett True (as The Legend) but in April 1983 they released a Laughing Apple/ Pastels flexi disc, which was given away with Creation's fanzine, Communication Blur. The Pastels track was 'I Wonder Why?' The relationship between the band and label was not a fruitful one, however.

Martin Hayward: I think Alan was still working at the Post Office when we first met him. He was feeling his way into what he would later end up doing, yeah running a club above a pub in London and putting out 7-inch singles here and there. Yeah, just starting to try and get a label together . . . it was just a bunch of people in London who were putting records out. It wasn't like a record company. Again, people who maybe shared a perspective on stuff but people who ran a club in London where we could play occasionally and we'd occasionally make a record for them.

Stephen Pastel: I loved Rough Trade, I thought . . . I just thought that was an incredible label and, you know, it was just the kind of thing that was unfeasibly brilliant. Both Dan and Geoff Travis at Rough Trade wanted to do Pastels singles and, with hindsight, we would have been better . . . we put out a couple of singles, neither of which we were very happy with. I mean we were so young and kind of foolhardy, you know, couldn't play or anything so needed to be extremely lucky to do something amazing and then we did some demos with David Henderson, from The Hellfire Club, and they suggested something better . . . a song called 'Something' became 'Something Going On' and it seemed to have more of a garage pop thing and it wasn't quite like the Postcard thing. It was kind of the first hints that we could do something original and really good. And Geoff Travis at Rough Trade never offered us a kind of ongoing deal so Alan McGee was starting Creation at the time and so we did a run of singles with them, and had a very kind of up and down relationship with them.

Alan McGee: I think I've just got an aversion to anything that says Pastels, so it's probably a default for me. I don't know why we ever did them.

Despite the relationship ups and downs with Creation, The Pastels had by now set a flag in the ground for Scotland's rebirth of DIY and underground music, at least on record. Importantly for them, they had also managed to release a one-off single on Stephen's beloved Rough Trade, a fully fledged release of 'I Wonder Why?', which had backing vocals from Rose McDowell and Jill Bryson from Strawberry Switchblade, another nascent Glasgow band that had formed in the Postcard flat. It also contained unspecified contributions from Dan and Jowe.

By the end of 1984 The Pastels had recorded and released 'Songs for Children' (released by Whaam! in 1982), the flexi disc for Creation that was later released as a full 7-inch on Rough Trade, 'Something Going On', 'Million Tears' (backed with 'Baby Honey') and 'I'm Alright With You', again for Creation.

While The Pastels were perhaps a little unsuited to Creation, The Jasmine Minks would find a perfect home there.

The Jasmine Minks: Creation 4

It was time for Creation to release another record, this time by their newfound Aberdonian friends, The Jasmine Minks. Creation 4, 'Think!', was released in February 1984.

Jim Shepherd: 'Think' was recorded at our rehearsal studio, Alaska, a studio that every early Creation band used, once we showed them how cool it was. We didn't have any money (although not long after this we had played enough gigs to save money to buy our own transit van). We brought our own two-inch tape with us to save money. Martin had borrowed it off someone. Pat Collier, owner of Alaska (and hero of ours from being in punk band The Vibrators), checked it over and said it was actually a video tape. But it worked okay, so we used it. Alan and us paid half each for the recording that day. Joe Foster produced. But really it sounded pretty much as we sounded in rehearsals, except for Dave Musker's organ playing. Alan brought Dave along with a horrible red keyboard, used on Orange Juice's 'Blue Boy' single apparently. I was the only big Postcard Records fan so it pleased me. The single came out in February 1984. It was pure mod in the artwork and punk in attitude. I don't think the press got that aspect at all. We were like 'Hurrah!' in that respect, full of attitude and good tunes. People are lazy when it comes to the arts and they think that a guitar can't be punk if it's not turned up full. I played my guitar hard, really hard, but it didn't have a punk sound so we were lumped in lazily with the sixties revival bands and the softer indie sounds of Cherry Red.

CREATION

Satellite City 1: the East Kilbride of The Jesus and Mary Chain, and Creation's first success

All around Scotland, small new scenes influenced by what they were reading in the weekly press about London were beginning to form. East Kilbride was no exception.

East Kilbride is a planned town on the outskirts of Glasgow, more commonly known as one of the new towns that included Stevenage and Milton Keynes. It was perhaps then known best for its brutalist architecture and less so for its music scene, essentially as it did not have one. Its most famous musical offering was Postcard alumni Aztec Camera, who had very quickly left for London. As no real scene had existed before them they didn't leave a vacuum. There was boredom before and boredom after, but young musical minds were avidly reading the music press in their bedrooms.

The Jesus and Mary Chain were initially just brothers Jim and William Reid, who had spent years making demos in their bedroom with a Portasound four-track bought with their father's redundancy money. They were soon joined in their escapist plot by Douglas Hart.

Douglas Hart (Bass, The Jesus and Mary Chain): I probably met Jim when I was 14. I used to write names of bands on my schoolbooks, and someone said, 'Oh, I know someone that loves all those same bands.' The three of us, Jim, William and me, were from East Kilbride and that's really where we started . . . and I was singing, Jim was playing bass, I was playing guitar, doing punk rock songs, and my voice is like a fucking little squeak . . . I was 14 but looked about 10.

Their lives were changed forever by a chance meeting with Bobby Gillespie.

Douglas Hart: Meeting Bobby was a really fortuitous thing and that was by sheer accident because we handed in a tape to a club called The Candy Club and I think we had seen The Pastels and we thought, 'Okay, we'll give the guy there the tape and he'll probably give us a gig.' And of course he didn't because unbeknownst to us he hated our stuff, but . . . on the B-side of the tape, 'cause we couldn't afford a new one, was a compilation with Syd Barrett and The 13th Floor Elevators . . . and he gave that to Bobby Gillespie, more for that than for us to be honest. And Bobby eventually listened to our demo and really loved it and called me . . . I mean I came home from school one day and mum said, 'Some guys called you about the band,' and I was like, 'Oh, really?' My mum said, 'I asked him if he was famous and he said "not yet".' So I thought, that sounds pretty good. So that was Bobby and I phoned him back and we literally were on the phone for two hours, you know, talking about everything, not just music but, you know, books and films, it was kind of real 'wow, kindred spirit'. 'Cause we were the three of us out in East Kilbride . . . we kind of felt like we were three freaks in the wilderness and to meet another one was . . . really important in the formative stages. And eventually he said, 'I've got a friend that, you know, lives in London, he's got a club and a label,' and we were like 'wow', and that was obviously Creation.

Joe Foster: Bobby Gillespie just decided, as he often did, that we should do something with them. And we very seldom ignored that. If Bobby was obsessed enough with something, it was good enough for us. So we got them down to do stuff and they, in some ways accidentally, caused a total degree of chaos that's beyond imagining and that appealed to us to a huge extent so we wanted to continue on with that. And that was that, and they were and are stars, and all we had to do was point them out. And push them along a bit and that was that.

Jim Reid (Interview, *NME*, 8 December 1984, with Neil Taylor): We talked about forming a group for ages but basically we were all so idle it took us over a year to get it together. We had the sound we wanted and we had the ideas but we realised that to succeed we have to get out of Glasgow because musically the place is an absolute shithole.

Alan McGee: The first time I ever met them was mad. Douglas Hart came in with biker boots, and leathers, and he looked like James Dean or something, he was either 16 or 17, and Jim and William looked as if they'd come in dragged via punk via the Rollers or something, and they were just held together by safety pins. Jim just used to soundcheck not 'One, two, three, four' – he went, 'Fuck, fuck, fuck, fuck, fuck, fucking cunt.' I was like, 'Fuck, what is this guy on?'

Douglas Hart: We came down with Murray (Dalgleish, drums) to play a few shows at The Living Room, you know, a room above a pub. The first time, I mean we were so mentally chaotic, and none of us are natural performers, so we'd had to get so drunk and when we got up there, there was a kind of weird . . . explosion (that) came out of sheer hatred and anger and it was quite intense and most of the people there didn't get it. You know, most of the regulars at The Living Room always reminded me of that scene in the original version of *The Producers* film, when they cut to the crowd after the first song in 'Springtime for Hitler' and they're all standing there like that [mouth agape], you know, in utter fucking shock. But McGee, to his credit, the minute we finished he came running up going, 'It's . . . I fucking loved it, I want to do an album with you.'

Alan McGee: Well I think William Reid is probably a genius, you know. Jim Reid's a rock star, it's built into his DNA, I'm a good manager/a good record guy. I mean my dad's a panel beater and my mum was a shop assistant so I've got no idea why I was good at that, you know . . . if I'm really, really into somebody and think they're amazing I will break you, I will make you a rock star for what it's worth. If that's what you want.

Creation Records put out the first record that made the company and it was the record that would also make The Jesus and Mary Chain. 'Upside Down', Creation 12, was released in late 1984.

Alan McGee: We put out a record and it exploded. I was on an Enterprise Allowance Scheme, that you got forty quid a week so they could take you as a statistic off the dole. And so I didn't have any money, I was just a working-class kid living in London.

Douglas Hart: We recorded that fairly quickly after doing the first gigs, and Murray played on that and then it kind of came to the point where I don't . . . it was kind of obvious Murray, our original drummer, was . . . I don't think he even wanted to . . . we had a tour of Germany lined up with Creation Records, with a Creation package, and I don't think Murray wanted to give up his job and go anyway so . . . and Bobby said, 'I'll do it,' and then there was a really pivotal point in the first rehearsal when we had Bobby on drums.

Murray Dalglish (Drums, The Jesus and Mary Chain): I left the band to do an apprenticeship and I knew that I wouldn't be in the band long. It was the right decision. I went on to play in Baby's Got A Gun and met my wife at a venue in Brussels. I think I can still get AAA passes when they're in town. Although there was some shit written when I left about me having a motorcycle accident and one from William's mind that I became a bank manager (I wish, lol). We've spoken about that one and he says he was so fucked up then that he would just say something daft like that. I hold no resentment for anything that was said, it was a way of getting publicity and I've been involved in much worse than that to get a headline.

The gigs shortly before and after the single was released became legendary excesses of chaos, violence and feedback. Lots of feedback.

Neil Taylor (*NME*, Ambulance Station review, 8 December 1984): They stopped the set after two songs. The sound system was kicked over, the audience were going wild, and just about every major paper seemed to be represented in triplicate. The two songs sounded terrible yet it was obvious that people were going to go away thinking the band was amazing – despite the fact that at the end of the evening Jim Reid was bawling into the mic, 'We despise you! Where the fucking hell were you six months ago?'

It's difficult to overestimate the seismic shift that was created in the independent music scene after the release of 'Upside Down'. The Smiths, on Rough Trade, had brought the indie sound and aesthetic into the mainstream, and to the mainstream The Smiths were the exemplar of what 'indie' was – fey, jangling, introverted and strange. The Mary Chain were a different animal altogether – loud – VERY LOUD   chaotic, aggressive and a whole host of other synonyms of negativity, anger and noise. Although they were still yet to break into the mainstream, the ripples from their early concerts and single made everyone in the music industry take notice. It also brought wider attention to Creation and set them on a course which would immediately elevate them to the higher echelons of the independent scene and set a manifesto for the next few years. It would also bring them the renewed attention of their fellow Scot musicians, especially back in East Kilbride, and sew further seeds . . .

Meat Whiplash

Meat Whiplash supported The Jesus and Mary Chain at their London Polytechnic gig in March 1985, which infamously developed into a riot. The two bands' shared roots go back a long way, and two members of Meat Whiplash would later become further vital components in the increasingly interconnected Scottish indie scene.

CREATION

Paul McDermott (Vocals, Meat Whiplash): We originally started the band out of boredom. All unemployed, no job prospects and a lot of spare time on our hands.

Thatcher was at her peak. It was grim. Industry and communities destroyed throughout the UK. No money and no future.

Jim and William probably started about the same time. We were all bedroom dwellers, loved music, learned a few chords and decide to try and create something.

Michael Kerr (Drums, Meat Whiplash): The moment Meat Whiplash was formed, we were sitting in my bedroom, and I can't remember if it was me or somebody else had said, 'Well, why don't we form a band for something to do?' Douglas (Hart) was playing guitar. I was playing drums. Eddie (Connelly) was playing bass and Paul (McDermott) was singing because he was the good-looking one.

Paul McDermott: Douglas was the original guitarist. He was closer to Jim and William, knew they were looking for a bass player and were probably more forward thinking than us. We had never considered playing gigs or even recording songs at that stage. They were well ahead of the game and certainly had a more polished sound and identity. Couldn't really blame him. After he left, we tried a bundle of guitar players. All technically brilliant but not what we were looking for. Although Stephen (McLean) lived in the same street as Michael, we only got to know him when he joined the band. Stephen went to Partick Thistle games with a friend of ours, Gordon Donaldson. He heard we were looking for a guitarist and contacted us through Gordon.

Stephen McLean (Guitar, Meat Whiplash): It was always something that I had liked the idea of but had no clue how you would go about it or anything. It only came about when a friend who also knew Michael, Eddie and Paul asked if I would be interested in joining Meat Whiplash. He told me that Douglas was leaving them to play with JAMC and they were looking for a guitarist. At this point JAMC had just recorded 'Upside Down' and it had yet to be released. I had known Michael for a while as he lived across the road from me and we had some mutual friends but we never hung about together or anything. I knew Paul a bit more and, again, we had some mutual friends and we would bump into each other around pubs etc. in East Kilbride but I didn't know Eddie before joining the group.

Paul McDermott: Stephen came along. A fast-talking, edgy bundle of energy and completely nuts. A perfect fit.

Stephen McLean: It sounds funny now but we only ever played one gig in Scotland before we went to London. It was a Creation night with JAMC, The Pastels and Primal Scream at The Venue on Sauchiehall Street. I can't remember how many songs we had – probably four or five. It was utterly chaotic but brilliant to do. We were all over the place. It gave us a taste for it and then we got asked to do the North London Poly gig.

The evolution of Primal Scream

By 1984, Bobby Gillespie had left The Wake and was focusing his attention on Jim Beattie's band, Primal Scream, which had now evolved to include Tam McGurk on drums, Robert Young on bass and John 'Joogs' Martin on tambourine.

Tam McGurk (Drums, Primal Scream): Well I always kind of fancied myself as a drummer for some reason. I don't know why. I mean, ever since I was a small boy I was always kind of obsessed with playing drums. I used to steal my mum's knitting needles and literally play on the sofa and stuff. And eventually, after years and years of nagging my parents, my mum and dad managed to get the money to go buy me a drum kit. I had done stuff with Jim (Beattie) before Bobby was involved in Primal Scream. Me and Jim used to go to The Hellfire Club with just bass and drums and basically do a Public Image thing, you know? It was just fun playing bass and me playing drums, sometimes he would play the guitar as well. But it was mostly bass and drums. So I'd known Jim for that period of time, and then when Bobby left The Wake, he kind of started coming on the scene, and then the Primal Scream thing took off.

John 'Joogs' Martin (Tambourine, Primal Scream): Bobby introduced me to Beattie and we started hanging out in Beattie's house in Mount Florida. That was the main hangout really. Before we all got a flat we all tended to hang out in Beattie's bedroom in Mount Florida. That's when he'd have his guitar out, making music, buying up albums, taking all this stuff back to Beattie's house and having a right good blast. By then I'd chucked my job, Bobby Gillespie had chucked his job, Beattie was just about to chuck his job – it was all coming together at that time. Always enjoyed Beattie's musical bedroom in Mount Florida, which was *the* meeting place at that early embryonic Primals period of 1984/85, discovering all these superb 1960s garage/psyche punk records. Had many a great summer session, with Beattie's cassette player blasting out 1960s compilations in the Queen's Park back then. Beattie was also the first guy I met who turned me onto Syd Barrett and his more obscure Pink Floyd/solo records, plus he also possessed those *Terrapin* fanzines, which dug even deeper into Syd's psyche.

Tam McGurk: In Glasgow there was a scene starting to stir up with Meat Whiplash and the Mary Chain, the bands from East Kilbride. And The Pastels . . . there was a guy called Elliot Davis. He was the manager of Wet Wet Wet. Bobby also knew him fairly well. You know, we actually did a demo tape for him. And he was going to manage us and he was going to, you know, take us to where we were gonna go and then it came down to our choice between him and Alan McGee at Creation Records.

Bobby's old friendship with McGee won out and Primal Scream became a Creation band. They began to play as a five-piece: Jim Beattie, Bobby Gillespie, Robert Young, Tam McGurk and John Martin. It is agreed that Primal Scream were officially born on 11 October 1984 at the Creation Artifact Night at The Venue.

John 'Joogs' Martin: Primals were getting some good early press in *NME* and *Melody Maker* and the odd fanzine so the word was spreading fast. That first gig (October 1984) as a five-piece was very memorable as it felt like a real proper band now – i.e. The Venue gig with JAMC, etc. We mostly played the odd gig here and there in Glasgow and Edinburgh in those early days until we got to England and started playing cities like Brighton, Plymouth and London, which were excellent!

Creation 11: The Pastels and 'Million Tears'

The Pastels' hiatus from recording was temporarily interrupted by the release of 'Million Tears' and 'Surprise Me', and the epic B-side 'Baby Honey'.

Martin Hayward: 'Million Tears' is recorded in London with Alan McGee and Joe Foster attentively present. Brian, unusually, arranges the bass – 'Just follow the guitar.' He also smuggles in some Flamin' Groovies.

My craft project bass is not something to be recorded and I borrowed my friend Aidan's bass for 'Something Going On'. McGee and the Creation credit card accompany Brian and me in a taxi to nearby Denmark Street to hire a Rickenbacker and grab guitar strings.

Joe is producing, making it look easy, and the small studio is great for communication. His unobtrusive keyboard adds body to 'Baby Honey'. On home turf, Jowe brings relaxed vibes and untethered trumpet.

I add backing vocals and bluff harmonica on 'Surprise Me', a song which feels naked and defenceless.

Our limitations are all apparent and somehow only add throughout to the day's three recordings – headed in different directions, expressive and uninhibited by any fixed idea of what we are doing or how. And still time for some Creedence Clearwater Revival fan chat.

The 'Million Tears' sleeve and Jane Simon's *Sounds* piece both use Carole Segal's chiaroscuro photos in late low sun in a Glasgow tenement stair. Brian has come straight from work and enjoys confusing by projecting this slightly out of place appearance in music contexts. I'm briefly rocking contacts [contact lenses] before deciding they are more trouble than I need, what with one thing and another.

With this single, and particularly with 'Baby Honey', I feel like we have established something.

'Brian wrote this after a recent trip to India,' Stephen deadpans, at a Living Room show.

We work 'Baby Honey' up as a band from Brian's guitar. Bernice's pattern and my bass are instinctive. Stephen's lyric of gently psychedelic fascination.

Once we have it, we never don't play it. It involves inviting in a little chaos, on which it feeds over time to grow monstrous. David Keenan describes 'staggered walls of blast furnace feedback' in 1987.

We record several versions because it is slippery and escapes definition. Live, Stephen, in control of vocal cues, can cut it prematurely if sulking, but mostly it goes on and on to a point of indefinable satisfaction.

Once at Waterloo Place, support by Primal Scream, some

voodoo between guitar feedback and mixing desk lands an alien craft on the roof of the building, and afterwards we find nobody knows quite what happened. William Mysterious appears and accuses Bernice of thinking she is Moe Tucker.

We never discuss it, but 'Interstellar Overdrive' and 'Sister Ray' are in the ether. You could find all sorts in there if you wanted. It continues to elude and intrigue over time and for a while is where we gather to explore. It's probably what we would all point to if you held a gun to our heads.

CHAPTER 4
1984-85

Rote Kapelle and the Shop Assistants

Edinburgh was ready for something different. The roots that had slowly been growing were about to become fully formed.

At the centre of the scene, fresh from his experience recording the Buba and the Shop Assistants single, was David Keegan.

If Postcard had its headquarters in Glasgow's West Princes Street and Fast Product in Edinburgh's Keir Street, Napier College was the breeding ground for the new Edinburgh scene, notably two core bands who were to shape Edinburgh's indie scene for the next five years. Many of the members of Rote Kapelle and Shop Assistants were in the same class at Napier.

Rote Kapelle soon settled on a stable line-up of Andrew Tully, Margarita Vazquez Ponte, Mal Kergan, Chris Henman and Johnny Muir; the Shop Assistants were David Keegan, Alex Taylor, Sarah Kneale, Ann Donald and Laura McPhail.

Chris Henman: I was at Napier College from 1982 to 1986, doing a degree in Biological Sciences. In 1984 Katy Lironi,

Margarita, Ann Donald, and David Keegan all started first year of HND [Higher National Diploma] Publishing. David Keegan had previously been doing Electrical Engineering in 1982, that's when I first met him. But he dropped out in his first year. Though I think he stayed in Edinburgh after that.

Laura McPhail was also at Napier College in 1984, possibly doing a different course. Peter Ellen (The Mackenzies) was also there at that time doing something like Electrical Engineering. He dropped out of that after his first year.

Jonathan Muir: Andrew (Tully) knew Alex (Taylor) from Edinburgh University. I knew she was singing in another band – I think we did a gig together at some point? Then at one practice session Andrew said she was going to leave to join that band – the Shop Assistants – full time. I'm not sure how Margarita came into the band – Andrew probably knew her through David Keegan. I thought she was great – really into music and film and art. And very funny when she wanted to be, although quite partisan about her likes/dislikes too.

Margarita Vazquez Ponte (Vocals, Rote Kapelle and The Fizzbombs; Drums, Jesse Garon and the Desperadoes): I left home to go to Napier College. I'll be honest, I didn't care what I went to study, I just wanted to come, so I picked, almost randomly, Periodical Publishing at Napier. And I ended up in the same classes as a lot of the people I was going to be in bands with and in the same college at the same time, and I think a lot of the scene came from the serendipity of all being in that place at the same time.

David Keegan: Alex got introduced to me via Rote Kapelle. She was singing backing vocals with them, and somebody suggested that she might like the kind of music that I was doing. So, we got together and she started singing as well and then, really quickly, we just seemed to really hit it off. And so, yeah, me and Alex decided just to do our own thing.

The others never really seemed to like the songs we were playing, that's the impression I got, and so Alex and I decided just to do our own thing. Then I went to college and Sarah (Kneale) was on the course I was on. By that time the Buba and the Shop Assistants single came out. I think it got a solitary play on John Peel. But over that we got loads of letters, like people ordering the single and so forth. I mean, there was only, what, 300 copies of it so it wasn't that hard to sell. So anyway, we met Sarah through my college course and she said she'd like to play bass, so that was good. We had a couple of temporary drummers and then Ann (Donald), who was also on the publishing course at Napier that I was doing, she said she'd play drums. That's great, we've got a proper band now.

Margarita Vazquez Ponte: Somebody asked me to be in a band . . . I was just waiting to be asked. I ended up at a New Year's party in the kitchen with various members of Rote Kapelle. They just asked, 'Do you want to come and sing?' and it was just like that. So I think then the next day, or a couple of days later, I turned up for a rehearsal at Niddry Street practice rooms, legendary at the time, where all of the Edinburgh bands practised. And I turned up for practice. And they handed me some words that Alex had written. And I sang those. And then I just had to make up stuff. Interesting.

Chris Henman: I knew Margarita from Napier (she started doing publishing in 1984, and was in the same class as David Keegan, Katy Lironi and Ann Donald). Perhaps I met them through David. We used to talk a lot in the college refectory. I realised we had some similar interests in music. We then started to go to gigs and other events together.

So I asked if she fancied singing in Rote Kapelle. Even though she had never sung before. She said she would give it a go. She came to our practice room. And after getting used to us, and the noise levels, she seemed to fit in and wanted to join. I think this was late '84.

By this time Johnny Muir had joined the band. He was four or five years younger than the rest of us. He was also from Balerno and went to Currie High School.

Andrew Tully: I remember parties up in Morningside and, you know, there just seemed to be this revolving troop of us. Alex went to the Shop Assistants. I ended up moving into a flat that Alex had shared in Morningside, so it was all very, I mean, I would hesitate to say incestuous, but we all kind of knew each other from parties and gigs and the pub. And as, you know, all the best things in life happen, you know, at parties at two o'clock on a Saturday morning, great ideas are formed. And the next morning when you're 19/20 years old, it's like, yeah, let's form a band.

Margarita Vazquez Ponte: David was getting the band together. He had Alex, and Sarah was also in our class, and he asked her. And Laura was in another class, in the same year, and Ann was in our class, because originally Shop Assistants had two drummers. It was much more female than male in our class, so that's how that happened. But it was never, ooh, David's gonna get a bunch of girls to be in a band with, never. Never really occurred to anybody.

Laura McPhail (Drums, The Shop Assistants): I was at Napier in 1984. I was in the same department as David, Sarah, Ann and Margarita, but not on the same course; I was doing a printing course, but it was a small department. In my memory, all the classes were next to each other, so we would see each other coming and going to class.

Ann Donald (Drums, The Shop Assistants): Went to Napier to do publishing and that was the class that Katy (Lironi, later The Fizzbombs) was in. Sarah was in it, Margarita was in it and David was in it . . . Laura was on the printing course. It must have just been a few months after that that David said, 'Do you want to be in a band?' I said yeah – there's no false modesty in this but I'm tone deaf and can't play. I'm very, very enthusiastic and I'd been going to gigs since I was 14. I went to interview Sandy at Fast Records when I was at school, thinking I was interested in radio and stuff and he was just lovely.

David Keegan: Sarah (Kneale) joined on bass in October and we had Grant on drums for the two Punk Rock Happenings in December. Moray helped out for another Waterloo Bar gig before Ann and Laura joined in March/April and that was the Shop Assistants.

Ann Donald: I remember we went up to David's flat once, at the bottom of Broughton Street, when he used to stay there. And he played us some cassettes from Buba and the Shop Assistants and I was like, oh wow, I had no recollection of who Buba and the Shop Assistants were at all. I just knew that we were this band that was put together. And obviously, you know, nobody's daft. Right. And one way you're putting a band together, there was still that novelty value. And I don't mean that in any dismissive way. I use it in terms of – it was not as common to have women in a band, plus a geezer, than a band full of geezers. So that's a fact. And David's not daft either. I'm sure there was reasoning behind his madness in getting someone who's completely musically inept. I only speak for myself, I don't speak for the others. Because obviously Sarah could play and I think Laura was, you know, just doing beats as well. So there's a canniness there; your band is potentially going to stand out more than others.

Jonathan Muir: Later, we did gigs supporting the Shop Assistants – one in Rosyth springs to mind – so we saw Alex around as her star rose. I think she was very unconfident about her voice. It sounded great.

Ann Donald: I do remember rehearsals. Either in the building that was the sauna or next to the sauna. So we were in that rehearsal studio in Niddry Street. And literally, the water coming down the walls and everything. And obviously David – I think he had to move his amp because it was so fusty. And I recall practice in there with Laura. We both played the same tune and beat, rhythm. But we had all been going to Green Banana Club at Edinburgh Uni as well. And that's where we first heard The Jesus and Mary Chain 'Upside Down', and, you know, when everyone says you hear a record that changes you? That was that record. And us fuelled by our 50 pence snake bite and blackcurrant – just used to throw each other about the dance floor in an excited way to that. I can't explain but you probably had the same feeling – it just took everything, it turned it upside down and shook it around for two minutes or however long that song was. We loved that sound. And David obviously loved the whole drum sound on it and thought, well, we'll double that with Laura and me.

Laura McPhail: Ann and I shared the drums and we went for what we hoped was a Jesus and Mary Chain style approach to the drumming. We all seemed to hit it off and we played through a few of the songs. I loved the band and the songs immediately.

Ann Donald: Because we only played about two beats anyway. So that suited my very limited capabilities. But the sound was great. And I remember when we recorded down at Newhaven. And he (engineer Peter Haigh) had a gas fire! Maybe he was throwing it out or something. But David had this idea – he said, 'Why don't you both play the gas fire?' And I said all right then and we stuck it in a bathroom to get the echo and everything, and it was just fantastic! I liked playing beside Laura. I know we look so physically different but it was nice to have a buddy to stand next to. It worked really well. We just kept to our simple beats and kept the wall of sound going, and it was easy.

ROTE KAPELLE AND THE SHOP ASSISTANTS

Laura McPhail: Looking back I think we started playing gigs almost right away. I think some of the first gigs we played were when The Pastels took us on tour as support and a bit later we supported The Jesus and Mary Chain.

Ann Donald: I don't think anybody actually thought twice about it until we started performing and then you got that absolute bullshit – 'Get your tits out' and stuff like that. Not least from Mr Bobby Gillespie, actually. We were playing one of our first gigs at the Hoochie Coochie Club, and obviously you're really close to the audience – as you are whenever you play any gig when you're just starting off. The audience is literally there and I think that's why Alex wore the shades as well. Just so she wouldn't see people. And I just remember Laura and I were at the back ready to play, and we heard this 'Get your tits out' and it was like, 'Bloody hell! That's Bobby Gillespie.' That's an absolute dick thing to say! Obviously I'm sure Bobby would be mortified at that sort of stuff now but that's the sort of stuff we did face on a very regular basis. But not usually from any of the bands we were playing with at all – the whole music scene was really lovely. You never thought twice about that as a girl but it was only when you heard some diddy audience member come out with that nonsense. Now you think back and I've certainly not heard that nonsense and I still go to gigs a lot. But you think back and you think, 'Jesus this is so neolithic and dumb.'

Chris Henman: I think any gap between us starting recording was caused by us studying. Personally the studying came second behind music. If we weren't practising, I would be going to gigs all the time, or out socialising. Even though we had very little money to do so.

There was just a few changes going on during this time. Malcolm was also away for nearly a year in Aberdeen, during which time we had a different bass player too.

Andrew Tully: I can see for those who appreciate a good narrative this could be the point where the band switch from 'exposition' to 'rising action'. From the inside we were still just the band and things were just 'carrying on'; we didn't know any different. We were growing as people, meeting new people, expanding our horizons, but fairly unwittingly. There was no masterplan, no 'let's make things happen' moment.

CHAPTER 5
1984-85

Back to Creation: the ascent of The Jesus and Mary Chain

'The Jesus & Mary Chain: Vile Evil From East Kilbride!', *NME*, 8 December 1984

After the release of 'Upside Down' in 1984, the JAMC's upwards trajectory did not let up. The unexpected success of indie meant that this was becoming common, so Geoff Travis from Rough Trade and Mike Alway formed a subsidiary label under Warner called Blanco Y Negro. One of the label's first signings was The Jesus and Mary Chain.

From the start, the band had been very open about their desire for fame, and that wasn't something that Creation could offer in 1984/85. McGee remained their manager but it was clear they couldn't operate as they wanted on Creation. Although they remained a Creation band ideologically, they were about to achieve unprecedented success. By 1985, the world of Creation and The Jesus and Mary Chain was about to bring Scottish music to worldwide headlines.

Max Bell (*The Face*, February 1985): 'The most revolting and disgusting group I've ever heard' – that's one description of The Jesus and Mary Chain. Some jealous rival maybe? Nope – that's what their own record company man reckons.'

As was the case for many bands before them, their records would be representations of the Mary Chain's creativity, energy and imprint on the world of music. However, like few bands before them, The Jesus and Mary Chain are also remembered for a gig that left an imprint on culture itself: the infamous North London Poly Gig showcasing Creation's Scottish roster – the Mary Chain, The Jasmine Minks and Meat Whiplash. I don't believe The Pastels were invited.

Douglas Hart: That year was insane, really, you know, incredible momentum, forward momentum, and incredible energy, including the riots at North London Poly.

Michael Kerr: We were on first . . . and it was typical Meat Whiplash style. We didn't have a clue about anything. We were meant to travel on the night before so that we'd be there in the morning and whatever. There used to be a bus from East Kilbride that left for London at ten o'clock at night. We turned up to get this bus and it was full so we couldn't get on and we basically had to go down on the morning of the gig. We knew that the North London Polytechnic was on Holloway Road because the advert in the *NME* said it was. We didn't know where that was so we ended up getting an *A–Z* to find out exactly where.

Stephen McLean: Looking back at that night, it is actually quite frightening, but at the time it was a mix of fear and exhilaration. It feels now as though the whole night had been building up to that, there seemed to be tension from early on. I think that the promoters maybe sold too many tickets and there were also loads of people outside without tickets so there was a bit of an atmosphere from the very start. I remember Bobby and Douglas letting folk in for free through a fire escape as well.

Michael Kerr: We turned up with our equipment at the venue . . . The Jesus and Mary Chain were already there. When it came to our soundcheck, Paul, our singer, was nowhere to be found. At that time the JAMC didn't do their own soundchecks. Basically their roadies did their soundcheck for them. We couldn't find Paul McDermott because he was in the toilet taking speed with Douglas Hart, so Jim Reid got up and did our soundcheck with us. We did 'I Wanna Be Your Dog' by The Stooges and Jim sang it with us . . . I just remember seeing all these people thinking, 'Why's he up there with them doing their soundcheck when he doesn't even do his own?' I'd like to have recorded that!

Stephen McLean: It pretty much started badly and deteriorated from there; we were getting things thrown at us from the first few minutes and there were guys down the front making threats towards us. We had been drinking beforehand and I took umbrage at the stuff being thrown at us and I lobbed an Old England Sherry bottle into the crowd; thankfully it never hit anyone, but, not surprisingly, it just made them even angrier. Shortly after that a couple of guys ran on stage and attacked Eddie. I managed to get them off of him and we left the stage. Alan McGee thought this was brilliant and it was then that he said we would be recording a single. He then encouraged us to go on and make a noise for the next ten minutes.

Michael Kerr: Anyway . . . we started drinking, as everybody did, and went out on stage. Now, we were not one of the greatest bands in the world so we just went out . . . I think we only had about four or five songs – 'Don't Slip Up' hadn't been written at that point – so we went out and started playing and there were some guys in the audience who were throwing things . . . then Paul did the 'Come on!' to one of them . . . and one of them came on. Paul ran off the stage and the guy ran after him. Eddie Connelly tried to stop him and the guy punched Eddie. At that point Stephen just threw off his guitar and went for the guy. Now, when this was happening the guy's friend got up on stage so we had the two of them up on stage causing bother . . . Stephen had managed to fight them both off stage. Now I'll go back a bit because I'm trying to think when the bottle incident happened . . . Eddie and Stephen were getting fed up with people spitting and throwing things. He'd bought a bottle of Buckfast at the off-licence and he'd been drinking that and when he finished it he walked over between two songs, went up to the microphone and said 'DUCK' and tossed the bottle out. It wasn't throwing it at somebody but it was throwing it in the air and see where it lands. That got everybody a little riled!

Jim Shepherd (The Jasmine Minks): I saw one member of Meat Whiplash punched full in the face as he played on stage.

Paul McDermott: Eddie always played his bass with his back to the audience. He was oblivious to what was happening and got punched on the jaw. He dropped his bass and came off.

Jim Shepherd: We went on after them. I was terrified. It felt like being thrown to the lions. I don't know why but the crowd didn't invade when we played.

Michael Kerr: After that The Jasmine Minks went on and one of them had put a hammer in his back pocket and as soon as the first song started he turned his back to the audience to show he had a hammer as if to say, 'If you want to try something then try something.'

Jim Shepherd: We had a claw hammer as part of our toolkit, used to nail Tom's drum kit to the stage (he hit them so hard that they wandered around the stage if we didn't), and Adam had it showing clearly from his jacket pocket as we walked to our places on stage. I had a suede-head and wore a Crombie coat, so I assume they thought we were tougher than we really were.

Michael Kerr: Then The Jesus and Mary Chain came on and did their usual fifteen-minute set . . . and madness ensued.

We were down in the dressing rooms underneath the stage and you could just hear this mayhem that was going on upstairs. Stephen had got his guitar nicked and before you knew it the police were turning up and we made statements . . . yeh . . . that was our introduction. That was the second time we'd ever played live.

Jim Shepherd: There is so much written about the riot at North London Poly with JAMC and Meat Whiplash. The place was trashed and the PA was turned into kindling. And remember that back then PAs were made from huge wooden cabinets towering high in the air.

Stephen McLean: The Jasmine Minks set passed without incident but when JAMC came on it just went mad. I can't recall exactly the order of events from then, but the whole place erupted, anything that wasn't nailed down was thrown or smashed and the PA was destroyed. The crowd were completely out of control and that's when it became really frightening. We managed to get out in one piece but the hall looked like a battlefield in the aftermath.

Douglas Hart: One of best things that North London Poly did was a support band from East Kilbride called Meat Whiplash, named after a Fire Engines song. They were kind of getting booed, and Bobby just whispered something into the singer's ear, and the singer walked out and said, 'This is the last song,' and everyone went, 'Yeh!!!!' And then he said, 'And it lasts twenty minutes.'

Michael Kerr: We went off and Alan McGee said, 'Just get back on and play a ten-minute song of just noise.' So we did. It might have been based around something but we just played and that riled them up even more . . . We went off and down to our dressing room and Alan McGee burst in and said 'WE'RE GOING TO DO A SINGLE' and then just left the dressing room. There were some other people we knew there and I can remember seeing their faces, thinking 'What's he thinking, releasing a single with them?'

Alan McGee: We'd conjured up madness.

Douglas Hart: Half of the crowd loved us, and half the crowd wanted to kill us.

Joe Foster: At the time, I was doing a postgraduate thing at North London Poly, and so I had to dive into the audience when they grabbed Jim Reid and pulled him in to try and murder him, and there was film of me doing that so that the college decided the best thing to do was not to praise me for saving someone – it was to fire me.

Douglas Hart: And Alan McGee hired some really heavy, you know, these were kind of ex-SAS guys, they were tough fuckers, and they quit after a few days, 'cause one of them would be knocked out with a scaffolding pole, and if these guys are quitting 'cause they can't handle it, what fucking chance have we got, skinny fucking cowards from East Kilbride.

Paul McDermott: Alan McGee called me over and told me to announce that we were going to be the next Creation single. The A&R guys from Warner's just looked at Alan as if he was fucking nuts. We finished, came off stage and were completely buzzing. Stephen and I headed to the student bar for a few pints and were greeted by the four guys that he booted off the stage. They were Geordies. They shook our hands, bought the beers and congratulated our spirited performance. Bizarre.

The Jasmine Minks' next steps

The mainstream media attention of 'Upside Down' and the riot would unsurprisingly force a huge amount of exposure towards The Jesus and Mary Chain but also to Creation itself. The Jasmine Minks, Meat Whiplash and Bobby's other band, Primal Scream, would benefit hugely from the attention, all of them entering the recording studio.

Jim Shepherd (Jasmine Minks): The success of 'Upside Down' was fantastic for everyone. We would go and watch JAMC for a while. The crowds were getting bigger and bigger. We all got a bit tougher after the riots and the label and our little scene became a lot more macho, a lot more cut-throat. Everyone wanted a part of what was happening with JAMC. Alan stopped managing us as he had to manage JAMC and run the other label, Blanco Y Negro. Kevin Pearce started managing us. He gave us confidence to do what was in our hearts regardless of what the major labels might want (they were always sniffing around at that time). It was a different story. We were trimming our songwriting; our reference point was the *Time's Up* EP by Buzzcocks. We scrapped our set and played a brand new set of nearly all new songs (which annoyed some fans, unsurprisingly). That was our reaction to what was around us. We recorded songs for a four-track EP at Alaska in one weekend – simple, direct, and what felt like our greatest moment. We were definitely tooled up and ready to go! But when it didn't come out as planned we retreated. We picked up our acoustic guitars and planned an album of pained beauty, organising a fortnight at our pal Iain Slater's [APB] house, using his eight-track machine. It's funny because Primal Scream simplified things too, shortening their songs and doing twenty-minute sets. Bobby and Jim Beattie had played with us at our first Living Room gig as a duo with a drum machine. We had become friends and ended up doing lots of gigs together over the next four years or so, over various Primals line-up changes. I went up to Edinburgh to help them record their first songs in the studio.

The Jesus and Mary Chain sign to a major

In February 1985, JAMC released 'Never Understand' on their Warner subsidiary, which reached number forty-seven in the UK charts. It was the highest placing for any of the new breed of Scottish independent acts so far.

The Warner's deal, with Blanco Y Negro, was on the imprint co-run with Mike Alway and Geoff Travis from Rough Trade. It had already released material by Everything But The Girl.

'Never Understand' was the label's first major single and its success led to a further release, 'You Trip Me Up'. While not as successful as 'Never Understand', it still sustained the momentum being created by the band. The Jesus and Mary Chain, and to a lesser degree the Shop Assistants, were

spearheading the re-emergence of Scottish underground music in the music press.

Biba Kopf (*NME*, 16 February 1985): Nine months in the making, the far from immaculately conceived Jesus and Mary Chain, from Glasgow, have alternately been heralded as new messiahs or dismissed as a bloody mess!

Max Bell (Sounds, February 1985): Jim, Bobby, William and Douglas have hit the cusp of their teens in a welter of concern about attitude, and they seem a trifle stunned (though they'd probably never admit it) at the amount of media fuss surrounding them.

Primal Scream's debut single

Primal Scream's debut single, 'All Fall Down' (Creation 17), was released in May 1985. Now, everyone who had missed their early gigs could hear for themselves what was being eagerly written about them.

Bruce Dessau (*Jamming*, September 1985): Recent events have pointed out the resurgence of quality music emanating from Glasgow. No scene, though, just bands making fine music and putting on gigs. Inevitably, one of the main impetuses behind this is the success of The Jesus and Mary Chain. But as they move on to bigger and better things, Primal Scream look set to emerge as the freshest blast to come out of Glasgow this year.

Bobby Gillespie (speaking to Bruce Dessau in September 1985 for *Jamming*): When Primal Scream started, all Jim and I used to do was make tapes of noise, then we progressed to writing tunes around bass riffs, and then finally about nine months ago we started writing pop songs. Essentially Primal Scream are a pop band, but we've got a huge range of influences, ranging from The Stooges to Irish rebel songs. All stuff with real emotion in it . . .

John 'Joogs' Martin: I think 'All Fall Down' was maybe recorded in London late 1984 but released in springtime 1985. I didn't play tambourine on it at the recording. I'd just joined in October 1984. So it was a four-piece on the sleeve cover of Bob G–Dungo–Beattie 'n' Tam. I remember Julian Cope coming out with the quote of 'Crucial' when he first heard 'It Happens' on the B-side with dramaba bas! Like most people at the time, I preferred 'It Happens' and I don't think Primals played it live for some unexplained reason, as Tam's drumming on it was pretty snappy! Felt strange to get a copy as I didn't play on it but it still felt exciting as we spent time in Creation offices folding our own pic sleeves of it!

The release of the single came at an unusual point in the band's career as Bobby had a dual role as singer for Primal Scream and drummer for The Jesus and Mary Chain. In the Creation hierarchy, the two bands occupied very different levels of importance at that point.

Tam McGurk: I noticed a change in Bobby from when he started associating with the Mary Chain. I think they must have taught him something that he didn't know to that point, something about how to deal with publicity and how to deal with the media, etc., etc., because it changed, you know, it definitely changed and literally overnight.

Meat Whiplash's debut single

As McGee had promised, Meat Whiplash had their turn to release a record, 'Don't Slip Up' (Creation 20), in September 1985.

Michael Kerr: In some ways, we rode on the coat-tails of The Jesus and Mary Chain because, you know, like we didn't have any huge ambitions other than starting a band. When Alan McGee said he'd booked studio time for us and we had to go down and record the single we realised that none of the songs we had were particularly great. And so we wrote some more songs. 'Don't Slip Up' was one of them.

Stephen McLean: I don't know about any of the other groups, but nothing was ever actually signed with us and Creation – it was all a very informal, 'Let's do a record' type of thing. As I said, Alan decided to offer us a single in the middle of the North London Poly mayhem and he was good to his word.

We had to come up with a song and we wrote 'Don't Slip Up' mucking about in our bedrooms after the London gig.

Alan booked us into Alaska studios at Waterloo and we did everything in a day. We had never been in a studio before but the Mary Chain were there and were able to give us a hand. We pretty much just played the song live and then Paul sang over it and it worked.

BACK TO CREATION

Paul McDermott: We had the bare bones of 'Don't Slip Up' but it needed some work. We finished it on the coach journey down to London, on our way to the studio.

Michael Kerr: I think that even the night before we went to London 'Don't Slip Up' was changed around. We had no idea it'd even work. We'd never been in a recording studio before. We did the same thing as before by turning up to go to London the night before and the bus being full . . . actually we did travel down the night before but I remember turning up at the studio absolutely knackered as you never sleep properly on those overnight buses. Absolutely horrendous.

By that time I don't think we'd played live again, we had no studio experience . . . totally fortunate that we were in that position – riding on the coat-tails of The Jesus and Mary Chain. The Jesus and Mary Chain produced that record as much as it's produced . . . You just went and played it live a couple of times and tried to get the singer to sing over that.

A lot of people say it's The Jesus and Mary Chain that played on that but it's not, it's just that they were there and it's as much as a single that's made in two hours can be produced.

That was that, and when the single came out, to our surprise it got really good reviews and did really well. I think Alan McGee thought at one point we might do okay. I remember him saying, 'Yes, you could probably be as big as Alien Sex Fiend,' and that just totally deflated me. I was just thinking, I wanted to be bigger than Alien Sex Fiend, you know? That was when, for me personally, I felt I needed to do something different and a wee bit more professional.

With Meat Whiplash we did gigs with The Weather Prophets

and Primal Scream that used to be something called The Creation Package where you'd go play Nottingham, Manchester, Birmingham . . . places where we'd all travel around in the same vans . . . so a bit like The Monkees.

Stephen McLean: I remember going back home to East Kilbride on the bus after the recording and I was absolutely buzzing. We all had a cassette copy of it and I was listening to it constantly. When it eventually got released it was unbelievable, it was really well received in the reviews.

The second single was a big disappointment. I think the song itself was actually okay but the recording of it just didn't work. I don't know if we over-thought what we were doing or not but it just didn't work out the way we wanted it to. I remember when McGee got to hear it he wasn't impressed at all. I think the idea was to maybe leave it a while then go back to it, but that never happened. Things kind of tailed off after this. Thinking back on it, I think that it left us kind of deflated and maybe we started doubting ourselves. I think that I certainly did.

We continued to play a few more gigs after this but, not too long after, we decided to have a break for a while and try to come up with more material and get some practice in. I think that was the plan anyway. As it turned out, we just kind of stopped. We didn't have a formal split or anything, it just fizzled out.

Michael Kerr: Growing up in East Kilbride was fine but it got to a point where you just thought, this town's not for me. Eddie was really one of my oldest friends and he ended up in Edinburgh because he was going out with Alex from the Shop Assistants, and I ended up just moving through. That's one of the reasons that I moved through because it ended up that I would go and see Eddie and I'd know more people in Edinburgh than East Kilbride.

Eddie and Michael leaving East Kilbride for Edinburgh was fortuitous, not just for them but also for Edinburgh's musicians. Eddie was soon to make a significant impact on Edinburgh's emerging new indie scene.

The Shop Assistants release a single

Fuelled by the success of The Jesus and Mary Chain, David Keegan was approached for a one-off deal by Bristol's Subway Organization, a like-minded bedroom outfit that had released a number of cassettes and was impressed with the Buba single. Subway's first 7-inch, The Shopping Parade *EP, the Shop Assistants' debut, was released on 16 August 1985.*

David Keegan: We were just playing our sort of music. It obviously was the kind of music that would . . . due to its kind of, I suppose, amateurish nature . . . it was ramshackle. It was recorded in a fantastic recording studio, but by people who had just learned their instruments. So it was the kind of music that only a small, independent label was likely to put out. And it was the kind of music that someone who was a fan of music, who liked music so much, they wanted to put some of their own money into, like, releasing your thing – which is the whole classic thing of independent labels. It's people who love a band

and want to put this out, want people to listen to this, which is where, with Buba and the Shop Assistants, Corky put his money into recording, releasing that with no expectation to get your money back, just because you wanted to put records out. The first proper Shop Assistants single was with a guy called Martin from down in Bristol. We were really lucky because he liked the Buba and the Shop Assistants record and said they'd like to put out something else by the band. So we almost, like, before we were even a band, we had the chance to make a single, which was pretty lucky actually. But again, it was an enthusiast who really liked the music who wanted to make a record label to put stuff out.

Ann Donald: I'm sure we recorded in Newhaven. And that's where I think we recorded 'All That Ever Mattered'. That's where we played the [gas] fire in the bathroom to get that sound on the drums. So that's just a snapshot that I remember. And I remember us going down to Waverley [train station], getting our photographs taken, because it's like a silhouette. And so . . . and there's the red colour, the blue colour, the yellow colour. Again, that came from David, you know, he's really smart. He knew, you know, if you wanted to sell three singles, you just bought the blue, the red and the yellow one. It was, you know, you're on. I think it was like the first stage and the re-pressed were red, next thousand blue, then went on to green, stuff like that, I think – pretty sure, because we definitely did different colours. And, but yeah, holding that in my hand, and I've still got it as well. It's just like, wow, I've made it.

Laura McPhail: I remember that it seemed to be a really quick recording experience. Essentially, it was all 'done live', with David adding guitars and Alex recording her vocals. David was a really good producer and had a clear idea of how to get a good sound. When we received test pressings of the single it was exciting – and I think we all listened to it together at David's flat. The sleeve was designed by the band, using photos taken by Angus McPake in Edinburgh city centre on a very sunny day. We added little hand-coloured sections to the front of the sleeve and it was ready to go. I seem to remember we were all happy with the whole EP.

It was an exciting time and there was a lot happening around us; all our friends were recording and playing live. It really felt that we were all in it together and there was always a new record, session, live review or music press interview that featured an Edinburgh indie band. I think everyone worked together, sharing equipment, rehearsal spaces, studio time and gigs . . . We would listen to John Peel and Janice Long; they played the music we wanted to hear and when they played our record, it was a great feeling, exciting – a rush, and a bit surreal to be on the radio.

Ian Hoey (aka Vince Van Yak, Vocals, The Dragsters): The *Shopping Parade* EP, that was huge, that caused massive ripples. Morrissey said that was a single of the year. But it's a great, great powerful record and really exciting and it sort of supercharged this scene. And, of course, the Shop Assistants got to support the Mary Chain and things, and there were real similarities. I mean, you know, David was very influenced by their style, but he's one of the great underrated guitarists as well –

what he brought to that band was fantastic. But there were so many elements... We have Alex up front... Getting nominated as the record of the year in the *NME* and stuff. Sarah, this sort of... wild bass player and then the two drummers, and just taking no prisoners and things. There was just this real excitement around *Shopping Parade*.

Margarita Vazquez Ponte: And they happened. They seem to get a buzz really fast. They were really great. David was an incredible guitarist, he was like a rhythm and lead guitarist at the same time. And he made a really full sound. And then Alex had this just lovely, wispy, gentle voice over the top of it. And her lyrics were very particular as well, they were quite poetic, and I think quite, I don't know, mature. And it just was a pretty unique sound at the time, even though it was referencing Buzzcocks and The Undertones and The Shangri-Las, but it didn't sound like them particularly. So everything seemed to click for the Shop Assistants really fast. And it was like a little snowball.

CHAPTER 6
1985-86

Meanwhile, elsewhere in the east

Rote Kapelle's first release

Three years after having formed, and two years after recording their demo, Rote Kapelle released their first offering, an EP titled The Big Smell Dinosaur, *in late 1985. They'd been having difficulty courting labels, possibly due to their abrasive sound, which did not sit so comfortably in the 1960s-influenced indie-pop that was becoming dominant. As with the Shop Assistants, their single was recorded with Peter Haigh at Edinburgh's Pier House studios. They approached Sandy at Fast Forward for advice, and this would lead to a fortuitous moment of inspiration for the next Shop Assistants single and a defining moment in Scotland's indie scene.*

Chris Henman: We wanted to put out our own record, probably because nobody else was offering to do so. We had heard about bands doing it.

It was part of the punk rock, independent ethos – anyone can be in a band and put out their own records. I guess it all started with Rough Trade and the Cartel.

We looked into it and spoke to Fast Forward in Edinburgh, and they said they could have a thousand singles made and distribute them around the UK through the independent labels and shops/the Cartel. They said it would cost £1,000 and they would need it upfront.

Jonathan Muir: We recorded at Pier House studios in Granton. Peter Haigh, who ran the place, was kind of an old hippy but he really put a lot of effort in to create a sound for us. It was a sixteen-track studio so the recording sounds slightly woolly now – some of the tracks had been bounced down, I think. But Pete knew how to get something good out of the equipment he had. I remember there being vocal overdubs for the first time and me recording an additional drum part in the stone-floored hall to get the reverb. There was spontaneity too – you can hear me and Margarita laughing over the end of 'Gas Fire' and Pete came in and crashed the hi-hats. We felt we had a proper record. When it was finished I was given a sheaf of sleeves to colour in. I think I did them in my bedroom and got some of my friends to join in too. It was amazing to see a piece of vinyl with your music on it. It's almost a kind of transubstantiation that those few minutes of you playing get preserved forever on those tiny wee grooves. I don't remember there being a lot of reviews – maybe one or two brief ones and they seemed to mainly mention the hand-coloured sleeve. I still think it sounds great when I listen to it now – the songs are punchy and the band sounds really together. We had rehearsed a lot for this. There are drum parts I could never play now – 'Fergus the Sheep' – I can hear my youthful vigour. I think the EP shows real promise.

Chris Henman: So as there was six of us in the band, we managed to raise the £166.66 each to do it. We recorded the EP at Pier Studio in Granton. However, after this we found out we still needed to pay for the sleeve. I think naively we thought that was included in the £1,000. So with nothing left of the budget, we got a thousand photocopies of a black and white design and hand coloured them all in, and put the record and sleeve in a plastic bag. As we all got fed up colouring so many sleeves, we asked our friends, including the Shop Assistants, to do some. Which I'm sure they enjoyed doing.

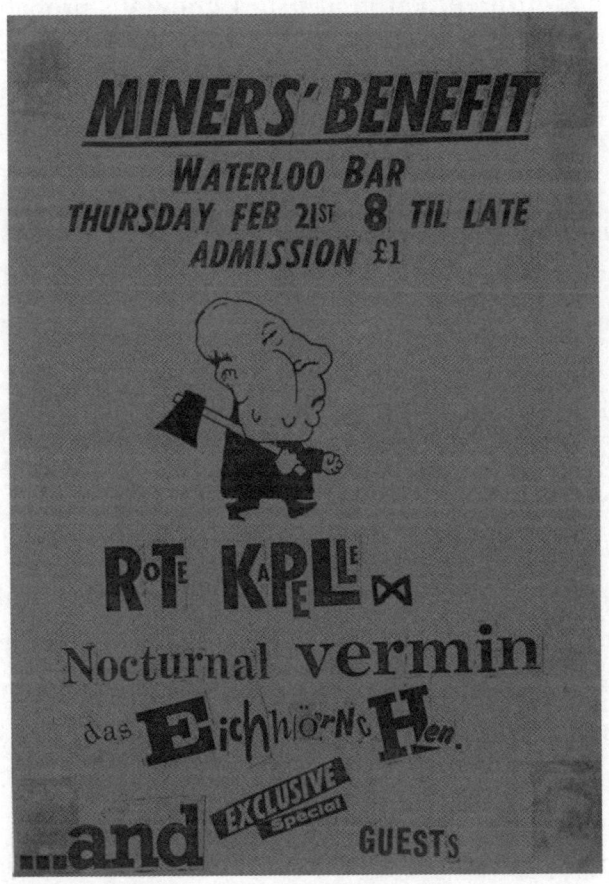

Nocturnal Vermin bring shame on Scotland

The Waterloo Bar in Edinburgh was becoming a focal point for many on the scene. One short-lived new band that arrived around this time were soon to 'bring shame on Scotland': Nocturnal Vermin.

Mark Allan (Vocals, Nocturnal Vermin): Rote Kapelle, who we played with at the Miners' Benefit in 1985 at the Waterloo Bar, were a different kettle of fish. I know it's probably not a popular opinion and I say it knowing Andrew Tully is a thoroughly decent guy, but they truly were the worst band I have ever experienced in the flesh, then and now. I appreciate that sounds a bit mean and I have mellowed a lot over the years but to my ears they were just unlistenable. They did get the best heckle I've ever heard, though (which admittedly came from the midst of our table): 'Bring back hanging!' Harsh, but I'd still maintain fair. Buba and the Shop Assistants opened proceedings that night (that dynamic would deservedly change pretty quickly). Moray Crawford of 35mm Dreams drummed for them that night (and played on their much sought-after single).

I suppose we [Nocturnal Vermin] were quite insular as a group and quite competitive so probably regarded other bands as 'the enemy'. Ha ha! Local bands we were on friendlier terms with were 35mm Dreams, The Architects of Fear, Rex Begonia and The Spooks (who used to play two sets a night, one in Beatles suits and the second in Sgt Pepper attire, which impressed me no end at the time). Bands I can remember going to see around then included The Napalm Stars and We Free Kings, who I liked a lot.

Not sure I was actually talented enough to use my influences on a musical level but my main listening was the likes of Crass, Discharge, The Dead Kennedys and the UK Subs. Angus (James 'Slippy Underfoot' McCready) was a huge fan of Paul Slack, the original UK Subs bass player, and as he was the main songwriter it's probably fair to say that they were an influence (which probably isn't a very cool answer). Listening to the guitar solo on 'Donger', it's more than probable that Arnold Bastard was au fait with The Stooges though. I will admit that my first 7-inch purchases as a youngster were Little Jimmy Osmond and Peters & Lee, so not sure if they surfaced anywhere in my output. Around that time I was introduced to the Misfits and was a late convert to The Velvet Underground after initially not being overly impressed with a compilation album I was given – hard to imagine now, I know, although in my defence it didn't have 'Heroin' on it! An outlier was Laurie Anderson, whose 'O Superman' single and the subsequent *Big Science* album were on constant play and was a big influence going forward but I would be lying if I said it impacted on Vermin. (We weren't that arty.)

Nocturnal Vermin may not have reached the level of influence that the Shop Assistants (or Rote Kapelle, for that matter) achieved but they were responsible for a couple of interesting pop culture morsels: their failed attempt at self-promotion in Dundee's Sunday Post *newspaper; and, in a stroke of bizarre foresight, their recording of a song called 'John Swinney (We Salute You)' about the future SNP politician, then aged 15.*

Mark Allan: Yeah, that undoubtedly came about from drunken pub talk. Think we all admired Malcolm McLarenesque shock tactics. It was intended purely as a laugh. Our pal Brian McGee wrote the letter [to the *Sunday Post*], never imagining it would get published. Unfortunately they edited it and didn't actually mention the band's name. So I was forced to write a 'rebuttal' the next week, making sure the band was mentioned. As a tactic it was successful in so much as we're talking about it now and it still makes me laugh. These days I play bass with Shock &

Awe (as Tommy Shock – I hate an alias me, ha ha!) alongside Murray Ramone (aka Bobby Awe), which has led to some great gigs over the years (last-minute call-up to support Scars at the Picture House being the highlight).

Satellite City 2: Bellshill

While the Edinburgh scene was now buzzing, the Mary Chain had moved to London and The Pastels were releasing singles only sporadically, still on Creation. Things in Glasgow were moving a little slowly but, as in East Kilbride a year earlier, things were starting to happen on the outskirts of the city.

One such place was former mining town Bellshill, where three schoolfriends were in the process of forming three bands that between them would create some of the most influential music to come out of Scotland. They would be The Soup Dragons, BMX Bandits and Teenage Fanclub.

Duglas T. Stewart (Vocals, BMX Bandits): Okay, well, I've lived in Bellshill pretty much my whole life. And it's ex-industrial, I guess what you'd refer to at one point as a ghost town. And when I was in my teenage years it was particularly at a real low point of lots of unemployment. It was probably a bit more violent than it is now and, yeah, it was a town that didn't seem to have very much hope. And it was also a sort of town where people who thought differently or dressed differently or liked to express themselves in different ways were kind of few and far between. So people who were a little bit like that tended to be drawn together. And I guess for me one of the things about Bellshill, about coming from that kind of town, is I think you're, very often, you're either kind of beaten down by it or you kind of do the opposite, it kind of makes you stronger, you know. And I think in my case it was the . . . it kind of made me stronger, it made me more determined to not be like the other people around me. To be different. And also encouraged me to have a reason for wanting to make music and create my own sort of worlds. Because if you're not very happy in the world that you find yourself in it's good to find a way to escape, whether that's actually physically escape, which I've never done, or just kind of escaping in your mind or with some of your friends and kind of by creating your own little musical adventures and fantasies.

Sean Dickson (Vocals and guitar, BMX Bandits and The Soup Dragons): My dad was basically a football manager and, you know, my mum was a housewife. There was nobody in my family musical. Still isn't, you know what I mean? I was the exception basically because I hated football. And in Bellshill there was two things you did: you played football or you were a poof. I was a poof so I made music.

Duglas T. Stewart: I was listening to a lot of stuff that other boys in the common room at the school I went to found very objectionable. I was listening to things like Jonathan Richman. The first album I bought with my own money, my parents would buy me records before that, was a record called *Jonathan Richman and the Modern Lovers*. And that was a real eureka moment for me. It sort of made me think, I want to make people feel how this makes me feel. This is sort of what I think I'd like to do. And it just, I think, you know, seeing . . . hearing that album and seeing some paintings by Matisse pretty much set my whole kind of aesthetic for life, of what I liked and what I was opposed to. And kind of coming out of the post-punk rock thing, what you were opposed to, I think, was just as important as what you were enthusiastic about and what you kind of believed in. And for me, I sort of hated the kind of archetypal hedonistic macho rock star. To me at that time that seemed to be epitomised by guys who were big fans of Whitesnake and The Doors and stuff like that and, you know, leather trousers and kind of macho posturing. And so I kind of set out to be kind of the antithesis . . . the kind of anti-Jim Morrison or something.

And . . . yeah, so it was definitely a lot of guys who had probably been very suspicious of punk, because there were an awful lot of people who were very suspicious of punk and were very, very aggressive towards people that they associated with that. And that's still in the early eighties and mid-eighties, it kind of carried on and if you didn't have a certain kind of poodle, permish type haircut or kind of feather cut . . . And you didn't necessarily fit in – just by wearing a flowery shirt or having a certain type of fringe you caused an awful lot of offence to certain types of blokes around Glasgow and places like Bellshill. And some people probably found that kind of frightening being on stage and facing these sort of guys but I loved it, I really loved the fact that these people were so offended by me. And I would try and figure out ways of being even more offensive and objectionable to them the next time they saw me.

Norman Blake (Guitar, BMX Bandits and Teenage Fanclub): I met Duglas in the art class at our school – we both went to Bellshill Academy . . . we were fans of Jonathan Richman, the

Modern Lovers. The *Rock 'n' Roll with the Modern Lovers* album was a favourite of ours. And I think because it was a pretty simple record actually, there's . . . you know, it's Jonathan with a drummer/percussionist and an acoustic guitar and an upright bass and it seemed that it was pretty simple, in terms of the . . . structure or whatever. And so, yeah, at the same time we started to get interested in the music that was happening in the city and we were both fans of Orange Juice.

Sean Dickson: When I was about 8 I was taught how to play classical guitar. 'Cause I think that's how my mother and father kind of thought, you know, that'll keep him busy . . . I used to . . . they'd hear me sitting in my bedroom playing Human League records and . . . I'd be playing their record collection, you know, Jackie DeShannon's *What The World Needs Now* LP, I played that to death, I've still got it actually. So they used to send me to classical guitar lessons, this guy called Sandy Holmes, I think a few of us have been to that guy. And I could read music for a while. I always hated it 'cause it was always on a Thursday night at the same time as bloody *Top of the Pops*, so it kind of ruined *Top of the Pops* for me, 'cause I only ever saw number one and the first track . . . 'cause I'd walk into his house and it'd be the first track on *Top of the Pops* and I'd be dragged into the other room for half an hour and then at the end of the guitar lesson I'd see what the number one was and that was it.

Duglas T. Stewart: I remember Norman once saying, in an interview I saw, about Bellshill being a dump, and it wasn't the best place but, actually, I was thinking about how grateful, in a funny way, I am that we came from Bellshill, because it was a

MEANWHILE, ELSEWHERE IN THE EAST

very important thing that the three of us gained some sort of strength through meeting each other.

The gang would venture into Glasgow to attend a drama group, where they were soon introduced to further collaborators and conspirators.

Norman Blake: Myself and Duglas were in Bellshill but we went into a place called the Dolphin Arts Centre in Bridgeton, which Duglas introduced me to. And we met some people there. Frances McKee, who . . . I guess together we started sort of making music, so it sort of developed from both of us and Sean. We augmented the band with the people who we met at the Dolphin.

Hugh Mclachlan (The Pretty Flowers): My sister Kim joined a drama group in the heart of the east end. At Bridgeton Cross to be precise, called the Dolphin Arts Centre. It was there that she first met Frances McKee and various other creative types that I would later get to know well. She initially had wanted me to come with her but me being the snooty young Dalmarnock oik decided it wasn't for me! Kim came home later that evening regaling me with tales of fun and chaos and how I was missing out on having a laugh for a change! I gave up my curmudgeonly ways the week after and so the adventure began. It was not long after that I met Duglas, Norman, Sean and Eugene.

Frances McKee (The Pretty Flowers; Vocals/guitar, The Vaselines: It was Duglas that I met first. He's gonna kill me when I say this . . . I went to an all girls school, so we didn't have a big experience of talking to the opposite sex, so when I was talking to Duglas, it didn't feel like I was talking to the opposite sex. We could talk about anything to each other.

Duglas T. Stewart: I met a girl called Frances McKee, and I thought she was, like, the most amazing creature, human being I'd ever met, I was just like, I just want to be around this person all the time, and Frances said to me, 'Oh, I'd really love to be in a group,' and I was like, 'I'm forming a group.'

Hugh Mclachlan: We all hit it off almost right away and as well as doing skits and am-dram stuff we found a common thread in music, especially Duglas. Not long after, we started going through to Bellshill and congregating in Norman's gran's house where we'd all try and write songs and help each other with ideas.

Their newly assembled band evolved into The Pretty Flowers.

The Pretty Flowers

The Bellshill collective were still just dreaming about making music together but they soon took their first tentative steps towards reality when Bellshill's equivalent of Big In Japan, The Pretty Flowers, was born.

Hugh Mclachlan: The one band that everyone was involved in at some point was The Pretty Flowers! Duglas had a perverse way of convincing you that kazoos and such instruments were the coolest instruments on the planet and everyone chipped in with his merriment. This would involve trips to the park to try out our new batch of tuneage that was probably written that afternoon. I think one was called 'Never Trust a Fish with a False Moustache'.

Norman Blake: I have a memory of us one summer being in a park in Bellshill. We thought it was a gig, but it was basically just us in a park playing to nobody.

Frances McKee: I can't remember how it came about but I went to Bellshill . . . this is how it all began . . . we decided to do this impromptu show in the park. Duglas was doing something and Norman and Sean they had their instruments and were playing away and suddenly it was my turn to do something. I thought, well I can't . . . so I sang this song that I used to sing in primary school and I was really embarrassed because it was really just a kind of nursery rhyme type song. Everybody was really supportive of each other, they thought it was a really great song and they really liked it and Norman put some music to it and it became one of our kind of songs that we sing in the band. That's how it really all started. No one turned around and said you can sing, but I was given this confidence, permission in this group to sing. And that's the thing, we weren't measuring ourselves by outside standards; we were measuring ourselves by our own, which was quite nice.

Sean Dickson (speaking to Duglas): I still can't believe we did this, and sometimes, I actually think, was this a dream, did we have a band called Child Molesters that played my school? We did that gig at my school, and Duglas sang 'I've got a little biscuit tin to keep your panties in,' so we got banned. We were quite happy at that.

Hugh Mclachlan: We did a poetry fanzine that Duglas later gave to Ivor Cutler that Duglas has mentioned once or twice. This led on to us booking a night at the Hattonrigg Hotel underneath the arrestable misnomer The Child Molesters!

I think we were threatened with a lynching that night! I believe I should've been anyways as I had been given a violin to play, à la John Cale, for most of the songs. I believe Norman had got it from the music shop that he had been working in at the time. I even got to sing for the first time one of my compositions.

Frances McKee: We were playing at a show at the Hattonrigg Hotel, and there was people outside boycotting it, because of the name, and I, I mean, I think that shows a sort of level of naivety with me, because I was like, well, what's the problem? Duglas phoned me up one night, and he said, 'Look, I'm changing the name to The Pretty Flowers.' I said, 'I really don't like that name,' and that's when I kind of took a back seat from it. For me, I felt more comfortable being, you know, a Child Molester than a Pretty Flower. Has this got an X certificate?

Duglas T. Stewart: Frances sort of said to me, 'Listen, I've decided I don't want to do Pretty Flowers any more, I think you know it's not really about me musically, it's, you know, about you and Norman and Sean and I want to do something with Eugene (Kelly, later of The Vaselines).' And, yeah, I was really sad about that and I wasn't 100 per cent sure I was going to continue doing things. I just had that moment of 'Oh well, that's that, all right.' I didn't throw a strop. I was of course very, very brave about it on the surface but inside I was an emotional wreck and then of course Norman went, 'Oh, I don't know if I'm really going to do this any more, it doesn't seem to really be going anywhere and, you know, people are telling me I'm a bit daft doing it.' So I was like, 'Oh man, is this . . . is the dream over?'

The Soup Dragons

The Pretty Flowers soon withered but their demise led to the emergence of two new groups, The Soup Dragons and BMX Bandits, shortly followed by The Boy Hairdressers and The Vaselines.

Sean Dickson: The Soup Dragons started first because I met Sushil, the bass player, through a friend who lived in Bearsden, and Sushil had a fanzine called *Pure Popcorn!*, which was quite popular in the scene . . . in those days there was a lot of people who used to sell fanzines at gigs and at parties.

Sushil Dade (Bass, The Soup Dragons): I was at Bell College in Hamilton studying Communication Studies and, inspired by the music scene at the time, I wanted to start a fanzine. Together with a couple of pals at college, Stephen and Paul and I put together *Pure Popcorn!*, named after a lyric in The Pastels song 'Heavens Above'.

Ross Sinclair (Drums, The Soup Dragons): I'd been playing with (Neil Menzies) for a few years and we had this band called Gods For All Occasions. And in fact, it was when we were playing, when I was in first year of art school, we played a gig at The Vic, at the art school bar, and Sean was there and saw us playing. It was after that that he said that I'm trying to start this band but we need a drummer, can you play the drums?

Sushil Dade: I put up a note on the message board at McCormack's music shop [in Glasgow] looking for like-minded souls to join a band. I listed my influences ranging from Orange Juice to Ravi Shankar, Kraftwerk and beyond. Original Soups guitarist Iain Whitehall saw this and he already had a link with Sean and we got together. At the same time Sean also had met Ross our drummer via the art school scene. We got offered our first gig supporting Primal Scream at Splash One. Iain was already booked to go on a camping trip. Enter Jim on guitar . . . the rest is history.

The Soup Dragons were initially Sean Dickson on vocals, Sushil Dade on bass, Ross Sinclair on drums and Jim McCulloch on guitar. Jim had entered the Bellshill orbit a few months earlier when he and his fellow Motherwell musical friends, Joe McAlinden and Francis Macdonald, met Sean, Duglas and Norman when they were all busking in Glasgow. This meeting was hugely important as these individuals went on to become the core of BMX Bandits, The Soup Dragons and the forerunners to Teenage Fanclub, The Boy Hairdressers.

Jim McCulloch (Guitar, The Soup Dragons and BMX Bandits): That's how we met, when we were going home on the train you'd meet these other buskers from Bellshill.

MEANWHILE, ELSEWHERE IN THE EAST

Joe McAlinden (Various instruments and vocals, The Boy Hairdressers, BMX Bandits and Superstar): We're getting on and off the same train. So it just naturally kind of started, you know, how's it going? And then you find out about them and then that's what naturally happened. And I think, obviously within that group of people, there was enough skill sets that it kind of stayed within that group of people. And we all grew. I didn't start as a writer but I was learning from and getting inspiration from the people around me. In my head, it was as natural as that.

Sean Dickson: The first thing that The Soup Dragons ever did, we'd been together for like about three or four rehearsals . . . in fact, I got . . . the one and only time I really worked when I was in Glasgow was I had a job for a summer just as I left school at the second-hand clothes shop in Queen Street called Flip and that's how I met Bobby Gillespie and all the kind of guys from Glasgow 'cause they used to come into the shop to, you know, everybody bought their clothes in that shop in those days . . . when the boss went out we used to put our own cassettes on. I was playing The Cramps and all kind of shit, you know, Sex Pistols, people coming in on a Saturday afternoon, The Jesus and Mary Chain are blasting. And I remember Bobby coming in and it was The Cramps that were playing and he said to me, 'Did you put this on?' and I was like 'Yeah,' and he's a big Cramps fan. So we kind of got talking and, you know, he used to come in, kind of say hi, and then he said to me one day, I had . . . it was like one of the first rehearsals or second rehearsals of Soup Dragons I ever did 'cause you always used to have a cassette recorder and record your rehearsals and I actually played it 'cause I was so proud of it, I played it in the shop on a Saturday afternoon when the boss slipped out and Bobby come in and goes 'Who's this?' and I go 'It's my band,' and he goes 'Oh really,' and he goes 'I run a club called Splash One – do you want to support Primal Scream?'

Ross Sinclair: It's like, 'Right, we've got a gig.' 'Wow, brilliant, where?' 'This Sunday at Splash One.' 'What?'

Sean Dickson: And then I realised that we'd never ever played a gig before.

Ross Sinclair: It's totally mad, like we sort of started playing, everyone goes mental, fuck, like, what the fuck is this, you know? That seemed like the moment where it all sort of came together.

Splash One: May 1985

While things were starting to happen on the outskirts of Glasgow, something pivotal was happening in the centre of Glasgow, where a club called Splash One opened to rival London's Living Room. It was run by Grant MacDougall, Bobby Gillespie, Joogs, Karen Parker and their friends.

Bobby Gillespie (*NME*, 3 August 1985, Neil Taylor): We've been organising gigs to help our friends. We hire a room every two weeks and put bands on. The first band we put on was The Loft, and they were followed by Big Flame. We'll be the third band, and then we'll get The Pastels, then maybe the Shop Assistants, and then . . . who knows?

MEANWHILE, ELSEWHERE IN THE EAST

John 'Joogs' Martin: A lot of bands had just started appearing around 1984. There weren't many gig venues in Glasgow. You had Joanna's, the Tech – Glasgow's Technical College – Night Moves, small venues like that. We'd already played Splash One under the Gigi moniker, along with Buba and the Shop Assistants and The Pastels in late '84. Around early '85 we all started talking about getting a club together. We put on all these bands we liked, for instance Wire, 23 Skidoo and Sonic Youth, but we also wanted to put on bands like Julian Cope and The The as well. Ten of us all got together. Grant MacDougall, Derek Louden, Billy Thompson, myself, Paul Harte, Paul McNeil, Bobby Gillespie, Beattie, Karen Parker and Louise Maxwell. Everyone got together as a committee, but me and Paul I don't think turned up for the meeting so we weren't involved. They all got together and decided they were going to start up a club for all these bands that we liked and all these bands that were just starting up. They thought Daddy Warbucks was that venue that we always seemed to like. Someone went along there and hired out the venue for a Sunday night.

It started off as maybe once a month in June 1985. The Loft were the first band to play, but within a couple of months they'd split up and returned another couple of months later as The Weather Prophets. I think The Pastels was the second gig. Through word of mouth, putting up posters, it really did spread like wildfire. All of a sudden all these young guys in moptops started to appear. Young indie kids with cardigans and anoraks started appearing. All these people just growing out of nowhere. Even Pat Nevin, the Chelsea footballer, started hanging out at Splash One because he loved his indie sounds. He was going into Creation Records at the time. It turned into a really good club. Different people, different choices in music – they didn't want it to just turn into a Creation Records special. Grant said why don't we put on different bands. There was a wee bit of a clash then between other people's tastes and theirs. They were putting on bands like Big Flame – thrashy, kinetic, Fire Engines type vibe – and then Sonic Youth. Obviously everyone liked Sonic Youth but not everyone was into 23 Skidoo, they were heavy electronic funk. They totally blew everyone's mind, when 23 Skiddo came on. Wire, there were big Wire freaks as well, so it was a really good mixture of bands.

We all wanted to get Julian Cope but he was really busy at the time. He was doing his *Fried* and *World Shut Your Mouth* stuff, so we couldn't tie him up at all. We really loved Matt Johnson's band The The at the time as well, tried to get them, but again they were getting bigger and bigger. Splash One as a club was just too small for them. That's how it all started up. Lots of people getting together, talking about it and getting the money together off Derek Louden. Getting the first band together through McGee, getting The Loft and that was it. Word of mouth.

MEANWHILE, ELSEWHERE IN THE EAST

Bobby Gillespie managed to get all the posters designed through an old print connection. Started with all these amazing colours like bright oranges, beautiful pinks and bright purples. Really beautiful colours the posters were, in the early days.

Grant MacDougall (Splash One organiser): It just became quite obvious that there was no sort of place that we could a) listen to music we liked, and b) see the bands that were starting to emerge. So we sort of thought about, well, what's a way of doing something ourselves? We got just over two hundred people attending the first night, so there was certainly, obviously, an appetite for it.

Duglas T. Stewart: Splash One was at a place called . . . I think it was 46 West George Street. It ended up burning down. And yeah, it was a curtainy-type nightclub place and Bobby Gillespie and a group of other friends, I think there was eight of them, decided that they were going to make their own nights. Rather than having Primal Scream or other like-minded bands playing on bills where all the other bands didn't really get it or understand and their audiences wouldn't get it, they would make their own place and there would be projections of films like *If . . .* and *A Clockwork Orange* and things going on in the background. And they would all make up one side of a C60 cassette and that would be the disco, like the eight people would have one side of a C60 cassette each, you know, and somebody would go up and change the tape and that would be the . . . and there would also be bands playing and it would be . . . like Sonic Youth's first Scottish gig was at Splash One and of course there were bands like BMX Bandits and The Pastels and The

Soup Dragons and Primal Scream and bands from England like Felt and The Loft and The June Brides and it just . . . at the start there was probably about maybe fifty, sixty people who turned up at the night going 'Oh, what's it going to be like? Well, this is like our own place, you know, wow.' You know, it's not like there'd be one record played by a DJ that we maybe sort of liked and the rest would just be like stuff that we weren't interested in at all. It would be stuff like 'What's that?' and you could go up and go 'What is that?' to the person that had made up that tape.

Frances McKee: That was our regular haunt every Sunday night. I am just going there and seeing all the contemporary bands to us and at that point we still weren't a band . . . There, you would meet all your friends, all your friends that you were going to be friendly with at some point, and it was just a haven. We were just starting to see things like The Pastels and a kind of realisation that you didn't need to be a virtuoso. You didn't have to play an instrument, it was more like I think quite different to what it is now – the capability was there but not necessarily the skill and . . . whatever the skill was it would come later.

Eugene Kelly (Guitar/vocals, The Vaselines): It was almost as if it felt like the first place in Glasgow where a big percentage of our audience weren't the enemy.

Although the club lasted less than two years, it acted as a huge catalyst and safe haven for the local indie kids, a place to formulate ideas, meet like-minded friends, hear new (and old) music and find inspiration. Nearly forty years later its legend still endures.

MEANWHILE, ELSEWHERE IN THE EAST

The Soup Dragons ascend

Nothing could stop The Soup Dragons' meteoric rise. If it was surprising that they'd had their debut gig at the hallowed Splash One, their next step was even more astonishing. It was also a demonstration of the power of fanzines, which were often a few steps ahead of the weekly papers, especially when they included tapes or flexi discs. In true impresario style, the best way to promote a band was often to produce your own fanzine, as was the case with Soup Dragons bassist Sushil Dade's Pure Popcorn!

Ross Sinclair: It was mad, you know. Sushil did this wee fanzine, *Pure Popcorn!* . . . It had this 7-inch [Soup Dragons] flexi disc on it with The Legend. Sort of a double track thing. The Legend, who we stayed with in London sometimes when we were down there, who was a great, really helpful, nice guy as well. Later turned into Everett True, of course.

Sushil Dade: Pressing up a flexi via Lyntone ('If You Were the Only Girl in the World Would You Take Me?') was an affordable way of sharing our music with folks via the fanzine. To our amazement it got Single of the Week in the *NME* (December 1985). Probably the only flexi disc to receive that accolade.

Sean Dickson: We actually recorded the track and made a thousand copies for £35, I always remember this. And put it on *Pure Popcorn!* And it got Single of the Week in *NME*, our flexi disc. We went completely from nowhere overnight. I had a phone call asking to go down and get interviewed for the *NME*. So

Norman came with me, we went down to London. I used to read the *NME* but I wasn't like crazy reading it every week so I didn't know all the journalists, but, little did I know, the journalist that was interviewing me was the guy that was always big on finding the new best thing. And they ended up giving us like four pages, four full pages, from nowhere to having four pages in *NME*. Next minute, the John Peel show contacted us, asked us, you know, 'Would you do a John Peel session?' And I was like 'Yeah, but we don't have any money to get to London.' And John [Peel] said if we go and meet him tomorrow at the Queen Margaret Union, 'cause he was DJing, 'cause they used to do that thing round universities in those days and that's how my friendship with John started. I went to meet him and he said can you come and do a session for us and I was like 'Well, we'd love to, we've got no money,' and he reached in his wallet and pulled out £150 and he said, 'Is that enough money to get to London?' And I was like 'Sure.' And always, right up to when he passed away, I always had this ongoing joke that I actually owed him £150 and I offered it to him one day and he'd never take it back, he refused to take it back.

Ross Sinclair: And again, it just, it just seemed like so easy. It just, it almost didn't seem remarkable. It was fantastic. But it was sort of, you know, when later in life, how difficult it is to replicate stuff like that, or to do again, or whether it's in art or music or whatever, to get that sort of level of interest going is really hard. And actually, the thing is that to do it with a sort of authenticity, you can't really fake it, you can't really invent a scene nor fake the excitement, or the dynamism in it. So actually, it was very genuine. And it was like, this really kind of exciting scene going on, so it seemed normal that some guy from the *NME* would come up and have a look and listen to this thing.

The impact of the Peel session and the fact that an unsigned band had an unprecedented four-page spread in the NME *immediately caused a sensation, not just among fans hungry to hear more but also among labels looking for opportunities to release great music.*

On 16 December 1985, The Soup Dragons recorded their first 7-inch single. Like the Shop Assistants, they recorded their debut in Edinburgh, with the Bristol-based Subway Organization. Unfortunately, the opportunity to show the world what they had to offer ran into difficulties and the band found themselves dealing with their first spot of misfortune.

Sean Dickson: The Shop Assistants had a single out on Subway Organization and they contacted us asking us to do a single. Which we did as a four-track EP called *The Sun Is in the Sky* and it shows you how naive we were because you don't know things like that . . . on a 7-inch record . . . if you have a certain amount of time on a 7-inch side it deteriorates the quality . . . so basically the EP didn't sound that great, it sounded awful in fact when it got pressed up. And the cover, the Letraset had slipped as it went to the printer's so the cover was just a complete dog's dinner. Funnily enough I actually love the cover now, because it just stinks of 16, 17-year-old naivety, which you can't buy as you know what it's like. But when you're 16 and 17 you don't want that, you want to be like all your favourite bands are like . . . And I remember us all sitting there nearly crying, you know, put it on, it sounded like shit and the cover looked like shit, we were like 'Shit, what do we do?' So we . . . we basically pulled it, much to the hatred of Martin that ran the Subway Organization but, you know, a lot of gratitude to him that he actually did agree to it then. 'Okay then, we'll pull it.'

While it was never officially released, The Sun Is in the Sky EP *did turn up in a few shops, making it one of The Soup Dragons' most collectable records. Despite their naivety of the music business the band had an innate belief in the quality of their music and a clear understanding that a debut single was potentially your only opportunity to make your mark on the world. To be fair to the band, nobody around them was advising them of any of the technical aspects required to release records. It's a remarkable testament to their quality control, especially in the face of the fast-changing world of music, that they held out to ensure their true debut not only contained a fantastic pop song but that it sounded enormous, and it did. 'Whole Wide World' has stood the test of time and is now recognised as one of the great singles of 1980s independent music.*

Sean Dickson: We made 'Whole Wide World' and we went the opposite way, 'cause I found out why our EP sounded so bad. So I was like, so it's all to do with grooves on a vinyl, so if we do a 12-inch of 'Whole Wide World', that means there's one and a half minutes on the A-side, so it should be the loudest record ever made. Which we did. There's like . . . it's the craziest-looking 12-inch, it's like the grooves are about that far apart [indicates with fingers]; they just spread right across. I remember going to the cutting engineer, he went, 'It's one and a half minutes,' and I went 'Yeah,' and he goes, 'Why are you putting it on a

12-inch?' I'm like, 'I don't know, 'cause it looks good.' He just went, 'I can only make the machine go this far with the grooves, there's still going to be a big runout on the groove,' and I'm like, 'That's cool.' And it is one of the loudest 12-inches ever.

We did a video for the first single called 'Whole Wide World', which cost £100, in Edinburgh, and it took an hour to make 'cause we went in with this VHS cassette of somebody fondling Daffy Duck through a box, and you can see it on YouTube, 'cause I put it on YouTube, and you know, they basically just wanted to play on top of it, you know, two images put on top. So this guy in this place that done it, I think he'd done commercials or talk-overs, he just didn't have a clue what . . . you know, it's just these four. I think we got drunk before it, so the four of us fell in this room and for an hour just sang the song into the camera. And then he placed the two, he took one take, it's not even edited, and just placed it on top of it and that was our video. And *The Chart Show* played it, which was just bonkers, you know, it was just kind of like 'Oh my God,' you know, but actually on Saturday afternoon – or was it Saturday morning? – *The Chart Show*, Saturday morning television.

John Peel is regularly cited as a hugely important figure in the independent music scene. His appraisal and playing of a record would introduce it to thousands of listeners on mainstream BBC radio. It shouldn't be forgotten, though, that The Chart Show *played an equally big role in promoting independent music. It first ran on Channel 4 in the early evening before moving to a Saturday mid-morning slot. Its indie chart introduced everyone from children to grandparents to the delights of Psychic TV and Nick Cave, US hardcore and jangling indie-pop.*

'Whole Wide World' received another coveted Single of the Week in the NME *and Andy Kershaw (28 June 1986,* Smash Hits*) said it was 'sure to please two kinds of customers. Those who cling, quite rightly, to an affection for the Buzzcocks, and those who may never have heard Manchester's greatest group of the Seventies, but will be enchanted by The Soup Dragons' fuzzed-up, galloping guitars and the semi submerged pale-pink vocal. It's all over too soon, and that's a good sign.'*

CHAPTER 7
1986

As good as Ramones Records: 53rd & 3rd Records

The energies of Edinburgh and Glasgow collided when Sandy McLean's distribution of Rote Kapelle's EP came to the attention of the Shop Assistants' David Keegan. The Shop Assistants and The Pastels combined forces with the Fast Forward distribution company to form 53rd & 3rd Records, one of the most game-changing record labels to emerge from the worldwide independent scene. The way was clear for the label to scoop up some of the best acts in Scotland and from further afield.

David Keegan: The idea for 53rd & 3rd came from Sandy at Fast Forward, who were the Scottish branch of the Cartel distribution network, and he suggested that they could put together a label to put out the next Shop Assistants record. We became the first release on that.

Stephen Pastel: Probably by then people could see that a lot of people like The Pastels and the Shop Assistants and other things were coming out and there was an opportunity to release some records.

Sandy McLean: 53rd & 3rd was based on a label under the wing of the Fast Forward distribution company, and it just gave us the opportunity to release records.

Stephen Pastel: I think David saw the opportunity to do a label. And I think David saw the potential for it. At first, I really just tried to kind of help him. I probably knew Sandy very slightly, just through him distributing records. Maybe he invited me out for lunch. I can't remember exactly. And then, so David and I thought we could do something and we thought there was enough kind of stuff going on in Scotland that we were interested in that we could document so it was really just to document the kind of music that was getting made. And that moment and the kind of sound, probably groups that were coming through just immediately after The Pastels and Shop Assistants.

David Keegan: I came up with the name, it's a Ramones song. I think I designed the picture on the label, which was Joey Ramone. There wasn't a plan to have a record label releasing certain kinds of music, it was always just going to be stuff that we liked.

David Keegan: I think everybody first contributed a band – I had my own band, the Shop Assistants. Stephen suggested the Househunters, which is Jowe Head from Swell Maps. And Sandy,

AS GOOD AS RAMONES RECORDS: 53RD & 3RD RECORDS

I'm not sure what Sandy's first band was, it was maybe The Beat Poets. So it was kind of just whatever we liked at the time. So there you go, super-varied.

The first release on the label was 'Safety Net' by Shop Assistants. It was a sensation, an immediate success, and leapt to number two in the indie charts. It put Scotland's home-grown industry back on the track furrowed by Postcard and Fast.

Mary Harron (*Observer*, 9 March 1986): The Shop Assistants have released their debut single on a new independent label 53rd & 3rd – the title of an old Ramones song – and there's no question where these girls' hearts lie. The charm here lies in the paradox between their sweet voices and the backing, which is a wash of mad, Velvet Underground-inspired guitars. Recommended.

David Keegan: Well, as soon as we very first played that song ['Safety Net'], we knew it was like a special song. I can actually remember the first time we ever did it in rehearsal and Alex saying, 'That's the next single.' It just seemed to be really special.

Ann Donald: We listened to The Ronettes and all that whole Phil Spector thing but without the crazy psychopathic side obviously . . . and I've still got 'Be My Baby'. It's the sound on that that is just incredible. And we partly wanted to recreate that as well as taking the excitement of Mary Chain guitar, which is what obviously David did. And that's what the beefed-up sound of Laura and I just battering two floor toms did and the sticks with the big furry pom poms on the end. There was nothing finer than battering hell out of that, you knew you were doing the right thing and it was just brilliant. Just somebody amped that up and blow up noise, great.

Laura McPhail: 'Safety Net' was for me one of the most exciting times. This was when it felt like things were changing. We felt the record sounded great, we were playing live more and more and we were on our own label – there was a sense of momentum and that something was happening.

Sandy McLean: AGARR1, the first 53rd & 3rd record, A-G-A-R-R, As Good As Ramones Records, and that one came out and did 25,000 the first week.

Ian Hoey: There was real excitement around that short period when 53rd & 3rd released 'Safety Net', which I still maintain is one of the best singles from the eighties, easily, stands up next to anything. You get that on a 12-inch record and the sheer power of it. And for me, that's setting the bar. I think when I heard that, I thought, 'My God, you know, there's something really happening, really exciting.'

David Keegan: When it was released, we were supporting The Jesus and Mary Chain, and that really had to, I mean, that was a feeling that something was really, really happening.

Andrew Tully: It was amazing seeing them, you know, doing things like 'Safety Net', and just how it went. And what was lovely about how it went . . . but without any, you know, the word, any publicists and the word. You know, people selling the

AS GOOD AS RAMONES RECORDS: 53RD & 3RD RECORDS

records to the radio or stuff like that. It just . . . I hesitate to use the word organic, it was just . . . and that's how things seem to be, it just . . . things just happened and it was lovely to see it happen.

53rd & 3rd and 'Safety Net' had set another benchmark for Scotland's revitalised independent scene. Importantly, this new scene was making a distinction between being a way to sell in to the majors, as the first wave of DIY bands had done, and utilising the means of production to form a genre in itself.

CHAPTER 8
1986

A new era for indie music

Scotland was now taking a pivotal role in helping create a new, identifiable sound. At the forefront were bands heavily influenced by Postcard and The Smiths: BMX Bandits, The Pastels, and Shop Assistants.

Simon Reynolds (*Melody Maker*, 28 June 1986): All this talk about indie-pop, about the death and resurgence of an underground, an alternative to chart pap. But is there really life beyond the major record companies' marketing schemes and, if so, what does it consist of? What does it sound like? Would you recognise an indie-popper if he idiot-danced on your toe? Simon Reynolds flips through the scene and discovers a heartening reaction to machismo, a return to innocence, a fresh way forward.'

Hugh Fielder (*Sounds*, 5 July 1986): 'Is there an indie revival in the air or just another battle of the bands? HUGH FIELDER tracks down the men at the top and pops the question.

Is this an indie revival we see before us? There's a new set of bands – Half Man Half Biscuit, The Soup Dragons, BMX Bandits, Rose of Avalanche, The Mighty Lemon Drops, Stump, The Chesterfields, the Shop Assistants – starting to make an impact on the indie charts on a new set of record labels – Subway Organization, Probe Plus, Fire, El, Pink, Ron Johnson, 53rd & 3rd . . .

Certainly the indie scene is in dire need of a boost. From the halcyon days of the early eighties when independent labels accounted for around 10 per cent of album sales, they've been pegged back to around 4 per cent.

The second 53rd & 3rd release was 'Cuticles' by Jowe Head, under the Househunters moniker, a debt to Swell Maps that both David and Stephen were delighted to put out.

The rise of Fast Forward and Narodnik

The immediate success of 'Safety Net' and 53rd & 3rd sent shockwaves through Glasgow and Edinburgh. The Jesus and Mary Chain had become a sensation after their release on Creation and their inspiring move to a major, but this was the first time since the days of Fast and Postcard that a locally based record label and band had had such a huge impact on the UK scene. It inspired further bands to form and gave them the belief that they too could release their own records. Sandy McLean was at the epicentre of this activity thanks to his huge experience with distribution, going back to the days of Fast Product and his recent success in distributing his own label.

He put the word out that he was open to more offers of collaboration.

Andrew Tully: The Shop Assistants filled out the scene massively and the scene, I would say the Edinburgh scene, if not entirely flourished from what the Shop Assistants did, it as good as did. I mean, I think it's undeniable that they brought all the attention and they brought, you know, they had the excitement.

Sandy McLean: Once I got out on my own I was just taken off the leash, I could go and phone up labels, phone up musicians, and just try to create things. I basically managed to get a credit account with a pressing plant called Making Records. Basically, the bands would just bring me the tape and the artwork and I would send it down to London and they would cut it and send us test pressings and then release basically finished copies a month or so later. And we would promote it and sell it and get the money back quick enough to pay the bill. As the money came in, we became more successful, heavy metal bands would come and want to put their record out. And I thought, well, I don't really want to do that on my label, but, I'll tell you what, I'll front you the money. And we created generic labels. We created a generic heavy metal label called Blast Furnace. The catalogue numbers were Kickass-1, Kickass-LP1, Kickass-18, a bit of an in-joke, but all the bands sold enough to make the money back. And I really genuinely enjoyed doing that. And it was just, it just felt great to be able to kind of create something like that, put it out to the world, and have it be successful.

A NEW ERA FOR INDIE MUSIC

Angus McPake: You basically arrived with masters and artwork, and he [Sandy] would get the record made and then get it distributed. And I think that was fairly revolutionary at the time, and it was almost like if you could afford to get somebody into a studio and record them, then you could start a record label or just put your own records out. And that was, I think that was very important and I think part of the explosion of the scene was partly down to that.

Andrew Tully: We were just like, ooh, how do we do this? And he [Sandy] would be like, 'Well, you bring me the recording and I can sort out getting it pressed up,' and stuff like that. So, you know, he was pivotal in facilitating it and letting it happen because we were just kind of fumbling around in the dark.

The immediate success of 53rd & 3rd led Sandy to offer distribution and manufacturing to other bands or would-be impresarios to run further labels. It's no exaggeration to state that Safety Net and Fast Forward kickstarted a renaissance in Scotland's independent music scene that would make 1986 one of the most fertile periods in independent music. Many of the releases would make their way to America and help influence the nascent Washington scene that would eventually make its way to the ears of Kurt Cobain. In the meantime, though, in Scotland it brought attention to The Soup Dragons and Shop Assistants and, in the wake of the earlier mainstream success of The Jesus and Mary Chain, the scene ignited. One of these new labels would coalesce East and West when East Kilbride émigrés Meat Whiplash would relocate to Edinburgh. This would result in bass player, Eddie Connelly setting up Narodnik Records with Fast Forward, as the frustratingly less celebrated sister label of 53rd & 3rd. It would also prove hugely important to future side projects of the Shop Assistants' chums Rote Kapelle... In many ways, if 53rd & 3rd was the Shop Assistants' label, Narodnik could be Rote Kapelle's, despite it never actually releasing a stand-alone Rote Kapelle record.

Sandy McLean: We were in Alva Street, and the bass player from Meat Whiplash got in touch, a chap called Eddie Connelly, and Eddie was on one of these government employment schemes and he was gonna set up a record label.

Michael Kerr: Eddie had started Narodnik on a Prince's Trust allowance scheme where I mean, you didn't sign on, and he'd got, supposedly, some money from an aunt or something like that, 'cause you'd need to show that you had a certain amount of money to start up this business. They weren't getting any huge investments for the label. And I think that he really liked Jesse Garon and he just wanted them to get a record out, so he was going to do it. And I think he then went to see Sandy McLean, at Fast Forward, and he did the distribution for it.

Narodnik Records never had the level of impact that 53rd & 3rd had, but nevertheless it became a classic label. Its releases were mostly by Edinburgh bands such as Jesse Garon and the Desperadoes, The Fizzbombs and The Vultures.

Much like their Bellshill counterparts, many Edinburgh bands quickly diversified, swapping instruments and forming side-project bands. Narodnik would be home to many of them.

A NEW ERA FOR INDIE MUSIC

One of the first of these side projects was Jesse Garon and the Desperadoes, whose single 'Splashing Along' was the first Narodnik release.

If the shared membership of the Bellshill bands seems complicated, the multitude of interlinking strands that had sprouted from Rote Kapelle would send shivers down Pete Frame's spine.

Jesse Garon and the Desperadoes

Rote Kapelle gave rise to multiple bands, often with core members playing different instruments. The first of these bands was Jesse Garon and the Desperadoes.

Margarita Vazquez Ponte: After a very short time in Rote Kapelle, Andrew [Tully] had another band, but they were just a half-formed band and they been called Das Eichhornchen, which means the squirrel in German.

Andrew Tully: [The Desperadoes started in] 1985, I think. Rote Kapelle's horizons had widened at this point by barging unceremoniously into the worlds of the nascent Shoppies et al. at Napier College and also Edinburgh's burgeoning garage scene centred around the practice rooms in Blair Street in general and Lenny and Angus in particular. We were young, 'gifted' and broke, drinking in the Green Tree and concocting great plans. At this point the next question after asking someone's name was 'Do you want to be in a band?' The serial musical bedhopping of Lenny et al. was infectious. If you fancied playing another instrument or a slightly different style of music, just ask around the table at the Green Tree or your new pals in the practice room next door. The Desperadoes had started off as a different set of pals from Currie High School who all fancied playing guitar – suddenly there was a whole set of new people to play with.

I'd always liked pop music. I always liked The Velvet Underground. Love the Monkees, and love Joy Division. And then they became New Order and did *Power, Corruption & Lies*, there was some really nice guitar stuff on that. And I thought, 'I want to play guitar'. And I can't sing very well but I want to kind of sing simple songs and just have a laugh. So it was definitely an offshoot of Rote Kapelle, the Desperadoes. And, again, I'd formed that with two friends back in Balerno and that was Kevin McMahon and Stuart Clark. Oh, and it was Eric on bass. So again, it was another bedroom band. And we didn't have a drummer. We quickly lost Eric on bass. So we had three guitarists. And we just did these kind of simple little pop songs. Very basic.

Margarita Vazquez Ponte: They all played guitar. So they were looking to expand, so after a little bit of time in Rote Kapelle, Andrew said to me, 'Do you want to come and play drums for our band?' So I was like, yeah, okay. Now, no, I couldn't play the drums. Did I know if I could? No, I didn't.

Andrew Tully: David [Keegan] was doing a kind of joint gig with Stephen from The Pastels . . . So they did a gig in Glasgow, where it was the Shop Assistants, The Pastels, Primal Scream, and another band in Glasgow. And then the next week, I think it was the next week, we all played in Edinburgh. And David had said, oh, do you fancy . . . or it might have been Alex in fact, said, do you fancy playing on the bill? And at that point, we only had one song, which was called 'And the Rain Fell Down', which became a trilogy, God help me, which was about a girl in Glasgow at the time that I was unrequitedly in love with, and I would go through every fortnight to see and we would go to gigs at Splash One and stuff like that. And then I would sleep on her parents' dining room floor.

But it always seemed to be raining in Glasgow whenever I went through. So I wrote all these songs about it raining and George Square. So we did this gig with The Pastels, the Shop Assistants, Primal Scream, and we were first on the bill. And we did the song. And there was an E chord in it. And I had difficulty holding the E chord down. So we ended up Sellotaping my fingers to the neck of the guitar, and I just had to go. Every third chord would go like that. So it was very primal. And then we went down really well. I think more people were indulging us. So then it was like, oh, we need to do another song. So the only other song we knew was 'Louie Louie', which fortunately was in E so I just, I think we did the first verse and chorus. And then that was all we could do. Then my abiding memory of that gig was, sitting glowering in the front row, The Jesus and Mary Chain. Who, if my recollection's right, had just done their first Peel session, and had just arrived back up in town, and we're kind of sitting there so I just remember these great shocks of curly black hair . . . They were at that point, just, you know, revolutionaries, and they're totally making it on their own accord and were causing this huge stir and stink. You know, riots at gigs and stuff like that. And they just seemed so glamorous and so seedy. I mean, it was like, it was like having The Velvet

Underground turning up in your living room. And it was like, this is amazing. So that was the Desperadoes' very first gig in a very kind of first line-up. And it went quite well. So we were then thinking, well, let's . . . we need to get more people. So that was where Angus came in, on the bass. And then Margarita, who'd been at the gig was, 'Oh, I've always wanted to drum,' it's like, well, yeah, why not? Let's just, let's just do it. And that's kind of how the Desperadoes started. That's kind of where we kind of started from.

Angus McPake: Jesse Garon and the Desperadoes had started before I knew them. They were arriving at rehearsal while I was leaving a rehearsal and they said that their bass player hadn't turned up. Would I mind standing in? And I was like, okay, but I wasn't even playing bass at the time. It was kind of this, just a strange thing to be asked, and I ended up in the band by accident.

Margarita Vazquez Ponte: Eventually, also, Fran joined, Fran Schoppler, who sang along with Andrew as a singer.

Fran Schoppler (Vocals, Jesse Garon and the Desperadoes): I was a student at Edinburgh University. I knew before I went to uni that I would really like to get into a band, or form a band. I'd tried to get into Kitsch and the Night Set (Paul Hullah's band) unsuccessfully and did a little stuff with an offshoot of K&TNS, The Disco Popes. I think I was on a year out from university and was living in a flat on West Richmond Street, Edinburgh. I moved into the flat with my university friend, Jacqui Small. A woman called Ruth Fraser moved in the flat over the summer of 1985. It turned out she was good friends with Alex Taylor of the Shop

Assistants. They had met while at university, in halls of residence. Alex visited Ruth one afternoon/early evening (it was light outside, it was summer) and sat in the communal living room drinking tea and chatting with Ruth. I was introduced.

We were all chatting away and Alex at some point told me about the band she was in. We were just chatting and having a bit of a laugh, singing a bit, what's the highest note you can sing, what's the lowest note? Alex mentioned she knew of a friend who had a band (Andrew Tully) who was looking for a singer. Would I be interested in going along to a rehearsal? I said yes, I would. The rehearsal rooms were in Blair Street. The rooms smelled like something had died in there and they were probably not the safest place to rehearse at the time. I remember the occasion as being a bit awkward. I didn't know anyone and I was quite shy I suppose. I was given some words to sing along to a song and I gave it a go. Nobody said after the rehearsal whether I was in the band or not required. I'm sure the verdict was told to me by Alex. I didn't realise the rest of the band all knew each other from college or school. I was definitely an incomer, an unknown quantity.

Margarita Vazquez Ponte: And then we had the never ending cycle of other guitarists.

Andrew Tully: You know, the Desperadoes haemorrhaged guitarists, like billy-ho. I mean, we had so many guitarists. If we ever have a reunion, we'll need to hire the Albert Hall. The Desperadoes were really quite different from Rote Kapelle. It was much more indie-pop, wearing our Velvet Underground and our sixties sensibilities on our sleeve a little bit more.

Fran Schoppler: Angus was in the band pretty much from the start. He joined a little earlier than I did. He was there when I visited the rehearsal room for the casual audition. We burned through so many guitarists! No, I don't think being initially a side project lost us guitarists. It was other reasons. Stuart Clarke realised once the band started planning tours etc. that he couldn't commit to that as he was at university and there was too much of a clash. He saw that it would have a big impact on his studies. John Robb (The Offhooks) and Bruce Hopkins joined after Stuart Clarke and Kevin McMahon left. When Bruce Hopkins left (or was it when John Robb left to concentrate on his own band), Michael Kerr (Meat Whiplash) joined the band.

Angus McPake: A lot of our influences were kind of nostalgia in a way. I think a lot of the stuff we talked about was about our youth. We certainly weren't all about the future and breaking new ground.

Margarita Vazquez Ponte: Andrew seemed to develop a secondary career as a bit of a stand-up because his monologues in between became longer and, well, he was very funny, although Angus and I used to heckle him like hell because it used to get really boring after a while and I definitely threw a few drumsticks at him.

Angus McPake: We played some really dreadful gigs in Edinburgh. And then I think, suddenly, just something clicked and we were actually quite good one night. And instead of thinking I'm just standing in for the bass player, I suddenly kind of went, I quite like this band. Perhaps I should stay in the band. And it was kind of a very, kind of fast trajectory after that.

Margarita Vazquez Ponte: Eddie Connelly, he used to be in Meat Whiplash, and was going out with Alex from the Shop Assistants, started putting out records [on Narodnik], so he put out 'Splashing Along'. *Billy the Whizz* EP was the other one. The second one was produced by Douglas Hart as well.

Andrew Tully: We'd started recording, and on the first day, about half-seven, Douglas goes, 'Oh, do you mind if we go to the chip shop next door?' And we're all like, oh, well, hmm, quite hungry. Yeah, yeah. And he went, 'Oh, well, no. I just want to watch *Top of the Pops*,' and we sat there and we got fish and chips and we watched *Top of the Pops* and the Mary Chain were on. And there's Douglas on there and we're like, 'It's you,' which seemed magical.

Fran Schoppler: I still get a thrill when I hear the early singles. The song and words for 'Splashing Along' were written by Andrew Tully. Each band member added their own touches to the song when we played it as a band, and the song was also helped enormously by that driving bass line from Angus McPake. The song was a love song to Glasgow but mostly a love song about a certain woman at the time that Andrew was smitten by. His muse! I'm sure 'The Rain Fell Down' was written about her too.

We travelled to Alaska Studios in London to record two singles. It would have been Eddie Connelly who had links with Douglas

Hart of The Jesus and Mary Chain, as Meat Whiplash were also an East Kilbride band and also on Creation Records. I believe, after reading a piece recently about Dave Evans's time in Biff Bang Pow! and The Jesus and Mary Chain, that Alaska Studios was the preferred recording studio for Creation Records, so there's the link.

I don't remember much about the recording process at the time. I would imagine for us that it would have been recorded with most of the band playing together in a live room, with a guide vocal, then some overdubs and the vocals put over the best take. I think I remember vocals were done with one run-through – the second is the take! It was my first experience of being in a recording studio. The band had only recorded a demo on a borrowed four-track recorder before that.

I think the reception for the 'Splashing Along' single was great. We got really positive reviews.

Margarita Vazquez Ponte: The singles did get a lot of airplay and did pretty well and did okay for us. And I think that we thought, maybe we thought, that what happened to the Shop Assistants would happen to us, but we were just too shambolic.

A NEW ERA FOR INDIE MUSIC

BMX Bandits

Soon after Sean put The Soup Dragons together, Duglas started building something from the ashes of The Pretty Flowers. The result was BMX Bandits, who were to become a central component of the Glasgow music scene and a breeding ground for new generations of talent. So many folk who travelled through its ranks have gone on to achieve successful music careers that it could be described as the Brit School of Glasgow indie.

Duglas T. Stewart: Sean was like, 'You've got a bunch of new songs that we've never done with Pretty Flowers and I've got a few ideas that we can maybe work on together, I think we should start a new group.' And I was like, yeah, but you've got, like, you're starting your own new group as well, and he was like yeah, but I want to do this as well. And so the BMX Bandits were born.

Sean Dickson: Because Duglas doesn't actually play any instruments he needs people around him to take his ideas and he's . . . I mean, Duglas is a very, very creative person and has a fantastic musical knowledge and a fantastic mind, you know, and I remember Duglas could give me . . . which is quite a hard thing to do, I know this 'cause I mean I've been making music for a long time, but there's not many people that can just give you an a cappella in a way of a song. You know, Duglas would write a song as a vocal and give you it and then it was my job to try and translate that into music, or it was Norman's job or whoever Duglas works with at that time. You know, I'm the one that usually comes up with the music first and then writes the melody or the a cappella on top and that's a unique gift that's he's got . . . In the old days Duglas would sing a song in front of me and I'd be like 'Right, okay, right.' I said just send me what's in your head, give me a tune in your head and he sent me this three-minute piece of music with him just singing the melody.

Duglas T. Stewart: We weren't sure how long it was going to last and we thought well let's pick something that's kinda . . . seems slightly crap but amuses us, you know, and BMX bikes were such a big trend at that time and a bit like Brian Wilson – the big trend when he started The Beach Boys was surf boards and he didn't surf. I'd never been on a bicycle. And so in my sort of head there was a little bit of a Beach Boys kinda tribute in the name, it was like a current trend that you would probably see as kind of a naff thing to take your name after and also it was something that I couldn't do. But we've never done any songs about cycling, which was, of course, Beach Boys did songs about surfing, but we kinda missed a trick there. We never quite managed to grab that market.

The band was initially supplemented by Soup Dragon Jim McCulloch, and Willie McArdle on drums.

Duglas T. Stewart: We made up a little cassette, BMX Bandits, which we recorded very, very cheaply in something like two hours at a studio in Glasgow just on Sauchiehall Street and it had four songs on it and it was called 'Figure Four' and I thought I'm going to give this to people whose music has inspired me and I wasn't actually thinking I'm going to get offered a record deal out of it or anything. And so I sent it off to people like Dan Treacy and Jowe Head from Television Personalities and Swell Maps and to Jonathan Richman and a few other people. And one of the people I gave it to was Stephen Pastel. I approached him at a concert in Queen Margaret union and said this is a cassette I made of my group, we're called BMX Bandits, and next time I bumped into him he said, 'Oh, I really liked, I really like the cassette you gave me, particularly there was a song on it called "The Day Before Tomorrow" I really like and I think you seem like a pretty interesting person. I'm just starting this new label and I'd like you to be one of the first groups on it. Would you record "The Day Before Tomorrow" as a first single?' And we were like, 'Yes! Yes! It's incredible.' And then we went and recorded two songs that weren't 'The Day Before Tomorrow' instead, because we knew better and it was like 'Oh, I still preferred "The Day Before Tomorrow", but yeah we like these as well.' So, yeah, we released that single and the rest is history . . .

BMX Bandits released 'E102' on 53rd & 3rd, the label's third single.

Duglas T. Stewart: Yeah, it felt, it felt incredible and because the record label headquarters was so far away and there was a tight turnaround, like, the singles were basically going to arrive pretty much the day before they were released. How I first got the single was going in like a record shop in Glasgow and buying a copy of it. And the front cover of it was like my face in a big star, you know, kind of smiling in a big star and kinda going up to the counter and going 'I'll take this one please.' And they were like 'That's you!' and I go 'Yes, it is.'

A NEW ERA FOR INDIE MUSIC

Sean Dickson: I think we've always been a way to try and confuse, even right down to the artwork of some things. I mean, that first BMX Bandits cover, it was thrown together on my couch, and we were rolling about because it was so bad, we were laughing at it, going, like, stick your face in a star, and it looked so bad, you know.

Sandy McLean: AGARR1 the Shop Assistants 'Safety Net', AGARR2 Househunters ['Cuticles'], AGARR3 I believe was BMX Bandits' 'E102', I think, and that came about... basically Stephen just brought them to us, said let's do a record, it was just going to be a single so that was fine. I used my friend Jo Callis's recording studio, Heart Street Studio, and his engineer Terry Adams to record the BMX Bandits. It was a Saturday night. And took them down there, introduced them, let them get on with it, six o'clock at night, woke up the next morning in Rose Street, my flat, and there was a cassette that had been put through the mailbox at some point at stupid o'clock in the morning and it was the BMX Bandits' 'E102'. Sean Dickson of The Soup Dragons was the main musical guy in them at that point and Jim McCulloch and a guy called Billy and a curly-haired guy whose name I can't remember was also in them, didn't last beyond the first single, and Duglas of course. So it was an amazingly happy record. I just loved 'E102', it was tremendous.

Unlike The Soup Dragons, who received almost universal praise for their debut, the reviews for the BMX Bandits' 7-inch were horrific.

Duglas T. Stewart: Well the very first review BMX Bandits got... it was funny because the first Soup Dragons release came out

I think about a week or maybe two weeks before ours and the review it got in *NME* was: 'This is possibly the best single ever made'... and then the BMX Bandits single came out and I think it was *Sounds* were like, 'This is possibly the worst record ever made.' And it was like these boys need to eat their porridge and it was like really, really ... 'this is real garbage', you know, was basically the gist of it, and being myself, the type of guy I am, I was delighted, you know, I was like ... I didn't think I could get anything better than that Soup Dragons review but this might be. And you know, I would carry a copy of *Sounds* with me everywhere and if I met anybody I was like wait until you see this review we got for a single and I think people were expecting to read 'This is genius, what a wonderful debut' and they'd be like 'Right, aren't you upset?' And I'd be like 'No, it's great isn't it? They really, really hate us.' But I was sort of pleased, it's that sort of thing. Funnily enough, I always remember, it might seem unlikely, that I saw an interview with someone from Fleetwood Mac who sort of said, 'Oh, we've never really been in fashion, but that's good because if you're never in fashion, you're never out of fashion.' I was like 'Yeah, I like that.' That's what ... we're going to be like that too.

Despite the poor reviews in the press, BMX Bandits were hugely popular and had come to the attention of Janice Long, who became a huge fan, while The Soup Dragons were lauded by John Peel. Inevitably, the demands of the shared band members proved unworkable and there was a splintering. The first departure from BMX Bandits was Sean Dickson, who was becoming increasingly stretched with his work with The Soup Dragons. Sean and Duglas remained lifelong friends, avidly supporting each other's projects. Jim McCulloch remained with the Bandits for a short while longer.

A NEW ERA FOR INDIE MUSIC

Joe McAlinden: The Soup Dragons, they were the first band, they really went. Jim and Sean, they were pretty much doing that. And I think Sean had to leave the BMX Bandits because he was doing The Soup Dragons. Round about then I took a lot more of an active role in the BMX Bandits for quite a time.

Jim McCulloch: That was tricky. I think that was difficult for [Sean] and Duglas on a personal level because it was the toing and froing of the other members of the bands and all that and I think they could see that. It was going to . . . it's going to pull apart, you know, because this was putting more demands on Sean's time and even maybe more than on my time because I was kind of more involved with both bands at this point. And it got a bit fraught, you know, there was a lot of arguing and argy-bargy about 'you can't do that, you need to do this' and, you know, but we just tried to make it work as much as we could.

Duglas T Stewart: Norman (Blake) started initially playing drums with us. Our first drummer was unfortunately not working out and Norman seemed like an obvious choice. So, after our first drummer left, Norman and Sean were in the band at the same time.

BMX Bandits' second single was the originally planned debut, 'The Day Before Tomorrow'/'What a Wonderful World', again on 53rd & 3rd, which received far better reviews. It still featured Sean but their next single, 'Figure 4', had a more stable line-up of Duglas, Jim, Joe McAlinden, and Francis Macdonald now on drums

Joe McAlinden: The second BMX Bandits record I was more involved in, I'd started to play with them live. So I was in the studio for, I think it was 'The Day Before Tomorrow'.

Francis Macdonald: I really enjoyed the BMX Bandits, it seemed a lot more fun and you know I stayed with them for a long, long time.

The Soup Dragons become part of Big Life

The Soup Dragons were making huge inroads towards the mainstream. After the 'Whole Wide World' single on Subway it was perhaps expected that they would follow the Shop Assistants onto 53rd & 3rd, but they had bigger plans. Their next release would be with Jazz Summers and Tim Parry's label, Big Life.

Ross Sinclair: I think we were doing a gig in London and they came to see us. It [the label] was called Big Life. It was him [Jazz Summers] and Tim Parry. Jazz was brilliant, sadly gone now, but I mean, he was great. He'd just done Wham! in China and it was like off the scale, like, 'Fuck, who is this guy?' You know, 'Why is he interested in us?'

Sean Dickson: This guy who used to comanage Wham! saw [the gig] and gave us a phone call and invited us to London and asked to manage us – Jazz Summers. And that's how our relationship with starting our own record label started back then, which was called Raw TV, and which eventually became Big Life, which was our managers' label.

A NEW ERA FOR INDIE MUSIC

Ross Sinclair: I think they wanted it to be big and bigger and bigger, which is their job, really, you know . . . They never really interfered with anything at that point, at that stage everything was pretty cheaply done and, you know, you'd record things for a couple of days. And you know, there wasn't any kind of, like, let's spend a month to record something and then scrap five of them and doing it was just you and . . . and did the songs that you're playing live and it's quite straightforward.

Sean Dickson: Raw TV was our imprint but it was kind of through . . . You know, we didn't really know how to run a record label that well but they just gave us complete and utter control. I mean we even like, we even had a secret deal with CBS Records for a while. 'Cause CBS wanted . . . you know, all these major record companies came out the woodwork and wanted to sign us and to be honest, you know, we weren't ready to be signed to a major . . . and you know, it wasn't really about money or anything for us at that time, it was more about let's just try and make some great records and we knew we were getting better as we were going on. And our managers were the same but they signed a secret deal with CBS that gave . . . I think they gave us like fifty grand or something to make records with the view that we'd sign to CBS. We never did – we just took the money and made records.

During this period, The Soup Dragons released some of their greatest singles. The follow-up to 'Whole Wide World' was the equally majestic 'Hang-Ten', their first for Raw TV. This was followed in 1987 by 'Head Gone Astray', 'Can't Take No More' and 'Soft as Your Face', all of which were hugely successful critically and in the indie charts.

Primal Scream's 'Velocity Girl'

Primal Scream, still on Creation, recorded their second single, 'Crystal Crescent' (Creation 26) in May 1986. The B-side was the now far more famous 'Velocity Girl'. It was around this time that Bobby left The Jesus and Mary Chain to devote himself fully to Primal Scream.

Tam McGurk: The two things were clashing. We actually asked him [Bobby], what you need to do is choose which one you want to do, you know? Because we were getting kind of fed up, you know . . . We were quite resentful . . . We didn't like it, Beattie, Robert and I. We thought, 'You're either in the Scream or you're not,' because at that time we thought, if you want to be in The Jesus and Mary Chain, go and do that and we'll try and get another singer. We were definitely thinking along those lines.

John 'Joogs' Martin: 'Crystal Crescent' was recorded in some studios in St John's Wood in London, complete with horns. It sounded pretty muddled on final release but the B-side, 'Velocity Girl', was a total breeze and so natural and that was recorded down a lane off Pollokshaws Road in Shawlands. Don't know why the Primals didn't extend 'Velocity Girl' to two minutes and release that as the A-side as it was the most catchiest of the two. As you know, a pic of myself bashing the tamourine (on the back sleeve) was a live photo taken by Dick Green at an Edinburgh Hoochie Coochie gig in 1985 along with Meat Whiplash and Weather Prophets, which to me was the best Edinburgh gig and at that time as a six-piece, as Paul Harte had joined as rhythm guitarist. It was around then also that I started to don a mask on stage for some unexplained reason! Maybe I was in some crazy spaghetti westerns at the time. Ha!

Tam McGurk: Just a brilliant song ['Velocity Girl']. One of the songs that you just know, as soon as you're playing it, and you're making up for the first time that it's just brilliant, and you don't get that feeling a lot, you know, but it was actually kind of more or less written and recorded on the same day. And we've done it in a day. And as I say, it was just made up and recorded on that day, and you just kind of got the feeling. Although it was very, very ridiculously short. It was just a really great pumping tune . . . One of the things about Bobby that used to kill me, right? We used to have moments like this where we would write these brilliant songs, just spur of the moment in the studio. We'd make them up, create them, and it was just au naturel, it just happened naturally. As Jim Morrison once said, it was like the music was writing itself, you know, that's what it was almost like. But Bobby would bastardise these songs, you know, and strip them down and structure them to the point where they were void of any life or any soul and he did that with a good few early songs. Bobby, you know, maybe him in his learning process of musical arrangement, whatever, but to me he ruined a few songs.

'Velocity Girl' defined Primal Scream's early sound and is one of the songs from the era that is remembered most fondly. It was the lead offering on the NME's C86 *compilation and it was number four in John Peel's Festive Fifty that year. 'Elephant Stone' by The Stone Roses bears some similarities to the song; years later, The*

Stone Roses would offer Primal Scream a support slot at their 2017 concert at Glasgow's Hampden Park.

The Green Telescope evolve into The Thanes

In Edinburgh the garage scene was about to go through some transformations, and in 1986, The Green Telescope went through a significant change.

Lenny Helsing: The Green Telescope were very much a going concern while both The Rubber Dolfinarium and The Beeville Hive 5 were in operation. When The Green Telescope were invited to play in Germany, including a spot at the Hamburg 6T's all-nighter at Fabrik, and also at De Stip in Amsterdam in August 1986, it was Angus [McPake] who played bass for us as

Alan [McLean], a teacher at the time, couldn't get the time off work. The track 'Make Me Stay' from our EP was selected for inclusion on the German label Glitterhouse's *Declaration of Fuzz* LP. It was an absolute thrill, and quite incredible really, to hold an actual copy of our debut EP *Two By Two*. I played it on every record player we could find, Dansettes, Bushes, friends' hi-fi set-ups . . . No I didn't hear it on the radio. I later heard that it was played on John Peel but I didn't hear it.

Alan McLean: The first EP was for Alan Duffy's Imaginary label and I'm still pretty pleased with that record. It didn't really have much to do with anything else that was going on in the Scottish or any other music scene so it was never really going to appeal to the burgeoning indie or twee Glasgow scene but it pretty well represented our sound and what we were into. Probably my personal favourite Edinburgh band of that time were The Hook 'n' Pull Gang. (They reformed a wee while ago with former Thanes drummer Cal Burt.) The 'Face in a Crowd' single was for Angus McPake's one-off Wump label. After that Gavin [Henderson] and I dropped out of the band and Steve [Fraser] took over briefly. Not sure if they gigged but they recorded 'Scream Thy Last Scream' for a Syd tribute compilation [*Beyond the Wild Wood*] and I know Steve is still pissed that I got a cover for his (much better) bass playing.

Angus McPake: Well, I started a record label myself at the time, called Wump Records, and put a Green Telescope single out. It's the one and only release. And we were going to do a second release of a band called The Dragsters.

Alan McLean: We reformed as The Thanes of Cawdor/The Thanes; Lenny, Bruce, me, and Calvin Burt on drums. Calvin at that point had just started on drums and we were pretty quickly in Jamie Watson's Chamber Studio recording our first album, which IMHO was pretty disappointing, with the band and Jamie not really being ready for that, at that point. Yes. I think Sandy McLean put that out, it was certainly distributed by Fast Forward. By the time we morphed into The Thanes there was quite a garage punk scene developing in Edinburgh. The Rubber Dolfinarium were Angus McPake, the late Ross Gallanders on guitar, Denis Boyle bass, Lenny drums and the late John Doe singing, later replaced by Smout when they evolved into The Beeville Hive 5.

Lenny Helsing: We just thought, we've gone as far as we can with The Green Telescope. People were kind of saying it was a bit of a sort of psychedelic name and we weren't really playing psychedelic music. The evolution seemed to go backwards and we were playing more kind of simplistic garage music, but, so, our bass player Alan McLean came up with this name, The Thanes of Cawdor. He thought it would be something that a teen in America sitting in the classroom, bored one afternoon, would come up with if they thought of having, you know, a teen group who came from Britain. And then we thought, well, what about all these great names like The Kinks and The Poets and The Dovers and The Damned, and so we just thought, let's just be The Thanes.

While the music was far removed from the more melodic C86 sounds of the period, the Edinburgh garage scene was a hugely important part of Scotland's eighties indie scene. Variety was integral to the scene but the outsider attitude and interpersonal support and encouragement were what kept it vibrant. The diversity of sounds nourished many from later generations and seeped into Scotland's music scene in unexpected ways.

Shop Assistants' album released on a major label

The success of 'Safety Net' had attracted major label interest in the Shop Assistants. It was perhaps not surprising, then, that their follow-up, 'I Don't Wanna Be Friends With You', was not on 53rd & 3rd but a major. The Cartel and the mid-1980s revolution in the British record industry had frightened the major labels. For the first time there was a serious threat to them and they were completely blindsided by the popularity and power of independent artists. Now they wanted a piece of that action. Unlike the earlier generation of indie bands, who gladly signed to majors, this new generation were far more savvy. They had seen a lot of artistic compromises being made and were less willing to damage their credibility. The majors would take a different approach and create an environment that was perhaps the best of both worlds – the indie on a major. This had been achieved with reasonable success when Geoff Travis worked with Warner's for Blanco Y Negro. Geoff Travis's latest deal, Blue Guitar, was a collaboration between Chrysalis and Rough Trade.

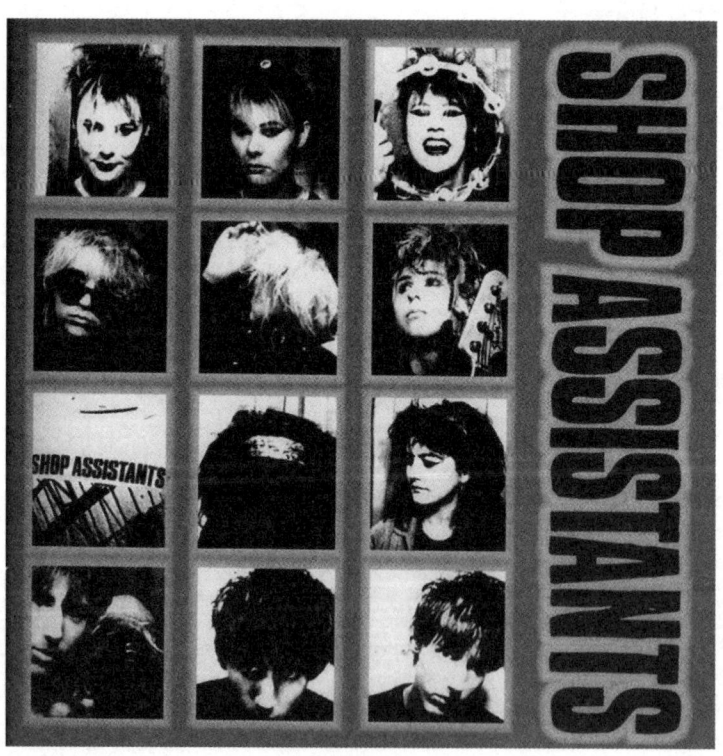

A NEW ERA FOR INDIE MUSIC

David Keegan: Well, initially we were approached by lots of different companies . . . but I really wanted to be on Rough Trade. I had lots of records by bands on Rough Trade, people like The Raincoats and Kleenex. It's like my favourite record label. So for me that would have been the ideal thing, but unfortunately at the time Rough Trade didn't have much money because it was spending it on The Smiths. And also, we had these ideas that we could record things properly and get proper distribution and all this sort of stuff. When you look at what 'Safety Net' sold, and how good the independent distribution network was, we would have probably been better off just staying on 53rd & 3rd and making the most of that. But like I say, I really wanted to be on Rough Trade.

Geoff Travis said, well, we've got the chance to form our own label as part of Chrysalis – Blue Guitar. So it will be like being on Rough Trade with the same artistic freedom and all that except you'll get paid the kind of money, you know, you'll get an advance as if you're on a big label. So it seemed like the ideal thing really. That seems to be the time-honoured tradition of bands from Edinburgh and Glasgow being starting off on a small label, a Postcard or whatever, and then signing to a subsidiary of a big label.

The single 'I Don't Wanna Be Friends With You' was released as support for the album, which was called simply Shop Assistants, *but it did not prove to be the hit everyone was expecting.*

The Dragsters

Labels were springing up everywhere, inspired by Fast Forward's unique offer of distribution and manufacturing. David Keegan, who had taken a small step back from 53rd & 3rd to concentrate on the Shop Assistants, surprisingly set up another label, Union City. While 53rd & 3rd specifically aimed to release and champion a diverse range of bands, Union City was set up specifically for one band: The Dragsters, originally from Greenock.

Ian Boffey (aka Roky Mountain; Guitar, The Dragsters): At Napier, I met Laura (now my wife) and David from the Shop Assistants – we all bonded over the Ramones and hung out at David's Rodney Street flat a lot. We would record songs because the world of the 'Portastudio' had arrived. We were all recording demo tapes with guitars, mics, drum machines and fuzz boxes. The guys from The Dragsters were up visiting a lot and Ian (Hoey, aka Vince Van Yak) moved up too – it seemed like lots of things were happening in Edinburgh around '86. Folks like Andrew Tully and Margarita were around – talented, funny, interesting people, and the Shop Assistants were incredible, one of the best Scottish bands ever. David remains my favourite guitar player to this day, and it was a joy to see them live – they were so good. Nevertheless, I think we were all slightly surprised at this funny little scene that was happening around us.

Ian Hoey: We didn't have money for studio time or anything like that, so basically, there was a band who had been, their label had paid them studio time in Edinburgh, and they finished and they said, 'We've got like a couple of days left. Do you want to go in and record a single?'

Ian Boffey: We somehow 'borrowed' some studio time from the Shop Assistants; David and Laura had cooked up some kind of plan to help us out – and so we dived in on a weekend with David behind the desk.

Jimmy Jamieson (aka Fabian McDonald): We recorded three tracks and 'Albino' wasn't originally bound for the A-side, but it just stood out to all of us. It probably wouldn't get played on the radio now.

Ian Hoey: It was about a minute long. We can squeeze that in on a 7-inch single. At the end of it, they said, 'You know, geez, "Albino" sounds far better.' And we're like, really? You know, it's a minute and twenty seconds. Is this a good idea? Because we don't want to be like a gimmick, like, look how fast our single is. It was like, but we thought, no, we'll lay it, we'll go for 'Albino'. And, thankfully, well, there was one or two people interested in releasing it, Angus being one of them. And we ended up not going with Angus's idea. We're still friends with Angus, so I guess it didn't bother him too long. Let's face it, it's not like 'Albino' was sold by the bucketload; that might have made things different if it had done. But yeah, David Keegan was setting up his own label, Union City.

Jimmy Jamieson: I think I heard it first when listening to Janis Long for a session by the Desperadoes and she put it on. My brother Peter was working in London and I called him and he got me the number for the BBC. I called up and went straight through to the show's producer! I told him thanks for playing our record – any chance of getting a session, and he booked us in for 21 December.

Ian Boffey: It's hard to describe how you feel hearing a song you wrote on Radio 1. 'Elated' is probably the best word.

Follow-up single, 'I'm Not an American', was less successful but it did help launch the career of Turner Prize-winning artist Douglas Gordon, who directed its music video.

Douglas Gordon: I made that video ('I'm Not an American'), well it was actually Super 8 when I was 19 years old. I think the budget was £50 and I think I borrowed the camera from somebody at Paddy's Market. I was living in the same flat as Ross Sinclair, this was when Ross left art school to go on tour with The Soup Dragons. Ross would go into my bedroom and go 'Pftt!', sneer in his Bearsden fashion. I went down to Greenock and shot the thing. I had never used a camera. I went to Jessops to get some splicing tape but it was shut so it was spliced together with Sellotape. I was a nervous wreck.

Somebody posted it on Twitter recently and I hadn't seen it since then. It's now part of this piece I had called 'Pretty Much Every Film and Video Work from 1992 until about Now', because that's the first film I ever made. I was watching it with somebody last year and she said, 'But it's got everything in it.' There are references to Hitchcock, I set things on fire and there's Mickey Mouse. It's a great song.

Shop Assistants tour the album

The release of the album Shop Assistants *(also known as* Will Anything Happen*) meant there would be the mandatory promotional tour. The band decided to take their friends along.*

Ian Hoey: When they were releasing their album they got a tour. Being the good people they were and are, they looked for some local bands to support them on that tour. I think it was mainly us and the Desperadoes and we'd share the dates. It was almost like one of these tours they talk about where it was like The Clash and the Pistols, though, and obviously I don't think for a minute I'm saying it was anything like that kind of thing. But yeah, so we're in a minibus. It's like the Shop Assistants, the Desperadoes, and us.

Andrew Tully: They said, 'Oh, well, we'll pay you fifty quid a night,' which was great, and then they said, 'Oh, and you can drive in our van with us,' which was great, and then they said, 'Oh, we'll put you up in hotels.'

Laura McPhail: It was a lot of fun – we were with our friends so it was a bit of an adventure and the gigs were great.

Ian Boffey: It was hilarious and full of 'hijinks and horseplay' to coin a phrase. Pop Will Eat Itself had been roped in and the folks from Jesse Garon were on board too – I remember lots of hare-brained drunkenness and mad singalongs in dressing rooms up and down the country. The Shop Assistants were never less than tremendous and PWEI were really hitting their stride as well. They were real characters – very funny and always in the music papers at the time, at a time when the three big music weeklies really had an influence. I went on to write reviews for *Sounds* later myself and, oddly enough, wound up reviewing PWEI in Edinburgh further down the line. But the whole tour was a bit of a blur; I remember meeting other bands like Gaye Bykers On Acid and then them and the guys from PWEI rolling around on stage with us a mad circus. I also remember bumping into the guys from Half Man Half Biscuit in Liverpool and how friendly and down to earth they were. Mainly though, it was just the exuberant nonsense you'd expect of a gang of young people haring around clubs and universities in a tour bus. The Electric Ballroom in Camden was a highlight – we were all very impressed with the drummer from My Bloody Valentine who shared the bill that night; he was like a young Keith Moon. The whole thing was great fun, if slightly out of control!

Ian Hoey: As far as I know, they were given a tour budget and they thought it was a tour budget for that tour, but that was their annual tour budget.

Andrew Tully: It was only afterwards that you got to know how the music business worked and it was like oh, well, normally you would have to pay to go on tour and then you would have to pay for your van and you would have to pay for your hotels, so you would come out of the tour thousands of pounds in debt.

Ian Hoey: They put us all up in hotels. They paid for the hotel rooms for the Desperadoes and probably themselves and The

Dragsters and when we stopped at the service stations, they bought us all food. And, because we're all skint. You know, I didn't have any spending money on that tour at all. The only drink we had, really, was on the rider at the gigs.

Andrew Tully: It was just like, wow, this is a different world, a different world. And it was brilliant that the Shoppies just let us, took us along into that world and, you know, and paid for us to be there.

Ian Hoey: And at the end of the tour, they handed us a hundred quid when we got out of the van, you know. So they're probably thinking, oh, well, there's some of it, some money left over. Might as well make a show of it all. And then, to their horror, they discovered, you know, that that wasn't the case.

In a completely unexpected twist, Alex left the band as the next phase of the tour was approaching, which would take them to Europe.

David Keegan: I think Alex really expected that we were going to become pop stars, and that the records would get into charts and so forth. I suppose we were kind of being led to believe that with the sales of 'Safety Net'. This is the thing, if you've been on a major label, and you've had that kind of distribution, and your record sold as many as 'Safety Net' did in the first few weeks. So I think we kind of thought, it's almost definite that whatever we do next will be, you know, it will be really successful. But it wasn't really. I think it ('I Don't Wanna Be Friends With You') got sort of number fifty or something like that, which is just fine . . .

All of a sudden, you're part of this kind of business thing you never particularly wanted to be part of... we did a John Peel session. And it was more or less when we're recording that Geoff Travis came up to say Alex is going to leave the band, which wasn't too much of a shock, to be honest. We weren't particularly getting on. And we thought, fine. We'll just carry on doing what we're doing. So, yeah, and we went off to France to play a festival at Christmas time and we're going to be filmed for French TV, which I thought was going to be really cool. But Alex just, yeah, she turned up to get the boat over and she said she'd forgotten her passport. And that was it. So she never played. So we had Sarah very quickly learn all the songs. There's video filmed of that, miming to 'Safety Net'. And it's the most horrendous thing. They put the camera on a pendulum. And it's a pendulum back and forwards. And I drank far too much on the boat over in good style and was really, really sick. And the next day it just felt like you're still in the boat. So if you look at the footage for that, it kind of makes you feel exactly how I was feeling at that time. Pretty, pretty damn seasick.

The Shop Assistants split shortly afterwards.

Further adventures of the Bellshill Beat: The Boy Hairdressers and The Groovy Little Numbers

The Soup Dragons were now one of Scotland's primary independent forces. The BMX Bandits, while perhaps not as critically acclaimed, were an equal force for enthusiastic audiences across the country. However, during this period, Norman Blake had taken a step away from musical activity.

A NEW ERA FOR INDIE MUSIC

Duglas T. Stewart: It's funny, when we started having that level of interest and success, it was almost like Norman had taken a wee break at first, and then I think he was like, 'Wait a minute, I'm missing out here, I'm getting back in with this.'

Norman recruited Joe from the BMX Bandits and artist Jim Lambie to form The Boy Hairdressers, with former Gods For All Occasions guitarist Raymond McGinley.

Norman Blake: I was friends with a guy called Jim Lambie, who's now an artist, but we hung out together quite a bit and I think did maybe a couple of early shows round Glasgow. The band at that time would be Joe McAlinden, Francis Macdonald, and we maybe even played one show, two shows and then we met Raymond McGinley who then joined the band.

Raymond McGinley (Guitar, The Boy Hairdressers and Teenage Fanclub): The thing is, I don't think I really felt the lightbulb moment with punk. My dad worked with this guy who had a massive record collection, and he gave me these records that were, like, Hawaiian guitar records, and musicals, and all sorts of mad stuff, Doris Day records, whatever, eclectic mix of all these things.

Joe McAlinden: I spent all my teenage years in orchestras. The reason I ended up playing the bass was Norman, his theory was, you play the violin, it's got four strings, so you should be able to play the bass. Didn't have a drummer, and I said, 'There's a wee guy, and he's brilliant, he's in a concert band, can play anything, you know.' He was a wee little 14-year-old specky guy at the back, not that I'm speck-ist, and I got him along to Norman's granny's.

Francis Macdonald (Drums, The Boy Hairdressers, BMX Bandits and Teenage Fanclub): I was going to school and I was playing drums in what they called a wind band . . . a concert band, the Motherwell District Concert Band. Which I suppose is like an orchestra without the strings, so it's brass, woodwind and percussion. And they didn't have a drummer and I was asked to play the drums. And also in that wind band was Joe McAlinden playing saxophone and Jim McCulloch from The Soup Dragons playing clarinet. And Joe . . . so I'm drumming and we're doing music from James Bond films and Morricone and different, slightly technical pieces for competitions, but Joe meanwhile was playing with BMX Bandits, his own band The Groovy Little Numbers, and was about to do the first gig with The Boy Hairdressers. The BMX Bandits didn't have a drummer and were recording a B-side; The Boy Hairdressers didn't have a drummer and had a gig at the Third Eye Centre; and The Groovy Little Numbers used a drum machine but they wanted real drums on a B-side, so Joe said to me one day, you know, 'We've got a couple of things we'd like you to try and do.' So immediately I was kind of, you know, playing kind of with three different projects but I didn't really have the same record collections as them. Splash One had been a bit too early for me.

Raymond McGinley: We had a regular rehearsal for a while, which was nine in the morning, on a Saturday morning – it was tough.

A NEW ERA FOR INDIE MUSIC

Norman Blake: And we did a lot of, I mean, great shows. We played in London with Dinosaur, before they added the Junior.

Joe McAlinden: We'd ask from the stage, 'Can anybody put us up tonight, please,' you know, that was before we played our last song. I mean, it was that, we just wanted to do music.

All three of the Bellshill bands – BMX Bandits, The Boy Hairdressers and The Groovy Little Numbers – rehearsed at Norman Blake's granny's house, often all at the same time, each band taking turns to use the instruments.

Francis Macdonald: The Boy Hairdressers and BMX Bandits were rehearsing at Norman Blake's grandmother's house, so the BMX Bandits had some kind of rehearsal, and Duglas sang some new song he'd written, and there's, okay, time for The Boy Hairdressers' rehearsal now, so Duglas sat down, Joe went from guitar to bass, someone left, someone came in, and now we were The Boy Hairdressers.

Joe McAlinden's band, The Groovy Little Numbers, released two joyous, melodic slices of pop magnificence on 53rd & 3rd. 'You Make My Head Explode' and 'Happy Like Yesterday' were sadly the only two singles they released.

Joe McAlinden: I'd just got a loan of a Portastudio and started writing stuff. It wasn't for any of these specific things, I was just trying stuff out. And I got a couple of girl friends – I don't mean girlfriends, like some harem – just a couple of girl friends, to sing on it, and we just did a demo with a drum machine.

And, naturally, being involved with 53rd & 3rd anyway, I popped the thing to them. And they liked it enough to say go and make a record, that was that. So, got into the studio and made the first [The Groovy Little Numbers] record, and that obviously was good enough to make a second one as well. Then that naturally ran its course. I had these grand ideas. I think the second record had a four-piece brass section on it and goodness knows what else. Flutes, and, you know, it was not a sustainable model. They were the first songs that I had written on my own. Being in cahoots with all of these people, it seemed like a natural thing. We were sharing it with everybody anyway. I gave it to Stephen and Sandy and they said, you should make a record. It was as simple as that. I think all through my career certainly, and even now, it is a lot about who you know. Talent doesn't seem to be enough, which is a shame. But I've been in a lot of the right places at the right time. Back then, we were all friends and that seemed to be a natural thing that happened

The continuing adventures of The Pastels – Truck Train Tractor

By now, The Pastels had left Creation and signed with Glass Records.

David Barker (Glass Records): I was aware of them of course, but Robert Hampton, later of Loop, who worked with me from 1985 to around 1988 when he went full time with his band, was a big fan and knew them, or had met them a few times at gigs. They wanted to make an LP, and Creation at that time, so I believe, didn't have the money or the inclination to do that. Glass was more of an album label than Creation were at that time. Also we had international connections. We met and got on and they came with us. They were very easy to work with, they knew what they wanted and I believed in them. Stephen Pastel is a close friend to this day. As for the gap, I don't think it was that long, compared to gaps between their records since . . . I let them do what they wanted and they didn't let me down. They wanted to work with John Rivers, who had produced Swell Maps. I'd already done four or five records with John so that worked out well. The recordings sounded so good.

Martin Hayward: I remember being thrown off Creation several times, I couldn't tell you if it was three or four times but that was the kind of relationship we had with them because we possibly wouldn't give them the respect which they seemed to want from us . . . We would take the piss in the press and we would just, well not just in the press, that was because the press happened to be talking to us, we were taking the piss all the time but not just out of Creation. Generally we didn't have a lot of time for most things to do with the music business so we were generally laughing quite a lot. But yeah, we were several times thrown off Creation for various misdemeanours.

Stephen Pastel: I think Alan McGee thought, when he cast us adrift, that our career would suddenly stop, but the best music we made, you know, in the eighties, was for Glass Records, and we were kind of left to get on with it ourselves. We did it in Leamington Spa, just away from everything.

Alan McGee: I mean, we put the records out but really it became apparent that, you know . . . I mean he's [Stephen] obsessed with being cool and I couldn't give a fuck about being cool so I don't care. We're the opposite, do you know what I mean? Total opposite people. So it was never going to work, 'cause I always wanted to win and Stephen likes a one-all draw.

Bernice Simpson: That did kind of change things, 'cause it was quite serious, it was really, really hard work.

Martin Hayward: Stephen finds us safe harbour with Dave Barker's Glass Records. Dave's approach is to gently support us without wanting to interfere in any way – repeatedly promising to take us for 'a few sherbets'. This seems ideal.

Bernice Simpson: My recollection is never really talking to any of our record companies, but Glass seemed to be benign and happy for us to crack on with what we wanted to do.

Martin Hayward: We have no real connections to anyone else on the eclectic Glass roster. This immediately feels less claustrophobic than Creation, where everyone seemed to have a furtive eye out. Josh (Robert), from Glass and a nascent Loop, hangs in Glasgow, modelling a classic Byrds bowl cut. He supports us solo on guitar pedal drone with song titles of cosmic nihilism, sat on stage on a plastic chair. He also plays a live one-chord after-show improv with Bernice, Brian and Eugene Kelly. Eugene is only pretending to play violin, but, importantly, looks like John Cale as he does it. It's good to watch Brian and

Bernice stretch out a bit together. 'I'll give you a fiver if Brian plays anything you've not heard before,' promises Stephen.

The first Pastels recording to emerge on their new label was 'Truck Train Tractor'.

David Barker: A breakthrough for the group, I think. Recorded by John Rivers before the *Up for a Bit* LP sessions. It's too long ago to remember sales figures but I believe it improved on their previous releases significantly. My then distributor, Nine Mile/ the Cartel, were very impressed. I saw it as the perfect set-up for the forthcoming LP.

Martin Hayward: Glass put us into Woodbine Street Recording Studio in Leamington Spa to make a single with John A. Rivers – Stephen's choice, because of Swell Maps.

John is super-neat and assured in his domain. No food, drink or cigarettes in the control room. He clocks us out to eat early evening, driving to a local with trestle tables and the feel of a canteen, for Ruskoline-coated fish, chips and peas and wistful Glasgow curry chat. He checks a cassette mix of Love and Rockets on the car stereo as the kind of set-up most people will hear it on. Sure, they can play a bit, but nothing we can't handle, in our own way.

A gold record for engineering 'Ghost Town' graces the control room wall, and John shares some Specials and Swell Maps war stories. WSRS is a step up professionally from what we have seen before, enough to make me feel a wee bit protective of our roughness.

Intending an A-side of 'Trains Go Down the Track', which we

approach first diligently, and nail to our satisfaction, 'Truck Train Tractor' is then largely created in the studio with the pressure off and a kind of collective demented glee.

Josh turns up to this session more in fan than in Glass liaison mode. Aggi has been shopping, and so, except for Brian who disdains such foolishness, our collective toy instrument racket establishes the mood. Bernice and I had Red Crayola's *Parable of Arable Land*, so a bit of nursery free form freakout seems natural.

Way back at a Night Moves soundcheck, I showed Stephen an open E shape on higher frets as a drone – at the time dismissed as 'sounding like jazz' but re-emerging in '25 Unfinished Plays' for not-Kid Jensen. To this Stephen now adds string bending.

We have worked up a cool middle part, which Brian visits as Steve Cropper, and I open out the coda with a recycled Cheap Gods line. Stephen brings new lyrics, Brian reacting to the 'farmer's wife': 'If he starts on the animals, that's it.'

I have a structured and Aggi a spontaneous backing vocal. Let's have both exit solo takes. I'm thinking 'Raw Power', Brian 'Lucille', but we both want piano percussion. Bernice is deadpan clockwork throughout – and we just about keep John away from the contemporary drum sounds.

Bernice and I drop Brian at his long-term flat-sit in Bishopbriggs. He has entered the world of legit work and now in this solo suburban flat is removed from the day-to-day lunacy that used to surround him. We stick the WSRS cassette on his posh stereo and take stock. We have surprised ourselves and Brian now wants to switch A-side.

Aggi wraps 'Truck Train Tractor' in a perfect pop sleeve and *NME* gets a slightly dirtier version of 'Trains Go Down the Track' (now 'Breaking Lines') for their *C86* project. This remains among the very finest songs to have been inspired by the Westerton–Milngavie branch line.

Bernice Simpson: For me this was the essence and energy of the band – I used to just sync in with Brian and Martin playing this live. I can still feel the joy!

The Napalm Stars

With a multitude of diverse releases outside of the jangly indie genre, 1986 was Fast Forward's most productive period. One of those releases was a single from The Napalm Stars, seeking to generate the sort of excitement The Clash did in 1977.

Martin Parry (Guitar): The Napalm Stars were an Edinburgh-based band formed in September 1982 and lasted until 1986. Originally we were a five-piece then we went through numerous personnel changes before forming a classic four-piece line-up. We mostly gigged around Scotland and the north-east of England with some forays into London playing the Moonlight Club. The music was influenced by the punk rock sounds of the late seventies. It was both refreshing and exciting and live – played with energy and enthusiasm. We released one single, 'Fiction/Workhard', recorded at Pier House studios in 1985 on an independent label, Stranded Records. The single reflected the intense energy we possessed, with shearing guitars, tribal pounding drums and soaring vocals delivered with an energy and verve. The single was well received but unfortunately didn't break the band, and finally, after recording one more demo, the band split up.

C86

C86 *is perhaps the most famous compilation of independent music. It was initially offered as a cassette by the* NME *in May 1986 but was also later made available as an LP via Rough Trade. It was one of the few compilations that seemed to spawn a whole genre by itself and came to define a type of melodic, ragged, guitar-based sound, such as Primal Scream, that echoed many bands of the 1960s. C86 would become synonymous with what would be known as 'indie music' as opposed to independently released music. It had a sound and a style. Ironically, 50 per cent of the bands on the compilation don't really conform to that definition. Big Flame, Bogshed, The Mackenzies and the Ron Johnson bands are far more reminiscent of Captain Beefheart and the discordant sounds of New York than Primal Scream's 'Velocity Girl'. Regardless, the definition has stuck.*

In a sign of how significant Scotland's music scene had become to the overall UK independent music scene, seven of the twelve bands featured in the compilation were from Scotland, including The Pastels, Shop Assistants and The Soup Dragons. C86 led to a huge explosion of similar bands and propelled the growing scene even further.

C86 TRACK LISTINGS

SIDE ONE

1.	'Velocity Girl'	Primal Scream	(1:21)
2.	'Happy Head'	The Mighty Lemon Drops	(2:43)
3.	'Pleasantly Surprised'	The Soup Dragons	(2:05)
4.	'Feeling So Strange Again'	The Wolfhounds	(1:42)
5.	'Therese'	The Bodines	(3:03)
6.	'Law'	Mighty Mighty	(3:39)
7.	'Buffalo'	Stump	(4:27)
8.	'Run to the Temple'	Bogshed	(3:30)
9.	'Sharpened Sticks'	A Witness	(2:30)
10.	'Breaking Lines'	The Pastels	(2:58)
11.	'From Now On, This Will Be Your God'	Age of Chance	(3:17)

SIDE TWO

12.	'It's Up to You'	Shop Assistants	(2:36)
13.	'Firestation Towers'	Close Lobsters	(1:46)
14.	'Sport Most Royal'	Miaow	(2:55)
15.	'I Hate Nerys Hughes (From the Heart)'	Half Man Half Biscuit	(3:43)
16.	'Transparent'	The Servants	(2:33)
17.	'Big Jim (There's No Pubs in Heaven)'	The Mackenzies	(2:36)
18.	'New Way (Quick Wash and Brush Up with Liberation Theology)'	Big Flame	(1:38)
19.	'Console Me'	We've Got a Fuzzbox and We're Gonna Use It	(1:25)
20.	'Celestial City'	McCarthy	(3:00)
21.	'Bullfighter's Bones'	The Shrubs	(3:45)
22.	'This Boy Can Wait'	The Wedding Present	(3:59)

CHAPTER 9
1986-88

Scotland is bigger than you think

The *C86* compilation and the huge success in the rebirth of independent music as a genre in itself led to an explosion of new indie music across the UK, one-off labels and bands forming in its wake. In many ways, 1987 was the pinnacle.

Glasgow and Edinburgh were not the only places where bands formed and thrived. While Bellshill had become established as one of the premiere music towns, the press still, frustratingly, referred to it as 'Glasgow'. The emergence of new bands would highlight the fact that (as in the rest of the UK) there were thriving scenes in other towns across Scotland, each distinct in its own way.

Irvine

Irvine is a small town, forty-five miles south-west of Glasgow, and, like many larger places such as Greenock and Bellshill, it had a small and dedicated bunch of indie kids. Perhaps the best-known band to emerge from the town was Trashcan Sinatras, but, undoubtedly, the cult band was The Big Gun, primarily known at the time for 'Heard About Love', a fantastic, blistering one-off slice of pop-fuzz. Today the band is recognised by a wider audience thanks to Mayflies, *the heartfelt semi-autobiographical book by award-winning novelist Andrew O'Hagan, who was a member of the band. It was adapted for TV in 2022. The Wishing Stones, born from the ashes of The Loft, were a London-based band but two of its members hailed from Irvine: drummer Andy Kerr and guitarist (and another excellent author) John Niven.*

Andy Crone (Bass, The Big Gun): There seemed to be a lot of bands through the eighties across the area. Most of the people we knew in Irvine at that time were in bands probably. Other than Irvine, I really only remember other bands from Kilmarnock. I suppose that suggests there wasn't a scene as such, more a case of lots of people doing their own thing and coming across each other at various points. The Trashcans weren't really on our radar though. We knew them but by the time they started doing something we weren't socialising in the same places. We were friendly with John and Paul Douglas (in fact, I think we may have stayed at John's flat in Edinburgh at the time when we recorded 'Heard About Love'), Davie Hughes (later member of the Trashcans) and I remember Paul Livingston as always being sound but I don't think I ever saw the band live. Pretty sure that will be the case for all of us? We were pretty much self-contained amongst our group of friends and possibly seemed like we were in a bit of a bubble.

Andrew O'Hagan (tambourine, The Big Gun): We were a bubble within a bubble. And one of the things about small Scottish towns in the 1980s is they could seem very sectarian. People were from 'the scheme' or the 'bought houses', 'the top end' or 'the bottom end', or they could be into disco or, heaven forfend, heavy metal. The more obvious divisions, Catholic or Protestant, never really affected me or my friends. In The Big Gun, for instance, there were two Catholics and three Protestants. The common theme was the music we liked and the places we drank. There were a lot of Irvine bands I never saw live. I never saw the Trashcan Sinatras. I edited a local fanzine when I was 15. We only got to two issues because we ran out of people we knew to interview. But Irvine could seem a very forbidding world beyond our group. Forty years on, you just have to say the words 'Sanderson Avenue' and a whole other world is conjured.

Allan Carruthers (Guitar, The Big Gun): There were plenty of aspiring bands around Irvine at that time and it seems that everyone in the pubs we frequented (the Turf, the Crown) was playing. We would seek out local hotels or clubs that would accommodate us putting on our own gigs ... By the mid-eighties, most of our friends had been playing in (punk) bands from the ages of 13 or 14. As our wider musical appreciation and influences developed, people would flit in and out of various incarnations of bands. The Big Gun settled around '86. Some of our friends had briefly played with some of the guys that went on to become the Trashcan Sinatras.

Andy Crone: I don't think there was a particular feeling about bands from Glasgow and Edinburgh. It's just that some of them were very good, with press attention well deserved. It's fair to say though that we weren't all fans of some of the bands.

Andrew O'Hagan: I loved Factory and was captivated by the Manchester scene. I loved the Sound of Young Scotland. I disappeared into a world of The Smiths, Felt, Go-Betweens for a good long time. I definitely had a strong sense of Glasgow bands – The Pastels, Primal Scream, The Jesus and Mary Chain – we saw all those bands multiple times, and I count it part of my general provinciality that I never went to Edinburgh until I was 16.

Allan Carruthers: We loved going to Glasgow gigs, they were big nights out, we'd been frequenting the legendary Apollo since our early teens. In the eighties we'd see most of the emerging bands including The Pastels, BMX Bandits, JAMC. Unfairly, but funny as fuck at the time, a lot of the bands took a lot of stick from some of our travelling crew. I think it was through too much alcohol rather than any intended malice. Apologies where required.

Andrew O'Hagan: What the band lacked in musical ambition it more than made up for in private jokes and good looks. But what they needed, very obviously, was a tambourine player, so I came along.

Andy Crone: Most of us were all friends from our early teens, some even before that. We were young punks together and stayed friends (and still are). There were various bands from our youth but The Big Gun formed with Keith and Allan, who were in Dead Souls, and Andy Crone and Andy Kerr, who were in Almost Evening (with John Niven and Basil Pieroni), getting together to play some songs. I think the other two bands were initially still going but pretty much ceased not long after.

We were all mates, quickly found playing songs together easy and enjoyable. Andy O'Hagan joined very soon after we started.

Allan Carruthers: All part of the morphing process. We had all known each other and swapped instruments and bands for years. I had played with Keith since school in Ground Zero and then Dead Souls. I played with Basil, Andy Kerr and John in BJ (Pieroni) and the Cuban Airmen. Andy Crone was the best-looking bass player in town and Andy O'Hagan just wanted to be in the coolest band in town.

Andrew O'Hagan: There was a single moment, okay a single period of a few nanoseconds, when The Big Gun were quite legendary in there. I mean, not The Rolling Stones at Altamont, but certainly The Stone Roses at Spike Island. As I say, it didn't last. We had homework and paper rounds.

John Niven (Guitar, The Wishing Stones): Up until the end of 1983, when I was 17, I'd been playing guitar in kind of sub-Clash punk bands with names like Suspect Device and Rebel Dance. Andy Kerr (later of The Big Gun, The Wishing Stones, then Spirea X, then Lucy Baines Band) was always our drummer. Andy was 14 when I met him and he was just so talented, the best musician on our scene by a long chalk. We did our first gig in my dad's garage. We were too young to play in pubs! There was such a great wee scene in Irvine at that time. There was us and Dead Souls, Graham and Tiny and Keith's (Martin, later of The Big Gun) band, and The Galloping Gunshot Boys (featuring Davy Hughes, later of Trashcan Sinatras) and The Kick and Warzone. We all used to play at the Grange Hotel on Kilwinning Road, which is now a restaurant called Si! George McDaid (later the original bass player in Trashcan Sinatras) was our singer for a while and Frank Reader and John Douglas (both later of the Trashcans too) would come to our gigs. Towards the end of 1983, 'This Charming Man' came out and the *Texas Fever* mini album by Orange Juice (we'd been a bit too young for Postcard as it was happening) and that was that. You went from wanting to be Mick Jones to wanting to be Johnny Marr or Roddy Frame overnight. Then, in the summer of 1984, my good pal Basil Pieroni (now of Butcher Boy) bought *Wild Summer Wow!* – the Creation Records sampler – at a stall in Irvine market and we discovered Biff Bang Pow! and The Loft. We thought the Loft track on that record ('Winter') was amazing. I left Irvine to go to Glasgow university in the October of that year and one of the first things I saw in the city were these fly posters with Captain Scarlett on them advertising some bands with a 'punk rock psychedelic soundtrack', at Daddy Warbucks on West George Street . . .

It turned out to be the first Splash One Happening, before it was actually called that. I remember being intrigued because, in 1984, no one was really using the term 'punk rock' to mean anything other than stuff like Discharge and The Exploited, and this clearly wasn't going to be that. We all went along out of curiosity and got our fucking minds blown hearing The 13th Floor Elevators and The Chocolate Watchband. The *Nuggets* stuff. All a wee bit ahead of where we were at the time.

The Big Gun eventually released their sole single, 'Heard About Love', on their own imprint, Hi-Fibre.

John Niven: I was in Glasgow – this would be 1986 now – living in a toilet of a basement flat on Ashley Street, near Charing Cross. The band photo on 'Heard About Love' was actually taken in that flat, by Paolo Righetti, from Millport, who later played bass in a short-lived band of mine and then tour managed The Wishing Stones. I'd known Keith Martin since the first year of primary school, since we were five, and we'd been around each other musically since we both started being in bands in 1981, when we were 14 or 15. But Keith had been a drummer at first and then a singer. I hadn't really thought of him as a guitar player, or a songwriter, so 'Heard About Love' just blew me away. Like it did all of us at the time. It was a bit 'Who knew he had it in him?' So melodic and well crafted. And then when John Peel picked up on it, it really seemed like they were off to the races for a minute.

Andy Crone: Keith brought the initial ideas of most of the songs and we worked them out together. All the stuff was really easy. Andy Kerr got almost every song bang on from the very start and Alan's guitar lines were quickly, perfectly in place.

Allan Carruthers: We never formally constructed songs as such. Keith tended to solely script his lyrics and offer up the guitar rhythm, Andy's bass would fill out the rhythm and we would then just jam it around till things fell into place, easy. Someone once suggested that I had ripped off the lead hook, linking the chorus and verse, from an Echo and the Bunnymen song – I have no idea which. For my part it was total improvisation. For the recording we went through to Pier House in Edinburgh. We chose it just because we'd seen other bands – I can't remember who – had recorded there. I still remember the reaction of Peter, the engineer, when on arrival our first question was 'Where are the nearest off-licence and bookies?' We done it over a weekend. Yes, Hi-Fibre was our own label.

Andrew O'Hagan: The whole thing was a burst of youthful energy and awkwardness, perfectly primed and ready to go.

Andy Crone: It was great to see the end product of something we'd put a lot of effort into. We also had a lot of help and guidance though from Fast Forward, who distributed it through the Cartel; and Mike Stout, who worked with The Wedding Present, who published through Cubic Music, was very generous with his time and advice.

Allan Carruthers: Almost forty years later it's still a thrill to hold and play your own band's records. I honestly still think 'Heard About Love' sounds great. I always loved it when people asked genuinely if the cover photo was the band as young kids. Although we funded it ourselves it would probably never have happened but for Andy Crone taking care of business. Thanks, Andy! There was no prompt that John Peel or Janice Long was going to play any of the songs. Coming in from a night out I put the radio on to catch the John Peel show just as he was giving the single quite a lengthy introduction. Through my elation I was still able to press the record button of my tape deck and caught most of it – it was amazing. First hearing it on John Peel was massive. The flexi had been played before so that was probably the biggest great surprise but every time hearing it on Peel or Janice Long (who actually played it more) was great. In retrospect getting the Single of the Week – in *Record Mirror* I think, but it might have been *Melody Maker* – and the *Smash Hits* Runner-Up Single of the Fortnight (to Michael Jackson) probably deserved more celebration than we afforded at the time.

Andrew O'Hagan: We only really cared what our mates thought. That's part of the arrogance and sweetness of youth. We should have been going crazy about getting so much press (we had no PR agent), but it hardly registered. Andy Crone, as I remember it, was a little more industry savvy and tried to build on our success and make connections and get gigs, but the rest of us just went to the pub. It seems fabulous now. We gained most of what we needed from the entire process just by being together and knowing we were with the right people. If you could bottle that: it's the essence of something wonderful. The band had vitality for its own sake, and I don't think we ever once discussed what it would be like to 'make it'.

Allan Carruthers: Like the radio play, the music press acknowledgement was amazing. Should Michael not be stripped of his *Smash Hits* title?

Andy Crone: [John Peel] was monumentally important to us. A guiding light with regards to music, so to be played by him was a big deal, a significant seal of approval.

Andrew O'Hagan: That was approval. He was like the God of Mates. To be liked by Peel was like passing all the exams you never sat. I was with him many years later and I told him how much it had meant to us, and tears came into his eyes. He wanted approval too. He didn't remember us, though. Bastard.

After the one-off single, The Big Gun eventually drifted apart.

Andy Crone: Keith and I spoke about this seven or eight years ago for the first time and neither of us could remember what actually happened. Andy Kerr moved to Glasgow to play in John's (Niven, the writer) new band then shortly afterwards followed him down to London to play in The Wishing Stones. We tried some different drummers, none unfortunately having the same easy feel as Andy, and also gave a drum machine a try.

We ended up having a wee break, not rehearsing for a few months, then before you knew it a year had passed. We basically just allowed it to fizzle out, I think.

In hindsight there's some regret with that. We'd had some record label interest, Go! Discs called up – I have no idea if it was any more than one phone call – and a fifty/fifty deal with Fast Forward to continue with our own label. This would also have allowed us to release stuff from other bands too, which might have been good fun.

Allan Carruthers: It is still an unanswered question; plenty of better bands just run their course. There was no formal disbandment, nor any acrimony ever. I tend to think that our biggest handicap was that three of the band were in full-time employment within local industry and therefore the band was a hobby.

We certainly had aspirations and hopes as we continued to create, but never professionally recorded, better songs (in my opinion) after 'Heard About Love'.

Andrew O'Hagan: It would be great to say there were musical differences, or that we'd bust up over a bad lyric or a girl or by reaching a dead end in percussive understanding, but in fact we just stopped because we forgot to say yes to the opportunity. Which is nice, I think. Sad and nice. The essence of pop.

John Niven and Andrew O'Hagan later became very successful authors.

Andy Crone: With Andy in particular, it was always obvious he would become a writer. John took some diversions en route but it was always clear that he'd want to be heard in whatever he did.

I wouldn't say there was a literary scene although there were people doing fanzines locally, including Andy O'Hagan, but all of our friends were big readers. We pretty much all loved music, books and films (the serial number of the single was ATOH1, referencing *A Taste of Honey*). And had impeccable taste in all of them!

Allan Carruthers: From a young age John could spin a yarn. At primary school on an Outward Bound course he'd have the dormitory awake and laughing all night with his mental hilarious stories. He's still Irvine's best frustrated rock'n'roll superstar though.

Years after The Big Gun ceased to be, I was in Northampton

and stood transfixed, in awe, at a bookshop window rammed full of Andrew O'Hagan's first published novel, *The Missing*. How happy I was that he'd thrown his tambourine to fuck and left us.

John Niven: We all loved books and movies. That's never changed. I met Andrew for the first time in the summer of 1985, at the YTS centre on Kilwinning Road, a kind of youth club where we played. He interviewed our band for his fanzine *Anytime Swing*. He'd have been 17, I think. A year or two younger than us. Andrew always knew he wanted to be a writer and wasted zero time getting there. It took me a good deal longer, what with being convinced I'd be a guitar hero until about the age of 24. And also being much thicker than O'Hagan slowed things up. When I did start writing seriously in my early thirties, Andrew was already ten years ahead of me and he was incredibly generous with his time, knowledge and contacts. I owe him an enormous debt. But, to come back to your question, it wasn't just me and Andrew from that time and place. There was Keith, God rest him. There's the Trashcans. There's Graham Fagen, who was the bass player in Dead Souls and is now an internationally renowned visual artist who exhibits all over the world. There's Basil and John Hunt who are now in Butcher Boy. It's a decent strike rate for a small Ayrshire New Town.

After The Big Gun, John joined The Wishing Stones, taking Andy Kerr with him.

John Niven: Andy and I were always in a band together, concurrently with him being in The Big Gun. The last incarnation being kind of a sub-Weather Prophets outfit called Celebrate Texas. What happened was we supported The Wishing Stones at Lucifer's (later the Sub Club) in late 1986. I met Bill Prince, who was the singer-songwriter-guitarist for The Wishing Stones and we got on really well. By this point we were discovering things like Television and Richard Hell and Creedence. Of course, Bill had been the bass player in The Loft, who we'd seen at Splash One and who had been on the verge of properly making it before they split up. They were real stars in our little universe. So, getting to know Bill felt like a big deal. Then, the following spring, spring 1987 – and this was like something out of a film – we were all drinking in The Griffin on a Friday night and the barman shouted out 'PHONE CALL FOR A JOHN NIVEN. IS THERE A JOHN NIVEN IN HERE?' It was Bill. He knew we didn't have a phone in the flat – couldn't afford it – and he'd figured, correctly, we'd be in The Griffin on the piss on a Friday night. He was ringing because he'd either just sacked Seth, The Wishing Stones guitarist, or Seth had quit, I can't quite remember, and they had a tour supporting The Wedding Present starting in a couple of weeks. Would I learn the songs and step in? I mean, for me, this was like getting asked to join the fucking Rolling Stones in 1969. They sent me train tickets to Euston. First time I'd ever gone to London on anything other than the Stagecoach. Big time baby! So I did the tour – I turned 21 on that tour – and it was great and then Bill said, 'Do you want to join the band full time?' Of course, being 21, I say 'Of course'.

A few months later John Willis the drummer leaves to join Loop. The Big Gun had kind of fizzled out by then and I said, 'Let's get Andy Kerr in.' Andy and I both moved to London together and joined the band. October 1987. The day after the massive hurricane wrecked the city. Then, inevitably, The Wishing Stones original bass player Karen O'Keefe left too and so we got Stewart 'The Bull' Garden down from Glasgow. Stewart had played rhythm guitar in Celebrate Texas and we'd been flatmates since 1984. Bill kind of taught him to play bass on the hoof. I guess it was that punk rock thing of taking someone you knew was right for the group rather than the best musician available. However it all happened, between the spring and the autumn of 1987. Bill somehow ended up with a whole new band composed entirely of Scottish guys four or five years younger than him! Not sure he'd quite planned that. God we were a handful.

Around this point, I started spending a bit of time back in Irvine for the first time in years and that's when I heard the Trashcan Sinatras' debut single, 'Obscurity Knocks'. Which was a bit like hearing The Big Gun a few years earlier. Holy shit! *This* is Frank and John and George McDaid? I couldn't believe it. It was so assured and fully realised. Just wonderful guitar playing from Paul Livingstone and brilliant lyrics and signed to a major label to boot. The full package. Obviously, it made me sick to my stomach at the time. How dare they be that good! How fucking *dare* they.

Despite the demise of The Big Gun, the Irvine indie scene continued for the next few years, as documented by Craig McAllister from The Sunday Drivers.

Craig McAllister (The Sunday Drivers): The Irvine Music Club becomes important at this point. Set up in the autumn of 1988 in the Redburn Centre (next to Castlepark Community Centre), the Music Club started up due to financial input from the council or government. I might be wrong on this, but I think that the area's postcode qualified the Redburn Centre for some arts grant or other, and so a converted prefab school hut was turned into a rehearsal room and occasional recording studio. Primitive stuff, really, with foam on the walls and a sticky carpet underfoot, but a space nonetheless for guitar hopefuls across the KA12 postcode to bash out their tuneless noise to their hearts' content and maybe even commit their atrocities to tape now and again.

Part of the 'deal' of having a rehearsal space was that we should document it somehow, and so in June 1989, *Bum Note* fanzine was born. Andrew O'Hagan may have interviewed everybody from the area, but only because he wasn't looking over his shoulder at what was coming next. A tidal wave of bands, all with roots in the Irvine Music Club, began making loud noise and impact. Surf Nazis. Sunday Drivers. Mary White Aryans. It was a healthy and competitive scene – 'my band's better than your band' kinda thing – but, just like the bands who'd shared backlines and billing at the Grange a couple of years before us, we pulled together for a couple of showcase gigs in The Attic.

We recorded a set of demos that became a compilation tape. Each band had two tracks included, one on each side of the tape. Along with a stick of Wrigley's chewing gum, the tape was attached to the cover of *Bum Note* fanzine. I was the 'editor', with a bit of help from Sean McFedries, stalwart of the local scene and guitar player in a number of bands. I spoke to the bands in the Crown (we'd moved on from the Turf by now), I'd 'interview' them at the rehearsal room and I'd then type their manifestos and raison d'être into fanzine pages. Sean would take a grainy snap of the band scowling next to a tree or an industrial unit and suddenly we had the bones of something that people might like to read.

I suggested we write to our favourite bands to try and secure an interview. As *Bum Note* featured new bands, I thought it'd be a good idea to ask an established band how they'd got to their level of success/fame . . . something that might act as a spur to the fame-hungry instrument abusers of Irvine. Nowadays you'd find the act on social media, fire them a wee message and, if you're lucky, someone might reply and you'd take it from there. Back in 1989, though, you had to send a letter to the band – often, there'd be an address on the back of a 7-inch single – and hope for some sort of reply. David Gedge of The Wedding Present duly answered one of the many letters I'd sent, inviting me to Leeds to interview him in a pub. The Wedding Present interview then became the main feature of *Bum Note* issue one. Gedge was a lovely guy. He sent me a postcard while the band were touring in Germany. He even added me, unasked, to The Wedding Present's guest list for the next few years.

I'm not sure why – cost maybe – but we printed just fifty copies of *Bum Note*. The first two out of the photocopier in the Redburn Centre's office went to David Gedge and John Peel. With Sunday Drivers having the first song on side one, I was hopeful of maybe getting some Peel airplay, so there was method to that idea, but that never materialised. So there were just forty-eight copies for general sale and it sold out instantly. Nothing like it for creating a scene!

The Irvine Music Club continued with compilation tapes, maybe twice a year for the next three years. The bands fizzled out, became other bands, grew up and got real jobs, but the fanzine continued for as long as the tapes did. We never again scaled the heights of securing an interview with anyone as lofty as The Wedding Present, but those fanzines documented our local band scene very well.

Grant McLean (Vocals, The Sunday Drivers): I always wanted to sing. I always wanted to be Elvis . . . or Morrissey. I saw The Nyah Fearties and I went 'Anybody can be in a fucking band! Anybody!'

John Niven: I'm an old man of 57 now, with some success behind me, and I can sit here today and hold us all in my mind's eye, all packed into the snug bar of the Grange Hotel, on a winter Saturday night in the mid-1980s – some of us dead and gone now: Keith, Larry, Tony – all drinking and laughing and talking. Roaring our way through our time. The air is thick with cigarette smoke, 'Upside Down' by the Mary Chain is playing through the PA on a cassette, and we have the whole road ahead of us. To go back there, just for five minutes. Well, you'd give all that you have, wouldn't you?

Of course, no exploration of Irvine's indie music scene would be complete without Trashcan Sinatras. Despite having been one of the first bands on the scene and despite signing with Go! Discs in 1987, they didn't release their first record until 1990, when their debut LP, Cake, *came out. Paul Livingston and John Douglas both joined in 1986.*

Paul Livingston (Guitar, Trashcan Sinatras): I was 15 and I was on the lookout for a new band to play with. I went to see this guy Paul, a drummer who ran the local rehearsal rooms, and he said, 'Maybe you can join my jazzy wee outfit, the Trashcans.' I thought that sounded awful but said I'd go and meet them at a gig in town. I'd already met John through his old band Easter Parade but it was my first time meeting Frank. Well, I thought he was just the coolest guy I'd ever met! Great style and kinda wild eyes. I took my guitar to his house the next day and we worked on a few songs with John. I loved how John played guitar and Frank's voice was incredible. So smooth and effortless. It felt like we had good chemistry from the get-go. I was incredibly enthusiastic about everything, which I think they appreciated at that point.

John Douglas (Guitar, Trashcan Sinatras): I knew the Trashcans only as a mythical, brilliantly named, band . . . the hippest dudes in town were associated with them . . . I knew they were something to do with Davy Hughes but he was no longer in them. My first meeting with the reality of the Trashcans was in the Crown . . . Irvine's music scenesters main haunt. Paul Forde (drummer) and Frank Reader (singer) got chatting to me and there was an instant meeting of minds. We hated the same stuff, loved the same stuff and laughed at the same stuff . . . It was a Friday night and they said they were playing a gig the next afternoon at the Volunteer Rooms in Irvine . . . they were so light and cavalier about the gig . . . no nerves . . . just fun . . . excited to be up on stage bashing out cool tunes. Frank mentioned a few of the covers they planned to play (Sweet Jane, Rock'n'Roll, some Elvis tune). Frank said he would show me the chords side stage next day. I was buzzing . . . I was used to rehearsals and 'getting it right' . . . it was back to being excited . . . bashing out a noise . . . just like the first days of plugging in and turning it up . . . total excitement. The gig was major life changer as suddenly I was on stage with someone who could sing . . . sing proper, with feeling and melody and own the space . . . no nervous clinging to the mic stand . . . no running around showing off . . . just singing great and loving the band. I was in . . . whatever they wanted to do, I was in all the way. After I joined, we played a few more raucous cover shows and then it was suggested by Paul Forde that we try to write our own stuff. Also get another guitar player. I could bash things out with the right spirit and I could come up with good ideas but I was no virtuoso . . . Paul Livingston had been spotted as the best around . . . he was approached and somehow persuaded . . . we had our first writing session in Frank's bedroom at his mum's . . . I had a few chord changes that I played and they were met with instant enthusiasm . . . other chords were added . . . melody was arrived at somehow and words were bashed on . . . we had a chemistry straight away and the ideas just flowed out of us . . . we regularly rehearsed and worked out the material.

Paul Livingston (Guitar): We wrote a few songs, played a few gigs, and just got to know each other after that. Not only could Frank sing, but he was a madman on stage. It was all just a total blast. We supported The Lilac Time in Dundee and their tour manager, Simon Dine, was about to start working at Go! Discs as an A&R man. He told Andy MacDonald we were good and it all snowballed from there. It had only been about a year since I joined but all of a sudden there were A&R people coming up to see us in shitty wee venues. We let them buy us drinks but we always knew we were going to sign with Go. Andy was cool and smart and was happy to let us find our feet for a couple of years before releasing anything. We didn't have an album's worth of songs yet.

John Douglas: A few line-up changes occurred, some were painful, but such is youth and its determination to have its own way . . . the ingredients were being honed till the chemistry landed and we became this full-time, all-in, focused, obsessed bunch who felt like world beaters in the making. The core of Frank, Paul Livingston and I was strong. Looking back, impressively so. We made demos and sent them out. Billy Sloan played us on his Radio Clyde show. Some record companies showed interest. We had a buzz around us and Go! Discs were the most appealing due to their independent mind set and their history of kinda weird, left of field success . . . with Billy Bragg and The Housemartins, etc. We really liked the folks there so somehow the reality of beginning to make actual records was here. A magical time, full of optimism and excitement. We were off the dole . . . and we had done it ourselves with our own material. The initial years after being signed were spent writing more songs . . . we had been signed on the strength of a few songs. 'Obscurity Knocks' was the song that had made the contracts come out . . . they were all just sniffing around until that song arrived. We bought the local recording studio/rehearsal space (Sirocco Studios) with our record advance, renamed it Shabby Road and camped there for the initial years . . . rehearsing, writing, recording constantly. From what I recall, Frank was the main overseer of all the songs . . . he would generally come up with melodies to fit what we all had worked on instrumentally . . . he would take sheets of word suggestions and grab what inspired him and turn them into songs . . . he was quite the magician at that time . . . None of us knew how to write a complete song so we were all chucking our ideas towards Frank and he had some alchemy type powers that gelled things into wonderful songs. All very magical for us but I'm sure Frank can shed light on the more hard graft aspects . . . We needed more of a hand to actually make a record so brought in Roger Béchirian to produce our first album . . . We knew his name from the early Stiff Records stuff and early Elvis Costello records . . . I think maybe someone at Go! Discs knew him and thought he would work well with us. He saw us through recording of what became *Cake* . . . lovely guy and very good with us. We felt like he was on our side and the record was soon coming together.

Paul Livingston: Recording *Cake* took a pretty long time, with a few false starts in there. We didn't really know how to make an album, so we just tried to make sure all the best bits from every demo we'd ever made were included. We dithered and focused on the wrong things and redid everything multiple times. It was a painstaking process but it was all done with good intentions. We were trying to make the best album we could. I had no concept of what to expect at all when it was finally released. Getting Single of the Week in *NME* for 'Obscurity Knocks' was about the most fantastical thing I could ever imagine happening.

By the time we came to make *I've Seen Everything*, we'd gotten much better live, and our songwriting had improved greatly. Honestly, recording it was a dream. Ray Shulman and Larry Primrose (producer and engineer) were an amazing team. We were confident and capable, and we had a good bunch of songs.

Again, we had no idea what to expect when it was released,

but I'm sure we were a little disappointed. When *Cake* came out, baggy was the big thing. By the time *I've Seen Everything* was released, grunge had taken over. We were always out of step with the fads of the day. Too early and too late. But recording it was a wonderful experience, and we're all very proud of that record.

In 2023, Cake *would make national headlines when its re-release on Last Night From Glasgow records made the UK Top 20.*

Paul Livingston: I'm not entirely sure how the *Cake* re-release got into the charts, but I feel like there's some sort of loophole being taken advantage of. Whatever, I'll take it. It's nice to get a bit of recognition at this point in the game. If you'd told me this would happen when we were making it, I would've said, 'It's gonna chart when I'm in my fifties? That's too late!' I was kind of a little shit in my teens.

Perth

Perth, often referred to as the Gateway to the Highlands, is a small city in Tayside. While it may not have as rich an indie heritage as Glasgow or Edinburgh, it does host The Twa Tams venue, a regular mainstay on the touring circuit. Its most famous musical independent sons are This Poison!

Derek Moir (Guitar, This Poison!): We had the nucleus of This Poison! from 1985 and had four songs that we were pleased with by early '86. We didn't have much money and didn't really know of anywhere to record in Edinburgh or Glasgow so we went to a guy who had a studio in a farmhouse in the countryside. It could have been Blairgowrie – it could have been Cupar.

We were quite pleased with it and sent it to all of the fanzines that we had been buying, like *Simply Thrilled, Are You Scared To Get Happy?, Baby Honey*, and we got good reviews. We didn't bother, or even think to send it to record companies, independent or majors. We would never of signed to a major anyway. Ideologically, we thought The Clash had sold out by not signing to Small Wonder, ha ha ha ha ha! I'm sure that we took that position from reading *Sniffing Glue*!

Perth always seemed to have its own musical micro-climate – Skids, Dexys, Siouxsie and the Banshees and Crass all played amazing gigs around '79/'80. Crass was a riot. Quite literally! They released it as a live LP, *You'll Ruin It for Everyone*, and probably helped set the agenda for being quite resolute about doing it for ourselves. Even from small-town Perth.

Although we regularly travelled to Glasgow and Edinburgh for Barrowland/Playhouse/Rooftops/uni gigs, we never were really a part of either the Glasgow or Edinburgh scene until we discovered The Onion Cellar . . . around 1985. They were putting on the likes of The Pastels, Wolfhounds, Jesse Garon and the Desperadoes. We had such a great time there – it was Edinburgh's Splash One and doesn't get the credit it deserves.

After the success of putting on The Wedding Present, by 1986 we had started our own club in Perth – Strasbourg Club – to do regular gigs, at the Riverside Inn in Bridgend. It overlooks the River Tay and the old bridge in Perth – snow-capped Grampian Mountains in the distance. How could anyone fail to be impressed? We put on lots of different bands from Jasmine

Minks and 1000 Violins to The Batchelor Pad, McCarthy twice, The Great Leap Forward. By 1987, This Poison! had moved into the top floor of an old Victorian flat overlooking the River Tay. It was built as Scotland's first Natural History Museum but was now defunct. It had a cinema on the second floor with the red velvet seats still in place.

The Wedding Present liked what we were doing and thought we could do a Postcard type thing with their Reception record label. It was more like the standard indie – 'Send us a demo and if it's good, we will release it.' We didn't have a clue about how that element worked. Perth didn't have its own Bob Last or Alan Horne so we had no template. We were ultra indie under achievers. Our objective was to release four great singles, a John Peel session and split up. We overachieved in our underachievement by releasing two great singles before Red Rhino spent all their money on George Best, the real one, doing promotion for The Wedding Present's first LP. That was a shame because we had a third ready to go and a brace of other great songs with the potential to be singles.

The riff for 'Poised Over The Pause Button' came out of nowhere at a Sunday afternoon rehearsal. We were a bit astounded. By the end of the session we had the basic structure – including the Bunnymen-esque quiet/loud idea. It was together within a week. It felt really exciting. We booked to record with Pete Haigh asap to capture it early.

Red Rhino had told us that this time we could have a second colour for the sleeve. Lites, as our chief designer in residence, designed the sleeve. It was a series of still photographs of the USAF supersonic X fighter project, nicked from PKDC library. The beaker that the pilot is holding is meant to capture the explosion of the music. When we got the first pressing of the sleeves we spray painted a series of them and they captured it perfectly. Unfortunately, the guy who was doing the job for us wanted to get the job done quickly and just did a few red brush strokes and sent them off to print. Disappointing but we couldn't afford to redo them.

Apparently, 'Poised Over The Pause Button' brought in the New Year of 1988. It was, we had been told, the first song that John Peel played on his World Service show. It is actually quite apt as it was about getting pissed on Jamaican Red Stripe beer ('The white stripe with the red . . .'), our favourite of the recently introduced international beers. Which we would have been drinking as it played over the international airwaves unbeknownst to us.

After 'Poised Over The Pause Button' we recorded a third single, 'The Great Divide', with Pete Haigh. We were relatively happy with it but really wanted the guitars to sound harder. We wanted to use Gang of Four's first Peel session as a template but forgot to take the vinyl along when we were mixing it (ah, the olden days!).

It didn't matter in the end as Red Rhino went bust after spending so much money on promotion for TWP's first LP, *George Best.* (I'm sure Gedge got that idea from the lyrics on the B-side of 'Engine Failure', 'To me perfection means George Best . . .')

We felt that we had done everything that we could from Perth and had to make a decision about relocating somewhere else – Edinburgh? Leeds? London? We decided on London. We would become pretty good mates with McCarthy and already had a bit of a scene down there and it's the logical place to go, so we ended up living in Brixton (I'm still there!). Most of McCarthy moved to Brixton, and we have been hanging out there on and off from the mid-1980s.

I turned down the offer of playing bass for Tim and Leticia (from McCarthy's) new band, Stereolab, and ended up becoming a history teacher. I'm now the Head of Humanities at BRIT school in South London (don't worry, it's a state school – nobody has to pay any fees – a major misconception!). Leticia and Martin Pike (Pikey), Stereolab's long-time manager, came in last year to do a talk on writing political lyrics. It was great to see them after thirty years.

Greenock and the South Clyde Estuary

On the coast, almost thirty miles west of Glasgow, lie the Inverclyde port towns of Greenock, Gourock and Port Glasgow. Despite being so close to Scotland's largest city, the towns had their distinct and individual music scene.

Ian Boffey: There was a small, thriving, indie scene in Greenock in the mid-1980s; the local bands were all very different, and some were very good. The Dragsters all grew up in the west end of the town and so gravitated to Gourock to play live. We landed gigs with our first school band, Laughing Gravy, at Janey's Under-18s Disco in the Bay Hotel at the Pierhead – sadly long gone. (We also played at a place called Davy Jones' Locker, which was a stone's throw from the open-air pool featured on a recent Blur album cover.) ... We were all aware of the great Beefheartian Glasgow band, Chou Pahrot, and their wild song, 'Lemons' – they all had crazy names like Eggy Beard and Mama Voot and we did likewise, just for a laugh really.

Gourock was important; it's where our favourite local bands played and we used to go and see a fantastic three-piece group called Apartment Six, led by a brilliant guitarist and huge influence on us all, Marco Rossi, at the legendary Ferry Café, handily located across the street from Janey's. The atmosphere there was electric; our version of The Cavern, in a way. Alcohol wasn't allowed so we could go to what felt like a small, packed club, even as young kids, and get to hear this incendiary live music. We were 'radicalised'.

Starting our own band was inevitable; Marco was actually the drummer at our first rehearsal and I remember playing 'Wild Thing' so fast he could barely draw breath; when we finished he said, 'Man, what a great version of "Get Off of My Cloud".'

Another big influence was The Styng Rites, a group led by George Miller, later of Kaisers fame. The Styng Rites were more in the Rezillos/Revillos vein and usually kitted out like characters from *Thunderbirds*, another fantastic live band and very supportive. Pete [Jamieson] was the guitar player and George [Miller] also did time on the drum stool for us – he's an excellent artist too and kindly painted our drum skin and 'psychedelicised' my guitar. So we would go and see them live a lot.

George Miller (The Styng Rites and The Kaisers): I was still at school in Greenock when Peter Jamieson and I started playing together, which gradually formed into The Styng Rites. We did the usual assortment of church hall/youth club/people's birthday party type gigs, then progressed to the pub and club circuit. We didn't have much of a clue what we were doing and were heavily influenced by the Rezillos/Revillos. The original line-up featured Marco Rossi from Apartment Six, an instrumental surrealist jazz punk trio similar to nobody except possibly Chou Pahrot. Although he was brilliant at it, Marco's talents were largely wasted on bass as he was undoubtedly one of the best guitar players Greenock's ever had.

The Styng Rites became one of the busiest live bands in Scotland and we went through quite a few line-up changes in the seven years or so of the band's life. I'd moved to Glasgow in my second year at art school and the band was gigging pretty much non-stop. Peter had left the band fairly early on and the best-known line-up, if that's the right phrase, featured Stephen Church on guitar, the late and much missed Iain Mathie (Bigza) on bass and big Jim Gallagher on drums.

I don't remember us feeling part of any 'scene' as such, although we played the same venues as all the other young bands. Although we did hundreds of gigs up and down the country, we always liked coming back to the Victorian Carriage in Greenock, where the audience threw bog rolls onto the stage when we played 'Wipeout'. When we played at the Klub Foot in London, we didn't feel part of that scene either. We were never a psychobilly band, but I remember writing one or two songs with that element of our audience in mind. I used to describe us as a 'souped-up beat group', which wasn't really accurate as I didn't know enough about the genre at the time to make such a claim.

Ian Boffey: Chris Davidson was very important as he started *Slow Dazzle* [fanzine], which we all snapped up at Rhythmic Records, the local indie record shop. Both Chris and the guys at

Rhythmic were supportive; we even had our own fanzine for Laughing Gravy called *Sniffin' Gravy*, which Chris kindly included in an issue of *Slow Dazzle*. So we got a lot of help, in a lot of different ways, from all these older, established figures on the scene.

Chris Davidson (Promoter and *Slow Dazzle* fanzine): In my opinion Greenock and its environs has always punched way above its musical weight over the past six decades in comparison to all other Scottish towns.

I had an idea in about 1983 to create a local music fanzine. I had thought about it long and hard for about a year, how to get it printed, distributed, etc., and it was not just to be about music. So, through Rhythmic Records (where else? Pre-internet/iPhone days!), I placed an ad on the wall in the café info centre asking who would be interested to contribute articles on music, film, fashion, books, politics, travel, pub reviews, football, a quiz, a letters page, etc.

Not sure if that broad spectrum had been done before. *The Face* and *i-D* maybe? Anyway, loads turned up at the meeting and all was sorted there and then, just about all aspects covered on the spot!

I also decided that I would make it a very unusual format – A4 landscape instead of the usual A4 portrait, with front and back coloured cardboard covers between the pages. I just thought it would be easier to fit photos and text in that way when photocopying reduced Boots developed pics and typewritten text to that layout – yup, all painstakingly hand done, real cut and paste, no computers back then!

The first issue in 1984 amazingly sold all of the 300 copies produced, mostly in Rhythmic, which good mate Andy H printed, with great help from Pat McErlane who also contributed great features throughout. Most of the type from my handwritten singles/LPs/gig reviews plus all of the stuff handed in by contributors were wonderfully typed up by my amazing wife Theresa Davidson. I honestly don't know how we managed it all in one year whilst both holding down full-time jobs and bringing up three wee girls!

The first of six issues – all in 1984 – had a yellow cover, with Bo Diddley on the front – my first ever interview. The next were Billy Bragg and Jonathan Richman! And the following five were green, blue, purple, orange and red.

Incredibly, by the final issue at the end of '84, largely due to getting rave reviews from *NME, Sounds, Melody Maker,* and Billy Sloan and John Peel, and mail order copies ordered from Poland, Japan, Germany, USA, Australia, Canada through Peel, etc., issue six sold a remarkable 1,200 copies of an unbelievable fifty jam-packed pages!

The iconic front cover was red on white, beautifully drawn by our very own George Miller, where I gave The Jesus and Mary Chain their very first ever interview and front cover. That legendary and fantastic cover now features in at least three books and two videos!

Other features in issue six were on Neil Young, The Mighty Wah!, A Certain Ratio, the miners' strike, a three-page interview with Pat Nevin, mostly on his brilliant musical tastes rather than his amazing football talents (I headlined it 'Pat The Trick Dispenser'!), Kurt Vonnegut, The Dragsters, four pages of letters (!), six pages of singles and LP reviews, George Orwell, The Styng Rites, four pages on Alan McGee, Joe Foster and Dick Green's then fledgling label Creation Records – their first ever interview and feature! – and finally a three-page interview with John Peel . . . I had a meal with Peel, and he incredibly let me sit in on one of his two-hour live broadcasts when he did a week of residency at BBC Glasgow. His wife Sheila was also in the studio, supping red wine – John affectionately sometimes referred to her as 'The Pig' due to the way she snorted when laughing out loud, so I headlined the article 'Breakfast With The Pig's Husband'!

Every issue of *Slow Dazzle* featured two pages on a local band – 56 Degrees North made this one – and also had major contributions from others, in this case mostly by James Brown, the legendary creator of *Attack on Bzag* (his fanzine at the same time as *Slow Dazzle* – we met in Glasgow), who subsequently created the enormously huge *Loaded* and *GQ* mags!

After *Slow Dazzle* a few other nice Greenock fanzines appeared, like *Surfin' Swordfish*, *Wax Bone Abdicate* and *Smalltalk*.

In 1986, Chris Davidson opened a club called Subterraneans in Greenock, together with Paul Barr and Thomas Taft.

Chris Davidson: Affectionately now known as 'Subbies', Subterraneans was a club formed under The Melrose pub at Barr's Cottage in Greenock by me, Paul Barr and Thomas 'Sheer' Taft in 1986, with thirty band nights and twenty-one disco nights attracting nearly four thousand customers over its ten-month existence, so that's an impressive average of about seventy-five for each night – 113 came on the opening night!

Inspired to recreate, match and surpass the likes of Paisley's Bungalow Bar Silver Thread nights, as well as Glasgow's Splash One events, we were able to do just that in less than a year.

Held in a small basement room, hence the name (that and the Bowie song, Kerouac book and brilliant Flesh For Lulu choon!), March '87 saw the record crowd of 182 for The Pastels, supported by The Groovy Little Numbers. Other crowds of over a hundred were for the likes of Felt, Television Personalities, The Weather Prophets, BMX Bandits, Marc Riley and the Creepers, Nikki Sudden, The Clouds and The Soup Dragons. We nearly always had a local support act, so the likes of The Dragsters, The Sherbet Tambourines, The Hardy Boys, The Next Projected Sound, The Mindpipes and The Roundabouts all got a slot.

Billy Harron from The Dragsters took great care of our lighting and Jim Barr photographically recorded most of it, as well as sorting broken fuse problems mid-set!

We were able to attract such a wide range of brilliant talent by telling bands that we could be part of a three-night weekend, by tying in with Rooftops in Glasgow and The Onion Cellar in Edinburgh on the Friday, Saturday and Sunday, which worked out a treat!

Apart from the door takings, the band nights were largely supported by the disco nights, twenty-one of them, mostly attracting crowds of over fifty. We gave the guys who are now Pineapple Soul six nights, and we called ours Psychedelic Punk Rock Happenings. Mostly me, Paul or Tafty DJed. The legend that is McD got his debut DJ set with us one January '87 night, after I had showed him how to work the decks!

One of the most pleasant surprises was the night that Swell Maps legend Nikki Sudden turned up with his Jacobites – turned out that his guitarist was Rowland S. Howard from The Birthday Party, and incredibly his drummer was Lindy Morrison from The Go Betweens! One hundred and twenty-two folks witnessed that . . .

The last night of Subbies was really something special – more than 150 turned up for The Weather Prophets (now The Loft) supported by David Westlake with Luke Haines, and The Orkneys. The managers, who hated us for some bizarre reason and couldn't wait to get shot of us, turned off the power before the end of the Prophets set. So, what did the band do? Invited the whole audience out to the street to finish their set acoustically, then everyone all came back to a big all-night party at ours!!!

Jim Barr (Photographer): There had always been a thriving local music scene in the early eighties, but things really started to develop around the time Rhythmic Records started in early '83. This created a hub for many of us who started to run club nights and attract a few bands from out of town. This accelerated when the fanzine *Slow Dazzle* started, for which I took a lot of the photographs from local and Glasgow gigs. Gigs were put on at the Bay Hotel in Gourock and Bogies in Greenock, but the pinnacle was around late '86 through to summer '87, when Subterraneans hosted some of the finest bands of that era. A club run by my brother, Paul Barr, Chris Davidson and Thomas Taft, based on the Splash One model. I was fortunate enough to take what I regard as some of the best photographs I've ever captured, and these still stand the test of time, nearly forty years later.

Falkirk and Grangemouth

One of the pioneers of the Scottish independent scene was Brian Guthrie, manager, label owner, promoter and distributor. His younger brother, Robin, was also in one of the most beloved of all Scottish bands, the Cocteau Twins (along with Liz Fraser, Will Heggie and Simon Raymonde). Simon and Robin later formed one of the most important labels of the last few decades, Bella Union.

The other important band from the Falkirk/Grangemouth area was Lowlife, who released records on Brian's Nightshift label.

Brian Guthrie: Lowlife came out of another band that I managed called Dead Neighbours. Dead Neighbours were described in the *Daily Record* as 'Scotland's answer to The Cramps', and they featured Craig Lorentson on lead vocals, Ronnie Buchanan on guitar, David Steel on bass and Grant McDowall on drums. I signed them to my management company, Nightshift Management, and I signed them to my original record label, Sharko Records. They did a lot of major support tours; they did three tours with The Alarm. They were out with most of the psychobilly bands of the day, like King Kurt and The Meteors. They also supported The Cult and various other bands. We produced three vinyl albums with Dead Neighbours and one cassette album in their incarnation. The final tour that Dead Neighbours were guests on was a twelve-day tour by Johnny Thunders in the era of his Cosa Nostra band. We did that support tour and at the time we had a situation where Ronnie Buchanan wasn't able to handle all the guitar parts. So we brought in Stuart Everest, who was a friend of mine and of my brother.

Stuart and Bill Heggie did apprenticeships in the BP (Grangemouth Refinery) together and obviously went their various musical ways. Robin and Will performed in a band called The Liberators, who I did a single with. I was co-writing the songs with that band. Then when the tour came up with Johnny Thunders and Dead Neighbours, David Steel had just got married and his wife wouldn't let him go out on the tour. Will had recently left the Cocteau Twins, and had been offered the chance to join Dead Can Dance but didn't fancy it, came back up to Scotland and I hooked him up with Dead Neighbours. He was able to learn their rather simplistic form of music in one rehearsal I think, held in a school hall in Grangemouth prior to going out on the Johnny Thunders tour. During the tour, a chemistry developed between Will, Stuart, Craig and Grant McDowall. What became the Lowlife line up came out of that. Ronnie Buchanan would eventually be sent on his way, as it were, but the final Dead Neighbours album and the first Lowlife release – the six-track mini album *Rain* – were recorded at the same time. Both put out within months of each other. Obviously the initial place we got with Lowlife was absolutely tremendous. It became clear that Lowlife were going to become the band and Dead Neighbours just faded into history.

Nightshift Management – obviously I was looking for deals for the bands. We'd come very close to getting a deal with MCA Records for The Liberators. We had several labels, including WEA, interested in Dead Neighbours, but the A&R people found the band and their general make-up quite hard to handle. Let's just say these guys lived the rock'n'roll dream to an absolute excess. They were very hard to handle. I was once asked by an A&R man how I managed the unmanageable, and that was a mantra that was to continue into the Lowlife days as well. Anyway, Nightshift Management then set up Nightshift Records because the deals we were being offered for Lowlife weren't great. There were very poor recording budgets, not much promotional budget. So we decided to do it ourselves and initially to get some money in, to get the first mini album done, I just got a bank loan. Any rumours that I was a secret closet bank robber or drug dealer were severely exaggerated. [Laughs] That's how the bands came together and Nightshift Records came together.

But Nightshift was not just a vehicle for Lowlife. I was running it as a label with other bands, some of whom I managed as well. I had a lot of Scottish bands on the label. People like The Matter Babies, Pioneers Corps, who were the first release outwith Lowlife – Pioneers Corps were made up of John Telford from the band Everest The Hard Way, an Edinburgh band who I managed. I was also involved in the Edinburgh and Medway beat scene, with bands from down south.

I got a bank loan when I had the Sharko label, and I used some of that money to record Lowlife's *Rain* mini album. That's what got it off the ground. That album and then its follow-up, *Permanent Sleep*; then *Diminuendo*, then *Godhead* I think – I can't remember the right order – those albums were all released to absolutely over-the-top press. We very quickly got a lot of radio play with people like John Peel and Janice Long at the BBC, as well as sessions here in Scotland with the Scottish-based radio stations. The press attracted a lot of record company interest, as I mentioned before, but the budgets that were being offered to us were miniscule. We wanted to make really good-quality records and have them really well packaged. I mean an album like *Diminuendo* had gold-embossed printing, reverse board and inner sleeve, and we were spending bigger budgets than labels like Rough Trade, Arista and various others we were talking to were prepared to offer. They certainly weren't prepared to offer much in the way of advertising and promotional support either. We already had the management company and we set up a label, so we used that. From the initial success of *Rain*, a bit more money came in and more interesting interest came from publishers.

Janice Long had two brothers. One was well known on the telly, Keith Chegwin. He had a twin brother called Jeff Chegwin, who was a major A&R person with Chappell music publishing in London. However, he'd [Jeff] developed a pretty severe alcohol problem and was removed from the company for a sabbatical, during which time he set up a company called Working Music with his wife, who was a former nurse from Inverness, up here in Scotland. I read about them in the trade papers and he seemed to have a budget behind him. It seemed that Chappell's were financing him to try and get going independently. We did a publishing deal and it was initially this that got us money for recording and tour buy-ons, because by the time *Diminuendo* came out we were doing major national tours with bands like The Go-Betweens. We weren't given those supports; we were buy-ons. Nowadays they call it cooperative advertising. You give the headline band and their management a few thousand pounds and you get the tour support slot, and you get a certain amount of stage space, etc. You get your logo in the adverts and so on.

The tour with The Go-Betweens coincided with *Diminuendo*, which was our first big break when we got into the indie charts.

And most of the releases we were doing by that stage were in the indie charts, the EPs, the albums, so we're up there competing with all the big names in the indie charts who were obviously selling a decent amount of product. So we were bringing in quite a bit of money but we were spending it quicker than we got it because the recording budgets continued to grow and grow. Famously I went to the Media and Trade Festival in France one January, when the band were recording what became *Swirl It Swings*, a four-track EP. On my return from France, I was invited down to the studios to hear what they'd been working on in the three weeks at top rates that they'd been in the studio. I was sat in the studio chair and these four wonderful tracks came blasting out of the speakers, and I thought, well, that's half of an absolutely amazing album, let's see the rest. And they said, that's it, that's all we've done, four songs. All that money and everything else, probably not helped by the fact that Keith Mitchell, who became a regular producer-engineer, was into the excess as much as the band were.

Let's just say there was a lot of whisky consumed and a lot of other interesting substances. Yes, they produced some of the best music I've ever been involved in, but it was a case of quality over quantity. So that was meant to be an album, it ended up being an EP. Keith Mitchell was an in-house trainee engineer for a guy called John Turner, who owned the Palladium Studios. Palladium Studios were a converted town house in Straiton Village outside Edinburgh. John was a session man, and he was a touring member of things as diverse as Demis Roussos, the Greek dude, and a lot of mainstream stuff like Lulu and Tom Jones. He did sessions on lots of records for lots of people. He owned the building and he produced more mainstream stuff, and had Keith learning the ropes. Obviously, Keith was very interested in what we were doing with both Dead Neighbours and Lowlife. My brother Robin had been involved in the earlier stages at Palladium as well, operating under the name George Spiggot. He produced some of the Dead Neighbours stuff.

That relationship between Robin and John Turner led to a lot of 4AD bands, like The Pixies, Belly and Throwing Muses, all recording in Palladium as well. Other producers from the States would come and work in this studio. We stuck with Keith for quite a few records, up to the *Godhead* album, which was the first thing we recorded out with Palladium. Elliot Davis owned a studio on behalf of Wet Wet Wet in Glasgow and their in-house engineer was a guy called Ted Blakeway. We used Ted on that album. Famously, all the songs on that album had been pre-demoed for me to hawk around at that year's Media and Trade Festival. They were done on Portastudios here in Grangemouth, mainly with Stuart doing most of the technical side since it was in his bedroom. It was TEAC four tracks, recording onto multiple cassettes and then mixing them down. Those tracks became what was known as *The Black Album*. There were 250 promo albums for me to take to MIDEM and to spread around the music business to try and get other deals, and so on and so forth.

Had everything gone to schedule, we wouldn't have ended up doing it at Wet Wet Wet's studio. We were going to be doing it at Axis Studios in Sheffield, which was a studio owned by The Comsat Angels, who were a band that I became very friendly with and loved a lot. They were going to produce the band and actually have them as a tour support. During the same time period, a guy called Charlie Gladstone at Chappell's had reached,

I think, the end of the road with working with Jeff Chegwin. I think his alcoholism kind of took over. Famously, we headlined the first ever ICA Rock Week on The Mall. And that particular night was the one that Jeff decided to drop off the wagon; he famously started fighting his wife outside the ICA on The Mall and the guys in the band got involved in protecting his wife, who he was laying into, and gave him a good leathering. So that kind of ended that relationship. But Charlie Gladstone had loved the band from the start, Charlie being the grandson of the Gladstone who was the prime minister way back in the early 20th century. He now lives up in Inverness and runs a smallholding I believe, but he took us on and he had an in-house label with Chappell called Idea Records.

So this album that was going to be produced by The Comsat Angels guys was going to be financed with the advance from Idea Records. However, at the last minute, Chappell's and Idea Records were taken over by Warner Brothers from the States, and Warner Chappell didn't want to be involved with our type of indie material at all, they wanted more mainstream stuff. The funding was stopped. I had Axis [Studios] lined up; they wanted paying for it and we couldn't do it. By that time I was also the Vice Chair of the Scottish Record Industry Association. I'd got to meet Elliot Davis, Wet Wet Wet's manager, and he came on board and said I'll let you use our studios to record your album as long as you use our engineer, hence the Ted Blakeway connection. He was also quite cunning because the same day that we started to go into the studios, he took out a court order against me for the full value of the recording sessions. He kept this in his drawer so just in case we didn't pay him he'd take action against me to get his money. That said, the money was coming in and this was pre the collapse of Rough Trade and the Cartel, who were doing our distribution, so we were able to pay him and the band moved on, as it were, at that period. So by that stage financing mainly came from the publishing advances. That gave us enough money to do the tour buy-ons and pay for studios. We were getting good sales and money was coming. Then, of course, in the late nineties, Rough Trade went bust, which cost me and the band a fortune.

The label was always going to be a vehicle for other bands I was involved with. I'd assumed initially that we'd get a big enough deal to take Lowlife to the next level. But I was concentrating on some of the smaller things I was involved in. I did a lot of Scottish bands, starting with Pioneer Corps. We did other Scottish bands; I managed a band called The Matter Babies, we did a couple of albums with them. I managed and released a band called The Steelchain, another one called Better Ways and a load of bands in that sort of indie territory. I got involved with the beat scene; I was very much a big fan of the sixties punky beat, as it were, so I got involved with bands like The Thanes and The Offhooks and things like that. I managed The Offhooks as well, and Calvin Burt, the drummer of The Thanes, who was the frontman of The Offhooks, he sort of partnered me with my current label TSB later on in life. He was helping me out with stuff. I think we had about twenty-five different bands and that was including bands from England and abroad.

It was quite an active label. By that time the label was handled via Fast Forward, who were part of the Cartel of distributors. We had a quid pro quo thing. I went and worked at Fast Forward's offices and helped them with distribution, release planning design and management, as well as telly sales management for them in return for the office and storage space. By this time I was able to facilitate, via them, what they called P and D deals: pricing and distribution. That would mean that Fast Forward, under the auspices of Sandy McLean and obviously the parent company Rough Trade in London, would advance money on sales in return for doing the pricing and the distribution, for which they got amply paid, but that was another way of financing things. There was always going to be other bands I was doing things with, because that pre-existed. I was managing bands before Dead Neighbours who then begat Lowlife. I'd been involved in the Scottish scene for a lot of years and I'd been involved as a promoter; in the punk and post-punk era I did a lot of promotions. I did concerts in Falkirk, Grangemouth and Bo'ness town halls. I did gigs in Paisley, Dunfermline, Edinburgh.

At that time, as we moved into the post-punk era, I was doing tours with people like Echo and the Bunnymen and The Sound, and still doing punk bands at the smaller end like Chelsea, UK Subs, The Members. I moved into the ska scene and did quite a few ska things, most notably on a regular basis with Bad Manners. I had a lot of careers running simultaneously. During this time I was also writing for *Sounds*, the weekly music paper, and I started doing some stuff for *Melody Maker*, even early issues of *Kerrang!* because it was the same editorial team as *Sounds*. I was doing radio by this stage as well; lots of stuff with BBC Radio Scotland and with the initial Central FM when they first were based in Stirling, before they moved to Falkirk – I did a regular alternative rock show. I did a three- or four-hour slot, once a week for about six months, and then of course the station got taken over by a bigger syndicate and moved their studios to Falkirk. They are now based back in Stirling but at that time, they moved to Falkirk and I lost my slot. I ended up doing a football radio show for them in Falkirk, but that's another story.

The Cocteau Twins

Brian Guthrie: Robin's career started at a very young age, he was probably playing in bands at 12 or 13, and was already doing major supports to bands like The Jolt, with a band called The Heat. He also joined a band called Warrior, who were formed by a chap in the old town in Grangemouth, Dougal Rae. They were doing sort of like pre-punk. Maybe it was just rock played badly, who knows. [Laughs] But they got interesting supports as well because one member of The Bay City Rollers, Eric Faulkner, actually came from Grangemouth and did gigs in Moray High School in Grangemouth, and it was Warrior that got the support. That also involved Stuart Everest, who later did his apprenticeship with Robin and Will Heggie. Robin and Will were then involved with The Liberators, who I co-wrote the songs for with Robin. The Liberators were completed with a singer called Michael Toner, and a drummer whose name I've forgotten. The Liberators – we did a single, which is the first thing I ever recorded with John Turner at his original Palladium Studios.

We put that out, self-distributed, it did quite well, got interest and I went on a trip to London because we had interest from Arista Records, MCA Records and RCA Records. RCA Records with an A&R man called Simon Cowell – I wonder whatever happened to him. [Laughs] I came back up from London from

SCOTLAND IS BIGGER THAN YOU THINK

the trip and headed to the rehearsal rooms. We used rooms in a semi-derelict building near Grangemouth docks. ETD Music it was called. It was a guy called Alan Dougall, who made flight cases and made-to-measure guitar cases and all that sort of thing. He had spare rooms and we used to rehearse in there. I came back from London with the news that there was a possible deal on the table for The Liberators. I arrived, went upstairs and heard this ethereal, other-worldly sound – a female voice. I opened the door and it was Will, Robin and Liz Fraser – what became the Cocteau Twins. Liz I knew of because I was running a club in Grangemouth at the International Hotel, the Nash, doing punk and post-punk shows, three days a week. Robin used to do some of my DJing, and Liz and her elder sister used to come down to the Nash for their nights out. The first time I met Liz she was completely bald. She'd shaved her hair off. But she had this amazing voice, singing God knows what, because there was not an intelligible lyric there, but just this wonderful voice which Robin, for his part, used as another instrument I think.

The deal with The Liberators naturally fell apart at that point. The Cocteau Twins' history was fairly brief because they went to a studio in Lesmahagow and did a demo, and rattled off some cassettes. Robin was a big fan of The Birthday Party. Him and Liz blagged their way into Birthday Party gigs. All over the country, sleeping in doorways, all sorts of things. The cassette tapes got their way, via Nick Cave, to Ivo Watts-Russell at 4AD Records and to John Peel and various other movers and shakers. Whilst they were still galivanting out on that tour, I took a phone call at our family home from Ivo, basically saying he wanted to talk to the Cocteau Twins. And I was like, that's my brother. And he goes, is he there? And I say, no he's actually following one of your bands around the country, sleeping in people's doorways. And he said, well I've got this cassette that's been passed on to me. I want to offer them a single deal. I said, well, his tour's meant to be over in a week or so, I presume Robin will be back home with Liz in due course. We left it at that and then a few days later, this handwritten letter – which I still have – arrived from 4AD. Ivo had decided he wanted to offer them an album deal.

Robin, Bill and Liz facilitated that relatively quickly. I think the deal they signed, they know now, was an absolute piece of shit because it didn't allow them the full return they should have had, and it allowed Ivo to exploit their back catalogue over the years and make lots of money out of it that the band members didn't see, but that's the nature of this business. Robin's obviously learned a lot more now; Robin controls his own business rights, totally 100 per cent himself. That's why he's now involved with a lot of the remastering and re-releases of Cocteau Twins material because he's controlling, and quality controlling, the remastering and the packaging, and got a better deal on the sales. Robin never wanted me to be the Cocteau Twins manager. There'd been too much water under the bridge by that stage and Liz wouldn't have me involved. Liz was determined that me and the rest of the Guthrie family were ruining Robin's life. There were many screaming hissy fits down in the family house in those days. The morning after my dad died she took Robin to live in Anne's flat. Anne didn't want them there and gave them the walk-in cupboards where you hang your coats. That was the space she gave them. It was big enough to put a mattress on the floor and was decorated with sparkly lights and frilly lace and this sort of thing.

For a short period of time that's where Robin and Liz lived together. With the whole bust-up around the time of my dad's death, that caused Robin and I's relationship to be pretty strained. But I was still the person he turned to when they eventually got a wee flat in Falkirk, next to East Stirlingshire's football ground in Victoria Road in Falkirk. I was the go-to person when they struggled. I would get phone calls saying, can you bring a Red Cross parcel up because there's no fruit. They'd have just got their Giros that day and I'd ask where has that gone, and Robin would say, oh she's bought chocolate with it. Sure enough, I'd raid the cupboards and take bagfuls of shopping up and she'd gone and bought a box of 144 bars of Cadbury's Dairy Milk with her Giro money. That was the way Liz was, and probably still is, but that's another story as well. The Cocteau Twins got their deal with 4AD, they'd only played one gig and that was in a nightclub in Stirling, and they never played anywhere at all in their hometown area.

They were a well-established touring band before they ever played in Scotland again. Even then it was basically only Glasgow and Edinburgh. My mum at least had the joys of seeing her son performing in the Usher Hall and the Barrowland. She'd have tears streaming, so Robin was everything that was right. I'm incredibly proud of what Robin did. Robin and Will musically, Robin primarily, created a style that's been often copied and compared with, but they were doing it uniquely and even the style of bass playing that Bill came up with was basically ripped off by Peter Hook of New Order. Bill never gets any credit for creating that sound, and I think that's a shame. But there you go.

The Vaselines

The Vaselines were formed by Frances McKee and Eugene Kelly in 1986. They had their roots in The Pretty Flowers, Duglas T. Stewart, Norman Blake, Sean Dickson and Frances McKee's Bellshill collective. And, of course, they are famously associated with Nirvana, who covered three of their songs.

Eugene Kelly: I was born in the shadow of the Barrowland, and one day, all my brothers left the house to go out on a Saturday night, and I went and I found Orange Juice's 'Blue Boy' sitting on the record player, so I put the needle on it, and then it was kind of an epiphany moment. Every time I'd come back from school, I'd play guitar. At one point, I only just had, like, the neck of the guitar, not even a full guitar, and I used to stand in the bedroom, like, so you could only see the neck of the guitar.

Charles Kelly (Drums): Eugene was finding his own way. We had a lot of old punk 45s and albums in the house along with indie stuff from '78–81 that I think he tried out, then he bought a couple of singles by electronic bands, discarding that sound swiftly for The Byrds, Orange Juice and The Velvet Underground type stuff, both musically and visually. He really didn't go for the type of post-punk stuff I was interested in. The first Velvets album had a big effect on him so it all began from there after he bought his first semi-acoustic red guitar from the Barras and started learning to play. He started a band called The Famous Monsters.

Eugene Kelly: Before I knew it, I'd written a few ideas – I mean, the words are terrible. The first song was about Henri Matisse, the painter from France, called 'Sunday Painter'. I remember my schoolteacher had seen me writing, and taking it out, and reading it out for everybody, and having a good laugh. I mean, you just watched *Help!* from The Beatles, and you thought you want to have a mop top, and run about, and have adventures. I didn't think it was possible to even sort of be in a band, or meet people who'd be in a band, or have a record deal, or have a hit record, that was kind of science fiction . . . The Famous Monsters was my first band. Line-up was Grant Rinaldi on vocals, Paul Cunningham on bass guitar, Gary Bell on drums and myself on guitar. Grant left after a few shows and I took over on vocals and Callum Cuthbertson joined on guitar. We only played a few shows with this line-up, one supporting The Pastels downstairs in the Barrowland, and Splash One with Shop Assistants and BMX Bandits. We didn't make it onto the poster.

Frances McKee: I was on the bus going to school, and then I went to a party with my sister, and Eugene was there with his brother, and I said to my sister, 'I keep seeing him on the bus.' So I made sure I spoke to him, after I'd had a sufficient amount of cider, and he was very coy, he played hard to get. That was how it all kind of began, the coyness ebbed a little bit . . . I started going out with Eugene. He said, 'You need to hear this, this record,' and it was 'Upside Down' by The Jesus and Mary Chain. And it was like, wow, that's, that's incredible. I had never heard anything like that.

Eugene was in a band with friends called The Famous Monsters so I was kind of taking a backseat from that but also, I think at the time I didn't want to be the girl in the band that just sang, I really wanted to do something else. So I started to learn to play guitar. And then Eugene and I were going to write a fanzine. Remember, music wasn't the most important thing it was, it was theatre and it was fanzines and writing. But the fanzine never really took off.

Eugene Kelly: We weren't proper musicians, we were not as skilled in any way, compared to a lot of the guys from Bellshill, I mean, it was a bit of a con. I thought, are we really a proper band?

Frances McKee: Eugene had some songs and so I said, 'Well, I'll try to play this,' but all the songs . . . were written around my skills, or lack of skills in the guitar, because they're all three chords and that's why we wrote them in that way, because I couldn't play a C chord, for example, or an F chord. Still can't! So that's why the songs are written in that particular way. And that's what we didn't know at the time but that's what was our boundaries really within the music that we created. And we would just bounce ideas off each other. Eugene always came up with the music side of it because I was really quite backwards in that sense, but the lyrics came from the chat that came between us, you know. The famous 'Monster Pussy' was literally a kitten that hid under my floorboards. You know, there was a certain level of naivety and Finbarr Saunders [a character from *Viz*] to our work.

Norman Blake: Even though they're heavily cited as an influence at that time I don't think that many people were interested in them. Myself and Jim Lambie had a club at Bennets in Glasgow, it was called Pink Swastika. They put on The Vaselines. Jim made an amazing poster for it. And there were maybe ten people there, something like that . . .

Eugene Kelly: We did play one headline show at Bennets, which was a gay disco, and we played a night organised by Norman Blake and Jim Lambie, who were both in The Boy Hairdressers at the time and that was the only show we ever played, headline show where it was the two, the duo, before we got like a rhythm section. And to be honest we weren't very good.

Frances had become friends with Stephen Pastel after meeting him at the Splash One club in 1985 and we used to meet and hang out with him in the Griffin bar or go to gigs or the cinema together. He'd encouraged Frances and me to form a band so we recorded some songs and Stephen thought we had some songs he'd like to release on his 53rd & 3rd record label.

Frances McKee: We wanted to give a kind of feeling that it was the two of us, not one or the other . . . So we really wanted to get a Sonny and Cher type of thing . . . We had a few names, but I used to always put Vaseline on my lips, and we were in the pub one night, and Stephen said, 'How about The Vaselines?' and we just went, 'That's brilliant.'

Eugene Kelly: Stephen had agreed with Sandy McLean and David Keegan at 53rd & 3rd to finance some time in the studio for The Vaselines to record three songs. We booked into a tiny studio in a basement in Berkeley near Charing Cross in Glasgow and, with Stephen and Annabel Wright, we spent two or three days working out how The Vaselines songs should sound. It was a lot of fun and our first time in a recording studio so we were a bit green but we were really pleased with the end results. There were good reviews for the *Son of a Gun* EP in the music papers and we done a few interviews and learned how to send the whole game up.

Duglas T. Stewart: When I first heard 'Son of a Gun' . . . to me that seems like a really cool iconic record. I don't think I'd made a record like that yet. You know, again, it wasn't within any group, it was a thing like, sort of, 'Wow, Eugene and Frances have achieved this . . .' It sounds to me like an iconic and important record, but doesn't sound like pretty much anything else before.

Norman Blake: Actually I think those Vaselines records are really, really important . . . in the context of the Glasgow music scene, they're really pretty amazing records. Lyrically, what Frances and Eugene were doing was brilliant. Amazing great, great songs . . . incredible, just really amazing songs.

*'Son of a Gun', released in 1987, was one of three songs later covered by Nirvana, most notably appearing on the post-*Nevermind *compilation,* Incesticide.

The Fizzbombs and the continuing adventures of Narodnik

Much like the Bellshill gang, the Edinburgh scene continued to diversify, swap membership and form new bands. One of the first of these new offshoots to emerge in 1987 was another Rote Kapelle splinter – The Fizzbombs. They immediately signed up with Narodnik, and 'Sign on the Line' became the third Narodnik release, after two Jesse Garon singles. In keeping with the previous releases, Eddie Connelly roped in his old Meat Whiplash bandmate (and JAMC bassist) Douglas Hart to produce and direct a video.

Margarita Vazquez Ponte: In the Desperadoes we also used to swap instruments. So, well, Angus and I used to swap instruments because Angus fancied playing the drums. And I liked playing guitar, even though I wasn't that great. So, we would inevitably swap for one or two songs, quite often it would be Blondie covers . . . so we decided to form another band with me playing guitar and Angus playing the drums. And that was The Fizzbombs. We looked around for two more people to be in that band.

Angus McPake: I was trying to learn to play the drums and wanted to do more drumming, and Margarita, who played drums with Jesse Garon and the Desperadoes, played a bit of guitar and wanted to play some more guitar. And Ann Donald, who was a drummer, wanted to play some bass.

Ann Donald: You want to be in a band and you want to play the bass? I was like, okay then. And this is, again, all comedy value. I remember playing at my house. Margarita coloured dots on the bass frets where I needed to play. I was really short-sighted but was too vain to wear my glasses. So if they put the orange colour dots, I could kind of do the side glance. It was just, it was fun.

Margarita Vazquez Ponte: And we asked Katy Lironi, who was also in my class at Napier, if she wanted to sing, I had no idea if she could sing or not. Again, we just thought, oh well, let's ask Katy. She might be able to sing. And so originally, that was that line-up.

Katy Lironi (Vocals, The Fizzbombs): I left school in East Kilbride. And I got into Napier College in Edinburgh to study publishing. So that was that, I just turned 18, left home, went off to Edinburgh. And I was extremely homesick, but very quickly met a whole lot of people in bands, which I'd never been in a band and I didn't play an instrument. Both my brothers were in bands and I spent quite a lot of time hoping that they would ask me to join the band, which they never did. So that was really quite nice to be asked to join a band. And I was just kind of told, we've got this band called The Fizzbombs. We're rehearsing tomorrow. You should come; so, okay.

Margarita Vazquez Ponte: I don't think we thought, at the time, this was going to go anywhere particularly beyond the rehearsal room because it was just all an avenue for us to be learning another instrument.

Katy Lironi: I was probably a late developer and leaving home, going to Edinburgh and suddenly being thrown into, you know, I guess what became known as the whole *C86* scene. It was great, because all your friends were in bands. And all you did was go and see bands.

Margarita Vazquez Ponte: Angus, he was just such a fast drummer. I remember at one of our sessions, the guy saying he had the fastest rolls in the business. They weren't always in time, but they were really fast.

Katy Lironi: We had our first few rehearsals and we had our first gig within a couple of weeks . . . it's that timeframe I think, it was quite a long time ago. If it wasn't within the first couple of weeks, it was certainly within a very short space of time. And that first rehearsal. If you remember, I mean, Ann was playing bass but Ann didn't play bass, and, you know, Margarita's playing guitar, and everyone's just learning, you know, everyone's just learning and I'm singing and I've never sung. And I'm writing lyrics and I'd never done that before. So it was a steep but good fun learning curve. But very difficult to open your mouth in front of that microphone for the first rehearsal.

Angus McPake: I know I'm not a good drummer, but I enjoy drumming. And I think that says a lot about what The Fizzbombs were about. I think we were just doing it because we enjoyed doing it, and I don't think any of us thought we were very good, so I think we were quite surprised once, after we kind of got barely good enough to do a gig, that Eddie from Narodnik Records said, 'Well, we'll do a single with you guys as well.' And it was like, all right, okay, well why not?

Katy Lironi: Pressure . . . so it was just like, okay. I'll whisper along to this and see how it goes, and then they stopped. 'You need to sing.' I'm like, okay, all right. So, you know, whisper a wee bit louder, and, of course, guitars and bass are quite loud, lots of feedback. So it just, it just kind of grew . . . Margarita and Angus were the driving forces and Ann and I followed in and did very little apart from our rehearsals and playing and doing what we were told.

'Sign on the Line' received excellent reviews and gave The Fizzbombs the opportunity to support The Jesus and Mary Chain at Glasgow's Barrowland Ballroom but the band eventually fragmented due to Katy and Ann finishing their studies at Napier.

Andrew Tully: The Mary Chain were playing at the Barrowland, and The Vaselines were supporting. Basically, we were told either the Desperadoes or The Fizzbombs were up for coming, getting on the bill as well. And I'm thinking, well, by seniority, it really should be us, but The Fizzbombs got the gig. And I can remember having to say through gritted teeth to Margarita and Angus, who were in the Desperadoes as well, 'Oh, that's brilliant,' thinking, that should have been me and, like Marlon Brando in *On the Waterfront*, 'I could have been a contender.'

Katy Lironi: It all just happened so accidentally. I didn't consider it as a career. I didn't consider anything as a career. I wasn't thinking about careers, but, I mean, I recall each course lasted for three years, and then Ann and I both went on to further study in Strathclyde and, at that point, left because it was like, well, we were not in Edinburgh. We're not with that crowd any more, so that's over with.

Margarita Vazquez Ponte: Eventually Ann and Katy left, and Sarah from the Shop Assistants joined, and we were in a three-piece. Yeah, so for the first single, it was the original line-up. And for the second single and the Janice Long session, it was me, Angus and Sarah. Yeah, it's complicated, isn't it? We did it for Calculus, which is Everett True, The Legend's record label. He managed to push us a lot in London, so we ended up suddenly having loads of London gigs. And it was, it had started as a joke, and it really had started as completely nothing serious and we didn't think it was gonna go anywhere and, suddenly, we were being courted.

Katy Lironi: Suddenly I thought, oh, right, maybe we should have kept going through there for rehearsals. It all just seemed like a bit too much of a hassle at the time. But yeah, that was a bit disappointing. And quite often, even still, people will say (referring to the second single), 'Oh yeah, I've got that,' and I'm, no, I'm not on that one.

The Onion Cellar

Edinburgh's blossoming indie scene also had its own club – The Onion Cellar. It was run by members of Jesse Garon, Jeff Duffy, Linda Irvine and promoter Stuart Cant.

Stuart Cant (The Onion Cellar, co-organiser): The Onion Cellar was set up as Dan Treacy pushed us into it. I'd been writing to Whaam! Records asking about TV Personalities gigs and when they eventually played ULU in London in March 1985 I was invited to Dan and Emily's flat before it for a cup of tea. Dan was nowhere to be seen but 1000 Violins, who were supporting, were there. Anyway the night was incredible. A couple of months later Dan and Emily started the Room at the Top and, as I'd recently started as a civil servant and was still living at home, I could easily afford trips to London. Over the next few months I probably went about eight times, seeing amazing new bands. The Pastels, The June Brides, The Membranes and many more. I used to go down Saturday morning, get a cheap hotel at Euston and go home Sunday. When Emily found out I was paying for hotels she insisted I stayed on their floor. Eventually Dan introduced himself to me and insisted he would come to Edinburgh if we did it. They managed to get a Coatbridge gig and a Moray House gig booked and told us to get an Edinburgh one booked for the Monday after. We (Jeff, Linda and I, who were very good friends) phoned around and booked The Mission. We had four bands on. The TVPs, 1000 Violins, who were on their way to a gig at Stirling Uni, The Green Telescope and The Beeville Hive 5, and it was great.

Dan . . . basically said go and start your club now and get The Pastels first as they always get a great crowd. Linda came up with The Onion Cellar name. We phoned Stephen, he said yes, and we had more than two hundred people on a Monday night when the first band didn't go on till about eleven.

At the beginning it was Jeff Duffy, Linda Irvine and myself but after seven or eight months we invited people we'd got to know during the gigs to join us, definitely Angus and Ewan, maybe Margarita as well. At the beginning we all still lived at our family homes in Clermiston and Corstorphine so didn't really know anyone on the scene. The three of us soon got a flat together off Ferry Road, which helped if the bands needed somewhere to stay. Normally we'd phone a band we liked and ask them and they'd normally say yes, though later on we had many bands phoning us. Jeff phoned Pop Will Eat Itself from the number on the back of their first single and they immediately said they'd do it for £90, which would cover petrol and hire.

Pretty much the same with The Wedding Present. I was with Dan Treacy in London to see The Mighty Lemon Drops and the Weddoes supported. I said to Dan how much I loved them and Dan said, 'There's David Gedge there. Go and ask him to play your club'. He said £100 and our pals This Poison! to support, a shake of hands and it was sorted. It all seemed very easy, especially when we never really had a clue what we were doing. We would only do one or two a month. We'd then get our very amateurish poster and flyer designed and get them copied (normally by a mate in the Forestry Commission who'd do it for free, saving us a tenner).

Then it was the dreaded fly posting, which we all hated. On the night we would arrive about 5.30 p.m., put up the portable stage, help carry in the PA, help the bands in with their gear and get on with the soundcheck. We'd head upstairs to Nicky Tams for a couple of beers while this was on. If we had time and it was a band we were friends with we'd head to Diggers Bar for an hour or two to show them a proper Edinburgh pub.

Doors opened at nine and we'd do the door and DJ till the first band about 10.30 p.m. We'd normally have three bands though sometimes only two, occasionally four, and the main band would go on about 12.30/1 a.m. It would finish about two then we'd cart the PA out, take down the stage, gather our records and get a taxi home. We'd get back about 3 a.m. and, being a Monday night, we'd have work first thing in the morning. Still don't know how we did it! The crowd varied greatly from about two hundred for The Pastels or Primal Scream to about fifty or sixty for the less popular bands. The crowd was mainly students and many came through from Glasgow if a Glasgow band was on. Almost every band went down great, as to go out at that time on a Monday night you must be keen on seeing the band.

Meat Whiplash becomes The Motorcycle Boy

The demise of Shop Assistants opened up an opportunity for Eddie Connelly's previous band, Meat Whiplash. It was suggested that an appearance of the now defunct band would give a Narodnik Records night at Edinburgh's Onion Cellar an audience boost due to their Creation connection. The band temporarily reformed with a dramatically different line-up, now including Alex Taylor taking vocal (and alternating drum) duties with original singer Paul McDermott. Original drummer Michael Kerr would now play guitar alongside the newly recruited Belfast guitarist David Scott. This line-up would be an intermediate between the original band and soon-to-appear The Motorcycle Boy.

David Scott (Guitar, The Motorcycle Boy): I played in a couple of bands in Belfast in the North of Ireland. The Urge, with whom I got to play the Harp Bar, and Pig Awful, with whom I got to play The Pound. They were important venues at the time, and I'm delighted I was able to play a small part of a wonderful scene.

Janie Nicoll (Vocals, The Vultures): I was going out with David Scott, who was Scotty, who ended up in The Motorcycle Boy, so I went out with him for about three years. And it was at that time that through me he met Eddie Connelly.

David Scott: I remember going to a bedroom with Michael Kerr in a flat not too far from the Meadows, getting our guitars out and just hitting it off with him musically. I loved playing with

Michael. Things progressed from there. I think Andrew Tully (Jesse Garon and the Desperadoes; Rote Kapelle) also lived in that place.

Paul McDermott: Eddie was finding it hard getting gigs for some of the bands. They seemed more interested in booking Meat Whiplash. He contacted me and asked me if I would do some of the gigs. It was completely different, the line-up varied, Alex singing or playing drums, Michael on guitar, etc. Just depended on who was available to do the gigs. After that Eddie found easier booking gigs for The Fizzbombs, The Vultures, Baby Lemonade and Jesse Garon and the Desperadoes.

David Scott: It did feel a little unusual with group dynamics, but I could never really put my finger on it at the time. I loved the Shop Assistants. I loved Meat Whiplash. I was just thrilled to be a part of something new and, to me, exciting. I spent a lot of time with tapes and/or Michael writing riffs and that part was as natural as it comes to me. I don't know how much the bands practised, but The Motorcycle Boy did a lot, as I remember. That helped with the newness of roles to some.

Michael Kerr: There was part of the Shop Assistants' contract that if anybody left then Chrysalis would have first dibs on basically what they were going to do next. And there was something else that if they did go and do something next they would get X amount of money.

Paul McDermott: Eddie and Alex approached Michael and then I became involved. Later on David joined us. We practised a few times, managed to get some money together for a demo (courtesy of Blue Guitar), gave them the demo and they were interested. By then I had left my job and moved to Edinburgh.

Michael Kerr: Me, Eddie and Alex went down to see Geoff Travis, I think just to discuss things. There were two guys there who ended up being our managers. They were The Mighty Lemon Drops' managers at the time. I think they'd asked Geoff, 'What's Alex Taylor doing?' and he explained the situation and they asked to manage us. They went to Chrysalis and said, 'Look, we want to give you a new contract.' The sound was to be as far away from Meat Whiplash as possible. Or far enough for it to be something new for us anyway. For us, back then using 'commercial' for an indie band was a swear word. I remember hearing a single by a band called Westworld who used sequencers. And obviously Sigue Sigue Sputnik. It was slightly like a Duane Eddy thing but with sequencers. I always found that quite interesting and that's the direction

I wanted to go in and make something more polished. Someone described us as 'rocky pop rather than poppy rock', or it might have been the other way around, rather than the sort of jangly tweeness, which I found quite an insulting phrase. Let's say it was something more polished that was to try and get a major record contract.

The first release by The Motorcycle Boy was the effervescent, breezy 'Big Rock Candy Mountain', again with a video directed by Douglas Hart. It was given a huge amount of radio play and press interest.

Michael Kerr: It got B-listed on Radio 1 and it was played every other show each day which [was rare] for an indie band at that time. It was released on Rough Trade because they thought they could get some publicity through the indie chart even though we were signed to Chrysalis at that point. That was a huge deal for a band at that point, for an indie band to be played on Radio 1. It got to something like number seventy-four in the charts . . . or seventy-six . . . and it just stuck there. Nowadays to get to seventy-six in the charts is quite straightforward but back then with the amount of singles which were sold, then we sold quite a lot to get to that stage . . . but it just stuck there and never got any further. I think if it got into that top seventy-five it would have been pushed a bit more and it could possibly have been a success but we'll never know.

David Scott: I really don't know why it wasn't a success. It should have, at least, set us up for future success. However, 'Big Rock Candy Mountain' probably came out too early. We had no other singles recorded at the time and I don't think we even had a full LP's worth of songs ready. As a consequence, we weren't ready to tour when the first single came out. At least, that's how I remember it. I could be wrong. In any case, the subsequent momentum wasn't as great as it could have been.

Michael Kerr: I think with The Motorcycle Boy we'd left it too long before releasing anything after 'Big Rock Candy Mountain'. I think that was our problem. I don't know why we didn't . . . well, we did record another single with Flood producing but we didn't like it and asked the record company not to release it and I don't think they were quite happy with that. We went back down to London and we went to the same studio we did 'Big Rock Candy Mountain' in and added more stuff but it still didn't work so that was scrapped.

I think after that we just waited too long before anything else was released. We went and recorded an album at Greenhouse Studios – that was never released and then after that Scotty was thrown out of the band and I left in solidarity . . . and they carried on.

Eddie and Alex moved to London and got some other people in the band but never released any stuff, but it never really worked for them either. I always just felt that if that album had been released and we stuck as the original band . . . I'm not saying we'd be U2 but we'd have had a modicum of success. I think the album was good enough for it to have done fairly well.

Up for a Bit with The Pastels

Despite being one of the first bands off the starting block, The Pastels didn't begin to record their album until late 1986, for Glass Records. Up for a Bit with The Pastels *was finally released in 1987.*

David Barker: They probably could have made an LP in 1985, but there were some issues with Creation, as I recalled earlier. Also, I was in the US and Canada for five weeks in July and August 1986, on the first Jazz Butcher US tour, which meant the recording couldn't happen till September. I don't think they would have been ready to make an LP before 1985. You have to remember they were not a full-time careerist group, dying to make it in the indie-pop business. They wanted to be successful, yes, but were more ambitious for the music itself than the life. They couldn't tour like other bands either. I think the timing was just right in retrospect. It was released in January 1987 and hit number two in the indie charts – Half Man Half Biscuit beat them to number one. It was released on Big Time Records in the US and Mercury in Canada through existing deals I had with both companies. Big Time went bust before any plans for US shows could be made, sadly.

Brian Superstar: *Up for a Bit* was recorded in Leamington Spa by a guy called John Rivers. It was the first time we'd ever actually been in a proper studio with . . . I was going to say with somebody who knew what they were doing but that's rather unfair on Joe. It was the first time we'd had a proper budget to record a proper record. I think we spent two weeks in Leamington

Spa working on that, with John Rivers, which was a different experience from what we were used to and he kind of insisted that things were in time and in tune, which was a novelty.

Martin Hayward: I think we enjoyed making it, I think that was a very interesting experience, but I think that our overall, well certainly speaking personally, I think this was shared, I think we were frustrated by the distance between what that was and what we'd wanted it to be or what we thought it could have been. I don't feel that now with some distance on it, I think it's quite an interesting record, but I think it wasn't what we'd wanted to make and I think that was overall what we came away from that with, which is maybe a bit of a shame.

Bernice Simpson: That was less fun, because before, it was just the band, really, We were kind of in charge, but once you got a producer, it changes the dynamics. And also, we were all living together for a prolonged period; it certainly starts to get tension, because if things aren't working out, everybody gets a bit . . . kind of because you've only got a certain amount of time, so it puts a lot more pressure on the group, as a whole.

Martin Hayward: Return to Woodbine Street, this time for an album. Guide dogs train on the surrounding streets, but we're not out much on working days – maybe for cigarettes or juice. Our guest house, run by a trim husband and wife, provides breakfast. He was in a band in the sixties on which he refuses to elaborate, despite some determined coaxing.

One evening, in the lounge, as five people, the guiding spirit of the cosmos sits us down all unaware to the UK television debut of *This Is Spinal Tap*. We are quickly hooked and then skewered with horrid fascination. How do they know so much about us? Bernice and I have seared into our memories an excruciating shared telepathic experience of the 'Jazz Odyssey' sequence, where David St. Hubbins' girlfriend Jeanine chances an onstage appearance for the first time, clutching a tambourine. We don't dare look at each other.

In WSRS [Woodbine Street Recording Studio], a bright room and kitchenette upstairs provide peace for last-minute writing, but otherwise we all want to be in the control room or studio, where the action is. Everyone is focused and present, making a good deal of stuff up on the spot.

One morning Stephen brings hesitant and spidery chords which Bernice, John and I push and push at to structure a waltz juggernaut. Bass taken from Tessa Pollitt on the original version of [The Slits'] 'Newtown' (I imagine she had heard Dave Alexander on 'Dirt'). Stephen adapts a letter from a US fan, alone in a town of Van Halen guys who want to kick his ass. Working title 'Lonely Wyoming'. He later receives sheaves of Wyoming State promotional material about what a great place it is to live and work.

The seventh chords on 'Communion Table Blues' (which becomes 'Up for a Bit') are me trying to approximate the great guitar on The Heartbreakers' offhand 'Can't Keep My Eyes on You'. Bernice brings a glam tom chug for the bass to swing around. When Stephen's lyric is done, the *Guardian* review section supplies text to the runout.

I am obsessed with the achingly cool opening bars of 'You Get What You Deserve' by Big Star. I use Brian's Baldwin whammy bar as a substitute for musicianship. A line half lifted from Pere Ubu's 'Cloud 149'. The psychosis my own. No one has heard 'Crawl Babies' before. Rather than teach it to the band it is quicker for me to record the guitar, with Bernice playing along, add the bass and a guide vocal, then hand it over.

I don't consider singing myself. A second lead would confuse things and we are a bit late to start that. It's not my nature to want to be up front anyway. This also lets me hide from my lyrics, so I can cut what feels like quite close to the bone.

I will split this and my other 'Up for a Bit' credits with Bernice to make a point. Drums are music too and this is a group often writing collectively. The old story. Bootsy comes up with the part and James is 'I'm glad I thought of that'.

Whoever decides to slow down 'I'm Alright With You', it now has just a hint of country and western – a reference point, but one we don't talk up so much.

Louise posts my cassette of The Hellfire Club demos so we can listen back to how we did 'Big Blue Bus', now revived as 'Get 'Round Town', with fuzz bass.

The Supremes' 'Automatically Sunshine' is a shared touchstone. Stephen has Richard and the Young Lions' 'You Can Make It' for John to stick on the studio turntable. We steal the accented beat and bells for his 'Automatically Yours', another studio construct.

Most timings are under the three-minute mark, so almost six minutes of 'Baby Honey' feels daringly lengthy, when really it could have been much longer. We layer the free noise, so I also enjoy mutilating a guitar. Order is maintained for the whole time we are in WSRS. Except for one late-night session with Lucy, Jowe's saxophonist friend, which the vortex of 'Baby Honey' helps to suck into late-night multi-room whisky-fuelled musical malarkey. The next morning John silently scrubs a Househunters sticker from his 'Ghost Town' disc while we all feel suitably ashamed.

For another classic Brian assemblage, 'If I Could Tell You', Stephen adapts Auden and suggests we all contribute verses. Bernice and I do. Brian characteristically declines, holding up a fag packet – 'There's some words on here if you want them.'

John leaves gaps on several songs until late in the sessions and hires a state-of-the-art Fairlight for a day to fill out several arrangements from his head. Our role to choose between alternatives and to say when. We let him get slightly too representational on 'Baby Honey', I think, but 'Ride' and 'If I Could Tell You' are garlanded.

'The Day That I Got Crucified' (with Lucy's sax and a Bearsden reference), 'Empty House' and 'Fateful' don't make the album. These turn up respectively as B-sides and as a donation to a *Censorship Sucks!* compilation supporting Jello Biafra and the No More Censorship Defence Fund when the Parents Music Resource Center go after him. No idea if Mr Biafra got anything from this or was even aware of it.

'Up for a Bit' is just us, a little Lucy and a lot of John, surprising ourselves and each other. I think we are all, for various reasons, initially a wee bit frustrated with the result and we certainly come to react against it. It doesn't sound as tough as we can be live. In retrospect John does a great job of disguising our weaknesses. We don't, at the time, listen to our own records much anyway – too personal and full of decisions which you would now change. It was a lot of fun to make, though.

Bernice Simpson: It was a very creative process, of which we were all a part. I felt it was our line in the sand and really captured the band. It still stands up for me.

Despite its recording not being a wholly enjoyable experience for the band, the album was regarded highly in the press. The band followed the album with a single, 'Crawl Babies'.

Martin Hayward: I think I surprise everyone with 'Crawl Babies' (Stephen's title – I can't come up with one) because we take the odd step of re-recording it as a single after the album is finished. I'm too flattered to object, which I probably should have done in the interests of moving forward. John Rivers asks us what we want from this new version. We don't know, John. Bigger? Better?

Aggi's sleeve is Brian's Bank Street tenement stair, picking up on the lyric. A key contribution, from 'Supposed to Understand' onwards, is her design work on almost all sleeves and labels. She establishes and develops a recognisable, sometimes oblique, visual vocabulary in conversation with and sardonic commentary on the band's output. This helps provide continuity as we ricochet between record labels.

Mark Flunder films a video for 'Crawl Babies' in Brian's stair and flat (I play bass as Frances whips gimp-masked Eugene's naked back) and on the rainy Clyde (Bernice plays the footbridge while Stephen nurses the carry-out). With Jerry and other writers, Mark's film and photography and Aggi's art and design, Bernice tells me she feels as if we have a team around us.

Where then should ill feeling come from? It comes early and builds gradually. Fragile egos (Stephen and I particularly) and a lack of communication all round. The pace we work at is slow as we are all doing this in limited spare time, giving both it and the rest of our lives less attention than necessary. We have a low boredom threshold – most of what we record is done as soon as we can play it through, if not before. We may get better at playing it later, or not.

Brian, Bernice and I mainly together wrestle whatever music there is. Stephen comes up with most of the words and vocals and does most of the talking, making connections and setting stuff up. Without which, let's be clear, nothing happens.

So – from, say, 1983 – chances are that Stephen's (parents) phone is engaged. If I'm checking in, usually from a far distant payphone, Brian's number is the one to call. Soon he and I seem to share a perspective that is different from Stephen's and one that naturally includes Bernice once she is aboard.

Music is credited to whoever came up with the chords that we build from and so Bernice and I are unacknowledged in this process. For a chord, best get a guitar. Stephen's ideas usually require more collective work. But this is all fine. Standard band stuff. I also need to say that each of the four can make the others laugh and this is how we spend a lot of our time. We take what we are doing seriously, but we don't take ourselves seriously. When this starts to change, things start to go wrong.

'One divides and the other chooses' mum would say when my sister and I shared food. Brian and Bernice also have siblings and know how to navigate shared space. I've known Stephen since primary – our earliest collaboration a picture of T. Rex on *Top of the Pops*. He is an only child, and when reality doesn't correspond to his imagination, this can be frustrating for him.

He demands and deservedly receives most external attention and that is fine with us three as well. None of us wants to be fronting this ('kissing babies', as William Burroughs puts it) and we are happy for someone else to do it. Some of it is for the group and some for Stephen, but it is the same work. Bernice and I discuss and can come to terms with the fact that this is essentially Stephen's band. After all, anyone paying attention can recognise our contribution and read the group dynamics.

Musically, Aggi initially contributes little – on stage briefly to add shrieked backing vocals. Yet somehow, as Stephen's girlfriend, she becomes a credited band 'member' during 1985 without discussion, and mainly without a role, unless this is to be in Stephen's corner. This seems questionable, but we accept it. What else would we do? My girlfriend is also in the band, but then, she is the drummer.

By late 1986, along with the *Up Pompeii!*-inspired design, Aggi and Stephen cover the 'Up for a Bit' sleeve and label with images of themselves, without discussion. This feels dubious, not because we would prefer to also be featured in this way – we are all represented on the inner sleeve – but because it is now inescapable that we are working with people whose instincts are to cover our debut album with images of themselves, without discussion. You won't find a great deal of Aggi on the record – some backing vocals. Now, she is literally all over it, in what feels a wee bit like an act of appropriation. This seems questionable, but we accept it. After all, people have ears. Don't they?

I have my moments as well. You can accept people being insufferable to an extent while the joint endeavour continues to move forward and to be fun.

With *Up for a Bit*, Stephen begins to handle more of the increased press attention solo. Mark shoots a couple of videos with Stephen and Aggi alone. A lot of this is efficient use of limited time, but it does subtly shift dynamics.

Despite being in a 'Glasgow band', Bernice and I never actually stay in Glasgow, unless you count overnights with my parents in Bearsden. Which you really shouldn't, according to Glasgow. Or Bearsden. Rehearsal can be a 140-mile round trip. We learn to do everything on the road. See driver for details.

Baby Lemonade and The Bachelor Pad

Eddie Connelly was still pursuing his Narodnik project. His next signings were Edinburgh's garage-pop band The Vultures and Cumbernauld's indie-pop band Baby Lemonade.

Janie Nicoll (Vocals, The Vultures): I'd met Eddie (Connelly) and Alex (Taylor) and all these kind of people. And it was at that time that Angus (McPake) recorded our demo on his, like, four-track recording deck thing. By that time we'd already played a gig. The first was at The Onion Cellar with The Beeville Hive 5,

The Thanes and The Stayrcase. And we were like, the first band on, so we were three girls and a boy drummer . . . probably ham-fisted and nervous. And then when we came off people were going 'When are you going to record your album?' We were like, 'Eh?'

Ian Binns (Drums, The Vultures): The Vultures formed as I knew one of them (Allison Young) as a regular of the Snake Pit. One evening she and her pal Anna told me they wanted to form a band though they couldn't actually play anything. I declared that I'd never played drums before but would give it a shot anyway. They enlisted Janie, who was a classmate of Allison's at Edinburgh Art College. Narodnik approached us, which we found a bit strange as at that point we really were struggling to play our instruments. For some reason Eddie thought it'd be a good idea to get us down to London to record an EP with Douglas Hart. But we were quite disappointed with the results and Eddie agreed that we could record it again back in Edinburgh at Pierhouse Studios, though with Jamie Watson producing. Can't quite remember why we didn't record at Jamie's Chamber Studios, but it might have been when it was still a tiny basement in Lady Lawson Street.

Janie Nicoll: We recorded the single at Jamie Watson's studio . . . he was brilliant. He was very hands on and kind of knew how to kind of get the best out of us. We recorded our 12-inch then and the sound quality and everything was a lot better . . . You get excited about it. And then it was months later that it eventually came out. It was just like a roller coaster, you know, it was a bit of a runaway train. So, then it came out and Eddie put out this really jokey press release. And put people off, I think, because he said we were like three beauty school dropouts. And it made out we were from America, and that we'd just landed. It was so off the wall that people thought, 'Who the hell are they?' We got a good review in *Sounds* and *Melody Maker*, but the *NME* review was quite critical because it was a woman that did the review. And we had the song 'Jack the Ripper' and I think she sort of took offence to, you know, she took the sort of feminist stance to Jack the Ripper and kind of slagged it off, you know, and I was kind of like, you're missing the point. Entirely. In those days it was like, because we did a Janice Long session. And it was like, 'Oh, but it's not John Peel.' And the same with getting a review, like we got a good review in *Sounds* or *Melody Maker* but it's not the *NME* is it? Just like, it's not quite good enough. So it was a bit of a fail really.

The Vultures' sole EP, Good Thing, *stands up as one of the finest in Edinburgh's garage scene and certainly feels like a pointer towards the forthcoming trend towards shoegaze.*

The next Narodnik signing, Baby Lemonade, released their single 'The Secret Goldfish' in 1987, after an earlier joint flexi disc with The Batchelor Pad.

Graham MacDonald (Bass, Baby Lemonade): I played bass with Baby Lemonade from the get-go. It was me and Mark Abbott starting off in the bedroom in Kirky (Kirkintilloch, near Cumbernauld) until I went to Falkirk Tech and brought Joan Williams and Paul Lally on board. I found original drummer Colin Campbell in Kirky too. We didn't feel isolated but liked Glasgow, especially the west end.

Narodnik picked us up after our demo was played on the radio, and nice to work with Douglas Hart of Mary Chain on the 7-inch. He should have done a video too. The first release would have been the 7-inch 'The Secret Goldfish' on Narodnik. It was played on Peel, etc. Great to hear it on radio, sold well, pop stars for a day.

Happy with the 7-inch reception. We also did a good version on the LP, wish we'd done another one. The B-side 'Real World' is lovely too, lovely vocal from a great singer. Album (*One Thousand Secrets*) recorded in five days, Chamber Studios with Mr Jamie Watson producing, not a bad record. Should have done a second one. Did a couple of gigs in Camden after this but game was up, ran out of new tunes and then old rock'n'roll grim reaper called it a day on us.

A good memory was supporting the TV Personalities at the Barrowland back in the day – great band, that was nice.

The Vultures EP was Narodnik's last recording. The label lasted a little over eighteen months and produced a run of releases that easily matched the quality of more celebrated labels.

The Baby Lemonade flexi disc was given away with the Are You Scared To Get Happy? *fanzine. Its flipside was by The Bachelor Pad, led by the wonderful Tommy Cherry, and their track 'Girl of Your Dreams'.*

Tommy Cherry (Vocals, The Bachelor Pad): That flexi made it as Single of the Week in *Sounds* so that was really funny. It also got us a lot of gigs up and down the country. I loved Matt Haynes' fanzine *Are You Scared To Get Happy?* He was a real passionate ranter and not at all twee. He was also really funny. My one big regret is not getting to know him better. I think The Bachelor Pad should really have been on Sarah Records. It was our natural and spiritual home. I also loved Bob Stanley's *Caff* fanzine. It was filthy and hilarious. Real punk rock Joe Orton sort of vibe. These were my sort of people. Good home folks.

Our second single, 'Do It for Fun', was the most fucked-up production ever, so after that the album sounded as smooth as a baby's bum to me. But then, I was incredibly stoned at the time. I wouldn't do any of it the same way again . . . once was enough!

For me, the best gig we did, it has to be the gig we did in Lincoln with The Telescopes. That and Grant Morrison writing us into the plot of a John Constantine *Hellblazer* comic book. A tape of 'Do It for Fun' is so noisy that we jam a nuclear bomb and save the world. What a gas to be in a DC comic. Thanks Grant. We used to do some gigs with Grant's band in the early days and on Grant's first television interview I dressed up as a nurse and administered him pills throughout . . . it was duly banned!

We should have called it a day the day Martin [Cotter] left as the whole thing was based on our dualist energy . . . we were Jack and Julian, I suppose. Be careful what songs you write, they may come true! In 2000 I recorded an album's worth of songs with Stewart Christmas under the name The Whores (of Perception) and we played a couple of gigs at the 13th Note in Glasgow. But that is a whole other story. In fact, I could write a book about it! Julian Cope was heavily involved. We imploded as fast as we created, yet despite this it was probably the best band I was ever in and the music was superior to anything else I ever did.

The Bachelor Pad, which had its roots in another wonderful Glasgow band, Martin Cotter's The Wee Cherubs, went on to release a series of fantastic music on Warholasound.

Tommy Cherry (The Bachelor Pad): I was a huge fan of Martin Cotter's guitar [when he was in The Wee Cherubs]. Then about 1985 a lot of things happened at once. The Cherubs broke up, I first heard The Jesus and Mary Chain and I went to a new club in Glasgow run by Bobby Gillespie called Splash One Happening . . . I instantly left the band I was in (The Oysters) and recorded some demos with Martin and also Graham. The songs were 'Jack and Julian', 'Girl of Your Dreams' and 'Norwegian Wood'. Splash One was amazing . . . the first time I walked through their doors I heard 'Treason' by The Teardrop Explodes. I felt I had come home at last . . . every record they played was fantastic. It was a scene. Within a year every major town in the UK had a copy of Splash. Then came the fanzines . . . it was like punk but with groovy Warhol kids instead of all those lumpy Clash fans and Sid idiots. I have a lot of fond memories of that period. We sent the demo to various fanzines and got a good response. Offers to play live meant we had to expand the line-up. Fortunately, I was sharing a house with a keyboard wizard, David Harris (who is a genius!), and Willie Bain from my old band The Oysters stepped in to play bass. Our first gig, thanks to Jim Honey of Simply Thrilled, was with Baby Lemonade and Jessie Garon and the Desperadoes. It was a gas. We signed up for a record deal with Mike Stout the same day Andy Warhol died so he called the label Warholasound.

The Wee Cherubs

Martin Cotter (Guitar, The Wee Cherubs and The Bachelor Pad): I had been in a band called Radio Ghosts, we had been playing and gigging for years and it was becoming stale, so I left. The Radio Ghosts were a kind of Gang of Four, noisy, angular agit-pop type of bunch, highly original and very guitary, but with a fair bit of attitude and much misery – most of it coming from me!

So by the time I left I was ready for something quieter and more subtle, where you could hear actual music, the guitar tones and so on, and where not every second was filled with spiky noise. I also wanted to write melodic but probably less commercial songs, songs that I had in my head but knew were wrong for the Radio Ghosts. They weren't even all songs – just fragments – but I wanted to let them out and experiment with them.

Christine was my true love at that time; she was playing guitar in a band called Rapid Dance. I can't remember if she quit or if they split, but she started learning to play bass in the new post-Rapid Dance band. We really were just doing it for fun. I was writing material that would never have been performed by the Radio Ghosts, and, so far as I knew at that time, would never actually go further than just personal enjoyment.

Then we started realising that a few of the songs had . . . something. We were very friendly with other Glasgow indie bands, notably Apes in Control. Their drummer Graham was one of my and Christine's closest friends, so he was absolutely perfect for us and was happy to split his time between the Apes and ourselves.

So we started rehearsing as a three-piece, and soon started

thinking about playing and recording, as the songs began to develop and mature. The music we were making at that time, I can't stress this enough, was being created entirely in isolation, independent of our contemporaries, and any other 'twee' influences.

If you'd known us at that time, you'd know that this was just the way we were. It was never deliberately anything – it was what actually came out. I always felt that bands such as The Pastels, who we never listened to at all, had a deliberate strategy and actively tried to promote their identity. They acted the way they wanted to be perceived; we, however, were way too stoned, and simple-minded, to even consider that. Certainly I was!

Well, we pressed a thousand [copies of The Wee Cherubs single 'Dreaming']. I do hear that it's quite collectable and this makes me quite sad and bereft . . .

The Cherubs were never 'big', even locally. So a few years after Christine had left and the band split up, I still had boxes of the single left. It never sold much then, because we were much too disorganised and unprofessional to have done anything like arranging any distribution for it. We just recorded it because that seemed like a good idea at the time.

So one day, maybe five years after the Cherubs split, I was moving house and rather than keep lugging around the ten or so boxes that I still had (each with twenty-five copies of the 'Dreaming' single) and having to find space for them in my new flat, I took them out and dumped them in a skip.

No wonder I'm sad.

This was Apes in Control's label, Bogaten. They had released a single called 'Funtimes/Joined in the Dance' and 'Dreaming' was the second single. As I said, we were very friendly with them and we had captured their drummer, so they kindly invited us to release 'Dreaming' on their label. They were/are very good folks, extremely creative and kind – but not business people, really. Or at all, come to that. Bogaten – if I recall, the name came from a Bob Hope/Bing Crosby road movie, and was also a monster in a later trashy sci-fi film. Why they thought it was a good name for a record label, God knows. Remember what I said about the blow.

It (demo tape *Rainforest*) was recorded before the session where we did 'Dreaming', I think, and had four songs: 'Poor Little Lost Soul', 'Pastures New', 'Waiting' and (seriously) 'Theme from an Imaginary Channel Four Documentary' (an instrumental).

The name for the last one, as well as being a reference to Sergio Leone's 'Theme for an Imaginary Western', came about because C4 was just opening and they were actually holding a competition to get some background music for their various logos. So we put this 'song' together (it was really just a spacey improvisation) but, as I recall, and quite typically of us, we never quite got it together enough to actually ever enter the competition.

We were, as I said, pretty independent, to the extent of being slightly isolated. I was listening to a huge range of music and I did of course know about Postcard Records, and it was part of the soundtrack to that time for me; I'd have to acknowledge it would have been an influence, stylistically, that would be unavoidable.

But there was no blatant attempt to sound like Aztec Camera or Orange Juice or whoever, much as we liked them. We'd be subliminally absorbing them and it would have shaped some of the nuances of our sound; but then again, our sound was so varied that I don't know that you'd categorise it as being Postcard-like.

If you'd been to any gigs, and if you listen to the two demos and 'Dreaming', you can pick up a major range of styles and influences, from the Blue Orchids to the Zombies. I don't even think there was such a thing as a Cherubs sound: I have an old video of us playing a gig in Kelvingrove Park in Glasgow, and every single song is musically quite different. The only commonality is that the same three people are making the music.

Christine moved down to England to answer a long-held belief that she should make shoes for a living. That was the end of our relationship and, with it, the end of the band. We did meet up again a couple of years later when she played bass in The Bachelor Pad!

A huge thanks to Roque Ruiz at Cloudberry Records for use of the interviews with Tommy and Martin.

Rote Kapelle, Jesse Garon and The Fizzbombs hit line-up snags

As the Bellshill bands discovered, swapping band members was all well and good – until the commitments of success made it impossible. The success of Jesse Garon's pop-friendly sound eventually led to frustrations within Rote Kapelle, and The Fizzbombs' success similarly affected Jesse Garon.

Andrew Tully: There was a fabulous article that The Legend did when he wrote for the *NME*, where he came up to interview the Shop Assistants. And when he came up to do a big interview with the Desperadoes, Rote Kapelle and The Fizzbombs. And we've got like a three-page spread in the *NME*. And the running joke in it was that Margarita was in all three of the bands. And you know, and he was kind of posing the same questions as you are, in that, how, how can three bands work? What happens when you are in three bands? And I would say for eighteen months, two years, it works, you know, because we were unemployed, at college, we had time. We weren't that professional about it. So it wasn't like we were rehearsing loads, it wasn't like we were doing loads of gigs, because there weren't loads of gigs to do. So it wasn't, you know, I don't remember any kind of real clash.

Margarita Vazquez Ponte: One time that *NME* came up and did a big thing on Edinburgh, and I was in three of the bands that they did, and I was in all the pictures and I know that caused some rupture. Some of the bands didn't like that. I think we were all quite loyal to each other. Really. I think the people who came in when you kind of always knew they weren't gonna stay forever, but the core remained . . . the core remained the same.

Jonathan Muir: Both Andrew and Margarita had left their university courses around this time so devoted themselves to music full time. I didn't feel they neglected Rote Kapelle as they had the time for all the different projects. Later on, perhaps they did, but Jesse Garon were doing really well and I personally wouldn't begrudge them giving more time to that. I remember Andrew described Rote Kapelle as 'the father ship' in an interview.

I think Jesse Garon had some great songs and were a really good live band too – Margarita was great on the drums.

Andrew Tully: Rote Kapelle had been the father ship, so to speak, and then the wee stripling comes along and overtakes them, so as that went on, it would become a bit awkward.

Chris Henman: I think Rote Kapelle kind of started to go by the wayside because Andrew and Margarita were involved in Jesse Garon and the Desperadoes and they were more popular and I think we weren't so much a priority. I did find it, in the end, quite frustrating.

Andrew Tully: There was a benefit gig we did at Coasters in Edinburgh, where I think Rote Kapelle had been asked to play, and then the Desperadoes were asked. And I do remember, quite understandably, a couple of members were a bit like, 'Well, I don't think you should do it.' Because, you know, it's kind of like, not quite two bites of the cherry. But that will detract from Rote Kapelle, you playing as well, because people will just be like, 'Oh, well, they're in that band. And, you know, which is the proper band and which is the main band?' So I do remember there being a little kind of tension about that. But generally, I would say it worked fine. But I would say that. You would ask me to ask members of Rote Kapelle. And I would understand if they went 'Well, actually, it was a bloody nightmare. They stole our thunder and ran off with it' kind of thing. Or stole my thunder. It's difficult knowing who. Was. We. I am. Oh, I'm getting all philosophical here.

The success and later demise of the Shop Assistants had generated interest and opportunities for other Edinburgh guitar-based indie-pop acts, and Jesse Garon seemed to be the perfect contender.

Margarita Vazquez Ponte: We had been on a roll. We had had a lot of airplay. We'd done well, in the indie charts. We were getting good articles in the *NME* and *Sounds*. And there was a big buzz about us.

Andrew Tully: There was a bit of a buzz happening about us. But we were just like, yeah, that's . . . well, isn't that how it should be, nice, it's really nice. And it flattered your ego, but it didn't seem like that big a deal. And then we got invited to do our first headline gig in London, at Great Portland Street. And it was two of the people from Lush were putting it on and said, 'Oh, you want to come down and play?'

Margarita Vazquez Ponte: We had this kind of showcase gig in London.

Andrew Tully: We're like, oh, yeah, that sounds good. And it was just a one-off gig. And we drove down that day. And we got there about four o'clock. Having driven all the way, set off at, like, eight in the morning from Edinburgh.

Margarita Vazquez Ponte: Basically, Geoff Travis was coming to it. And that was the golden ticket as well. Rough Trade, that would have been nice. And the *NME* were coming to it and various people. So it was a big deal. And, of course, what happened to us?

Andrew Tully: As Scottish bands do, we went to Green Park and we got pissed. And we, you know, 'cause we were 21, 22 years old. It was just like, well, we're in London. Someone's paid for us to come down here. Let's go to the off-licence. Let's get some drinking. So I remember sitting in Green Park for a couple of hours just chilling out. And then we had to drive to the venue. And I remember we drove up to the venue. It was a huge queue snaking round outside and when we went to the soundcheck we hadn't been able to soundcheck initially because there was a drama group having rehearsal in the basement where the gig was, so I'm thinking it [the queue] must be something to do with a drama group perhaps, a performance going on upstairs or something. And then our roadie Charlie, bless him, said no, they're here to see you. At which point we all went, 'Oh, really.' And it turned out that I think the *NME* was on strike that week. So *Sounds* and *Melody Maker* were the only papers, music papers, that were available. And someone we knew was working on the gig guide for *Sounds*. And he'd said all the Desperadoes are playing. Let's put a big half-page picture in, saying Gig of the Week. So everyone had seen this, like, oh, Gig of the Week. And there was a bit of a buzz about this.

Andrew Tully: So we had the editor of *Melody Maker* and *NME* and *Sounds* there. Geoff Travis from Rough Trade was there. All these heads from record companies were there because they'd heard we'd supported the Shop Assistants. So by the time we went on stage, we were absolutely shitting ourselves because suddenly the place was packed. And suddenly we realise the enormity of it.

Margarita Vazquez Ponte: Anybody with sense would have rehearsed 24/7 and sorted it. I think we maybe had two or three practices. And it just didn't happen for us. And we played a really shambolic gig. We turned up at the gig and it was a bigger venue than normal. And there was a queue around the block. It was a big crowd come to see us, there was a lot of anticipation, and it just didn't happen. We played badly. It wasn't clicking with the audience.

Andrew Tully: And normally I used to make lots of jokes on stage and was quite chatty. And I was suddenly aware, people are expecting me to be quite chatty. Oh, oh, so I just started mumbling. And yeah, it was rubbish.

Fran Schoppler: Oh my God. That night. The showcase gig did go badly. We were really lacklustre when we should have sparkled. We had been playing live for a few years by then and had some great gigs under our belt.

Margarita Vazquez Ponte: It was a disaster. And then subsequently, we had a meeting with Geoff Travis from Rough Trade the next day.

Andrew Tully: It was like getting called to the head teacher's office. Because we didn't have a manager or anything like that. But we'd heard he might be interested. So we trooped in, and certainly, half of us were huge Smiths fans. So, this is like being summoned to see the Pope or something like that. So we're like, but we trooped in in our shabby, charity chic that we'd slept in, all hungover. And he gave us a real talking to. And you know, my recollection of it is he was aware that we were Smith fans. And when he found out that we'd been drinking he said, 'You do know that Morrissey on the day of a gig doesn't speak at all to save his voice.' And I'm like, really? And, and he said, to Fran, I really liked your voice. I like a couple of tunes, but you need to do a lot more. So he sent us away with homework. And he said, I want you to go away. And I want you to write twenty songs. And then pick the five best, and then come back to me with those five best songs. And then we'll talk, and we're all like, oh, yes, Mr Travis, absolutely, Mr Travis. And then we kind of walked out. And we just went fuck, because by that point, the Desperadoes have been going, perhaps eighteen months. And we'd written fourteen songs. And I'm thinking, twenty songs, that's going to take us two years.

Margarita Vazquez Ponte: It was a disaster for us. We were then dismissed by the music press. And I don't think we ever really recovered. We carried on but we never really recovered or gained the momentum that we had had. Had we played at our best, maybe, it would have been different. I think.

CHAPTER 10
1988-89

The landscape is changing

Sarah Records and The Orchids

Bristol's iconic Sarah Records, run by Clare Wadd and Matt Haynes, was hugely influenced by Postcard and in many ways was a perfect home for jangling Scottish guitar-based bands. Glasgow's The Orchids were one of those great fits.

John Scally (Guitar, The Orchids): The band started when Chris, James and myself were in our later years of high school. We had the idea and started to discover our musical influences. Once equipped with our first musical instruments, we started to rehearse in my house.

Chris Quinn (Drums, The Orchids): We didn't appear to fit in with the other scenes.

John Scally: We didn't fit in anywhere. Still don't!

James Hackett (Vocals, The Orchids): There were a few songs written in our time that we practised in our local community centre, and without having any sense of perfection or craft, we thought it would be good to demo some and get ourselves some gigs. We did, I think, four songs in a three-hour session in a reasonable cheap recording studio. We handed them out to a few places including a club night called Texas Fever, and Karen McDougall was one of the folk involved and she was suitably impressed enough to send it to her fanzine-writing friends and Clare Wadd got back in touch about putting a song on a flexi disc for one of her fanzines. Of course we were overjoyed. We had only been writing songs a short while and already it was getting noticed.

The flexi (From This Day) *appeared in 1987 on the Sha La La imprint, the precursor to Sarah Records.*

James Hackett: The flexi was a success and when Clare and Matt got together and asked us for a single, again, we were so chuffed. We had written a few more songs buoyed by the success of our last demo, we had recorded a few more. Again, very cheaply. We sent them the songs and they asked if it could be their second 7-inch release. We jumped at the chance, they seemed to be good people. We were pretty ignorant of the fanzine culture, we had no preconceptions, they just seemed really enthusiastic and wanted us to make a record.

Chris Quinn: We never thought that handing our demo into them to secure a support slot at one of their gigs would lead to us releasing records with Sarah Records but it did . . . It was incredibly exciting to be offered the chance to record for a brand new label and we didn't care where it was based.

John Scally: Matt and Claire are lovers of music. They are also two great people who are still supportive to this day.

Chris Quinn: We liked the way they operated. We loved what they stood for, as we'd grown up despising the way the industry operated so it was really refreshing to be involved with people who were doing this just for the enthusiasm and love. We were very fortunate. We did hand a demo tape to Alan McGee after a Biff Bang Pow! gig in Glasgow in 1987 but he never contacted us . . . but we never really expected him to! We were still called Gentle Tuesday at that time and Primal Scream had been signed to Warner's by then so we definitely thought the song would never see the light of day. McGee's comment when I handed him the tape and he saw the band's name was 'Gentle Tuesday? That's The Scream's next single.' It was at that point we decided to drop that as the band name and come up with a new one. I guess that says something about where we 'fitted in'?

James Hackett: Of course, it would have been great to have a budget to record them better, but we didn't want to ruin any chance we had of making a record. You couldn't fault them [Matt and Claire] for their effort and enthusiasm, they did a brilliant job. All their hard work, living on a tight budget and sacrificing their own quality of life to get records out, was beyond most folk. There was a certain amount of love and nurturing between ourselves and Sarah that saw us all thrive. I suppose being with a label that wasn't local, and maybe because it was a bit late to the scene, may have set us apart, but it was down mainly to our own lack of making connections, but we were still in awe of our peers and really socially awkward. That's probably the biggest reason for being apart from the local scene; it didn't seem that friendly and we had a certain amount of mistrust that became a chip on our shoulders.

John Scally: Personally don't remember much other that it was in a studio in Paisley. The recording engineer was recording St Mirren's Cup Final song the same week; we were drunk as usual. Was great to see our song released as a single, big achievement for us, dream come true.

The band's first single, 'I've Got a Habit' would be Sarah Records' second release.

Chris Quinn: We definitely never saw ourselves as part of the Scottish independent scene at the time. We always knew we were a wee bit different and that was always going to be the case from the very beginning. Our mainstream influences and our contrary attitudes to everything probably contributed. I recall after our first ever London concert in February 1988, we travelled back up to Glasgow on a train and The Soup Dragons were in the same carriage travelling back up too. We were whispering to each other, 'Fuck's sake, there's The Soup Dragons, can you believe that?' but then we got really drunk and boisterous and loud. We never did speak to them for the whole journey. It seems a bit strange and nowadays if I saw any of them I'd go up and speak to them but back then they were in another world from us and we knew it. We were far too shy to go and have a discussion with them. Back to that 'not fitting in' thing again!

The Soup Dragons sign to Sire

The Soup Dragons' upwards trajectory was continuing with incredible momentum. The next step was inevitably to sign with a major label.

Jim McCulloch: We had 'Majestic Head' and 'Soft as Your Face', they were still under the aegis of Raw TV.

Sean Dickson: I always remember 'Soft as Your Face' because that was the first record that Radio 1 daytime actually took notice of and we got this message saying, 'Oh, it might be up for the playlist,' which like, in those days, was kind of the holy grail. You know, it was like, 'Oh my God, we might get on the playlist and get played during the day.' And there used to be a programme on Radio 1 called *Round Table* . . . it used to be every Friday night and it was like they put . . . they'd be like somebody out of a band or some famous person and they'd play a few records and people would talk about what they thought of the record. And our record was, we were all told our record was going to be on *Round Table*, which was usually a lead-up to if it got good reviews you'd end up on the playlist the next week. And there was this idiot that said it sounded like 'Springtime for Hitler' from the Mel Brooks movie and I was just sat there going like 'What the fuck,' and it was like the guy went 'Yeah, yeah, yeah, that just sounds exactly like "Springtime for Hitler",' and we were like . . . and because that was put in (the minds of) these people that run the playlist's heads, we never got on the playlist.

The lack of a mainstream hit record did not deter major label interest and the group were still darlings of the NME. *The band signed to Sire Records, which had a track record of being able to successfully bring leftfield music to the mainstream, keeping integrity while making money. The band's first album,* This Is Our Art, *came out in 1988.*

Sean Dickson: It was like decided because, you know, it was like about three, four years into the band and we had to start making money to live, you couldn't just keep signing on the dole all the time so we signed to Sire Records, which was, you know, the Ramones were on Sire, The Undertones were on Sire, Madonna was on Sire, so it was like, 'Yep, that'll do for us.' And Seymour [Stein], the guy that ran Sire, was a sweet guy, we met him and he seemed very into us.

Sean Dickson: That LP was a bit random because in those days, I never really had any intention of making albums. It wasn't something that was an interest to me. Seven-inch singles was what I was interested in. I just wanted to make 7-inch singles for the rest of my life when I was about 20, you know. By that time actually I was about 19, so I was still like 'Oh, my next 7-inch, oh my next 7-inch,' and it was like . . . then suddenly you are making an album.

Jim McCulloch: It basically involved two different producers. The first that was involved with a guy called Pete Brown, he's the son of Joe Brown, the Cockney geezer kind of musician guy. But he [Pete] was a young guy, same age as us, and was thrown in with us. And I think it got too much . . . he was getting a lot of pressure from us . . . pressure from the management company, and with a half-finished album – he kept doing mixes and management were not happy, and we weren't happy. And then he just couldn't satisfy both sides. So he just threw his hands up. And that was him one day, and then some other producer came in as well. And we've eventually got something that was a happy house. The music was changing so quickly. They were using so many different things, you know, listening to so many different types of music. It's just this big mishmash of sounds, you know, but just that's the way it was with The Soup Dragons.

Sean Dickson: I think the reason that *This Is Our Art* is so all over the place is because it was recorded in sections all very far away from each other. 'Cause they were all just recorded as tracks. 'Cause we used to just go in the studio and record whatever we were rehearsing at that time or whatever songs we came up with.

Jim McCulloch: 'Kingdom Chairs' [the single] was the first official Sire release, which meant it was going to go in the official Top 40 charts, it wouldn't go into the indie charts because it was straight. So that's when the first big dip happened in our trajectory, or whatever. And that's when alarm bells started ringing maybe. It was when the record company were saying that we didn't get a hit, you know, so that's when they started to slowly pull the plug on it, you know. So that was our first major crisis, basically.

Sean Dickson: And by the time it ['Kingdom Chairs'] came out that was when Ross our drummer made the decision that . . . he had the chance [to go back to art school] 'cause he'd left Glasgow Art School, to do the band full time, that's where I met him.

The album was not a success and only reached number sixty in the UK charts. Sire dropped the band soon after.

Jim McCulloch: By that point, we had no kind of problems with press or, or just any, no crisis of confidence or anything because we were, we knew what we were doing. We knew how to do it and we were just really happy with the way it was going. But then it's like, oh, this is going to be the end of The Soup Dragons here, you know, and in kind of a way it was the end of that Soup Dragons because that was a time that there was a big hiatus and we didn't have a record company and we had no money and so Ross decided to leave the band and go back to art school to finish his degree.

Sushil Dade: Being signed and being dropped by labels is part of the pop equation and not unique to our experience. We were thrilled to be on Sire . . . home to the Ramones, Undertones, Madonna, so we were in fine company while it lasted. I remember signing the contracts and our meeting with Seymour Stein . . . crazy times. I really respected the decision Ross made to focus on his art studies and at the time making music was all the rest of us really knew so we stuck at it. Things happened. There were bright times, there were dark times. There was always light at the end of the tunnel.

Jim McCulloch: And we were left kind of scrambling about. What are we going to do? Do we want to continue or not? And so that kind of left us in a strange place for the first time ever really.

The Vaselines' second EP

The Vaselines had been quiet for a while but they were eager to get back into the studio to record more. Their line-up was supplemented this time by Eugene's brother Charlie Kelly and bass player James Seenan. Their first release, the Son of a Gun *EP, had been a big critical hit. The second, the* Dying for It *EP, while still delighting the weekly press, was to have a huge impact further afield, when it reached the ears of K-Records' Calvin Johnson and Nirvana's Kurt Cobain.*

Dying for It *contained the tracks 'Dying for It', 'Molly's Lips', 'Teenage Superstars' and 'Jesus Don't Want Me for a Sunbeam'. Having covered a track from The Vaseline's first EP, amazingly, Nirvana later covered two from this second one – 'Molly's Lips' as a Sub Pop singles club release and 'Jesus Don't Want Me for a Sunbeam' on the seminal MTV* Unplugged *album.*

Eugene Kelly: We felt lucky to have released one single and a second one wasn't guaranteed but a year later Stephen told us we could make another one. We didn't see a year between singles as unusual as we didn't know any better. We went to Pier House studio in Edinburgh with our bass player and drummer to record as a four-piece for the first time. The studio owner treated us like children. I think he was jetlagged or just a knob. He gave up on us and handed the engineering over to Ian Beveridge, who was great and we got on well with. He went on to become the monitor engineer for Nirvana and my band Eugenius.

Stephen asked David from Shop Assistants to add guitar to 'Dying for It' and his contribution transformed an okay song into something that sounded like a real band.

Charles Kelly: Eugene and Frances decided they wanted a more raw sound for their live performances instead of the drum machine they had used initially so he asked me and I in turn asked James to join. I looked forward to it and figured I could make a basic racket influenced by Moe Tucker and in turn Bobby Gillespie.

Frances McKee: It was just whatever felt quite natural. 'Molly's Lips' is a high-pitched song, it felt more comfortable for me to sing it. That's really all it was. I don't know if it was my emerging kind of feminism and all that. Certainly not . . . you know, the girl that does backing vocals in the band.

Charles Kelly: The only memories I have is the two musicians who played on the recordings. Sophie Pragnell, who played the viola on Jesus, I think Frances knew her possibly, she was a sweet kid, and David Keegan from the Shop Assistants playing a bit of mad guitar on one song. Stephen Pastel was there to give advice and encouragement during the recording. I think we made the recordings fairly swiftly, maybe in two days I guess. I remember Eugene borrowing a massive USA flag prop from Peter from Secession for the cover and I think it was my old girlfriend's polka-dot shirt which I borrowed and an old Teddy Boy leopard skin waistcoat my older brother Bernie brought back from London that Eugene sported in the photos.

Eugene Kelly: Oh the horn! Now we have to play every night. And it was Stephen's idea. And the thing about that was it wasn't even a proper horn because the horn has two noises – an in and out. So we had to sample it and play the first sound twice. So we were there. We were visionaries. We were using technology before, you know, before sampling, before The KLF and before anybody. Great.

The Hardy Boys

One of the rarest indie-pop singles to emerge from Scotland was 1989's 'Wonderful Lie' by Greenock's The Hardy Boys. In those rare times it comes up for sale it can command close to £500. This is the story of that one-off release, as told by its singer and songwriter, David Douglas McArthur.

David Douglas McArthur (Vocals, guitar, Safe Houses; Bass, The Hardy Boys): Ian McLachlan, Hardy Boys drummer, and I had played together in a hardcore punk band called Distemper. The band formed in 1982 at the peak of the 'new punk' revolution. I vividly remember sitting in my O-level English class writing the lyrics for the four songs that would become our first demo tape (recorded at Pattern Sounds in Greenock in early 1984).

I was heavily influenced by the anarchist punk scene and along with (Sheer) Thomas Taft, my best friend from school and later Creation Records recording artist, we would travel up and down to Liverpool's Aigburth Anarchist Centre to watch bands such as Crass, Flux of Pink Indians, Chumbawamba and Bjork's KUKL. Distemper appeared on numerous compilation tapes, released a split single with Oi Polloi and were interviewed by hundreds of fanzines. We were even interviewed by the bible of hardcore punk music, *Maximum Rocknroll*.

However, around the middle of 1985 I began to be drawn more to indie-pop and the likes of The Pastels and The Wedding Present, although I couldn't get on with the 'cutesy' aspect of the genre. Later, when we were on Bubblegum Records, I found some of the behaviour really contrived and frankly annoying. In 1985 I was also becoming a Velvet Underground obsessive. Distemper were very much still in existence but we had sacked the guitarist, recruited a singer and I moved to guitar and we developed a more indie-pop sound. After one more rejected demo we sacked the bass player and recruited Derek Mullen on bass and Johnny Hanson on keyboards. And changed our name to Safe Houses.

I had known Alan Bannister from The Hardy Boys for a few years as he was part of the Greenock punk scene. Safe Houses, now with a much more poppy sound, were starting to play gigs around the country with The Hardy Boys. It was clear that Alan and John White were unhappy with their rhythm section and I was unhappy with Safe Houses' keyboard player. Alan, John and I met in Gourock one Sunday morning to discuss merging the two bands. John and I were really keen on a six-piece band with John on vocals and guitar, Alan and I on guitars and backing vocals, Michael Bonini on keyboards, Derek on bass and Ian on drums. Alan, however, wasn't keen on having two lead guitarists so we compromised on John and I playing in both groups. Safe Houses became me on vocals and guitars, John on guitars and vocals, Johnny on keyboards, Derek on bass and Ian on drums. Safe Houses went on to record two extremely good demo tapes, the first of which brought us to the attention of Eleanor from *Baby Bites Back* fanzine, who released 'If I Should Die' as a flexi disc.

Safe Houses were tight as fuck. We married a harder indie-pop sound with overtly political lyrics. At the peak of the band's powers we supported the James Taylor Quartet at Rico's in Greenock. We were incredible!!! A tight eight-song set finished with the instrumental 'Simon Templer'. We walked off stage and back to the dressing room to bask in the glory. The James Taylor Quartet had just been in the charts with 'Theme from Starsky and Hutch'. James had a nine-piece band including Steve White on drums. They walked on and wiped the floor with us in around thirty seconds!!! A harsh lesson. Afterwards James was really encouraging, telling me to keep at it and how good we'd been on the night. I knew at this point that the band was about to implode so Safe Houses split and I joined The Hardy Boys full time.

Safe Houses were rawer than The Hardy Boys and I felt 'Wonderful Lie' was too poppy for the band. John's voice suited the song better than mine. I was also savvy enough to see that two people playing in two different bands was a ticking time-bomb on a relationship level. Generally bands start off as a bunch of mates who you would do anything for and end up loathing the sight of one another!! Safe Houses were imploding for other reasons too and the clever move was to split the band up and focus on The Hardy Boys. I spent a year playing bass in The Hardy Boys and I'm absolutely not a bass player. I play bass on 'Wonderful Lie'. In November 1989 Alan had decided that he'd had enough, two weeks before we were due to play some English gigs. I moved to guitar and Derek joined on bass. Derek is a fabulous musician and we spent every night rehearsing in various flats before playing the gigs, which were great.

I wrote 'Wonderful Lie' in the same way as I wrote all my songs at the time: on an Aria acoustic guitar that I bought from Ad Lib Music in Greenock. I would sit in my living room with a pad of paper and would write the lyrics at the same time as the music: words with chords above them. Very primitive! I was 21 at the time and songs just fall out of you at that age. I had everything written but needed an introduction and a bridge, so I 'borrowed' the chords from 'Stay Free' by The Clash! I have never disclosed that to anyone before. None of the band picked up on it either.

We then reverted to the trusted method of sending tapes to loads of independent record labels with absolutely no success. One night Michael (he was the only one of us with a phone!!) got a call from Neville Street from Stella Five Records: 'I love the tracks man!!!! I want to put out a 12-inch single.' Stella Five pressed five hundred copies so if you have one, hang onto it! Radio Clyde and Radio Scotland gave the single airtime, as did regional radio in England. Neville was and still is one of the nicest people on earth. Stella Five had already released the brilliant *Headhunting in Toytown* album by The Geekais. Neville quickly became the band's manager and remained with us even when we reformed in 2010. In 2022, I travelled to Shrewsbury and played five Hardy Boys songs with a 'house band' to celebrate thirty years since Stella Five released their final record. Nev's quirky English positivity was the perfect balance to our dour west of Scotland misery.

Neville Street (Stella Five Records): The band had approached me about playing a gig in Shrewsbury and sent through a demo tape called 'Montgomery Cliff'. I thought it was great, so booked them to play. They were tight musically and their set was brimming with indie guitar classics (and I don't say that lightly). They stayed over at my house – the first of many occasions – and we talked music into the early hours. I mentioned my label Stella Five and that I'd got a distribution deal with Probe Plus in Liverpool, which was part of the Cartel. One thing led to another, the band signed to Stella Five and before we knew it 'Wonderful Lie' was recorded, ready to be pressed and released. The launch gig in Shrewsbury was in support of a band called The Fat Lady Sings. The Hardy Boys seemingly popped up all over the place, also supporting a Liverpool band called River City People. Talk about chalk and cheese! River City People were all ponytails and Simple Minds *Waterfront*-esque bass lines. While it didn't sell by the bucket loads, 'Wonderful Lie' was well received and has since become an indie classic, selling for three figures on eBay Japan.

The Hardy Boys would later reconfigure as Flame Up!

David Douglas McArthur: Flame Up! was a total blast!! Flame Up! consisted of the same members as The Hardy Boys but without Kate. We released one double A-side 7-inch single, 'Mr God'/'Need I Say More', on our own Viva! Genius label in 1991. We were arrogant enough to give the record the catalogue number TALENT1. The songs sounded like The Charlatans being beaten up by Fugazi while The Fall held the coats.

We recorded a second single called 'Sinister Minister' but

deteriorating relationships within the band and our general lack of finance meant that it was never released. 'Sinister Minister' did however provide me with one of the funniest moments in my musical life. At Christmas 1992, I was invited onto the local Christian radio station in Greenock to play my five favourite Christmas songs and to talk about 'Sinister Minister'. The song was about the recent sex abuse allegations in the church and I was told by the presenter that I could not mention the name of the song or what the song was about, it had to be called 'currently untitled'. When recording the song we decided there should be a free for all in the middle eight, where we would shout the first things that came into our heads. The five of us were gathered around the microphone in the Trashcan Sinatras Shabby Road studios shouting anything and everything and one of us 'played' a trumpet. It was mayhem but the one that does cut through is Ian clearly shouting 'Fucking bastards!!!! FUCKING BASTARDS!!!!!! FUUUUCCCCKKKKKIIING BAAAASTARDSSSSS!!!!!!' The DJ loved the track so much he played it twice.

When I visited Michael in Canada in 2016 we talked extensively about what we had musically and agreed Flame Up! was the most creative period we ever had as a band. Freed from the limitations of indie-pop, Flame Up! was great musically: we were hugely influenced by bands such as No Means No and The Jesus Lizard and The Fall and by Glasgow bands like Dawson and Badgewearer, but we were fraught with tension, as The Hardy Boys were previously.

CHAPTER 11
1990-91

Endings and new beginnings

Sarah Records had unfairly come in for criticism for embellishing many of the so-called 'twee' elements associated with the scene. A huge media backlash and excessive negativity had severely damaged the credibility of the once vibrant and innovative scene. Heavier sounds from America were on their way via bands such as Dinosaur, Sonic Youth and Hüsker Dü. More obviously, another underground movement to rival punk was reaching mainstream culture and its shockwaves would soon be felt by the independent guitar scene. While New Order had helped pioneer a hybrid of electronic and guitar music, other bands from Manchester were taking things even further. The Happy Mondays' 'Wrote for Luck' in 1988 was a near year zero moment for the crossover of guitar and dance music and its energy and beats were soon to find their way to Scotland. In the meantime, both Rote Kapelle and offshoot Jesse Garon and the Desperadoes would have a last attempt at indie guitar success by recording their albums. Rote Kapelle's *No North Briton* and Jesse Garon's *Nixon* were both released in 1990.

ENDINGS AND NEW BEGINNINGS

The end of the line for Rote Kapelle and Jesse Garon

Jonathan Muir: The musical world was shifting on its axis around then, due to the rise of Madchester and dance music, but I couldn't believe Andrew and the others didn't feel they had more to say. TBH I kind of shudder now when I hear 'Bring Down the Grand' [Jesse Garon's 'Grand Hotel'] as it seems to endorse the IRA (I've lived in Belfast for the last twenty-five years), even though Andrew denies it does this. I always wonder what they would have gone on to do. They were never going to follow Primal Scream into mainstream success but they would have done music with a kind of wry heart and soul. The mix of singers and instruments and the sensibility in the music could almost place them as precursors of Belle and Sebastian.

Ian Binns: Johnny had left by then and at some point after it was recorded and its release I decided I'd had enough, partly as I thought we'd run out of steam and partly due to some stressful relationships within the band. Judging from the fact that the band folded shortly after I'd announced my departure, I guess the others also felt we'd run our course.

Chris Henman: We were going for the whole of the eighties. In-Tape asked us to put out an album – we finally got to do a full album – but by the time we'd finished it the band had pretty much imploded. Everyone else was too busy with other bands, I think the interest had gone. I mean, the album [*No North Briton*] got released in 1990. But the band had already split.

Fran Schoppler: *Nixon* was recorded late in December 1989 and mixed over a few days in January 1990. The recording of it was a bit of a nightmare. The guys were writing guitar lines and embryo songs in the recording studio and delivering cassette tapes to me to listen to, of songs that they wanted me to write lyrics and vocal lines for. I had come down with the flu and missed the majority of the studio time. Getting a respiratory illness is a singer's worst nightmare! I recorded my vocals in early January 1990 when we were in the studio for mixing the tracks. We were under pressure. I don't think we were properly ready for the studio. There are only a few songs on *Nixon* that I like. It still pains me.

Angus McPake: *Nixon* really was our first LP although we had already issued *A Cabinet of Curiosities*. I think we regarded *Cabinet* as our first LP at the time, as all the previously released tunes on it had been re-recorded for its release and there were a few new ones to boot. It seems now that most people regard it as a compilation so I'm not unhappy to call *Nixon* our only real LP. We had got involved in Kevin Buckle's Avalanche organisation, I think mainly because Andrew and Margarita were working in his shop at the time, and he had a good relationship with the Cartel distribution network. So, Kevin funded the recording sessions, which took place at Chamber Studios, back when it was on Westfield Road. Jamie Watson was engineering and nominally producing. I'm not sure how many days we were booked in for but it seemed like a long time, certainly longer than we'd ever been in a studio before. With the exception of maybe three songs ('Grand Hotel', 'Hold Me Now' and possibly 'Stand Up'), we had nothing ready so there was a frenzy of activity trying to get some new material ready in time. I was sharing a flat with Margarita at the time and can vividly remember writing 'Goodbye Misery' in her bedroom. Apart from that it's a bit hazy as to where the other songs came from. 'Eight-Lane Freeway' was musically all mine but my lyrics were rejected. As I remember my lyrics were a bit of a gloomy insight into the band's recent failings and were seen as being too negative. They were probably terrible too, although thinking about it they could now be highly poignant in hindsight! Andrew's replacement lyrics were a bit too Bruce Springsteen for my liking but then he was the literary genius of the band so what did I know?

The recording was split into two sessions and I think at the end of the first one we were quite pleased with what we'd done. I remember I had recently bought my first Hammond organ, insisted on sprinkling it liberally all over any track they'd let me, and congratulated myself on how good it was all sounding. By the time of the second session, maybe about a month later, we had quite simply run out of material. I suggested we do Lulu's 'Love Loves to Love Love' to fill the gap and I think the rest of the songs were written on the spot in the studio – very Rolling Stones! 'Eden' was a guitar riff I'd come up with and Fran had some words that fitted. I remember the acoustic twelve-string I played on it had quite a high action and being in agony trying to get to the end of the song. Our revolving door of guitarists was probably rotating at its fastest at this point and it's difficult to remember quite who's playing on what. I do know that along with bass and keyboards I played a fair amount of guitar on the sessions, along with Andrew, Michael Kerr and Dave Evans. Guesting on congas was Jeremy Black, who would later play guitar live with us too.

When it came to the mixes we were very argumentative as a group. I've always said democracy in music very seldom works and we should really have let Jamie and perhaps one other member do the mixes but unfortunately it was not to be and it all became a total mess, sounding very flat and dull to me now. A sleeve and a title were required and that also led to a bunch of arguments – I think the title and packaging are still a bone of contention to some members today. The critics were very kind to us on its release but it did sink without a trace, most probably as we didn't promote it very well. We also rarely played any songs from it. After the many setbacks endured throughout our existence I think the finished album was possibly our last disappointment. *Nixon* was the writing on the wall and we split up within a year of its release.

Fran Schoppler: We still were gigging, doing small tours and getting some decent gigs in 1990 with bands like The Pale Saints, Trashcan Sinatras. We were pretty busy. It was in 1991 that the band folded. I think there were too many band changes and we struggled to keep a stable line-up. We weren't writing enough songs either. Gig attendance on tour was not as good as it used to be. Other members of the band had other things they wanted to do. Priorities changed. I think we fizzled out. We had a lot of fun. It wasn't fun all the time, obviously, but we did have a good laugh being in the band. Andrew was so funny on stage, he always had us in stitches, in between songs. He's a natural show off. The audiences loved that too. We encouraged a bit of audience participation. There are many photos of us all laughing at Andrew's jokes and silly banter on stage. Playing live in general was great; it's the time in between – travelling, the time between soundcheck and actual gig performance – that were the hard parts.

The first recordings in Alaska Studios in London were a thrill.

The Janice Long session at Maida Vale was a very special moment, as was hearing it being broadcast on the radio. We recorded the session in between gig dates on a small English tour.

Every record release was a big moment.

I feel proud of what the band achieved, even if we never secured a major label record deal. In a way, I'm not sure why we all chased that. Perhaps it was the expected route for an indie band and we saw other bands around us do that. There would be perks like support slots for bigger bands, possibly a name producer and more studio time. But we would have lost our creative freedom. I think we were ambitious and we pushed ourselves forward, out of sheer determination and a love of the music we were making.

Chris Henman (Rote Kapelle): Dance music came along. The music scene had changed. It had run its course: the sort of shambling twee guitar thing, I don't think is meant to be like a long-term thing. All these bands who'd started as teenagers in the early eighties had just run their course and burned out. it was time for something new

Finitribe

The glory years of scratchy indie-pop spanned 1985–88 but there were soon to be huge changes in the music landscape. Edinburgh outsiders, Finitribe, started years earlier as a spikey, post-punk band similar to The Visitors but very quickly advanced their sound

way beyond guitar music. In many ways they were one of the most pioneering of all Scottish independent bands and had a part in the development of what became known as acid house. They released their debut EP, Curling and Stretching, *in summer 1984, on their own Finiflex label. Of all the bands in this book, they had perhaps the most unexpected career trajectory, helping to shape the UK's contribution to early acid house and – certainly – helping to shape the huge commercial impact of US industrial music when one member later joined Ministry. Their in-house production team also hugely contributed to the development of the late-1980s indie/dance crossover by helping The Shamen add further electronic dance elements to their sound. This is how they did it.*

Chris Connelly (Vocals, Finitribe, The Revolting Cocks and Ministry): Well, in 1984, the really exciting music of Edinburgh that we grew up with had grown to a kind of halt. And at that point, in 1984, my listening changed at that time, there were bands like Test Department. Einstürzende Neubauten, Danielle Dax, that was a big one for us, and Foetus, bands like that. Some bizarre bands were really capturing my imagination. I kind of felt let down by Edinburgh. In fact, we all felt let down by Edinburgh at that time, I think because the vibrancy of the early eighties had turned into people crawling to be signed to major labels, which is fine, but they were really blanding out their sound. And that's not necessarily a bad thing. But it wasn't what excited us at the time, you know. Fire Engines became Win, who I loved but it was all about the biggest deal you could get and, you know, people like Jesse Ray were signing to Polygram for hundreds of thousands of pounds and we're all on the dole, collecting, like, rent supplements and all living together and we're so fucking poor. So 1984 was a bit of a pivotal year, it's like, it was a split in the road where people who really wanted to make it as, you know, blue-eyed soul, for example, bands like Wet Wet Wet. That was the norm – Texas and stuff like that. And we were like, 'TRAITORS!'

John Vick (Finitribe): When the band formed, we were at school. We didn't all know each other particularly well. But we were maybe all the ones who were a bit more interested in music, maybe a bit more interested in listening to John Peel, for instance. And also, maybe not into the commercial side of things. We got together and met each other a little bit, and we got on well. Andy and Chris knew each other well, they were family friends. I was like an outsider. Phil was an outsider. Davie was a couple of years older. And Simon was my sister's boyfriend, but he was a drummer. We asked Simon if he'd come and drum and we just did this kind of music which was more experimental, I suppose. Maybe, I'm gonna say, Captain Beefheart, sometimes. I know it might not have sounded like that but that's how we would get on with it.

Davie Miller (Finitribe): I don't think there was any local influence. We got to know The Visitors very early on. And they were the same. They were kind of very separate from the old Josef K, Fire Engines thing. They weren't part of that either. And we just naturally gravitated towards them. And maybe it's because we met them first. Who knows what we would have done if we'd met The Fire Engines first. But we met John and Derek and Colin and Alan and that was that. And they were going to release our first record. The Visitors were going to release a Finitribe record. We were going to be the next record on their release schedule, but it never happened. I think that was the influence, other than the external stuff. There was nobody else like it. I guess we gravitated towards The Visitors because they weren't . . . They stood out and they stuck out and they were vocal, noisy, and everything. We didn't have Beach Boys albums in our record collections. We had lots of industrial records in our collections and that's where we started.

John Vick: We would zone in and do stuff with repeating things and make these pieces which were not particularly . . . we had no idea what we were doing structure-wise, but they had structure. In the end we decided we'd try and make a record. That was called 'Curling and Stretching'. And we didn't have distribution with Sandy for that, because we didn't really know him at the time. Davie didn't have the job at Fast at the time. There was the Cartel, which had a set of people – I can't quite remember what they were called. Sorry about that. They were in Leamington Spa. They were part of the Cartel. We phoned around and they said, yes, they'd be interested in distributing. So I went down and met them. And they said, yeah, we want to do this.

Davie Miller: Fast was something in the distance. We didn't know them, we didn't really know anything about that side of things. But they were obviously part of the Cartel. 'Stretching' was our first record. I guess we decided that, okay, we've got, we're making music. How do we get this out to people? Let's make a record because that was what people did. So John from The Visitors produced the record. WI did it at Pier House studios in Granton, which I believe is still there. Again, it was just kind of, we just thought, well, let's make a record . . . we sent it to a few people. And I think John Peel picked up on it. And from that, we got a John Peel session, and things grew from there. That line-up stayed together for two or three years until we were doing tours.

Chris Connelly: We got it in its component parts: we got their records from one place, and we got the sleeves from another place. I remember it was the middle of summer. And I was living with John and everybody else was away on holiday. So we sat in his bedroom and just collated the record ourselves, which I'm so happy we did that, because I'll find it in record shops still. And I was, 'I touched that forty years ago. My spirit is in there. We sat down and put it together.' But it was interesting because I was so naive, I just thought a record was going to change everything, but really it didn't. You know, it was a good learning process.

John Vick: I was working, so I'd pretty much paid to get the thing going. Andy was a graphic designer, he was at art college. So he did the sleeves; he learned how to do sleeves. I learned how to do the mastering and all of that stuff. And we released this record, but very quickly after that, Davie got his job with Fast and of course the next thing would come through Fast and that would be [the label] Cathexis.

There was quite a few gigs between that record and 'De Testimony', and I'm going to say we got darker and more industrial and more electronic. We still had electronic parts within 'Curling and Stretching', it just wasn't as advanced because we didn't have the money, we didn't have the instruments.

Chris Connelly: Before 'De Testimony', it was very much guitar, bass, drums, keyboards and vocals, and it was a very traditional set-up for a band, but we were absolutely hell bent on not playing them traditionally. But we still like melody. And, you know, we were really, really blessed with having Simon McGlynn our drummer, who was just so versatile and able to do things with time signatures that were well away from the four-four, standard rock time signature, and we would write things in strange time signatures, which made me do lyrics in strange time signatures, and that we weren't verging off into the nasty prog rock territory. That was the arch enemy, of course, and we were really into the band Wire. And I still am, of course. And we were aware that they, at the beginning, were perceived as a four-piece punk band, but they leapt away from that so quickly and kept the same line-up and the same instrumentation.

Davie Miller: It was just our way of exploring different elements of music and theatre. And we were all interested in music and theatre and film. So it was more of a kind of a broader thing for us. It wasn't just about being in a band, being in a band had become quite boring, with drum kit, bass guitar, vocals, it just seemed dull. We quite quickly brought in other elements. We would use tape echoes and we weren't into melodic pop music. Although we would then go on to listen, I mean, I think 'De Testimony' is actually . . . some of the rhythms are based on a Madonna song. But we liked to mix things up: we would record things and then we would cut up the tape and then edit the tape and kind of make tape loops . . . we found ourselves kind of running with those ideas and making something that wasn't the norm. I don't even know if we even thought about it that much. It was just what came out in our rehearsal studio. We probably got too stoned too much. We were all quite different but we all liked very similar music and we're interested in The Velvet Underground, which, you know, Glasgow bands were as well, but there was a cross between Velvet Underground and Throbbing Gristle.

John Vick: A company called Ensoniq made this thing called the Mirage Sampler. I had just enough to get this Mirage Sampler with a special filter, which meant that if I was recording sound it was much higher quality. That's what I wanted, for it to be high quality. A friend of ours, Malcolm, said, 'I've got these tapes, I don't know what's on them but do you want to see?' I had these reel to reels for doing four-track demos, even music, because it was a good four-track. I played it back and it was church bells; I thought great, I'm going to sample these onto the Mirage. And it became such a great instrument. We then wrote a song, I put it all together with the band as well playing these church bells, and of course it was 'De Testimony'. I was with Chris Connelly, we'd sit there and play da da ding ding ding and we just put it together, so I was with him when we did that. Then we said, hey listen, we've got this stuff going on, what's everyone else going to play, and we got it together. We got a nice percussion going and we made sure it was good, we went into the studio and recorded there. And, yeah, it worked.

Chris Connelly: I remember clearly the night that we came up with the church bells because it was me, I think it was me, and John and Philip for sure. And probably Davie, in Philip's flat on Leith Street, and his roommate had given him a reel-to-reel recording, which had church bells on it, and we sampled the bells and we're just fucking around with melodies, all of us and we came up with a 'doo doo doo'. And that was it, you know? That became the centrepiece of that piece of music. And it was a fluke, in a sense, but we were very, very specific about the dance direction, it was very different for us, because we messed around with so many time signatures before and now we're making something that you could actually dance to.

John Vick: I would always drive echo units and so the music would always be a tune on a keyboard of sorts, going through an echo, structuring the time, and everyone would go for it. With guitars or singing or whatever it was, but that's the core of it. And of course when we came out the other end of that we were more electronic, even though we still had drums. But yeah, Cathexis. Robert King said he wanted to release this record. And we were really pleased, because it meant that even though we might be able to get the money together to do it, somebody who was more experienced was going to be able to sell it and do a better job.

Cathexis was a fantastic label run by Robert King, a successor to his earlier label, Pleasantly Surprised. Cathexis released work by Pink Industry, Test Department and many other wildly original acts.

Davie Miller: We'd made 'De Testimony' in 1986, which, unbeknown to us went on to become a record that Alfredo picked up in Ibiza and started playing in these clubs in Ibiza. Danny Rampling, Pete Tong and Paul Oakenfold were going out to Ibiza in 1987. They heard that record there. They took it back to

London and it became part of the whole Shoom thing, the acid house thing.

And I was actually driving. I was on tour with The Pastels. I was a Pastels driver for a tour they did in England and we stopped in Leeds. And James Brown, who went on to become editor of *Loaded* and was an *NME* journalist, said to me, 'Do you realise that your record is huge in Ibiza?' We didn't know anything about Ibiza, or what was about to happen in London with acid house. And then all of a sudden, we get a phone call from Pete Tong. I'd started working for Fast distribution at that point so I got a phone call from Pete Tong at the Fast offices. And he said, 'We want to license this record.' And I think he offered us a thousand pounds. A thousand pounds at that point was a huge amount of money. And I think it went a long way to us recording our first album.

While 'De Testimony' was being played in the summer sun of Ibiza, the band were still slogging around the UK touring circuit, struggling to fit in with many of their Scottish contemporaries.

Davie Miller: Most of the Edinburgh bands at that time were very jingly jangly. We couldn't play our instruments. Maybe, I guess The Pastels weren't great musicians either, but they've got that kind of . . . it was more melodic. We were much more let's hit things until we make a noise and record that noise and see what happens. We did a show in Glasgow in 1986. It was with The Boy Hairdressers. So, The Boy Hairdressers and Finitribe in Glasgow. We set fire to the place. We had a big cauldron of oil, which we bought and we kind of made a massive, massive hoo-ha and we made a lot of noise and we're banned. We were told not to come back. And still when I walk past the CCA to this day, I hurriedly walk past because I think someone's gonna pull me out.

John Vick: What we realised was there were more people doing experimental music in other cities, in other places around the world. You've got to remember, we were young and we hadn't been exposed to the big world as much. We realised this was great, there's more people out there doing this sort of thing, or who are interested in this sort of thing. We carried on down the route of trying to do experimental music, heavily using the sampler and electronics. We got lots of support gigs and we were able to support people, so we managed to start playing with other bands around the UK. And it was interesting, it was good. I'm gonna say, instead of being part of a small cult in Edinburgh, we were part of a bigger cult in the UK. Instead of playing Edinburgh ten times a year, we played Edinburgh once a year. We had local support but we weren't looking to go down to the pub to play a gig and our mates come in; we were looking to play around the UK, and we'll play Edinburgh but not so often. We will do it as best we can and when it happens, everyone please come along because we're not going to do it once every month for you.

I started working in Southern Studios. I'd go down to London and help people do their music there. That opened things up for me as an engineer and I ended up learning more. John Loder, he's gone now but he was the owner and he and his wife lived upstairs in this nice house up top. He would come down to make sure I was okay and then leave me to work with whoever I was meant to be working with. I don't know if you've ever heard of Lene Lovich? She and her husband, they did her music, and they just needed a hand running the studio. They were much more expert than me in many ways but I was there to be that engineer who plugged things in, made things work, sorted things out, you know. There were various other people – Björk would be recording there. It was one of these things where I would just be setting things up . . . Adrian Sherwood, all these people worked at Southern Studios. It was this den of very good people. Keith LeBlanc – all these people, they'd either come from America or from London. Lee Scratch Perry. These are all the people who were there when I was there.

One like-minded local was Mr Egg (James MacDonald) and his band, Ege Bam Yasi. James had been the bass player in The Fakes, one of the early punk bands from Stirling. He became one of the leading figures in Scotland's acid house scene. And he only speaks in 'Egg language'.

Mr Egg (Ege Bam Yasi): If I took anything from The Fakes it was probably keep playing, I wis too naive and innocent musically back then to have a path ti follow.

The name Mr Egg all came out of the song title 'Misdirection'. The lyrics were in a sampler at Wilf [Smarties] Planet [Studio] in Broughton Street where we used ti record and while someone was playing around with the sampler on the word misdirection they were editing the word and it stared misdirection and was cut down – misdirect, miramati, misderec, misderec, mirec . . . it soonded ti me like Mr Egg. I thoucht 'That for me . . . '

Musical interpretations are all different. I would not call the energy or sound of acid house ti be punk related other than it was new and different. Punk and acid were underground but acid house has started underground and stayed underground.

No other music has done the samegg . . . every new genre of music that started underground has been lifted out . . . punk, teggno, drum.n.bass . . . am glad ti say acid house has kept it real.

I am sorregg ti say EBY did have a dash of commercialism only because at that time others were in the band (altho ultimately EBY was me) and various people were involved over the years . . . so survival time was one of those moments in time where things took a twist . . . that grouping of people got together as myself and Fred Parsons lived in Stirling, the singer Karen (Smyth) joined after she saw EBY play at the Wee Red Bar in 1984/85-ish.

I had been doing acid stuff in Stirling mid-eighties but was playing no gigs. Back then acid was not even a name, it was a sound. The name came later. I use ti listen to John Peel at nights and he would play the odd acid tune and the sound connected wi me.

The music was played on the Roland TB303, which I had back then, but I did not know that machine made that sound I was hearing on JP.

Working with the Finitribe was a massive help and things could havegg been different if we had turned different corners.

EBY played La Sorbonne in 1984 and Wavy Davie frae the Finis came backstage and asked if we were going to do stuff wi them, supports, etc. and it all went from theregg . . . back then the Finis were a bit nuts – visually, musically different – but EBY was a bit nuts live and musically different but we hit it off.

Finitribe's 'De Testimony' was also spreading beyond Ibiza and had made its way to the ears of US indie label Wax Trax! via their joint association with Southern Studios.

Chris Connelly: I was working at Fast Forward and we'd get records a few times a week for us to hear because we sold the records over the phone. You know, there's a new Television Personalities record or blah, blah, blah. And one week there was three records that came – one by The Young Gods, 'Big Sexy Land' by The Revolting Cocks, and there was a Ministry 12-inch single called 'Nature of Love'. And all three of these records really spoke to me, I was like, 'This is the future.' To me, this is great. I finally have found something that I can really connect with. And, you know, I got in touch with Wax Trax! Records. And when I went down with Wax Trax! to sell Finitribe I met Al Jourgensen. He was working in the studio at the time on what would become the album *The Land of Rape and Honey*. Bill Rieflin, Paul Barker and Al Jourgensen were all living in a flat in north London and so they were in the studio 24/7. And so Al was up and about, or he'd been up, you know, for a month or something like that. And he listened to my song. It's like, that's fucking great. We've got to get you on Wax Trax! Let's go do a song now. So he just dragged me into this studio and put me behind a microphone. And we started working together then and we kept in touch.

Davie Miller: They liked what we were doing. That helped immensely to get them (our Wax Trax! releases) to college dance charts. And that, again, raised our profile.

John Vick: And for us it was like, okay, once again we're not with Finiflex but this is bigger and better, so we did some records for Wax Trax! Records. One of them was a rerun of 'De Testimony' because they wanted that on their label somehow. Then we did 'I Want More', which was a Can song.

Davie Miller: Then Chris got a call from Al Jourgensen.

Noisy Scottish music was no stranger to the Ministry/Revolting Cocks team, who had met The Jesus and Mary Chain while both were working at Southern Studios.

Paul Barker (The Revolting Cocks and Ministry; Interview from Industrial Accident DVD): (Al Jourgensen) wanted his sound to be harder than it was. Al asked me to go to England to work on new material. Al and I stayed there straight for six months and we worked at Southern Studios. We were in there whenever it wasn't booked. The Jesus and Mary Chain did their first record at Southern so they were wrapping up when we got there and I really think that first Jesus and Mary Chain album really sprouted that whole 'whatever the fuck that scene is'. Just be as obnoxiously loud as you fucking can possibly be. Just 'Fuck you!' It's just so bad-ass.

Chris Connelly: I went over (to Chicago) a couple of times before I actually moved myself over there. I went over to record and rehearse for a live Revolting Cocks album – he (Al Jourgensen) had this idea that the second Revolting Cocks album should be a double live album. Because it was such a sort of fuck-you statement to the music business. So I went over for a month in the summer of 1987. And we worked and worked up the set and worked in a rehearsal space, and then played this gig which got recorded. And I got back to Edinburgh, that's when I started to become disillusioned with the Finitribe. Because I didn't feel we were working fast enough on music. And so, you know, that's, that's how it happened.

And eventually, about a year later, I just moved myself over to Chicago, and that was that. I've been there ever since. Well, you know, it's sad and I regret it to this day, to be honest with you. I probably should have stuck with it, but that's that. We had gotten to a point with the Finitribe where we were taking an awful long time to write songs. And I feel like we had, you know, we've done 'De Testimony', we'd moved into a larger rehearsal space in Leith. And we spent a lot of time doing up that space, sanding the floors, painting the walls. And there wasn't an awful lot of music being done. And I was itching. I was feeling itchy, I was feeling my feet burning as, like, I need to move on. And I'd already met The Revolting Cocks and things like that. And, you know, that was exciting to me. But, of course, the future was still exciting to me. But I just got to a point where I was like, I can't, I can't. I need to move on, I need to move on. And you know what, it was the best possible thing, although I say I regret it, it was the best possible thing to happen. It really hurt at the time but then the Finitribe went on to have this great success. And to me at that point, it was like, well, this is what should have happened. Otherwise, it wouldn't have happened, we would have been sitting, the six of us, in a rehearsal space trying to come up with parts. But we needed to split into two, we had to leave and then all of a sudden you know, they're having, you know, there's *Noise, Lust and Fun* and the 12-inch singles and stuff like that. And they became really popular. And I went to America and, you know, did cocaine or whatever.

After Chris became the new singer for The Revolting Cocks, Finitribe were now a three-piece, and 'De Testimony' had just received an Andrew Weatherall remix that took it to even greater heights.

John Vick: For me at the time I felt, oh, Chris, this is what we've done. But at the same time I remembered sitting in the piano room at school plunking away on my own. I knew that this wasn't going to stop me doing music. I'm just not going to be working with Chris any more. We are very good friends. I was left with Phil and Davie and was like, I don't know what I'm meant to do. I'm into my electronics, I help all these studios, I'm just gonna keep doing stuff. They said, well, let's do it all together. So we carried on doing it.

ENDINGS AND NEW BEGINNINGS

Davie Miller: Danny Rampling invited us to Shoom and we went, we went to Shoom, and we, we kind of got immersed in this, we were quite amazed by what was happening in London. And so this is interesting. It's different. It's interesting, and it's something we had an affinity to. But we weren't too concerned about really being part of it. We just, we were just happy to play music and make music that people enjoyed. And the electronic thing developed.

John Vick: That's when we very much went into the electronic world. Chris was like, I'm gonna say, a front person. We weren't really front people. We are, but we're not, you know? We weren't holding the microphone screaming and shouting, we weren't like that, though we're into doing words and saying things and sending messages. We ended up just the three of us. *Noise, Lust and Fun* was with Sandy, an album that had [Little] Annie on it as well. It was one of these things where we just got on with it and it was going to be a new thing. There were lots of things carried forward, but it was new. And it was really enjoyable because it was more electronic, and we'd moved away from being the band with drums, guitar, bass. So it didn't matter if there wasn't a drum kit; it didn't matter if there wasn't a guitar; it didn't matter any more. And in fact, there wasn't. It became much more uniquely electronic. Even though it wasn't cool club music electronic, it was more just electronic.

Davie Miller: I guess with dance music lots of people started making records and distributing them. It was a different type of music and it required a different selling technique. It was very quick so you'd make a dance record, it has to go out, has to sell that week, has to get to the right people. It was white labels. It wasn't big sleeves. it was a quick business, cutting a record, getting out. And people were driving around the country in vans.

Thanks to Finitribe's cutting-edge mix of electronics and their experience of working with producers such as Andy Weatherall, they were much in demand as producers themselves, especially for guitar-based bands who were starting to experiment with electronics and dance music. Once such band was The Shamen, previously a guitar-based C86 band called Alone Again Or, who were increasingly travelling in a more electronic direction.

John Vick: I used to repair studios, and there was this one in particular I worked at doing my electronic engineering, called Planet Studio. There was a guy there called Wilf Smarties, he was the producer and he was working with Wet Wet Wet. A band used to come down from Aberdeen and I can't remember what they used to be called, but all of a sudden they were called The Shamen. They liked the electronic stuff that I did so they said, would you help us do some of the music for our album? I did, and they really liked it, and of course that was *In Gorbachev We Trust*. I did quite a lot of things on there. It was more like setting up so that it sounded electronic. They had lots of guitars and everything, but I made it sound much more – I don't know how to say it but I produced it how I thought would be different. And it was and they then signed to One Little Indian. That was quite bizarre. We didn't follow them to One Little Indian but One Little Indian keep coming back into this, don't they? They were great. It was purely because these guys would turn up at the studio and they'd come all the way from Aberdeen. They were particularly nice. There were two brothers too; I'm not sure if they were twins or not. Keith and Derek. They were just ever so good and ever so nice. Quite often bands, don't say this, but Wet Wet Wet were maybe quite aloof, quite popstar-like, whereas The Shamen were just like, hi John, how are you, we want to do this, we want to do that. They almost pulled me in as a friend of theirs to help out, as opposed to there's that lad who plugs something in and all of a sudden we can hear something. There we go, that's how it was. They were great, they were nice.

The Shamen's album, In Gorbochev We Trust, *released in 1989, was a truly pioneering work in the progression of indie music into dance. Certainly, the launch single, 'Synergy', had a December 1988 release that predates the 1989 Paul Oakenfold WFL remix of Happy Mondays' 'Wrote for Luck'.*

While 'De Testimony' and Finitribe's activities in general are seen as pioneering steps in the evolution of music, it could be argued that Finitribe's most infamous legacy is their 1989 EP, Animal Farm.

John Vick: We went to a place called Monimail in Fife with a mobile studio. Nothing fancy but enough to make music. I wrote this song and realised it was really good, and that I wanted the words to be – well it was called 'Animal Farm'. I've been a vegetarian since I was 15. They slag me off, saying I invented vegetarianism. I didn't, of course I never. I thought McDonald's was bad . . . there was a TV documentary about them burning down the rainforests in the Amazon to create space to grow beef. The song was called 'Animal Farm' and the chorus was 'blood red gold'. It was great. It wasn't like 'De Testimony', it wasn't popular, it wasn't anything, but it was this good song, and it had this message . . . and One Little Indian said to us, do you want to do a big poster – a big campaign to fuck them off? We were like, well, how would we do that? And they said we'll pay for it all because it's expensive. There was a graphic designer and I can't remember his name but he was really keen to do it. So we did it and made five thousand 'Fuck off McDonald's' posters. It was 'Fuck off McDonald's, Finitribe EP, Animal Farm' with pigs looking through the big 'M'. We went out on tour, five thousand posters made. And we got a phone call. I don't know how we got a phone call but somehow or other, seventy-five posters went up in London and the police raided Rough Trade. They didn't know this but they thought they were getting all the posters. But we had been dispatched a thousand posters because we were going on tour. They said they'd only made four thousand posters and seventy-five had gone up. They confiscated 3,925 posters and thought that was them all. We said we wouldn't put any more up. They were livid but as long as we didn't put any more up, no more action would be taken. We went out on tour and at the back of the van there was just this thin bit underneath all the equipment. Mr Egg was our merchandise man. There was a thousand posters, and honestly they all sold out. We did maybe ten gigs in this tour; maybe a bit more but roughly around that. It was just around the country, but the posters. The posters! People came; I don't know that they liked the music, but they loved the posters. We sold them for £2 each. One Little Indian's Derek said, 'That's your tour support by the way.' You know what tour support is? What happens is, most bands can't really afford to go and promote records – it's quite expensive to go out and do gigs. So it was like, you can use that money to support your tour. We sold £2,000 worth of posters. £2,000 went into the bucket to pay for the vans, the crew and for everything. Otherwise you wouldn't be able to go and promote records. You've got to get a hand doing it. In the end through sales of records it comes back. They always take it off the sales but it's called 'tour support'.

As Finitribe were having critical and commercial success with One Little Indian, Chris was having equal success, now fully relocated to the States with The Revolting Cocks and Ministry.

Chris Connelly: It was very different to the Finitribe, but at the same time, you know, I mean, we weren't altar boys. Not at all, especially me. But The Revolting Cocks were full on. It was far more. As a young man, it was kind of like it was far more angry and sort of Sex Pistols-ish in a way in attitude. And it's funny, because when I left, that was at the beginning of rave and acid house, right. And that was sort of peace and love. And I went over to this completely toxic nightmare of, like, audiences just full of people out of their heads on bad drugs, like not peace and love drugs, just like, whatever. I don't know. And the band too, well, certainly me and Al, ha ha, though we did have a couple of scientists in the band who kept us on the straight and narrow, thank God.

I left right at the beginning of acid house. In a sense, I remember feeling it a little bit. I remember the Finitribe being in London, and we went to a party where there was a warehouse party. And it was kind of new . . . this was kind of the beginning of people tripping and listening to music. I don't know why that happened. I don't know how it happened. But I went over to Chicago and it wasn't like that at all. It was, you know, it was cocaine and speed and whatever. And the music was aggressive. But the music that I left behind was getting less aggressive and more friendly towards the audience, and it was definitely geared to dancing. But the irony is when I first moved over, Chicago house was booming. And it was all being recorded at the same studio where we were recording. And I know to this day, I still know a lot of these players. Vince Lawrence is a good friend of mine and he was here, he helped write the first house record. And he was recording in the studio at the same time as us and we were also like frenemies, you know. We would make fun of

ENDINGS AND NEW BEGINNINGS

each other all the time. Because of their stupid dance music. We had our stupid dance music but we worked when, you know, we worked well together.

Chris Connelly: The (Ministry) record *The Land of Rape and Honey* came out on Sire. Sire always seemed to be in a bad mood with Al [Jourgensen] for whatever reason. He was the bad boy of the label. He wasn't Madonna, and he wasn't Morrissey. They didn't put anything into the *Land of Rape and Honey*, I can testify to that. And the record took off in a major way, not in a major sort of Bruce Springsteen way, but it sold a lot more than Sire thought it would. I think they were like looking for a way to get rid of Al or something like that. But then all of a sudden, oh, people are responding to this. And they did respond. And so then they got interested. Because they're a major label. They like money, they don't give a shit about, you know, us. And I really, it's a testament to Al's, and

Paul Barker's as well, their tenacity with what was the sound that they were making, which was a new sound. This was, to put it simply, kind of crossing synthesisers and electronic music with fast guitars, which really hadn't been done that much before. And they did it. And to me, when I heard that it was like the loudest, most aggressive syncopated music, it was candy to me, it was just like, 'This is great.'

During a break from Ministry and The Revolting Cocks, Chris released a solo album, Whiplash Boychild, *a hidden treasure by a Scottish artist. On one level, it is far removed from any of his other work but at the same time it fits in with everything else. It's essentially a beautifully constructed, twisted pop album that still contains all the danger and experimentation of both Finitribe and The Revolting Cocks. While it is claimed that Nine Inch Nails influenced both Scott Walker's* Tilt *and David Bowie's* Outside, *I suggest they might both have been listening to* Whiplash Boychild *too.*

Chris Connelly: Wax Trax! Records, they were very nurturing of their artists. I said, 'I really want to do a solo album,' which is what I did. Then Jim Nash, who was the CEO, he's like, let's do it. What's it gonna be like? And I was like, yeah, I don't really know, I just want to try, and it's like, okay, so I, I've always been interested in pop records, you know. I mean, pop records as in things like The Velvet Underground and stuff like that, you know, the chord changes and these are things that we never used in the Finitribe, or things we never used in The Revolting Cocks, either. Like picking up a guitar and playing D, A, G minor, whatever. And I started to get into that and started writing these songs.

ENDINGS AND NEW BEGINNINGS

I was so obsessed with Scott Walker at the time, which is how that cover version came about. And, you know, it was at a time where, you know, *Tilt* hadn't happened yet . . . I've got a good singing voice. And I wanted to sing on a record. It's weird, because I got to this point in Ministry, where after every single concert, in every single rehearsal, I had a little headache, because I was singing LIKE THIS!!!! all the time. And I was a heavy smoker at the time, which did not help. So I was like, 'I need a break from yelling.' So we got into doing this, me and a couple of friends of mine, a girl called Jessica Villines, who's a filmmaker. And a guy called Stuart Zachman. We went into Chicago Trax studio and started working together. And Bill Rieflin from Ministry also played on the record as well. And it was far more of a melodic sensibility, it was far more of an introspective sound as well. But that's what was going on in my mind at the time. It's easy to burn out in Ministry . . . You can burn out after like, ten seconds of a song because it was so loud. And it was so full on all the time. It was kind of overwhelming, you know, and Al is such a character. I mean, he's wonderful, but he's got to be Al all the time, you know, and with that comes a lot of humour, of course, but at the same time it brings a lot of danger as well. So *Whiplash Boychild* is me stepping to the side and just taking a breather.

If it hadn't been for the Finitribe, which I started with my friends, like, in 1980, I probably would have gone off the rails, but this was the thing that guided me through my teens and my early twenties. And there was a very strong bond, and there still is. And, you know, I can thank these fellows for keeping me on the straight and narrow. We taught each other about playing together. And I've used this my whole life, like, how to be democratic in a small group, you know, now I'm a teacher myself. And I still find the rules that apply to the Finitribe really apply in the classroom, to help for cooperation, for empathy. For peers teaching peers rather than teachers teaching you. We didn't go to anyone for outside help, we had our mentors and The Visitors but we taught each other, you know, and that was a really special thing, I think.

In many respects, Finitribe splitting two ways demonstrated that Scottish alternative music had far-reaching influence beyond guitar-based music. Finitribe were instrumental in the development of UK acid house and the indie/dance crossover via their production work with The Shamen. Chris's work with Ministry and The Revolting Cocks would become a part of the US underground's move to mainstream success, importantly showing no compromise.

The Soup Dragons proved to be another important stepping stone in the shift from guitar to electronics.

The Soup Dragons emerge from their hiatus

The Soup Dragons came under attack from the weekly music press, which accused them of jumping on the indie-dance bandwagon. This was both unpleasant and undeserved but unfortunately the tag has stuck to the present day. There is little evidence to support it; in fact, it can be argued that the opposite was true and that, while they were not the actual pioneers of indie-dance, The Soup Dragons were involved from the very start. It is an unfair label but perhaps typical of the UK press at that time.

ENDINGS AND NEW BEGINNINGS

Sean Dickson: Ross, our drummer, he'd left Glasgow Art School to do the band full time . . . And he made the decision that he wanted to carry on his degree so suddenly we were drummer-less before the *Lovegod* album. And that was like '89. And then me, myself and Jim, sat one night and . . . decided to use a sampler and drum machines cause that's when . . . '89 was the year like samplers all started getting used and things, and they were bloody expensive then but we bought ourself a second-hand Akai S950 and an Atari computer and it was my job to learn how to work the bloody stuff. And that's kind of how *Lovegod* started, you know, drummer-less.

Jim McCulloch: Basically we were looking about for a drummer. And we had songs half written in demo form. And we had shows booked as well. So it was a lot of things, a lot of pressure for us to do something. So we went back to Bellshill and found a guy called Paul Quinn, who, you know, part of the musical miasma anyway, and we knew him. And he was a much more straightforward rock drummer. And basically, the demos that we've been making, Sean programmed with a TR-909 drum machine because we don't have Ross. And then it was getting Paul in to help with that and so there was a crossover element in the drum machine and Paul, and then just try to go in for a kind of Stooges thing and into like the John Waters movies and just trash American culture thing. And that was kind of continuing or what the band visualised, really visual music. And it was just trying to take it up to the next level basically.

Sean Dickson: There was a great engineer I used to work with called Marius De Vries, who made a lot of our records around then that taught me a lot . . . he went on to make Madonna's records and things. And he taught us a lot . . . some of the stuff we did around, you know, *Lovegod* and *Hotwired* was actually quite groundbreaking technology-wise. We were never ever given the credit for it, you know, because there . . . there was a huge backlash towards us from the press with 'I'm Free' becoming such a big record.

The funny thing is, the way it happened was . . . and, you know . . . people have always hinted that there's been a lot of stuff covered up about this. I really don't need to cover anything up now . . . I DJ all over the world, I'm proud of what I did and there was no lies involved in it, it was a completely organic thing, you know. Like everybody else, we were necking ecstasy and going clubbing . . . it just didn't . . . it wasn't just happening in Manchester and London, it was happening in Glasgow as well. The difference with Glasgow was we were dancing to old soul records. There used to be a club called, I think it was called Universe or Universal or something, and upstairs was acid house and downstairs was more kind of break beaty, kind of soul stuff. And if you listen to *Lovegod*, that's what all the influences are: they're not from acid house, you know, they're from more the kind of dubbed-out, kind of slower grooves. 'Mother Universe' was the first track we recorded and we worked with the engineers Marius De Vries and Steve Sidelnyk. And, as I said, you know, the amount of technology that was going on was unreal. And it was just like all of a sudden I could make the records that were going on in my head. That's what it was all about. For years . . . leading up to then, for years I was struggling with wanting to move forward all the time. I'm never one for going backwards, I'm always moving forwards and . . . the 12-inch of 'Mother Universe' came out (in 1989) and suddenly all these DJs that we'd never heard of, it was like a whole new world was opened up to you. You know, 'cause up until then we were just an indie guitar band and suddenly there was . . . like the *NME* came up with this term: indie-dance.

CHAPTER 12
1989-90

Splits and ends

The fragmentation and transformation of Primal Scream

By 1989 only two members remained from Primal Scream's original line-up, Bobby Gillespie and Robert Young. Andrew Innes, an old friend from Glasgow, had replaced founding member Jim Beattie on guitar and the wonderful Martin Duffy, who had played on all the albums, became a full-time member. They relocated to Brighton and underwent the first of many huge transformations.

Both Tam and Joogs had said their goodbyes to the group during the recording of their 1987 debut album, Sonic Flower Groove.

Tam McGurk: I feel Bobby just wasn't happy with the personnel. Bobby wasn't a guy you could disagree with. It was his way or the highway. I've never been a yes man ever in my life. I've never been a troublemaker either. But he wanted his own people.

SPLITS AND ENDS

Well, thirty years down the line he's got his own people because there's not one original member left. It's just him. Well, how did it end? It ended with all of us in Union Street, Glasgow, in a baker's with a downstairs bit where you could sit in and have a coffee or breakfast or whatever. And we had a meeting, we were all there: myself, Alan McGee, Bobby, Jim Beattie, Joogs, Robert Young and Stuart May. You knew something was wrong, right. And basically it was a case of 'We're not happy with the level of drumming that's on the album . . . and we're gonna let you go.' And I was like, well, fine. Because I kind of knew it was bullshit. Anyway, you know, it wasn't to do with the drumming. It was more political than that. But to be honest, by that point I just wanted out anyway, I was fed up. I was thinking I was actually happier being second man on a train down to Carlisle than I was in fulfilling my childhood dream, which was to play the drums in a rock'n'roll band, which is quite a sad conclusion to draw after four years, so I was quite happy. Towards the end, I was Bobbied out, I'd had too much of him.

John 'Joogs' Martin: When we finished up with the Julian Cope tour, we were basically just whisked away on a minibus to Rockfield Studios in deepest Wales. It was on the bus that I was talking to Bobby Gillespie and he's going, 'You can come along, John, you know, Joogs, for a couple of weeks, but we don't really need you on tambourine,' and I was like, 'Why not?' 'Well, we're gonna get someone else in to play tambourine, I'll do it.' I said, 'Why am I here?' 'Well, you're here just to come along for the ride and get a feel of a place and, you know, keep the groove going. The vibe.' And I was, 'Riiiiiiight.' I didn't like the sound of this feeling already. Like I'm not playing on the album. He didn't really trust me playing tambourine. Maybe I was too off-beat for him. I don't know. So that was that. It was then decided obviously behind the scenes what I wasn't to be that Tambourine Man on the record.

Jim Beattie left shortly afterwards, and he and Tam went on to work together in Spirea-X.

An unrecognisable and surprise remix by Andy Weatherall of 'I'm Losing More Than I'll Ever Have' from the second album was released as 'Loaded' in February 1990, following much the same template set by Finitribe's earlier production of The Shamen. The Primal Scream remix led to 1991's Screamadelica, *regarded as one of the finest cultural moments of the 1990s. The band, as of 2023, are still touring it in its entirety at retro festivals.*

John 'Joogs' Martin: It was really strange when 'Loaded' came out. That was the first single before *Screamadelica*, in about 1990. I kept hearing the song in clubs and thinking Primal Scream sound totally different now. How far is this going to go? Then all of a sudden it shot onto the Top 20, like holy shit, they're in the Top 20. I could never have envisaged that one, especially with an album like *Screamadelica* and 'Loaded'. I thought it was a great song, great album. There's nothing you can really do. I thought, those guys with all the dividing, they took it right through and got lucky with Andy Weatherall and created a magical album, to tell you the truth. It did bug me at the time, hearing it everywhere, coming out of cars and clubs and pubs and things, but what can you do? Fair play, they stuck in there and they got it. There's not a lot you can really say to that.

The Pastels' second album

In 1989 The Pastels released their second album, Sittin' Pretty, *this time with Eugene Kelly and David Keegan helping out.*

Eugene Kelly: The Vaselines had played our first shows as a duo supporting The Pastels and later when we added Charlie and James on drums and bass we toured with The Pastels in England. Sometime in 1987 Stephen asked me to join them to play guitar, piano and violin. I could only play guitar but the piano parts were mostly one note rhythmic banging and I stuck a pickup on the violin and played some drones. It was fun for a while but I never really felt that I fitted in with the rest of the band and I always felt that The Vaselines was my number one creative concern. I recorded on The Pastels' second album but the producer made me feel like an incompetent dick as I was being asked to contribute on instruments that I couldn't play properly or at all. After a short Scottish tour I decided that I didn't want to do it any longer.

Martin Hayward: I was even less happy with that one, I think. I don't think it's a very good album. I think it would have made a good EP. Some of the stuff on it I think is fantastic but as a body of work I don't think it works.

Martin describes the recording process of the album.

Martin Hayward: Brian, Stephen and Aggi rent an Easter Road flat, Bernice a few blocks north. We begin commuting to REL (Studios) together, but don't keep it up. 'Reminds me of my best girl's hair,' Stephen cutely dismisses both the vista of Salisbury crags and the romantic tradition, as we head up Queen's Drive.

Richard Mazda is producing again. 'Comin' Through' provides grounds for optimism, but we break apart making this record, in a way that is unclear at the time. We are more atomised and less intense than for previous recordings.

A VHS comfort rental of *RoboCop* for the lounge goes largely unwatched. It's impossible to settle to anything, including going out for a walk. I make Oddfellows in Forrest Road and try to write, before deciding the song is probably complete. Time to get back.

'Nothing To Be Done' is one of the first things we tackle. As with 'Crawl Babies', Bernice and I are the band, and I record a guide vocal. I have in mind the duet oppositions of Lee [Hazlewood] and Nancy [Sinatra], and I'm thinking about resources and how to use them. 'You sing this bit, you sing that.' Stephen and Aggi rise to the occasion. Brian has borrowed a secret weapon amplifier from Cameron Fraser of The Cateran which is more expensive than anything we could afford. His guitar overdub is fabulous. I'm thinking of Prince introducing surprising instruments to an established palette and find a Eurodisco keyboard setting.

The same recording approach for 'Ugly Town'. Brian on slide.

'Baby You're Just You' is Brian in Neil Young and Crazy Horse mood with nicely disconsolate words and vocals from Stephen backed by Eugene.

'Anne Boleyn' is vintage idiosyncratic Stephen over Bernice and me, Brian adding single finger fretting lifted from 'Train Kept a Rollin' by Panther Burns.

I write what becomes 'Sittin' Pretty' straight after catching Paul McCartney do Duke Ellington's 'Don't Get Around Much

Anymore' on telly. I don't mention this to anyone, but Brian's subconscious may be reaching for the same song in his phrasing. I know he has Willie Nelson's version. I'm also thinking Mickey & Sylvia's 'Love Is Strange' as covered by Johnny and Patti on 'Copy Cats', specifically the irresistible muted arpeggios. A straight Modern Lovers style rock'n'roll callback, but Stephen's lyric and vocal feel careless, and not in a good way.

Much of his work on this record seems strangely indifferent, or worse, really for the first time, and this gives it a flat feel overall, for me.

David Keegan drops by to put guitar on 'Swerve'. Since the Shop Assistants split, he has been lending his talent to various things, like The Vaselines' 'Dying for It'.

I don't know how 'Sit on It, Mother' ends up on the record. Only Richard's moothie [harmonica] is new and the original on 'Comin' Through' is better.

We record a live metallic 'Baby Honey' early on, all playing in the same space. Stephen adds a disengaged vocal. Our rhythm section backing will later turn up (after the rhythm section has been sacked and without our knowledge) as an inferior version on 'Truckload of Trouble', with the urgent metal squall removed.

A brisk and tuneful version of Mike Nesmith's 'Different Drum' also never sees the light of day.

We do the live thing again with the extended version of 'Pablo Picasso', which has been in the set for a while, channelling Bo Diddley and Ivy Rorschach into semi-structured drone noise. We have a thunderous backing track down, including cello and viola. In the control room we listen to the playback loud, thinking the bass is in. Then the bass comes in.

Stephen was keen before we started that no one was going

to quote the 'Repo Man' version. I wasn't sure why, until he puts a new lyric over it, which I hear for the first time without warning on playback as 'Ditch the Fool'. On one hearing I am able only to catch a new emotional register, and I let it go. In the self-correcting earlier band, this scale of unilateral decision wouldn't have been attempted.

It soon appears to me as the worst of several bad choices on this record and I regret going along with it. Reviewers will later have to pretend that they 'get' the 'irony', to accommodate this lapse in taste. I don't think so. There is no kind of truth to be found here.

It is also hard for me now not to read this as a 'response' to 'Drop the Boy' by Bros. Stephen is genuinely and puzzlingly perturbed by the rapid success of Bros. For some reason they really seem to boil his piss. I should have steered us away from fantasy vendetta and back to Jonathan Richman.

The record takes too long to make, then too long to mix and then release is delayed and delayed. At one point we are touring a record that isn't available – 'Smell the Glove' style.

I tell Stephen I think *Sittin' Pretty* would sound complacent as an album title. He disagrees.

The front sleeve photo is in the bed of the Kelvin, just off Great Western Road. We find a location of fallen trees and arrange ourselves. Bernice perches elegantly on a tree trunk. Wordlessly our photographer backs away and Stephen and Aggi follow. He backs further away. Again, they follow. Bernice gives a belly chuckle of disbelief. Brian exhales smoke – 'Fucking let them get on with it, if that's what they wannae do.' 'Nah, I'm not going to' – stepping from background to middle ground. The only thing missing is a best before date.

SPLITS AND ENDS

'Speeding Motorcycle' (1991) was the last Pastels record to feature the original line-up.

Martin Hayward: The last thing we are involved in recording is what becomes a rather lame version of Daniel Johnston's 'Speeding Motorcycle' at Pier House in Granton. Tone Loc donates a beat. The atmosphere is increasingly toxic, but I'm not in the mood to take any hints. Say what you mean. Norman Blake provides some fresh air. Not long after, Bernice and I receive individual copies of a letter, signed by Stephen, Brian and Aggi, informing us that we have been sacked. Bizarrely there is a statement about who gets to keep the band name. As if. A lawyers' letter divides our meagre equipment assets, and he then attempts to repossess the 'Comin' Through' session tapes, left in Edinburgh with Bernice. Good luck with that. The level of formality is completely alien and it all feels like massive overkill. More might have been achieved with a sit-down, but then that would have required eye contact. Simultaneously, Stephen is quoted by a tame writer in one of the weeklies saying we have 'left' and he is 'baffled' as to why this might be. Bernice and I are, at exactly this moment, splitting up from our own relationship and have enough to be getting on with, thanks.

Bernice Simpson: I had hoped that Aggi might support our female contribution but that was never a bond. It was always you and I versus them. Quite sad that there was no sisterhood but hey ho. The men were the leaders, right? An axis of power dictates the outcome of our artistic voyage. Sad, but inevitable somehow.

The Pastels continued, despite losing much of the harder-edged punk attitude that Martin and Bernice brought to the band. Much like with the original band, Stephen brought in other musicians to help realise his vision. Mobile Safari *was released in 1995, featuring the great John Hogarty on guitar and some equally great members of Teenage Fanclub.*

The Wendys

Another guitar band who experimented with the new sounds emerging from dance had a more direct link to what was happening in Manchester. Edinburgh's The Wendys were right at the centre of the scene and signed to the coolest label of the day – Factory.

SPLITS AND ENDS

Ian White (Guitar): In 1988 we got the support to Happy Mondays on their *Bummed* tour at The Venue in Edinburgh. Backstage we got talking to the band, with the late Paul Ryder being really friendly. I would meet him again several times over the years at AHW's In The City music conference and he was always good value for a chat. Derek Ryder, Shaun's dad, said he loved our set and told us we should send our demo to Factory. Previously I had no idea who to send it to so I made up a name, Wilerassim, made up of the names of three of the main players at the label. We kept in touch with Derek for the next couple of years and kept sending our latest demos. In spring 1990 I got a call from Phil Saxe, Factory A&R, who said he wanted to come see us. We had a gig in Galashiels organised by local band The Pralines, and Phil came by plane, train and omnibus. When we came off stage he told us he wanted to sign us. It was mind blowing. By November, contracts had been negotiated, a demo/trial production had been recorded with Ian Broudie, and we signed at the opening of the Ben Kelly-designed new Factory offices opening party in Manchester. Johnny our drummer was kilted up, traditional style.

Some XXX photos were taken by Pete Walsh and thankfully never surfaced. In attendance were, amongst others of the Manchester scene glitterati, Vini Reilly, Johnny Marr, the Mondays getting gold disks for *Bummed*, New Order, Rob Gretton, and, excitingly for us, Pat Nevin! We had landed on another planet. Very sore heads the next day. Later at a Happy Mondays show at Barrowland, Alan Erasmus told us that when they were moving office they found one of our earlier demos down the back of a filing cabinet so they maybe heard something they liked from those first recordings.

SURPRISE SINGLE OF THE WEEK

THE WENDYS: The Sun's Going To Shine For Me Soon (*Factory*)
This effortlessly elegant debut from the recently-signed Edinburgh crew makes virtually every other pop single this week sound creaky and cobweb-infested by comparison. Check out the sun-flecked simplicity of melody, gently rippling guitars and dreamily whispered lyrics before you turn on the cynicism.

The mellower moments of Happy Mondays' first LP sounded like this, tribal percussion buried beneath rudimentary tunes, while the gliding vocals call Northside to mind. Is this a Factory House sound we hear before us, or just the stamp of shared producer Ian Broudie? No matter, what's important is the radio-friendly subtlety that will catapult The Wendys on to Mark Goodier's turntable and into Charlatans fans' record collections. The sun will be shining on them soon.

The Wendys: fresh from the Factory farm

Ian White: We didn't move to Manchester but we're down there quite a lot visiting the Hac and the Factory offices. Just like New Order etc. didn't move to London, Factory didn't think we needed to move to Manchester. Phil, A&R, became our manager and he lived in a Manchester suburb so we were often there on tour . . . There was a real buzz and air of confidence around Manchester and it was a great time to be there. The only time we played with other Factory bands was the Happy Mondays at Revenge at Calton Studios just prior to signing, and those bands who we played with at the Cities in the Park festival at Heaton Park. We were very much peripheral to the Madchester scene and being truthful sort of expected a more independent Factory rather than a label who had an eye on the charts and daytime radio. Post-industrial, post-independent? It was still cool as fuck!

Tony (Wilson) was great. Such an inspiring figure but few at Factory would ever be asked to be guest speakers at a business school. For a while he seemed to either always be rolling a spliff or smoking one but also lucid and interesting to speak with or, as in most cases, listen to. Tony was very supportive and I believe if it wasn't for the financial issues they would have supported us for several years. He liked us as outsiders from the scene and we were pretty grounded and called him Howie, which he seemed to like. Tony and Factory gave us a feeling of freedom and the only thing he insisted on was that the 'Scottish drinking song' as he called it, 'Something's Wrong Somewhere', with the 'It's going down smooth, it's going down smooth' refrain, was to be the first track on the album. Factory had all the right attitude and history. Maybe we signed at the wrong time. We wouldn't have been ready but signing in '88 or early '89 would have been a better time for us I think. The financial woes were terminal but being on that label got us some great press, and Single of the Week in the *NME* is not to be sniffed at and was a landmark in our short full-time professional career. We were in the Top 10 of the indie chart at times and in all sold around fifty thousand units across the two singles, EP and album. We and others, like our Warner Chappell publisher, saw us as a fifty thousand sort of band. That suited us fine. Indie kids to the end.

Phil suggested Ian Broudie as producer. By then he had recorded the Sundays and Northside but for us it was the Bunnymen angle that interested us. Ian wanted to make sure we could work with each other before committing to an album.

He came to Edinburgh and booked two days at REL. The session was great. We got on really well with Ian and, although rushed, we got a decent version of 'More Than Enough' recorded, and a straight to two-track recording of the embryonic 'Sun's Going To Shine for Me Soon', which we would later record again and which got us Single of the Week in *NME*. 'More Than Enough' was pressed as a promo-only 12-inch and went to DJs around the country. It seemed to make sense at the time that it would be a bit arrogant but thinking back I don't know why we didn't re-record it as part of the album sessions. I guess none of us knew just how soon the Factory demise was to be... We recorded it as part of the album sessions, starting in a semi-rural old schoolhouse near Stockport before sacking off that studio for the famous and iconic Amazon Liverpool. At Amazon we finished recording and did all the mixes. Ian Broudie and Cenzo Townsend were the producer/engineer pairing and worked really well together. Cenzo is still a sought-after talent and is particularly well known as a mix engineer. We stayed in hotels with Cenzo during the sessions and got on pretty well. The first digs were a former (and probably shut down) old folks' home in Bramhall with bin bags on the mattresses, dust on the marmalade and butter, cat furballs everywhere and a landlady who told us she recycled the cling film in the dishwasher. We stayed two nights then on to a place in Poynton for several days. It was full of engineers getting shit ready for the first Gulf War. We then decanted to the Cherry Tree in Kirkby for a week, nearby to Amazon Studio.

Like for much of the indie scene, financial woes were about to take their toll on The Wendys.

Ian White: [The] cheque bounced, having spent £3,000 at Sound Control. Factory owed us £30,000 from the EastWest deal . . . we later found out it was allegedly taken in paper bags to Peter Gabriel's studio to keep the New Order album recordings going.

Jez was to produce our next album but after a couple of rehearsals and a bit of arrangement chat the label crashed so the project halted.

The huge independent music institutions that had been built up so successfully to genuinely compete with the mainstream music industry was rapidly imploding. It was shortly about to reach a crescendo.

Ripples throughout the industry: the Cartel and Fast Forward collapse

Sandy McLean: One of the things that we needed to address was dual distribution. And the two biggest labels, Mute and Factory, were putting their product through two separate companies – through us and Pinnacle distribution. So it made total sense for them to have two companies competing with one another trying to get their records into the shops. So after doing this for a few years, Richard Scott at Rough Trade realised this wasn't in our best interests. So he basically organised a meeting with Factory – Tony, and 4AD and Creation and some of the big ones, and just said, dual distribution is over. You got to come with us or you go with Pinnacle. And Tony Wilson basically said, 'Cheerio,' and off he went to Pinnacle. Creation came with us and 4AD came with us and Mute came with us but never did sign the contract, which came to bite us later. So that became sole distribution and we became the sole distributor. And that was part of the kind of growing-up process, the kind of maturing of the marketplace. But . . . I was really annoyed to lose Factory because I really liked the label. And I had a very small relationship with Tony Wilson on the phone, because he would phone up and plug his record or records. And he knew Bob Last and liked Bob Last as well. So he kind of had a soft spot for Fast and Fast Forward. And I was really disappointed to lose it. But I saw his point. But at the same time I realised we had a business to run and we couldn't just scratch out a living by living on crumbs, we had to actually make some hard decisions, and that was one of them.

What had made the independent record industry – the Cartel – a viable alternative to the mainstream now imploded spectacularly. The first casualty was Red Rhino at the end of 1988. Fast Forward limped on for most of 1989 but finally succumbed in early 1990, with, unimaginably, Rough Trade itself ceasing to exist a few months later. In a little over ten years, one of the most pioneering and successful forms of DIY would be no more and indie would never fully recover from it.

The trail of destruction was widespread. BMX Bandits, Jesse Garon, Rote Kapelle and The Vaselines would be heavily damaged and it is no surprise that, with the exception of BMX Bandits, nobody was able to carry on for much longer.

Independent music, as it was in the 1980s, was effectively over with the demise of the Cartel. Dance music required an entirely different operational structure, with a fast turnaround of white labels, and many of the majors once again swooped in, this time under the umbrella 'indie' imprints.

Sandy McLean: Well, it just got bigger and bigger and bigger. And we had to keep so many balls in the air basically when, you know, there's only so much space in those offices in 21 Alva Street and only so many staff you could fit in there. And things got more expensive. You know, all of a sudden you find you're doing videos, you're spending thousands of pounds on a video for the BMX Bandits that might be shown on *The Chart Show* for ten seconds. So you're doing that for umpteen different bands. You're chasing that or you're trying to spend money on remixes and things like that or you do stupid things like release a David Bellamy record. What really stopped Fast Forward was the fact that our landlords, Red Rhino, went bankrupt, and that invalidated our lease with the landlords, which I managed to hide for about six months. But eventually, when the landlords found out they basically just gave us our notice, and I couldn't keep all the balls in the air at that time. And I was also coming under pressure from the new boss at Rough Trade, Richard Powell.

Part of Rough Trade getting more professional was they hired outside people, they hired consultants to go headhunting people. And all of a sudden, the people they brought in were a Virgin boss and one was Pinnacle's boss. So obviously we had these two guys who weren't really our political shade running us and trying to turn this new thing into the old thing. And he (Richard Powell) just said you can't run a distribution company and be working for us selling stuff over the phone. So he basically did his best to get rid of me and nearly succeeded, but we got rid of him first. And things changed, you know. All of a sudden we're working from desks behind the house. The new guy at Rough Trade, George Kimpton Howe, he looked at the balance sheet and said, hang on, you've got six offices. You don't need six offices, shut them all down, and we'll do it all from London, and that had been predicted by Mr Red Rhino. He said at some point that will happen. Any accountant will look at these overheads and just draw a line through these. You don't need six warehouses. You don't need six offices. You'll do it in one. So we got called to Birmingham in 1990, all the regional offices got called to Birmingham, to a hotel. 'Oh God, here it goes.' And we were basically told you're all getting paid off. We all got a thousand pounds to go away. So that was it. That's basically what happened. We went back to our rooms, drank the minibar. The next day, went back up to Scotland and our friends went back to Bristol, York and Norwich, and Leamington Spa, and started winding the offices down.

Richard Scott (Rough Trade): The Cartel ended because the Rough Trade group fell apart. It had sort of decomposed, it blew up. In the year before it blew up the sales side sold £70 million worth of records. How could you cease to function with that kind of money coming through? But all senior management at Rough Trade had fallen apart or left. And it just blew to pieces, just like a Catherine wheel where the pin isn't bang in the middle of it. It just suddenly exploded. Just completely fell apart.

Brian Guthrie (Nightshift Records and Management): When Rough Trade went tits up, it was an absolute nightmare. Their north London warehouse became a free-for-all. You could go down there, vans would be turning up, boxes of stock and everything would be loaded up; God knows where they were going. There was a profligate amount of stealing going on but also for me, because they were doing my pricing and distribution by that stage, via Rough Trade's hub in London, a lot of my master tapes and original artworks went missing. Consequently I then faced a battle not only to keep the label afloat, but to prevent mass bootlegging. I mean, I've got versions of Lowlife albums that are bootlegs from Spain and Italy. At that time back in the seventies, eighties, nineties, there were no legitimate record labels licensing things from you properly in Europe, especially in Spain and Italy, so the bootlegs were pretty shabby reproductions of the UK albums. The sleeves were poorly printed, the records were horrendously, horribly made – they must have been pressing them in cheese. It was a bad time. At one point I was facing personal losses of over £60,000.

The ripples caused by the collapse of the infrastructure severely damaged The Vaselines, who were then on the verge of releasing their debut album, Dum-Dum.

Vaselines record *Dum-Dum* – and then split

Charles Kelly: I think we played a few tours of the UK with The Pastels during this time. I remember keeping my leather trousers and jacket on in bed in one hostel we stayed at as the walls and mattress were sprayed with arcs of junkie blood from someone hitting up! We had a good laugh on tour as we were not taking ourselves entirely seriously and we were certainly not careerists. I was always excited to play London though, places like the ULU. I used to drink far too much also, so those years can be very vague.

Eugene Kelly: I think for us, Frances and I were kind of clueless. We talked to 53rd & 3rd and they agreed to give us money for an LP. That was the first thing we recorded without Stephen in the studio. So we had to knuckle down and create more songs and because . . . it was a kind of part-time adventure, you know, we were both at uni and college, it was just being in the band and you tour on your holidays, so you weren't sitting writing songs every day, so we had to then sit down and write enough songs for an album and I think we kind of eventually got there but it took a while.

Frances McKee: I didn't have an air of confidence when I was younger. Had I gone on and been able just to bluff it but . . . in a moment the cracks would appear. That sort of stage fright or something was always sort of lurking in the back of my consciousness. To eradicate that we would drink buckets, so on stage we were just so drunk that it was impossible. We played a show. [Laughs] We got asked to support The Jesus and Mary Chain in Barrowland . . . this would sum us up . . . we hadn't rehearsed, of course, and this is when we had Charlie and James in the band as well. And we got on stage with the soundcheck and realised it was going to be rubbish so we went to the pub and got so drunk. Got on stage. No one was playing the same song. It was just madness. Got off stage. Stephen came backstage and he was, like, 'Guys, you've blown it! You've totally blown it!' We were just knotted with laughter. We couldn't stop laughing because it was an absolute riot. So we didn't take it seriously. Just as well, because there's always that kind of this could just go any way. And it usually did.

Charles Kelly: Playing gigs was a very brief experience as we only used to play on average for twenty to twenty-five minutes. We never really got a bad reception apart from one time we supported JAMC at the Barrowland but we were all half pished anyway and after various catcalls and someone chucking a can of beer at Eugene I gobbed on the audience . . . while in Rome and all that. Norman used to drive us on tour. I have a memory of him driving us round in circles beside Buckingham Palace trying to figure out how to get to our destination and some back-seat driver giving him a hard time while the rest of us shouted abuse to Liz and co. out the window of the van.

Eugene Kelly: No, we didn't think like *Dum-Dum* was going to be our defining statement about The Vaselines. It was a bit of a scramble just to get songs, there wasn't an over-arching concept, it was like we just want to get some songs and make a decent rock record. And it was kind of made up as we went along in the studio, that was . . . going to the studio, record and see what happens and hopefully come out the other side with something that everybody's happy with. So it was kind of, it's good – I mean that's the way I've always worked since then, just kind of make it up as you go along and not really spend a lot of time planning stuff and demoing stuff 'cause it takes the life out of it. Just keep it exciting, keep it spontaneous.

Frances McKee: We really thought long and hard about it. [Laughs] We didn't. We were writing lyrics and . . . you know, 'we need lyrics for this song' . . . I think, ahh . . . 'Love Craft' was one where we just . . . don't tell anyone, but we can't actually remember the lyrics. So any time we play we have to have the lyrics in front of us because they don't make sense . . . so because we both sing all the way through we have to make sure we do the same thing. But no, it was . . . again we didn't know what was going to happen. We had no idea and Jamie was really good at honing our talent, whatever that was, just really nudging us in the right direction.

The songs were new. We never gigged them. And when the album came out we eventually split up so consequently we never played them live.

Charles Kelly: The main memory I have is during the recording of 'No Hope', that the studio was so small there was no space to stretch out anywhere. I had to lay down on the ground in the recording booth as I had the worst hangover ever and Frances standing over my head singing the words: 'Better under the table than under the ground/And I can't give it up.' Life imitating art

Eugene told me that him and Frances were splitting up and that was the end of the band. I felt sad, for my brother and Frances, as well as not being able to play gigs any more. I had no intentions of joining any other bands as I never classed myself as a musician, more a music fan. I've never been overly ambitious and realised everything has a lifespan. I went along for the ride on the coat-tails of the more talented people and had a great time.

Eugene Kelly: [*Dum-Dum*] was recorded 1988/89, and then 53rd & 3rd and the distribution company went bankrupt so there was no money for a release. So it sat on the shelf for quite a while and Rough Trade in London agreed to finance the release of it so that's when it came out – I mean, about a year or so later. And by that point the band had splintered and we'd started drifting apart, Frances and I, so the band was over by the time the record came out and we didn't kind of – as we've said in the press releases – like split up, that was just us kind of dramatising it a bit. It was that we, the band, had drifted apart and the kind of, the spirit had gone out of it. So it was good to have the record out but it felt a bit of a failure as well . . . it was good to have a physical copy of your record and your pictures on it . . . the buzz had died and the band was over so we just kind of . . . [Long pause] It was out and we didn't tour or play any shows really for a while after that.

Dum-Dum *limped out in December 1989 with no label to promote it and a distribution company that had essentially vaporised. But the foundations it laid became a template for many bands who followed in the new decade.*

John Robb summed up much of the animosity revolving around the twee jangle-pop of the second half of eighties indie.

John Robb (*Sounds***, 11 August 1990):** 'We got labelled with the post-anorak tag,' notes Raymond [McGinley, of Teenage Fanclub]. 'The so-called dirty movement, when everybody got into the "sex thing" . . . Like it was amateur sex and I'm not into that.'

'The whole thing was a reaction against people calling it anorak music,' adds Norman [Blake]. 'Which was a joke anyway, it was only people in places like Bristol that took it seriously.'

The much maligned 'anorak' era, which eventually became the stereotype of indie music, all started because of Stephen

Pastel's tongue-in-cheek 'rak. The piss-taking cynics on the Glasgow scene quickly picked up the garment and the joke soon got out of hand.

The subsequent 'dirty' movement, hosted by The Vaselines' tongue-in-cheek pop sleaze, was a reaction against the 7-inch versus 12-inch crap that most of the airheaded fanzines of the time were involved in.

BMX Bandits album, *C86*

The collapse of Fast Forward and the Cartel had severely affected the BMX Bandits' releases too.

The first album made available to the public was a live offering, Totally Groovy Live Experience!, which was recorded for Fast Forward but instead came out on Avalanche Records, to Duglas and co.'s great surprise. Their studio debut was also a casualty, released on their own imprint, Click, in the new year. It was archly named C86, the same title as the NME *tape release from three years earlier. The line-up on this album was Duglas T. Stewart, Joe McAlinden, Francis Macdonald, Gordon Keen and Norman Blake, who had temporarily rejoined the band after The Boy Hairdressers dissolved.*

Norman Blake: Me and Duglas were friends, we hung out all the time, we were still living in the same place when we weren't recording or playing. We'd be watching whatever movies . . . we were friends without the music. So I suppose I was around.

At the time we'd written quite a few songs together, myself

and Duglas, for the (BMX Bandits). I think at that time Sean had become quite busy with The Soup Dragons, they had some success and so just through hanging out in Bellshill in our bedrooms, we ended up writing some songs together. And those . . . ended up on the *C86* record.

Duglas T. Stewart: The first BMX Bandits album was called *C86* because again it was just me kind of sticking up two fingers to who I saw being the enemy, and the *NME* were part of that. It was a bit like, 'Well, you don't want us to be on your *C86*, well we'll have our own one, and we'll do all of the tracks.' So it was, yeah, it was just like a little bit of a kind of cheeky joke, rather than making it like 'Oh yeah, we were . . .' almost a thing that would beat us down, 'We were one of the bands that weren't selected to be on this amazing thing.' We kind of turned it round to be in our heads a kind of positive funny thing, you know. A little bit like, 'What *C86* do you prefer? That tape or our one?' So, again, that was being a bit mischievous. I remember when I bumped into people like Stephen and I told them, 'Oh yeah, we've got our first album out and we've decided we're going to call it *C86*,' he'd be like, 'Ohhhh, that's just . . . you know, that's just going to annoy or confuse like these people that don't like you even more. They're going to like really not like you, or kinda go . . . are you trying to make a fool of us?' But we are, we are trying to do that, we do want to annoy them, you know, and we want to please the people who care about us and like us. So it amused us so we decided to do it.

Joe McAlinden: In the BMX Bandits there was a natural leader in Duglas. He had a vision that, I wouldn't say we all followed, but he was happy to take in all these other influences. Into a big melting pot. And it just seemed to come out that way. We would try stuff, and if it was good, it was good. If it wasn't, it was a laugh, it was funny, or we moved on to the next thing.

Gordon Keen (Guitar, BMX Bandits): I became good friends with Norman and he called me to ask if I'd be interested in playing with the BMX Bandits in London at a show they were doing with, I think, The Vaselines, The Pastels. This was on a Wednesday I think and the show was a few days later, so it was a pretty steep learning curve. Musically BMX Bandits songs can be quite challenging. The band where I was lucky enough to learn with, and from some really great musicians.

The album release was hugely damaged by the collapse of the Cartel and it affected Duglas's plans for future releases, not just for BMX Bandits.

Duglas T. Stewart: *C86* was never going to be for 53rd & 3rd, it was gone by then. The original idea was I would get a loan and release the BMX Bandits and Teenage Fanclub's debut albums. The two albums were recorded back to back in the same studio. There was a short time when 'Right Across the Street' was considered for *A Catholic Education* [the first Teenage Fanclub album]. When the Cartel went down, like a lot of people I was in a bad situation. I was a few thousand pounds in debt but couldn't get royalties due or any of my remaining stock. Teenage Fanclub thankfully didn't get caught up in the mess as they quickly got proper labels interested in releasing their album. I was their friend but didn't know anything about releasing or promoting records. I was pleased for them . . . Losing all that money, being in debt and having all of these copies of our album just disappear was one of the big factors to me being put on antidepressants for the first time. Those are the tablets mentioned in 'Serious Drugs'. So if the Cartel hadn't gone under and fucked me up I would never have written 'Serious Drugs'. So the end result was a good thing for me overall.

CHAPTER 13
1990-94

A new guitar sound for Glasgow

The birth of Teenage Fanclub

Many of Scotland's pivotal bands had fizzled out by the start of the decade. The Edinburgh scene, which had been especially vibrant only four years earlier, was now almost non-existent. But on the west coast, from the ashes of The Boy Hairdressers (who had made only one single, 'Golden Shower', obviously on 53rd & 3rd) emerged a band that was to become an international influence and would themselves become bona fide (nearly) teenage superstars. This was Teenage Fanclub, a band that both encapsulated what had gone before but also became the future. At the time of writing, they had just released an album, Nothing Lasts Forever, almost thirty-five years after their conception.

Norman Blake: We [The Boy Hairdressers] just ran out of steam really. But myself and Raymond kept working together, we bought a little four-track and so some of the newer songs that we'd been writing became embryonic Teenage Fanclub songs. And from there the band sort of transitioned. Boy Hairdressers sort of dissolved but me and Raymond were left and that transitioned into Teenage Fanclub.

Francis Macdonald: I think Norman and Raymond had found in each other kind of a good balance and . . . people that want to work together and collaborate. And so they began doing four-track demos with a drum machine. And Norman had said we're going to make this record, would you drum on it, you know, as he does, 'Would you . . . that'd be great . . .' 'Okay.' So I was on board to do the drumming.

Norman Blake: Yeah, with the first Fanclub record it was . . . well like I say the band started as me and Raymond and then we asked Francis, who played in The Boy Hairdressers, to play in the band. And then we met Gerry, Gerry Love, just again through . . . Glasgow's a small city in that way, so you get to know people. And I think we met at a show one night and asked him to play bass there and then and to come and join the band. Which he did. But at that point the songs had pretty much been written for that record so he came along and the four of us recorded that, those songs.

Gerard Love (Bass, Teenage Fanclub): I'd seen Boy Hairdressers play. Norman's quite an engaging guy so he's not a difficult person to get to know but I didn't really know them so much socially before I was asked. I knew Duglas a little through Joe and Jim. I knew people they knew but . . . the first time I probably remember having a conversation with Norman he was asking me would I fancy joining him and Raymond and it was like of course, you know . . . but, yeah, there was not really much discussion because it was the aftermath of The Boy Hairdressers.

Francis Macdonald: I knew Gerry because Gerry briefly played in the band with Joe, The Groovy Little Numbers, so I met him through that. But I remember Gerry saying to me, 'Oh, Norman's just asked me to play in his band.' And Gerry had liked The Boy Hairdressers, I think he'd bought the single. So I was like, all right, great, you know, so that was going to be Teenage Fanclub mark 1, I suppose, Norman, Raymond, Gerry Love and me, but I did from the outset say, 'Well, I'll play on the record but I can't tour 'cause I'm going back to uni.' And what was interesting was Norman and Raymond, they weren't saying we're going to make demos, they were saying we're going to make an album, which was quite interesting. It was quite a confident approach.

David Barker (Paperhouse Records): Stephen Pastel told me about them. He said my pal Norman has a new group, they're really great, so I said get him to send me a tape . . . and he did. I thought it was tremendous. Norman had actually played bass for The Pastels on some European gigs in '87 or '88. Their bass player Martin Hayward couldn't get time off work, so Norman deputised. Gerard Cosloy, who had been at Homestead in the US, had a new label called Matador and wanted to release them there. They had a gig in Glasgow – it was a John Peel night at the uni – so I booked a flight up. Then Norman called to say they had a gig in London the night before at the Bull and Gate in Kentish Town, so I met them there and went to Glasgow the next day. How could I resist a group that announced themselves 'We're Teenage Fanclub and we're Glasgow's top singers by the way'?

Gerard Love: Three-quarters of the first Teenage Fanclub record is songs that The Boy Hairdressers were doing, so it wasn't as if it was a brand new thing. It was like, it was the culmination of work in progress.

Francis Macdonald: I didn't even go back to the sessions to hang and share my twopence-worth. I kind of felt, 'I played my drums and I'll not be an extra cook in the kitchen.' That was definitely my mind at the time, you know. And so then they needed a drummer and I don't know how they got hooked up with Brendan O'Hare. I think when Brendan was on board and Norman was now not singing falsetto but they hadn't quite made the leap into the full-on distortion pedals sound of most of *Catholic Education*, well not most of it, of 'Everything Flows', that's the point I'm trying to make. We did a version of 'Everything Flows' which was maybe just the guitars were a bit cleaner and it wasn't quite the thing that it then became. And they decided to remix some of the record and re-record some of the tracks. Which was the right thing to do, 'cause they came back with 'Everything Flows', which all of a sudden sounded really exciting and had that, you know, Raymond's solo on it and that became . . . So, actually, you can see the record, I'm on seven tracks, Brendan's on four. But those four point the way to the *Bandwagonesque* sound and going forward.

Gerard Love: The first record was comprised of two different groups. The first group was Norman, Raymond, myself and Francis Macdonald, who was at that time in BMX Bandits.

David Barker: I think I suggested 'Everything Flows' as a lead-in 45 in advance of the LP. It got an instant reaction in the press and a lot of gigs for them. Matador arranged for them to come to New York to play at CBGBs as part of the New Music Seminar. July 1990, I think. I went over with Laurence Bell (later founder of Domino records) who had another label at Fire, Roughneck, plus a couple other Fire people, Juliet Howles and Dave Bedford. I introduced the band to Don Fleming, who I'd become friends with the previous year. Don had been in Half Japanese and B.A.L.L. and they loved them so were keen to meet him. By some lucky chance, Wharton Tiers' Fun City Studio was free for a couple of nights and 'God Knows It's True' was cut there with Don. Fun City was where Sonic Youth, Dinosaur Jr., Pussy Galore had worked and Teenage Fanclub were big fans of all that stuff.

Raymond McGinley: People from the *NME* would have been in New York at the time we played, and they took notice of us playing at CBGBs with Urge Overkill and Superchunk at the Matador Records night and then reported on that back in the *NME*. So immediately it made us look more exotic. Their seeing us doing something somewhere else worked quite well. At that point we had no sense of careerism, we were just enjoying the fact that we were doing stuff and enjoying, or not enjoying, the detail of whatever we were doing that day. We had no sense of, oh yeah, we need to do this, we need to do that. We'd no idea. Maybe people recognised the lack of desperation in us, and liked it.

A NEW GUITAR SOUND FOR GLASGOW

Teenage Fanclub's momentum was incredible. In little over a few months they had released one of the greatest Scottish singles of all time 'Everything Flows', an album, A Catholic Education, *two further singles for Paperhouse and a US single for Matador. Due to the nature of its construction, the album was understandably patchwork, but the singles paved the way for a modern, forward-looking sound that perfectly chimed with the underground sounds of America that would shortly be responsible for remaking the US mainstream. Nirvana were on their way and Teenage Fanclub were their Caledonian equals.*

Norman Blake (speaking to Keith Cameron in *Sounds***, 3 November 1990):** I think what I did in the past was okay! I'm not embarrassed about The Boy Hairdressers, I liked it at the time and still think it was a bit different from what most people were doing. Okay, it was really slated, but that doesn't bother me. Actually, a lot of Teenage Fanclub songs were Boy Hairdressers songs that just didn't happen. Me and Raymond worked them out and then the band fell apart.

[So where's the missing link?]

Erm, I'm not sure, maybe we just sat around in Glasgow for two years. We were trying to open a studio at one point, me and Raymond, but we couldn't get the money together. So we had to wait.

Y'know, I really enjoyed the scene. It all began as a reaction to bands like Simple Minds and their terrible art rock thing and I think it's a bit of a shame that people are so down on the whole anorak thing – there was nothing wrong with it! People are so against the whole cutie thing, but I think it was okay. I mean, take the BMX Bandits, Duglas is pretty camp but it was more campy than wimpy.

Bob Stanley (*Melody Maker,* June 1990): I saw Teenage Fanclub a couple of months back. They played seven songs of loud, sloppy Beatles-meet-Dinosaur pop – the vocals were inaudible, the sound was dirty, but the impression was that, given a sympathetic soundman and few less pints of ale, the fab pop choons would shine through.

The Soup Dragons hit the big time

The summer of 1990 held a huge surprise for the Glasgow independent scene. After their near continuous excellent press coverage and climb up the musical ladder, the failure of The Soup Dragons' Sire period was sore. The previous year's experiments with drum machines and samplers for 'Mother Universe' chimed perfectly with the rise of the indie-dance crossover. Nobody, however, could have dreamed that the reborn band would soon reach the upper reaches of the pop charts. This is the bittersweet story of the album Lovegod *and the single 'I'm Free'.*

Sean Dickson: We were actually the first band ever to get coined it – indie-dance – which was just, it's complete bollocks, it's just journalistic wank like everything else. And they loved it because they gave the name and they'd like invented this thing. What they didn't like with The Soup Dragons was that out of that whole scene we had the biggest hit record with 'I'm Free', so they had nothing to do with that. They didn't, weeks up to 'I'm

Free' come out, go like 'Oh my God, this is the best record ever made.' Suddenly this band who, you know, used to sell X amount of records went straight into the Top 5 in the UK and it wasn't off the back of them. So of course when that happens that's when the knives come out. And they didn't understand . . . you know, and the other thing as well, which I really believe in, was we were up in Glasgow. We were asked to move to London millions of times, which I just refused point blank . . . funnily enough I live here now, back then I was like 'I'm not living in London.' So we didn't hang about with the journalists, we didn't hang about in the right clubs, so people didn't know us as people, you know. I think they thought we were maybe being opportunists. Which I kind of understand in a way, you know?

Jim McCulloch: Primal Scream had done it as well. They went from kinda jingly jangly to this dance crossover thing as well. People always said that The Soup Dragons jumped on this indie dance bandwagon thing but we'd been putting out remix stuff for a while – 'Can't Take No More' had remix stuff, you know, and that was just . . . we were just kind of following where the music was taking us basically.

Sean Dickson: So we had 'Mother Universe' come out (in 1989) and that record was really applauded within the dance culture scene at that time and a lot of DJs were playing it and all this. We were recording *Lovegod* off the back of that and one day, about three or four o'clock in the morning after being out somewhere, off my face, I came home and I saw The Rolling Stones *Live at Hyde Park* on the TV. I'd never seen it before. And the next morning we were rehearsing . . . I said to Jim our guitarist,

'Did you see that song "I'm Free" by the Stones?' And he was like, 'Yeah, yeah,' and I was like, 'I've never heard that song before,' and he goes, 'It's some obscure B-side or something.' I go 'great song', and we literally just started jamming it. And all I could remember was 'I'm Free, do what I want any old time', and if you actually listen to the version of The Soup Dragons' 'I'm Free', half the lyrics are wrong because I didn't have the lyrics and I didn't, we didn't actually go back to the movie to study it, we just jammed the version of 'I'm Free'. And then a few days later we were in the studio, you know, recording and we decided to do 'I'm Free'. And how we decided to do it was completely unlike any record we've ever made at that time. We were just like 'Let's put eight minutes of a drum groove down and invent a record on top.'

Sushil came up with the bass line, which is nothing like 'I'm Free' of the Stones, and we just said, 'Right, let's make this section the kind of Jimi Hendrix guitar section,' which is there 'cause the actual 12-inch 'I'm Free' is how it was recorded, eight and a half minutes. The version on the LP was cut down. And then it was like 'Let's get a gospel choir' and we actually looked up *Yellow Pages* for a gospel choir and found one in London. We phoned them up and the next day thirty-five people came and sang 'I'm Free'. We just made it up as it went over the next few days. And one of my favourite records at the time was S'Express, the 'Theme from S'Express', and I asked the engineer if he would mix the track down and he came a few days later and we mixed the track.

Sushil Dade: To be honest I think it was a collaborative effort. My musical fingers were not quite on their best behaviour during that session so what you hear is me playing on the chorus and part synth/keys (clavinet) doubled up on the verses. Man and machine in perfect harmony. I'm sure Sean probably whistled a primitive verse of the line and I fleshed things out from there.

Sean Dickson: And then when we finished it we played it to the record label and the girl from the record label started crying as she heard it, 'cause she just thought it was like the most amazing record she'd ever heard. And that's made us all kind of sit there and go 'Shit, what have we just done?' And we released it about a month later, it was really just . . . actually it was one of the quickest turnovers we've ever had on a record. We released it and it was in the Top 40 for eighteen weeks; it came out and it was basically the whole summer of 1990, that record stayed in the Top 40, it just . . . it would go up and then it would go back down and then it would get to number five. The highest it got to was number five and we done *Top of the Pops* like umpteen times, it was all completely bizarre. And then as you said, you know, the press and like the *NME* and *Melody Maker* and *Sounds*, *Sounds* not so much, it was more the *NME*, kind of, 'cause we were still the little *C86* band, you know, and they turned against us.

Sushil Dade: It was incredible to be on the iconic show as so many bands we loved had been on the show before and we'd watched them on our TVs at home. Buzzcocks, Orange Juice, Strawberry Switchblade, etc. It changed things as the band got so much exposure through it and opened up other doors, I guess. Never did *Crackerjack* but got on *Top of the Pops*. We were happy with that.

Jim McCulloch: We had our eye on America by this point. And because we were looking to go over there, we had never been to the States before. And we were desperate to get over. So we went. So we had signed with another company by this point, Mercury, they were quite keen to get us over. And so we decamped. And after 'I'm Free' it kind of went downhill for us in the UK.

Sean Dickson: When you have such a big hit record you enter a world which is completely bizarre. You know, you do things like TV-am and things which, like, you know, I mean we ended up getting banned from TV-am basically because our manager forgot to tell us we were on TV-am, so we went out clubbing the night before and it was about five o'clock in the morning when we found out we were on TV-am so you can imagine what state we were in. And we were taken to TV-am and nobody would come with me, you know. I was like 'Somebody come with me,' so our drummer came, Paul, and it was, it was entertaining.

It was me and Lorraine Kelly. Lorraine wasn't happy. 'Oh you're from Bellshill? I'm from East Kilbride.' And I'd be sitting there sitting there shrugging. I think I shrugged my shoulders through this whole five-minute interview, 'cause our LP had come out that day. And I remember the record company, 'cause we . . . at that point in time we were like on Big Life, which was owned by Polygram, which these days is Universal. And there was all this pressure from our manager on me about 'Remember that you've got to say your LP's out today,' 'cause there's all that stuff you start to learn, it's like you're given space when she goes 'What are you doing next?' You're supposed to say, 'Well, my LP's out today, The Soup Dragons, *Lovegod*, go and buy it right now.' What did I say? I said, 'I don't know.' So in front of like eighty million people or something on TV-am, our biggest plug, I turn around and go 'I don't know'. And it all came crashing down ... then there was this quote that I supposedly said that I've always had a dance element to our music. Which I never ever said that quote but even when I said I didn't say it I was called a liar. So you couldn't win.

'I'm Free' reached the UK Top 5. Despite arranging the track, which forms the basis of almost all subsequent versions, The Soup Dragons received no royalties for it. The album, Lovegod, *received mixed reviews but has been reappraised over the years and is now regarded as a classic of the genre.*

The Vaselines support Nirvana

Kurt Cobain was famously a fan of The Vaselines, who briefly reformed to support Nirvana at Edinburgh's Calton Studios in October 1990.

Keith Cameron, journalist and friend of Andrew Tully, had been documenting the rise of Nirvana from their earliest days.

Keith Cameron (*Sounds*, October 1990): If any of the US underground bands are likely to break through into the mainstream, then it's got to be Nirvana. Currently being courted by eight major labels, they'll probably take the money and flee their Sub Pop nest but they'll be taking their dignity and powerful pop with them.

Eugene Kelly: Yeah, well, Stephen Pastel had sent copies of our first Vaselines EP to Calvin Johnson at K Records in Olympia, and he would play it on his radio show. And I think at that point, Kurt was living in Olympia. So, he'd heard and got interested in the band and played it to Kris and Kris liked it. I think they were fans of us way before, from the very beginning. It's only when they started making, like, ripples over here that we found out about them and found out they were fans of us and played our songs in their set. And eventually we met when they played in Edinburgh at the Calton Studios. I think it was just when 'Sliver' was released, maybe before that, so it was definitely before *Nevermind*. And we got a phone call from their agent asking us to support them and the band had split about a year before but I was interested in meeting them and getting out of Glasgow for the night.

Frances McKee: It didn't have an impact on me because I was a school teacher and . . . I keep hearing on the radio all this early nineties house music, but that's what I was into, I wasn't into guitar music. I sold my guitar. I never really wanted to listen to guitar music. I was into beats, you know, and parties, didn't want to go there. So Eugene phoned me and said, 'Do you want to play this show, there's a band called Nirvana who seem to be playing one of our songs,' and . . . I thought about it for five minutes and I thought why not.

Charles Kelly: Eugene contacted me to say that a group called Nirvana had done a couple of cover versions of Vaselines songs. This might have been a year or more before Kurt contacted someone to get a hold of Eugene to ask us to support them in

Edinburgh. We had a hastily organised rehearsal in James's flat. I had no drums or sticks so I improvised by getting two bamboo sticks and sellotaping two nut bolts to either end and playing on a shoe box . . . *Vision On* eat your heart out . . .

Eugene Kelly: We rehearsed in Frances's front room on acoustic guitars and then borrowed all Teenage Fanclub's guitars, electric guitars and amps, took a van through to Edinburgh and met them and played with them and it was a great night, especially to see Nirvana in a small venue way before the rest of the world was interested in them. It's pretty amazing.

Frances McKee: We did it, but we didn't rehearse as usual. And we went along . . . my sister, my younger sister, and she had only gone to raves and we went to this venue in Edinburgh and she says, 'What is everybody doing?' I said, 'They're standing about having a pint.' 'Why?' [Laughs] Just a whole kind of different experience. So we said we're going to listen to the music soon. 'Why isn't anyone dancing?' Well, we don't really dance. They just stand and hold their pints and listen. So we were just laughing at that. So I'd never heard Nirvana and never seen them . . .

Charles Kelly: When we arrived I was, as usual, very hungover and jittery and noticed this guy clocking us when we were setting up for the soundcheck, a short guy with short straggly bleached hair with roots showing and eyeliner. I said to Eugene, 'Who's that guy that keeps looking over here?' He said, 'That's the singer from Nirvana.'

Frances McKee: But . . . backstage it was just . . . I was . . . I grabbed Eugene and said, 'You need to go over these songs with me because I haven't a clue how to play them.' And we're sitting there trying to play, I can't remember what song, but Kurt came by and I thought, 'He's going to think we're idiots. [Laughs] We can't play our music. This is terrible!' I was a bit embarrassed about it all. Little known to me at the time he was in awe of us. It seems bizarre. He was quite quiet until of course the end of the night and everyone got quite tipsy.

Andrew Tully: I went to the first Calton Studios gig more out of curiosity. Intrigued by The Vaselines appearing and they were good friends of Jamie Watson's. I was curious about Sub Pop at the time, mainly due to the fact that my pal from university, Keith Cameron, was extolling the label's virtues at the *NME*. Also The Cateran, who we had belatedly befriended – a bit too rock'n'roll initially for us indie-pop kids – were constantly touring with the likes of Tad, Dwarves and these upstarts Nirvana. Mudhoney were the Sub Pop band at the time, Nirvana seemed like enjoyable also-rans to file alongside Tad, etc.

Frances McKee: My sister and I were talking to Kris and said, 'You remind us of someone, who is it? Who is it? Oh my God you look like Chevy Chase!' [Laughs] So he didn't take it very well . . . the night ended really on a high, but Nirvana weren't very well known there . . . Nobody would have known it was going to go that way.

Norman Blake: I think that one of the biggest influences on Nirvana was Eugene. I was there the night that Eugene met Kurt Cobain for the first time and Nirvana had asked The Vaselines to reform and come and play with them in Edinburgh. And this was before their success, you know. But I remember we get to the venue and we, I think we meet Kris and he . . . Eugene introduces himself and he [Kris] says, 'Oh, Kurt's upstairs, he really wants to meet you.' And so we go into the dressing room and Kurt, it was when he was wearing the really heavy eyeliner, and I remember Kurt Cobain saying, 'Oh, Eugene Kelly, I can't believe I'm meeting Eugene Kelly, I'm such a big fan,' and he really was, you could tell that he was, you know, kind of blown away by meeting Eugene.

Charles Kelly: During our short performance I noticed Kurt again at the front of the smallish crowd filming us with a camcorder . . . I often wonder what happened to that recording . . . after the show he gave us Nirvana T-shirts, the black-and-white ones with the circle of hell on the front and the crack smoking (on the back).

Norman Blake: And of course Eugene took it all in his stride. And I think . . . you know, if you think The Vaselines were a very melodic band, great songs, really great songs, we recently . . . myself and Duglas, toured in Japan with Eugene and we played a lot, playing the songs acoustically and they work as well in that context because they're great songs. So I think if anyone was an influence on Nirvana becoming a more melodic band it would've been Eugene. And Frances, of course.

Eugene joins BMX Bandits and they record their second album, *Star Wars*

Fresh from the excitement of the Nirvana gig, Eugene found himself without a band.

Eugene Kelly: Yeah it was quite depressing, you know, just not making music, not having, you know, lots of people round you who it was fun to be with and travel and watching your friends getting on, being a bit more successful. And I was working in a pub in Duke Street up the east end and I was on my break and I walked by a TV shop with a wall of TVs and it was The Soup Dragons performing 'I'm Free', like, sort of their big hit single, so it felt kind of, you know, everybody else had taken a step up and I had just regressed back into the bedroom.

Duglas T. Stewart: Eugene was in BMX Bandits just before we joined Creation. We were making the album *Star Wars* and The Vaselines had split up and I think Eugene was feeling at a little bit of a loose end. And I became pretty good friends with Eugene . . . and . . . yeah, I was like I'd like Eugene to be in the group, I think it would be a lot of fun, and it was a lot of fun. Norman was less able to play with us on a regular basis, 'cause Teenage Fanclub were really happening, and Sean had left a few years before to concentrate on The Soup Dragons. And yeah, he [Eugene] brought a new element of humour and nonsense and mischief into the mix. A kind of irreverence.

A NEW GUITAR SOUND FOR GLASGOW

Gordon Keen: Before Norman asked me to join the Bandits he'd told me that Primal Scream were looking for a guitarist and encouraged me to audition. I never did, and felt that I wasn't cool-for-school enough to go along!

Eugene Kelly: I think I'd known Duglas through all those years from the early eighties onwards and he knew I wasn't doing much and got me in the band to replace Norman, who'd left, and I toured with them for, I mean, a year or two years. I can't remember how long but it was good fun . . . I mean, the Bandits were the best band to be in just for sheer enjoyment and laughter and we got to travel to places that I'd never been before. I always thought it unlikely to get to a place like Norway or Japan . . . or England. BMX Bandits, when I was in them . . . it was like what it was like to be in The Goons or Monty Python, it was just silly and great fun.

Gordon Keen: We recorded *Star Wars* at Riverside Studios. It was a wonderfully collaborative album in terms of the songwriting and notable in that Eugene Kelly joined the band at this time. I'd broken up with my then girlfriend just before we started recording, which led to me writing 'Life Goes On'. Duglas then finished writing it with me and Joe writing the great sax solo at the end. The song 'Disguise' had Eugene and me playing alternating guitar solos together for the first time, and it was this song where I think Eugene heard something in us playing together, and towards the end of the sessions he asked me to form Captain America with him.

Eugene Kelly: It was great, I mean it was . . . but I had to leave because I was starting Captain America and that had to be, that was starting to be more like the main thing that was going to keep me busy.

Francis Macdonald: I was in Japan with BMX Bandits in the Gordon, Eugene line-up, and we were doing a soundcheck or Eugene was going to play a song maybe in the BMX Bandits set or . . . it's vague . . . but I just remember drumming and I remember Gordon and Eugene exchanging a look and so then I was asked to play on the record they were making and I did the drums I think over a weekend.

Duglas T. Stewart: And while he was in the BMX Bandits he (Eugene) hooked up with Gordon Keen, who was one of the BMX Bandits guitarists, and decided, do you know what, I really should have my own group again, and he started a group called Captain America, which became Eugenius and he ended up, like, you know, doing pretty well with that. But I think, yeah, being in the BMX Bandits for a little while encouraged him not to, not to quit, you know, to continue and do his own thing again. And of course then Eugenius have a major American deal and Gordon ends up leaving the band as well to go there. But that's always been a kind of story of BMX Bandits, like kind of people drifting through the line-up and staying for a while and then moving on and doing something else. And then sometimes returning many years later, you know. Or Norman's appeared on every BMX Bandits record or every BMX Bandits album since he's left the band. He may have left the band officially but he still occasionally will pop up at shows and pop in the records.

Star Wars was widely well received and played a large part in the next stage of BMX Bandits' career.

Captain America

Captain America, Eugene's band after The Vaselines, had a far more US underground sound; but it should be said that this influence was in part due to The Vaselines' influence on the US underground scene itself. It had come full circle. On this side of the Atlantic, the new band brought their own unique touch. It may be a controversial view but I always preferred Captain America to The Vaselines, with their power-crunching guitars, heavy drums and well-crafted songs.

Eugene Kelly: I think we chose the name just because I like *Captain America* comics. I'd always liked the name and I've never been very good at thinking of band names . . . I think at that point I was watching our friends be in Teenage Fanclub and I was excited to see them perform and I went to quite a lot of their early shows and I think that was a big, kind of, inspiration for Captain America. You can even hear it in the music, we tried to sound like them and even the first couple of shows we had Brendan on drums. So it was just like 'I love that band' and I kind of . . . that's what I want to do and it was quite derivative but if you're a songwriter you just want to write songs and you want to play them so the songs I was writing at that point were quite influenced by Teenage Fanclub. And the same things that they were influenced by, like Big Star, because that's . . . we all kind of swapped music and we all kind of had similar interests and influences. So it was just like 'Let's do something and let's get out of the pub and get on the road.'

Gordon Keen (Guitar, Captain America): The initial line-up was Eugene, myself, James Seenan on bass (from The Vaselines) and Brendan O'Hare (Teenage Fanclub) on drums. Frank Macdonald (Teenage Fanclub, The Pastels, etc. etc. etc. etc.) took over from Brendan after a while. Andy Bollen joined on drums after Frank Macdonald. I don't really recall specific influences at the time. Velvet Underground, Neil Young, Dinosaur Jr., all kinds of west coast psychedelia was what I was listening to, but from my days in the Bandits (which I was still in at the start of Captain America) we listened to such a range of music that all kinds of stuff seeped in, I think.

David Barker: I remember seeing Eugene Kelly in the bar at King Tuts and saying if you get a new group going I'm up for it. I loved The Vaselines. This was maybe late 1990 or early '91. Captain America played in London with Mudhoney in early 1991 and Brendan O'Hare was helping out on drums. Must have been there I talked to Eugene seriously about doing something.

Gordon Keen: Dave Barker had Paperhouse, which was one of a small collection of labels under Fire Records at the time . . . It was a bit of a whirlwind, as Dave had signed us after our first show. I also met my (future) wife Yuka and mother of our daughter Misa at this time, so life had suddenly changed for me in every respect. It was quite overwhelming at times, plus we were drinking and partying quite a bit, so it's also partially hazy!

A NEW GUITAR SOUND FOR GLASGOW

Eugene Kelly: First Captain America record, 'Wow', was just a, I think it was just a 12-inch. I seem to have just released 12-inches and hardly any 7-inches and . . . I don't remember much about it, I mean it was just kind of a recording, we'd just signed to Fire (Paperhouse) Records, which, I mean Teenage Fanclub had been on briefly and . . . 'cause they seemed to be interested in what was going on in Glasgow and they were scooping up everybody that was here. And I think it just felt good to get a record out and be able to perform live again. I don't remember much about it . . . vague, vague, a lot of that time was spent on alcohol.

Gordon Keen: We recorded with Jamie Watson at Chamber Studios in Edinburgh. Eugene wanted to record there as he'd recorded The Vaselines with Jamie . . . I had no expectations really. We were getting a lot of attention suddenly but there was no plan, it's not how we rolled. We were getting to put out a record on a London label, that in itself felt like the achievement.

Eugene Kelly: When you think you're never going to really reach any great height, you don't think anybody's going to hear about you so you think you can get away with calling your band something that's, you know, that is somebody else's trademark and copyright. So, I mean, that was a big mistake

A double whammy of legal woes befell the band. The first was, bizarrely, clothes chain C&A taking issue with the homage to their logo, as used on Captain America records. The second, more serious, issue was Marvel sending a cease and desist letter to the band and demanding they change their name.

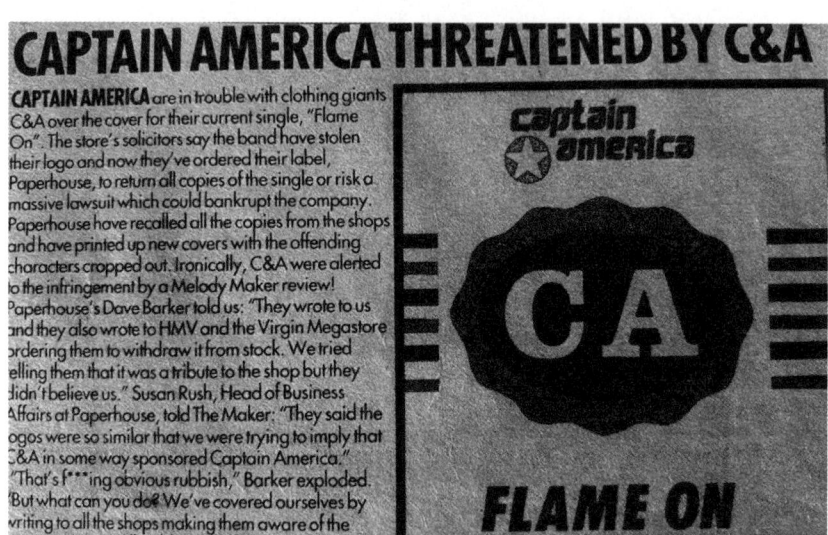

Eugene Kelly: And then we had to change the name very quickly and we made a bigger mistake by changing it to Eugenius, which probably could be the worst name ever for any band. But yeah, we chose Captain America and it would have been great if, you know, if we didn't get a bit of interest from major labels and they didn't tell their friends at Marvel comics that they'd just signed a band called Captain America. And if they didn't decide to try and sue us. It would have all gone really well.

Roy Lawrence (Drums, Captain America): This time for us was so mixed, but it certainly didn't feel like game over. They happened at different times: C&A was when we were still at Paperhouse and it actually felt quite surreal, almost comical, and because we were still an indie band it held the hint of the rebellious and I think actually gave us some publicity – I still have some clippings! The record still did well enough in the indie

A NEW GUITAR SOUND FOR GLASGOW

charts, even though I think in the redesign of the sleeve we forgot to put the barcode on to clock up sales.

The Marvel one happened when we signed with Atlantic Records (in the US). My memory is that we were in *Billboard* magazine where Atlantic announced our signing, which caught the attention of Marvel and then subsequently their lawyers. *Oomalama* hadn't been released and we had to change our name so the album came out as Eugenius. I remember feeling a mixture of positivity and exhilaration because we had just signed to Atlantic Records and despondence that we had to lose our cool name, which I thought could be damaging, firstly because it was a great name and secondly because any momentum we had gathered had been as Captain America and people might not make the connection or want to wear a Eugenius T-shirt in the same way! However, our first album hadn't even been released and we were lining up for our first American and Canadian tour with the wonderful Mudhoney so I felt our world was opening, not closing.

Oomalama, the debut album, eventually came out. Some copies did carry a sticker stating 'Captain America' but inevitably a name change for any band causes upheaval and damage. In my opinion it is one of the classic UK albums of that era, full of melodic scuzzyness and a sure influence on many of the next generation of indie bands from Glasgow.

Gordon Keen: I think we garnered mixed reviews for the album, and the expectations around the album had got a bit out of hand in my opinion. Maybe people weren't expecting that the album was reasonably lo-fi in production as an aesthetic. We didn't have a really settled line-up as yet, that came when Roy Lawrence joined on drums and Raymond Boyle on bass, that's the line-up which was our finest, in that we really gelled as a band and as a group of people. Roy and Raymond were as good a rhythm section that existed at that time, I used to love rehearsing with them. Some of our best work was probably never committed to tape. That said, we do have hours of unreleased material we recorded, post-*Mary Queen of Scots*, which would be nice to share with the world at some point.

Roy Lawrence: [Why did the album not do as well as expected?] It's a big question that probably needs a lot of views to construct a narrative that explains it, like everyone in a room drawing a picture of a lightbulb. It's there, we all see it from a different angle, and only when everyone's pictures are seen collectively can we see the whole lightbulb!

A NEW GUITAR SOUND FOR GLASGOW

Some of my thoughts – as mentioned before, the fact it was Eugenius and not Captain America that released [*Oomalama*] I believe will have had some impact, either through people not knowing, or no longer liking or caring for us as passionately. We had a good following as Captain America and gigs were busy (see the Buttermilk video, which was filmed at a real gig in Windsor the night the castle burned!).

This is also a perception in the UK, because I think the album did well on college radio in America. I remember seeing a college chart somewhere where we were number one while on tour with Mudhoney. There was a real break between the UK and America when we signed to Atlantic. Atlantic weren't too concerned about the UK and wanted to break us in America so we spent a lot of time touring there, and in Canada and Japan.

I think that led to a drop in our profile and popularity in the UK, because we weren't focusing on it, because of Atlantic's plans. I also believe this led to the music press, who were so England/London-centric anyway, to have further reason to take a dim view of us. You have to remember, they weren't much better with the Fanclub and gave them a hard time for *Bandwagonesque*! We had writers like Everett True giving it a kicking, though without the courage to admit that when he was in Seattle (if you read the review he says he liked it when he was with Kurt, but didn't when he came back to the UK). So we started to get some traction in America, Canada and Japan and get more resentment back in the UK. Such are the choices we make.

Despite the mixed reviews (which I think were entirely unfair) the album did reasonably well. As mentioned, the band were hugely being pushed in America, most notably by Kurt Cobain. Nevermind *was about to be released and would change the landscape of the US charts. Anything remotely connected with Nirvana or grunge was now big business and the band Kurt talked about most was his hero Eugene Kelly's new band.*

Nirvana played the Reading Festival on 23 August 1991. This was a month before the release of Nevermind *and three days before 'Smells Like Teen Spirit' was shared with the world. Not everyone was aware of the tsunami awaiting them, but the audience were more than sure they were the hottest band at the festival.*

In November and December, as Nevermind *mania hit the world, Nirvana took Captain America on a tour of the UK as support. They revisited Calton Studios, where Eugene had played with the reformed Vaselines a year earlier, now to a hugely different reception.*

A NEW GUITAR SOUND FOR GLASGOW

Andrew Tully: It was pandemonium. About five weeks before *Nevermind* came out, Ewan Mathieson, who was now working for Rough Trade, sent us up a taped copy of the album that he had been given by our mutual friend Keith Cameron. As soon as we put it on in the shop it was like Moses and the burning bush – a revelation. We ended up playing it in the shop three times a day. What was lovely about Nirvana was how they seemed to fit into that Scottish thing of being pals with the bands that you like and taking them on tour with you 'cause you want to hang out with your pals!

CHAPTER 14
1991–95

Further adventures of The Orchids, Garage and a new golden age of indie

The Orchids' debut album

The Orchids had kicked off 1990 by releasing perhaps their greatest song, 'Something for the Longing'. A mini album, Lyceum, *was followed by their debut album proper,* Unholy Soul, *in 1991.*

James Hackett: I was trying to put method into writing and thought, something that would drone on for a while, more rhythmical, and a big chorus. It gave a lot of space to be more adventurous and it worked.

Chris Quinn: It felt with the song and video for that one like we were a proper band in contention for bigger things. It was definitely more mature than other stuff we'd released up to that point. It probably just came naturally through experience and the development of the band as a whole. We were always wanting to make the next thing we created different from the last thing. We'd started to mature a bit as individuals and as a band and put a lot more thought into the songwriting and the studio process, making it less immediate. Up to then we'd probably just pretty much played what we played live and didn't use too much in the way of overdubs and had more fixed song arrangements. Ian Carmichael talks about this development in the book about Sarah Records by Michael White (*Popkiss, The Life and Afterlife of Sarah Records*) when he said we were now starting to think ahead.

John Scally: As a band our sound was developing, and recording in Toadhall with Ian Carmichael we had someone who got us and knew how to capture our ideas. Our sound was getting bigger and more colourful but still with the delicate touches.

Chris Quinn: In the video for 'Something for the Longing' we'd also come a long way from the 'Underneath the Window, Underneath the Sink' one. We looked like a proper band on the 'Something for the Longing' one, probably thanks to Toad Hall's moody lighting and creative filming and editing! The sleeve was awful. We were limited to two colours for those earlier sleeve designs and we placed this one in a gaudy orange colour sleeve with writing that was a very similar colour. So it's difficult to read the band name and song title (in a basic rubbish font) in a certain light. We weren't happy with the 'Made in England' thing that had to be added so we insisted on adding 'Recorded in Scotland' on the back of the sleeve.

John Scally: *Lyceum* being on 10-inch was never thought of as our first album, more a small collection of songs, these were songs that have been well rehearsed and gigged for some time. *Unholy Soul* had a completely different feel and vibe, we knew what we were working towards, and getting more confident in ourselves and as a band. It was clear that the album had a feel and a flow, it was exciting. We took up residence in Toad Hall and everyone was in a good place. The Old Swan and Ali Shan kept our energy levels up. It was a great time. As an album it's aged well.

James Hackett: The first album was such fun. We now had a great relationship with Ian and he knew we were working or at university and not able to attend together all the time, so he did a lot of the work when we weren't there. We started to feel at ease with recording and we created a few of the songs in the studio. We also heard Pauline Hynds sing backing for Ian's band One Dove and thought her voice was brilliant and asked if she would help us out and she agreed. A lot of things were coming together at the same time. The reaction was so enjoyable. Most people need to hear that you have done something of worth.

Chris Quinn: We'd only had a couple of singles between the release of *Unholy Soul* (very well received in 1991) and 'Striving' being released in 1994. That's a long time in the music industry. To be successful you need to keep building momentum quickly, so I think that would be a factor. We never maintained any momentum after that either because of other circumstances. The fact that we'd lost momentum in 1992/93 and then failed to continue any momentum after the album's release would have contributed to lower sales and lower chart placings than previous releases. I think there was still a place for the album despite the press and other bands moving on from the influences we'd had up to now. Things had definitely moved on. So had The Orchids but just in a different way and over a longer time period. We weren't the type of band who were going to be driven to change our sound based on that movement. We were still contrary and ploughing our own furrow!

Unlike their contemporaries, The Orchids agreed to stay with their original label, Sarah, rather than moving on.

Chris Quinn: We maybe never really had the confidence, the right image or the hard work to carry that off, though. For certain the compromises required would have been far too much for us to take. We sent things away to EMI or Go! Discs – I still have the polite rejection letters. We'd sometimes be proactively contacted by some of those types of labels but we just thought it was bullshit – a new young A&R person putting out feelers and we knew it wouldn't come to anything. On occasion you'd hear that someone from a label who was interested was going to come see us live but they either never showed up or had slunk away right after (or worse, during) the gig with no further contact made. We always viewed ourselves as a wee bit different from others in the scene. Our more melodic mainstream influences may have had a bit to do with that. Who knows? Of course we wanted our music to be heard by as many people as possible but I think things would have been very different had we taken that path. It wasn't to be and we definitely have no regrets over that.

James Hackett: We didn't fall out or anything. We had a practice one night and it wasn't fun, it was becoming a real toil. On the way home I said to John that I wouldn't be calling anyone to arrange a practice and he agreed. No one did. John, Chris and me would meet for a few pints quite often and would suggest to make some noise but never seriously. Well, for fifteen years anyway.

John Scally: Real life got in the way.

Chris Quinn: We just had a very long break! The long sabbatical began in 1994 and it was down to a number of factors, not just because of one thing. By then we'd been nine years in existence, six of these as recording artists. Several of the band turned 27 that year so there was maybe an element of 'if it doesn't happen soon' to things. We all had other jobs by this time. We were starting to think of other priorities in life. Relationships, jobs, our other careers that actually made us some money, even properties and marriage and families, I guess.

Edinburgh's garage scene revisited

The Edinburgh garage scene had mostly dissipated by the start of the new decade. Obviously, Lenny and Angus were still keeping the flame alive, mainly by appearing in a plethora of bands. There would also be The Kaisers and The Pterodactyls. But perhaps the most surprising would be the fruits of the endeavours of two very, very young schoolkids from Fife, John Gibbs and Steve Mason, who, surprisingly, had been a part of the original eighties scene.

John Gibbs (Bass, various): Steve Mason and I, we were at school together in the same class. In 1984 I had become obsessed with 1950s Woolworths rock'n'roll reissues and was given a cassette off my brother, which had Link Wray on one side and very early Cramps stuff on the other. So I started a rockabilly/psychobilly band, The Surfabilly's, with my mates Keith Douglas (guitar), Richard Petrie (drums) and 'Fido' (on tea chest bass).

It was all just a knockabout laugh and a hobby until we got offered a show along with other bands from school and in the process of trying to get ready we realised that poor Richard had no sense of rhythm at all . . . But, we knew that Steve Mason had a snare drum and was doing drumming lessons so we replaced Richard with Steve in that awful kind of underhand way that teenage bands do! At this point we changed the band name to the UrangaTwangs.

Steve bought a very cheap drum kit and became a part of the 'gang' as I suppose we were. As the next few years went on,

Steve was getting better and better and he started playing in The Second Generation as well as us. By this time we had renamed ourselves again to The Batfinx.

Steve and us parted ways and I moved from rhythm guitar to double bass and replaced Fido and we played a lot of shows around St Andrews and the area (mainly supporting local heroes Joe Public). Waaaaay more shows than a bunch of teenagers should've been allowed to do.

Steve Mason (Drums, The Second Generation and Batfinx; Vocals, The Beta Band): I was doing a YTS scheme at William Low supermarket in St Andrews and I got a phone call. I was part of the Scottish mod scene. I was going to various mod nights in Perth and Falkirk and Edinburgh and somehow, somebody must have found out that I played the drums. So I got a phone call one day from this mod band in Edinburgh called The Second Generation. And they were halfway through recording an album. And they said to me, 'We just fired our drummer, we've heard you play the drums. Can you come and finish this album?' I was totally stunned. I'd never been in a recording studio and the idea of being in one to me was the most exciting thing in the world. The idea of playing on an album that was being released was just like, I couldn't believe it was happening. But unfortunately, this band were absolutely shit. It's one of the very few things, and there really, really aren't very many, that I'm embarrassed about and they were shit . . . Nick Kennedy was a guy who was in a lot of those bands. He was a keyboard player. And he was a really cool guy and he played in The Second Generation for a bit. Why I don't know – he was so much better than anything that we were doing.

Nick Kennedy (Keyboard, The Pterodactyls, The Second Generation and The Thanes): It must have been around about the end of 1987 that The Pterodactyls then played a gig at the Calton Studios with The Thanes and The Second Generation. At this gig, Rod Spark asked me if I would play a session on their album, which I of course agreed to do. They were already in the middle of recording I think, so it might actually have been the beginning of 1988, and they were recording at Jamie Watson's Chamber Studios. In the studio, Rod and the other guys then asked me if I wanted to become a full-time member of the band and get a full credit on the album, which did actually happen, although I did only play on about four tracks. They had got a record deal with Tony Class's Unicorn Records. We then did play a few gigs south of the border to promote the album at a Blackpool weekender, and we also played a big festival which I think was called Mod Aid (a couple of years after Live Aid) – or was it called Modstock? But it was at a hall in Wimbledon and we went on second last before The Boys, who I think at the time were being managed by Paul Weller's dad.

At the time Steve was the youngest in the band; I think he was only 15 or 16. I was only 18 at the time and I think Rod Spark was 20. What I can remember about Steve is that he was most of the time in a bad mood and was kind of the grounding voice of the band, especially when Rod was having some pretty crazy ideas about what we could do or what we could sound like. But we did have a laugh with Steve, especially when everyone was taking the piss out of Rod. What also caused a lot of bad moods in the band was that when we played gigs away from home, there was often only one room booked in a B&B with one double bed for the four of us. And this was also for me eventually a reason to leave the band. Rod organised a two-week tour of Europe with no money guarantees and at the time I just couldn't afford to pay my way through Europe. So I left the band. Apparently they did go ahead with the tour and Rod's mum played organ. Everyone was pretty pissed with me but I just couldn't do it.

Around about the same time as I started playing for The Second Generation, there was also a line-up change in The Pterodactyls. John Watson was somewhat unceremoniously kicked out of the band and Calum took over the lead vocals and Claire Scrivner joined as rhythm guitarist. John Watson went on to form Jonny and the Deadbeats. The Pterodactyls with this new line-up then were in a local Edinburgh newspaper being quoted as 'We are not a boring psychedelic band!' Got involved with The Thanes around 1992 as the then organist Bruce Lyall wanted to leave the band and Lenny asked me to join them. I gigged regularly with The Thanes and recorded, again in Jamie Watson's Chamber Studios, 'Dozen Thought Buzzing/Antenna Surprise' in 1993, which was a single on Screaming Apple Records, then 'I've Seen Darker Nights/Happy Chain' on Distortion Records (I'm not exactly sure of the year for this one). And also 'Dissatisfaction/Shipwreck' on a Misty Lane EP with the Italian band The Others in 1995. I also recorded on a track for *Not So Pretty*, the Pretty Things tribute album.

Steve Mason: We used to rehearse in Niddry Street, where the caves are. It was like going into another world. It's so hard to describe . . . it was like being in a cave system. You had to walk down these long sort of tunnels. In the middle of the tunnel would be a plank of wood, like just planks of wood going all the way down, far, far into the distance. And you could see somebody had just run a load of wires down top, with lightbulbs hanging down. And then you'd go into these . . . and then the guy would say 'Aw, you're in room 12' or whatever. And there wasn't, there was never any numbers on the doors. You just found a room that was empty that had a lot of power sockets. And these power sockets were just hanging off the wall. And all the rooms were smashed apart. They were all smashed up. There was like a light bulb hanging from the ceiling and power sockets hanging off the wall. And the funny thing is, I remember one night we came out of there and The Exploited were coming in and I fucking hate The Exploited for a lot of reasons, a lot of fucking reasons, but mostly because they played that song 'Fuck the Mods' and a lot of mates of mine at the time had their fucking heads kicked in because of that fucking song . . . Anyway.

That was an amazing place because it's pretty much every band on the go at that time in Edinburgh rehearsed there. What was amazing was me and a mate of mine, Pete Rankin, probably about fifteen or twenty years after that, one day we were bored and we decided to go on this ghost tour. This is long after that rehearsal room closed down. We decided to go on this ghost tour of the caves. So we turned up and went in this place. And I said to Peter, 'This is just our old rehearsal rooms. I've rehearsed in every single one of these rooms.' It was fucking ridiculous.

John Gibbs: I moved to Edinburgh in 1988. I joined a busking band with members of Charlotte and the Rogues called Zoonie and the Moonmen, who spent years successfully liberating coins from folk on Princes Street. It was through this that I became good friends with Calvin from The Thanes and The Offhooks (creaking open the door to the extensive Edinburgh garage punk scene).

Through mutual friends at that time I then hooked up with ex-Styng Rite, George Miller, who was playing a kind of glam rock punk with Eugene [Reynolds] of the Rezillos. We started a basic rock'n'roll/rockabilly band called The Hitsville Greaseguns who played relentlessly throughout Scotland. Towards the end of The Hitsville Greaseguns we brought in my old friend Johnny from The Radium Cats on drums and, after a tour of Germany, almost overnight we transformed into The Kaisers.

The Greaseguns' equipment was all being stored in my flat after our last German tour. I woke up one morning and decided it would be great to play/record some Beatles in Hamburg stuff on the four-track I had lying around (*The Beatles Live! At the Star Club in Hamburg* was and still is my and George's favourite record). Johnny by this time was living in my flat so we set everything up and started trying to record (badly!). I phoned George and asked him if he could help out on guitar. We loved doing it so much that the band was born that same day. (In fact I think George might even have gone to Live Music on Leith Walk and traded in his Peavey amplifier for a croc skin Selmer Truvoice combo.)

George Miller (Guitar, The Kaisers and Country Teasers): The Styng Rites, like a lot of bands, just kind of fizzled out. I think we realised it had run its course. Shortly before the end I moved to Edinburgh and subsequently joined Eugene Reynolds' new band Planet Pop (later Rockatomic). Eugene had a great flat in the Haymarket area and myself and Johnny Maben, the future Kaisers drummer, rented rooms in it. (Eugene produced The Styng Rites second record and I learned a lot from him about how to arrange a song.) When us lodgers were skint, which was most of the time, a bunch of us including Johnny would go busking, doing mainly rockabilly stuff. This led to the formation of The Hitsville Greaseguns, a rockabilly covers band that featured Greg Moodie from Edinburgh, a fine guitarist and, as ever, wasted on the likes of us. John Gibbs played double bass and subsequently electric bass in The Kaisers.

The idea for The Kaisers came about on the way back from some gigs in Germany. We stopped off in Hamburg in order to see the remaining beat music sights of Saint Pauli and generally soak up the atmosphere. Having always loved The *Beatles Live! At the Star Club* album and the whole early sixties Hamburg beat scene, it kind of felt like the ghosts of these beat groups were somehow still there. I thought it might be an idea to bring one back to life, albeit one that had never existed. An experiment in artificial nostalgia, I suppose. I also felt we were somehow not really qualified to play rockabilly, but beat music, that felt more like home.

Johnny, John and I had a rehearsal or two, then were joined by Matt Armstrong on rhythm guitar – a real beat fanatic with an impressive collection of old guitars and rare records, which influenced us immeasurably.

Teenage Fanclub breakthrough: *Bandwagonesque*

One of the most successful and influential albums of the 1990s was Teenage Fanclub's Bandwagonesque. *It was a triumphant year for Creation, their new label, which also included* Loveless *by My Bloody Valentine and* Screamadelica *from an almost unrecognisable Primal Scream.*

America was a huge influence on Teenage Fanclub, not just sonically but socially as well. While the C86-era bands had by this time mostly withered in the face of the onslaught of electronic dance music, there was an equal onslaught of grunge and the US underground. Teenage Fanclub were not just riding the wave – they were part of the tsunami. Their Boy Hairdressers incarnation had given them early experience of playing with bands such as Dinosaur and they had developed in almost exactly the same way. Teenage Fanclub, by the turn of 1991, were as influential as many of their US peers.

Norman Blake: I think we had always felt an affinity with Nirvana, through the connections with The Vaselines and K Records and even with, I suppose Sub Pop and what they were doing, and we'd sort of known Sonic Youth and those people so we met a lot of those, the American bands, Yo La Tengo, people like that. And, you know, I think Nirvana . . . I don't think they could really handle or come to terms with the success of that record (*Nevermind*). Certainly I don't think they particularly enjoyed it, you know. Becoming a phenomenon as opposed to a touring band. But we did see them when they were a smaller band and they played much smaller shows, so we sort of saw both sides of what that could be. But, obviously, after that they became so big, Nirvana, that it was just this juggernaut that I don't think any of them really probably felt . . . I'm sure they enjoyed it to an extent at the time but it just became this out-of-control thing.

After A Catholic Education, *Teenage Fanclub quickly embarked on a series of influential singles and two back-to-back albums, one of which would help change the fortunes of both Creation and the band.*

Norman Blake: Francis went to university and basically told us that he couldn't commit to being in the band. Which was fine, obviously. And so we met Brendan O'Hare, who then joined the band.

Raymond McGinley: What I think can happen to bands is the classic thing of people want to – the good thing with us is we'd made the record before anybody knew us. So we decided who we are, and on what terms we were going to exist. And that was out with any reflection from anyone, out with just us. We had no one giving us an opinion of, maybe we should be like that, or maybe we should be like this. We just, out of ourselves, made this thing.

Gerard Love: When we were in New York, we met with Don (Fleming) and we recorded the 'God Knows It's True' 12-inch in New York. We just got to know him you know, with a few drinks, and Don was a big stoner. So we just hired a studio and just recorded tonnes of stuff, tonnes, you know, tonnes of cover versions and stuff. Dave Barker was a big fan of The Beatles. I think maybe that year would have been John Lennon's 50th birthday possibly, so we released a one-sided single of 'The Ballad of John and Yoko', which is like, it was almost like *Auf Wiedersehen Pet* – a rabble, but it was very in keeping with where we were as a band at the time and we were let loose in New York. And it was good fun, but I think the 'God Knows It's True' 12-inch is nice, but 'The Ballad of John and Yoko' was a limited edition. But, after *A Catholic Education* that was the next recording session we did. Maybe a year later, we moved into Amazon Studios down in Liverpool and started recording what was to be *Bandwagonesque*.

Raymond McGinley: And again, we just made this record in our own little bubble with no reference other than to each other and Don Fleming who we're working with, then you come out the other end of that, and, you know, record comes out, then seems to start doing pretty well. People seem to like it. And then a certain degree of madness ensued, where I think people thought we were gonna be the next Nirvana or whatever.

Norman Blake: I think very often with those kind of things you're kind of in the right place at the right time and the press want to champion something and it just so happened that that record (*Bandwagonesque*) was the one. Maybe partly because there were harmonies on it and that was unusual when we were making the record . . . so we recorded it with a guy called Don Fleming, who played in B.A.L.L., and we met him through Sonic Youth and Don had produced some stuff – he's good friends with Thurston [Moore]. And I think, at that point we wanted to make *Catholic Education 2* and make another noisy record and Don had heard us singing and he's said, 'You guys do really good harmonies, why don't you do that, because no one really does harmonies nowadays, it'd be a really unusual thing.' And we kind of thought, 'Well, yeah, I suppose that may be worth doing.' And so we did, with Don's encouragement . . . he said, 'Yeah, do some harmonies on this part,' and maybe it became a little bit more musical in a way and less noisy and maybe . . . the success of the record was partly down to that, in that it was maybe different, sounded different, than other things that were around at the time.

FURTHER ADVENTURES

The band relocated back to the UK, with Don Fleming in tow. However, before Bandwagonesque *was released they released another album,* The King, *recorded in just twenty-four hours.*

Norman Blake: *The King* was an album that we made, I think kind of for a bit of sport really. We were kind of midway through the recording process, we recorded at Amazon, just outside Liverpool, Kirby. We'd been working quite intensely and we needed a break so Don Fleming suggested let's just record some random stuff, so we started to think about what we could do and we would do something like, we would say let's record a guitar riff, flip the tape over and then record the same thing again and then play some drums over that and then sing over that and then flip that around and then sing over that again. Or let's put the tape at triple the speed and record something then slow it down again and play the piano over it or whatever. And so this all happened in one . . . over the course of one night, and we recorded a bunch of songs then some cover versions, we covered songs that we didn't have lyrics to, but this was pre-internet so you couldn't find the lyrics, so we just had to guess at what the lyrics were.

Norman Blake: We thought it was kind of fun or whatever so I think we suggested to Alan (McGee), 'Look, would it be cool to like maybe press 500 of these and just sell them or whatever?' And then there was a miscommunication at some point and they ended up pressing a lot more than that and so it hung around for a lot longer than it was supposed to. That's really how that record came about, it was a twenty-four-hour project . . . it was fun and in many ways epitomises the kind of mood in the camp at that time. The whole band at that time and, well it still pretty much is, has always been . . . it's been a fun band to be in.

Raymond McGinley: We knew, whatever happens, we made the record first and the other stuff came after. We just followed that template ever since. We saw a lot of madness and bullshit once we started to get more popular, but we saw that as something that followed on from our thing that we did in isolation, and people seemed to like this thing we'd done in isolation. If somebody tries to influence us, the way we worked, we never really tell people to fuck off. We're going to listen to them politely and then we go and do what we want. And that's worked quite well. By the time we came to make *Bandwagonesque*, we had this madness where people in the American major label world had got strangely turned on by us, for whatever reason.

Norman Blake: The first (proper) album that we made with Creation was *Bandwagonesque*. And it was a funny one actually, we really like this about them, we didn't sign a deal with Creation. Alan came and met us and said, 'Look, we'd love to make this record, so why don't you go into the studio? We'll pay for it.' And so we thought, 'Okay, contract?' and he was like, 'No, don't worry about that.' So we didn't sign a contract with them so in theory we could have recorded the record and then said, 'Thanks a lot, see you later,' but . . . So we kind of liked that they trusted us or whatever . . . We spent a few months recording, finished the record and then eventually signed the contract with them. And the album was released around the same time as *Loveless* and *Screamadelica*, I think those were the three . . . those three albums I think were being made at the same time actually.

Creation put out The King *quickly and briefly, but* Bandwagonesque *was the real triumph, not only of each member's musicianship but also of their songwriting. As* A Catholic Education *had mostly been written for The Boy Hairdressers, this was the first Teenage Fanclub album of new songs, and it was a democratic process.*

Gerard Love: I have to say, Norman was very encouraging of myself and Brendan and Raymond to come up with ideas because I think, it's for probably two reasons. It's maybe to make it seem more like a band. But also maybe it allows Norman to maybe pursue these stronger ideas. So this spread around but definitely made it more interesting as a sound, hearing maybe different people's ideas of what I saw . . . I always had the kind of melodic sense. My family are great musicians but we're not trained musicians, not classical music. I can't read music, I can play music. It's an instinct, isn't it?

Norman Blake: Yeah, I think if a band has three songwriters it makes it a little easier to produce albums, you know, of course it does. You think if there's one person writing everything there's . . . it's a lot of work . . . it's difficult to write twelve great songs, you know. It's difficult to write one great song. But, if you have three people writing it just takes the pressure off all of you and of course you will influence each other. If someone writes something you really like, you'll think, 'Okay, I'll try and write something that can match that or will stand up to that.' So that helped. I think we kind of really opened up our songwriting at that time. We thought, 'Listen, we can all write, there's no . . . let's all write, you know, just if anybody has an idea just do it.' And that really changed the dynamic of the band at that time. We've kind of stuck with that since then; the band from then on has been the three of us writing songs.

Gerard Love: Well, you don't really have to be able to map it out in order to make it. I'm sure it's the same for most people. There's a story in that. I think maybe that allows you to make something which is maybe slightly more unique rather than something which has not been tried and tested. You've got to use your imagination. The more limited you are in some things, that comes from making mistakes, some things having a chord which shouldn't but which creates another chord, which creates a new dynamic. It's good to feel something but not really know the rights and wrongs of something. I think music is instinctive anyway.

I think it goes back to watching local talented people make music, like BMX Bandits, The Boy Hairdressers and The Soup Dragons really do well and make records, and see these guys come up with songs. I think it makes it seem closer to you. Plus I see that, obviously the punk rock thing, the idea that any of us can do this and it just inspires you, the fact that – why not have a go. And as I say I was always drawn to music, I was always drawn to melody . . . But I didn't think I'd ever get the chance to record a piece of music that's on a piece of vinyl. I think the madness of *A Catholic Education* plus the encouragement of Norman and other people, it was very much like, 'Have you got anything?' and I'd play him something and he'd be very keen and enthusiastic about it.

Norman Blake: Do you know, I really have no idea why the *Bandwagonesque* record did as well as it did . . . I suppose the thing in the US that was the strangest was the media stuff, like I said the *Saturday Night Lives* and the TV things that we did and the MTV things that we did. That was just bizarre in a way for us. Although I'd never heard of *Saturday Night Live* when we were on it so we turned up there and we . . . by this point for a very brief period we had an American manager, I don't know what we were thinking but anyway . . . we were backstage and kind of just sitting around drinking wine or whatever and he said, 'Are you guys not freaked out?' and we were like, 'No,' because we had no idea what it was, you know. He said, 'This is going out live to like' . . . [gestures millions of people] 'Yeah, what?' So . . . but it was . . . and it was great, they were great experiences, it was great fun doing that stuff, you know, and it was amazing to see that. Around that time we also toured with Nirvana on the *Nevermind* tour and that was incredible . . . to be able to witness a phenomenon like that was bizarre and amazing. We did the entire European *Nevermind* tour and the record had really just broke at that point and . . . I've memories of just watching thirty thousand people jumping up and down, singing along to 'Smells Like Teen Spirit', it was quite something, you know, to be around and witness that.

Raymond McGinley: People at the label were getting really upset, because we weren't really taking it seriously. We were just, like, showing up at a television station, and, you know, getting pissed, and going out there.

Gerard Love: There's lots of great people at Geffen [their US label] that we got on really well with, who were on our wavelength, but I think just the structure, of that type of . . . you know, classic major label was difficult. Once things start to go wrong it just becomes a bit of a maze, where the buck doesn't stop anywhere. I mean it got worse when Creation folded. We ended up on Columbia, that was the absolute perfect example of a major label. I mean Geffen probably started off as an independent and it just became too successful so it had . . . it embraced the major thing but . . . obviously the idea that they signed Sonic Youth and they signed Nirvana, but obviously they had credentials . . . it wasn't as if they were trying to sign the next Michael Jackson. . . . I mean Sonic Youth are an interesting band and it was a smart move to sign Sonic Youth, because they're like a magnet . . . you know, Sonic Youth go to Geffen then Geffen must be cool because Sonic Youth don't really make mistakes, you know. So . . . I think Geffen were an interesting label and there were lots and lots of great people there but, yeah, it was difficult . . . the difference between Creation and DGC, who . . . it was an arm of Geffen called DGC that was maybe the more independent side. But there was a massive difference between the way Alan [McGee] conducted business, which was like madness.

BMX Bandits sign to Creation

For Creation, 1991 was a huge year and they were keen on exploring more music from Scotland. The BMX Bandits would be next.

FURTHER ADVENTURES

Duglas T. Stewart: The way I remember, Alan McGee and Creation becoming a part of our story was that Teenage Fanclub had a studio over in Motherwell and Alan was coming up to hear some new demos of songs that were going to make up the first Teenage Fanclub release on Creation. And we [BMX Bandits] had just finished recording a track called 'Serious Drugs', we'd just finished making an album called *Star Wars,* and after we'd finished that we had this song left over we recorded. And I think that would be 1991 and Alan heard this track and I don't sing lead vocals on it, in the original version it was Joe McAlinden, whose voice can sound a bit like Norman. And Norman was playing the track and Alan heard it and assumed it was Teenage Fanclub and he was like, 'This has got to be a single!' And Norman was like, 'Eh, that's not Teenage Fanclub,' and of course, I mean, he loved all the Teenage Fanclub stuff he was hearing as well but . . . Norman was like, 'That's BMX Bandits,' and Alan was like, 'What? I thought the BMX Bandits were like some real cringeworthy kind of comedy group. I'd never really heard them but I just didn't think I'd like them.' And then I think we were playing at a place called The Garage and Alan came along and was like, wait a minute, they've actually got lots of good songs and they're really fun and entertaining to watch. I want this band to be on Creation.

Joe McAlinden: The reason I ended up singing, it was because of the key that it was in, 'cause it came together really quickly, and I think that's why it's so good.

Alan McGee: Why did I do it? Because I love Duglas Stewart, big Duglas, genius.

'Serious Drugs' was the hoped-for big break single for the band.

Francis Macdonald: I could understand 'Serious Drugs' confusing people. I mean, 'Serious Drugs' was interesting, we probably wouldn't have got to Alan McGee if Duglas and Norman hadn't been pals and Norman was in Teenage Fanclub. And then, you know, Alan McGee heard the right song at the right time. 'Serious Drugs', I think it's probably the best thing the BMX Bandits ever did. And so when that was our first release on Creation all of a sudden this kind of, the poor cousins to Teenage Fanclub, nose pressed against the window, were on Creation releasing a really creditable single and it was Single of the Week in *NME* and *Melody Maker* all that week. I think the next week we were back to being the worst band in the world again. But, yeah, it was fortunate we got McGee at the right time and he supported us for three albums.

Duglas T. Stewart: Radio producers were all like, record of the week, that's amazing, yeah, and then Radio 1 had their anti-drugs week, the week it was released, and suddenly, people were like, 'It's our anti-drugs week, we cannot have a single [where] the hook line is "get some serious drugs".' So it got banned by Radio 1, and unlike what happened to Frankie Goes to Hollywood, or 'Je T'Aime', getting banned did not take us straight to the top, but made it kind of go down.

Guitarist John Hogarty, previously from The Clouds, would become the next BMX Bandits recruit.

John Hogarty (Guitar, BMX Bandits and The Pastels): I joined/ auditioned 15 July 1992 (I remember the date because, as a result, I got onto the Pavement guest list at the old Cathouse), then played my first gig with them in Tokyo, October '92.

'Serious Drugs' was, however, fortuitous for Joe McAlinden as he also joined the ranks of Creation as a solo artist and put together a new band, Superstar.

Superstar

Joe McAlinden: I was writing, and I think even though I was possibly playing with the BMX Bandits I don't know if I felt fully a member. It's not a bad thing. I always used to think of myself as the guy that could play a few things. So I'd get, come on Joe, can you come down and do this? So I was just working away and learning a bit of guitar and doing all that kind of stuff. So I just made that song ('Superstar'); made a demo and gave it to Alan McGee. Purely because I'd met him through working with the Fanclub. It was a natural thing. And he loved it. And he said, go and make a mini album. I didn't have a band at that point so I had to find a band. It felt, at that time, important to me to have new people. I could easily have gone in and done it with the same bunch of people, but I just wanted to find other people. And I wanted it to be a new thing. I was still heavily involved with the BMX Bandits at that point. And Superstar made that mini album, recorded in Glasgow, and it came out and it was very well received. And again, still playing with the BMX Bandits quite a bit. There came a point actually where it was fine, my time was fine, and it was all based in Glasgow.

But we ended up, after Creation, Superstar signed to EMI in

America. We'd just made a record and I was working on the BMX Bandits album, *Life Goes On*. There's quite a few songs I wrote on that record. Co-wrote as well. And I actually sang. I sang 'Serious Drugs' and 'It Hasn't Ended'. But my record company in America wouldn't let the version of 'Serious Drugs' come out as a single with me singing it. Because they felt it would cause some confusion in the marketplace. It must have been a very small marketplace but that's why there's a version with Norman singing it. Because it was a great song, and it had to come out as a single. I had to just step back, and I was kind of gutted. But the version that I sang is on the album anyway, and we're all friends and I didn't want to muck anything up for the BMX Bandits. I thought it was rubbish that EMI thought this way, but it was what it was, and we had to just deal with it. Shortly after that I had to leave BMX Bandits and focus purely on Superstar because there was always going to be this conflict. I didn't want anything to impinge on what they were doing. I didn't want any of these problems to arise again. So after quite a few years of doing that, I moved on to just doing Superstar.

I've still got all the faxes. My mum's just moved house and I was sure that I'd kept a whole load of stuff, and I could never find it . . . Then, clearing out the garage, and there's five huge boxes of stuff. Going way back. Loads of brilliant stuff. I've got loads of photographs. The launch of the Superstars' *Greatest Hits Volume One* goes down as a legendary night because it was in the Apollo. Not the big Apollo, the underneath Apollo in Glasgow. But the bill that night was: the Fanclub played, The Soup Dragons played, the Bandits played, The Boy Hairdressers played. I'm pretty sure Eugene played. Think he did. That was just an amazing night. We were just giving out records and playing our songs. It was one of those bills; it's like, it did actually happen. And that was the only time it ever did happen. But we all played. And I think they all did a couple of their own songs, and a cover version. I can't remember which ones, I'd have to dig all of that out. But yeah, that was a great night . . . I remember Go! Discs were desperately trying to sign us at the time. And they turned up with all of their staff, and bags of Buckfast, trying to lure us into some kind of thing. But we were like, ah that's great, and we just started giving it out to people in the audience. [Laughs] Everybody ended up a bit plastered.

The Pearlfishers

Around this time, David Scott's The Pearlfishers appeared, crafting elegant, Brian Wilson-esque pop. Unsurprisingly, David soon became firm friends with Douglas T. Stewart and Norman Blake.

David Scott (Vocals): Hearts & Minds (1986–89) was a pop-art idea that got a lot closer to surviving collision with another major label but did not survive the producer-go-round and my inability to say no to anything.

Hearts & Minds had fantastic songs though, and the band was good and I was kind of cute and – even after we got dropped – we could pull a crowd and people who heard it went why is this not huge? A lot of bands, pure of heart and sincere of intent, wind up asking the same question.

So, we kept going, and people kept coming, until Hearts & Minds became The Pearlfishers more or less overnight in 1990 when I discovered there was an American group of the same name signed to a major label. It was a beautifully convenient excuse to start again and we loved the sparkle of the new name. DF's Stuart Clumpas, promoting an upcoming Hearts & Minds show at The Garage in Glasgow, wasn't as thrilled but we all got over that.

Eventually, three things came together leading to the first Pearlfishers releases.

First, around 1989/90, we took over the running of a space on Yorkhill Quay in Glasgow called The Recovery Room (it had been an actual recovery room for injured dockers up to the late seventies) and ran it as an artists' collective rehearsal room. I installed my eight-track studio there and we worked almost every day, all day, rehearsing and recording. The band eventually settled on a line-up of drummer and vocalist Jim Gash, bassist Mil Stricevic (formerly of the group Big Sur), Brian McAlpine on keyboards, and me, and we found our true voice in that little rundown shack with our cheap microphones and with magnetic space at a premium on half-inch eight-track tape.

From there, Bruce Findlay, newly separated from Simple Minds, made a huge impact during the short period he managed us, first by being such a miracle of a human being but most profoundly by insisting that I regarded the recordings we were making at The Recovery Room as masters, not demos, and to be confident about self-producing. He was completely and groovily direct in saying I/we should trust our instincts and that 'success' needed to manifest itself in the first instance in the making of beautiful things. He also introduced me to Stewart Cruickshank at BBC Radio Scotland – another miracle of a human being – who became a major champion of the band and later my mentor, friend and guide when I started presenting radio shows.

Finally, I was able to raise some money from a long-standing Virgin publishing deal – the one unequivocal positive of my time as a 'major' music industry dweller – and match it with a grant from the Prince's Youth Business Trust (only Jim Gash was strictly 'a youth') to incorporate My Dark Star as a record label and plan two releases, the first of which was the *Sacred* EP.

The song 'Sacred' had originated from a rhythm I heard buskers playing from some distance on the Paris metro with a bass line I improvised 'in my head' and 'in the moment'. The writing demo had all of the bits already in place so when we recorded it properly it was about getting the ideas down strong and steady with a bit of performance edge. It's a good recording and sounded fantastic on regular radio plays, helped by a great mix by Andy Thornton of Big Sur and a brass section of Hermie Longalong, Matt Jenkins and Robert Henderson, arranged by my long-time Falkirk compadre Bill Wells.

A more obvious Bill arrangement is found on one of the B-sides, 'Working & Wasting Time', where he put a snaking sixteenth-note feel against the slow gospel 4/4 of the piano. Distinctive and memorable. Both 'Sacred' and 'Working & Wasting Time' were mainstays of Pearlfishers shows in those days and the latter was still in the set list of the most recent Pearlfishers tour in 2019. Elsewhere on the *Sacred* EP, released on 12-inch vinyl only in 1991, the song 'Twisting & Turning' pointed more firmly towards a direction I'd take later on, where Brian Wilson – specifically through his 1988 solo return – had re-established his rent-free occupation in my brain. The manufacturer had a mastering deal with Abbey Road Studios so Jim Gash and I travelled to London in a beat-up car to worship at the altar. Quite a moment mastering those songs, cut on eight-track in an ex-dockers sick room, at the Church of the Fabs.

The Soup Dragon's second album and US success

In 1992 The Soup Dragons essentially relocated to America full time, where further developments of their sound hugely resonated with US audiences. It is also worth noting that Hotwired *came out in 1992 and its fuzzed-up blues with dance beats would not be too dissimilar to what Primal Scream went on to offer in 1994 with their follow-up to* Screamadelica, Don't Give Out.

'Divine Thing' was a Top 40 hit for The Soup Dragons in the States, and led to a US stadium tour.

Sean Dickson: *NME*, 'cause we were still their little *C86* band, they turned against us, so the best thing that we did is we just thought, sod you, we'll go to America. So it was really refreshing just to get away from it, and go to a country that just took us for what we were. You know, I remember going through immigration, and the guy opened my passport, and he went, 'You're from that psychedelic band,' and I remember thinking, 'That's the coolest thing anybody's ever said to me.' And we spent the next two years in America, touring and selling a lot of records.

Sean Dickson: We went back and made *Hotwired*. 'Divine Thing', the single from *Hotwired*, which done kind of reasonably okay in Britain, it went Top 20 in America. It was the most played video on MTV that year, which was crazy 'cause you just couldn't walk anywhere, you know, you'd have people sleeping outside your hotel door. It all became very scary. It was bizarre because your face was just on somebody's TV all day long and in those days MTV used to actually play music, especially in America. It wasn't, as you know, these days it's all chopped up in channels. It was just music, music, music, music. And Nirvana's 'Smells Like Teen Spirit' had come out, so the four big videos of that year were like 'Smells Like Teen Spirit', The Red Hot Chilli Peppers' 'Give It Away', there was some Pearl Jam thing and something else, so it was just like a constant rotation of these records and, you know, Nirvana opened up this huge thing as well. All of a sudden at all our gigs, it was stagediving.

You know, nobody used to stagedive at Soup Dragons gigs but all of a sudden, every town we went to in America . . . You know, that's how I've got no tooth, 'cause somebody stagedived and broke my tooth in half. I was standing, I could see the guy coming and he landed right in my face and broke my tooth off. It was once again in America . . . the dance culture thing didn't happen as big in America like it'd happened in Britain, but what happened is, the whole kind of like grunge thing became huge in the States. And that's when we were out there touring. But we were, I mean we were completely different to all those kinds of bands, but people still saw us as the psychedelic rock band and, as I said, 'Divine Thing' . . . which was quite a groundbreaking video because 'Divine Thing' was actually one of the first videos to have A-list rotation on MTV with drag queens and transvestites on them. And I actually don't think at the time MTV actually realised what they were playing. Iggy Pop once got interviewed on MTV and mentioned it, how much he loved all the drag queens and transvestites in the video, and we were like, 'Oh shit,' but they still kept playing it. And I'm . . . it's one video I'm really proud of is 'Divine Thing'. It was quite groundbreaking for its . . . the way it looked and all that as well. Especially in America for MTV to play that. And then it got nominated for an award so we had to do the whole MTV Awards thing, so it was all pretty mad times. And then we got to take, we took . . . we were starting to play really big places in America and we were asked who we'd like to support us. One of my favourite bands is Tom Tom Club so crazily they said yes.

So we had half of Talking Heads support us every night. It just got mad. And then . . . and we were just contained in this bus, you know, it was like a travelling soap opera. You know, 'cause you can only go so long in these . . . we were doing like four-, five-month tours. Four-month tours, whatever, in the back of this bus, you know, these bunks in the middle of the tour bus and I think we just basically all got on each other's nerves and, you know, kind of hatred started 'cause people kind of break off into groups and camps and all this, so . . . and it does get a bit Groundhog Day, you know. We done a tour once supporting INXS where it was like forty thousand people a night in basketball arenas, so suddenly you're presented with another. It was kind of weird, it was like every now and then you'd be presented with something that's alien to you. You know, suddenly you're on *Top of the Pops* and then suddenly you're touring America, then suddenly you're playing basketball arenas every night.

FURTHER ADVENTURES

Creeping Bent and Shoeshine

Two new labels emerged in Glasgow during this period, Douglas MacIntyre's Creeping Bent and Francis Macdonald's Shoeshine, both releasing quality music and taking many of their friends into the new era.

Douglas MacIntyre (Creeping Bent Records): I was bored with my life in the 1990s and had always harboured the desire to start an organisation that combined music and art. As a teenager starting off with [my band] Article 58, I was a fan of the Fast Product and Pop:Aural labels, which acted as a spark to initiate Creeping Bent in 1994. The timing of my desire to create Creeping Bent as an outlet coincided with artists like The Leopards, Alan Vega and Revolutionary Corps of Teenage Jesus and The Secret Goldfish making records that I felt should be released. After releasing singles by these artists we quickly picked up coveted Singles of the Week in the *NME* and other weekly music papers. This led to John Peel being an avid supporter of the label and asking Creeping Bent groups to record sessions for his BBC Radio 1 programme. The music papers started writing articles about Creeping Bent artists, all of which created forward motion that in turn led to other artists joining Creeping Bent, most notably The Nectarine No. 9 and Adventures in Stereo.

Creeping Bent started a monthly club at the 13th Note in Glassford Street. The club was called Record Player and lasted for a year, with artists like Future Pilot AKA, Bill Wells, Jock Scot and Appendix Out performing at the club (all of whom would go on to release on Creeping Bent).

Adventures in Stereo was Judith Boyle and Jim Beattie; they approached me about releasing their first EP and we continued working together. Judith's voice was angelic and perfect for delivering the skewed underground pop that Jim Beattie was producing. We released further EPs then two albums by the group and organised several concerts. John Peel curated the Meltdown Festival in London's Royal Festival Hall and invited Creeping Bent to programme a label night. Jock Scot was compère for the evening, with Adventures in Stereo headlining a bill that included The Nectarine No. 9, The Secret Goldfish and The Leopards. It was the first night I met Vic Godard and he jumped on stage with Adventures in Stereo to sing their encore, a version of Subway Sect's 'Nobody's Scared'. Vic became part of the Creeping Bent fold and went on to collaborate with The Leopards, The Secret Goldfish and Port Sulphur.

The Secret Goldfish were formed by members of *C86* groups The Fizzbombs (Katy) and Mackenzies (Paul). Their idea was to do a fuzzed-up version of sixties girl groups; the Goldfish quickly became favourites of Peel and recorded two sessions for his BBC Radio 1 show. Katy went on to perform with Vic Godard and the Subway Sect at the Bowlie Festival organised by Belle and Sebastian, and also collaborated with James Kirk (Orange Juice).

Creeping Bent always ploughed our own furrow and remained resolutely independent throughout. We always sold enough records to reinvest in the next project and that was our modus operandi, we never had any intention of competing with bigger record companies as we did not want to be dictated to by market forces. An album by Port Sulphur, *Speed of Life*, was released in 2022 and reached number one in the Scottish album chart and number four in the UK independent chart. Along with releases by Gareth Sager, The Kingfishers and The Sexual Objects, we have managed to keep ourselves amused and to connect with an international audience at the same time. Creeping Bent releases are now manufactured and distributed by Last Night From Glasgow, who have proved immensely encouraging and helpful to a plethora of artists operating independently across a multitude of genres.

Shoeshine was a celebration of many of the acts Francis Macdonald worked with.

Francis Macdonald: Well, I was kind of too young for Postcard first time round, but I appreciated that Postcard was a touchstone for Norman, Joe, Duglas and all the other people that got me into this kind of world. And Postcard seemed to have records that had sleeves that were uniform, you know, so I had this idea that I'd start doing 7-inch singles on Shoeshine and all the covers would be the same and just the labels would be different, so that people would hopefully want to collect them all. So that was probably a bit of borrowing from Postcard. The other thing was, I was in a band for a wee while called Speedboat with Finlay McDonald, who passed to the BMX Bandits line-up and also passed to the Teenage Fanclub's line-up, and he's back to the BMX Bandits now as we speak, Finlay and Scott Walker, not *the* Scott Walker but *a* Scott Walker, very talented recording engineer and songwriter, Alisdair Vann, Finlay's half-brother. So we did some what I thought were four-track demos but Scott recorded them and they sounded so good and they didn't have a label and so I was like, 'Okay, we're starting this label, I could put out a Speedboat single and album, I could put out a BMX Bandits single. I was playing in a country band with Brian Taylor. Gerry Love played our first gig but later on Martin Heyward, who had been in The Pastels, became the bass player in The Radio Sweethearts and we were very influenced by country rock music and I had to cut a Radio Sweethearts single. I did a song with Norman, we did a single together called 'Frank Blake'. I knew that if I went to him with a concept of 'Frank Blake' it might appeal 'cause he likes puns like Mellow Doubt, Neil Jung, so 'Frank Blake'. That was the first four singles, the fifth single was a live single I think with . . . from an Alex Chilton gig when I was drumming with Alex Chilton when he came to Glasgow. Can't remember the sixth one but anyway the label began and I was playing on all the singles. It was partly a way to release music by the bands I was in and partly just to get things going. And it was later on that I put out records by things that I just liked and wasn't directly involved in. So I don't know who I was taking influence from there, I was just kind of rolling up my sleeves and getting on with it I suppose.

It's a different buzz. One of the first things I did when I was getting a feel for Shoeshine was I dropped Alan McGee a line. And I said, 'Alan, you know, thanks Alan for all your support' – you know he funded three albums and a lot of tour support and he got some of us publishing deals to get some money and he had a bit of promotion, probably particularly around the first, the BMX Bandits *Life Goes On* album with 'Serious Drugs' and 'Kylie's Got a Crush on Us' on it. But, you know, nobody else was going to do that for that band at that time. And we maybe always just had that thing of 'Oh, how come they're getting that, we're not getting this and oh, we're dropped now, you know,' and when I started Shoeshine I was behind the desk now, I was the guy writing the cheques or not writing the cheques, writing the cheques and watching them bounce off the end of the desk. So I dropped Alan a line to say, 'Alan, I just want to say thanks 'cause all the tour support, all the money, I don't know who else would have done it.' And he sent a nice wee brief line back going, 'Thanks for this, yeah it's easy to be the bad guy when you're on the other side of the desk really.' However he put it. So it was different, in a way I got my cake and ate it 'cause I was putting out records but I was on the records. When I heard Michael Shelley, 'Think With Your Heart', I thought God, I could put that on my label, what an amazing, amazing thing.

That's like . . . he's my Ben Vaughn 'My First Band' for 53rd & 3rd, this great American songwriter that no one knows anything about but he writes amazing songs. Or when I heard Laura Cantrell and got four songs by Laura Cantrell, I thought she's my Emmylou Harris, this is amazing. I get to be the label that promotes this. What a buzz, you know. I don't even think it's the next best thing to being the artist – it's the other thing from being the artist . . . 'cause the artist without anyone in support or shouting about it or promoting it, they need that, you know, and to feel part of the story in that way is a very different buzz, it can be great. It can be tough and it's getting tougher. I remember Alan McGee saying, 'Francis, it's changed so much in the last five years' – that would've been . . . 1996 or something. I mean, so in the years since, it's changed beyond all recognition, which is why I put less records out now. I do other things.

CHAPTER 15
1992-97

New blood and old success

a.c. acoustics, Thrum and Whiteout sign to majors

New bands, inspired by the earlier generation, began to appear at the start of the new decade. Three of them – a.c. acoustics, Thrum and Whiteout – were signed to larger labels in 1993 and were slated to have a huge impact. Unfortunately, the level of fame expected was never reached and their individual stories warn of an industry whose main interest was success.

The history of a.c. acoustics runs through many of the later 1990s Glasgow scenes, despite them never actually belonging to any of them. They were outsiders to begin with and in many ways remained outsiders, but their importance to this story, and especially to the subsequent generation, is significant. They were a band of huge talent and charisma who left a series of superb records that never reached the level they very much deserved.

NEW BLOOD AND OLD SUCCESS

Paul Campion (Vocals, a.c. acoustics): There was a famous music shop in Glasgow, called McCormack's. I'm sure this was the origin of an awful lot of bands across the generations. It had a board where folk looking for like-minded types with a view to getting together to form bands would pin up a note. Roger Ward from Dumfries and by proxy his friend Caz Riley, also from Dumfries, met me and me them. Caz is a brilliant bass player and a brilliant human being. I can honestly say that I don't remember him ever hitting a bum note either live or in the studio. He just always got it right. He could play bass and talk at the same time, with a fag hanging out of his mouth. The connection was a shared enthusiasm for The Wedding Present, Mary Chain and, in sharp contrast, Nitzer Ebb, Front 242 and industrial hardcore. I think the important thing is that we had a lot more *not* in common than we had in common, and that was key to the quite eclectic nature of our output.

There were very few opportunities for emerging acts to play in Glasgow by the late 1980s and, to remedy the then 'pay to play' infrastructure, a.c. acoustics took matters into their own hands despite having formed only recently.

Paul Campion: It seemed more sensible to engineer a support with established bands, get a support and play to a big audience. Spacemen 3, a band we loved, were on a UK tour (in 1989) and we saw that they unusually had no tour support.

Caz Riley (Bass, a.c. acoustics): We got the initial early gigs mostly by lying: we'd phone the agents and tell them the venue wanted us on the bill and then phone the venue and tell them the agent wanted us on the bill . . . by the time they spoke, they both thought we were on the bill. Roger and Paul were very good at that stuff.

Paul Campion: I phoned [Spacemen 3's] manager in London and convinced him that we were possessed of a huge and growing following in Glasgow and he told me that if the promoter was happy he was happy. I then phoned the promoter and told him that Spacemen 3 were huge fans and we had been contacted by their manager and asked if we would support them. He told me that if they were happy he was happy. With zero following we supported them and played to the best part of a thousand people in Glasgow. One of our first gigs. That was at a time when people actually watched support bands.

Despite an incredible ability to crash support slots for touring bands, the nascent a.c. acoustics soon ground to a halt.

Paul Campion: We realised that we were somewhat creatively limited and it was obvious we needed a drummer. Dave Gormley was in Thrum at the time. Dave was, and in my view still is, the most extraordinary drummer on the planet. Dave does a lot more than play drums when he is playing drums. It's very difficult to describe.

Caz Riley: We met Dave through the Apollo crowd and watching gigs, hanging out, we met Thrum. Watched a few gigs. Monica later sings backing on 'Hand Passes'. And that's where we decided to steal their drummer. We had been full-on industrial, drum machine, post-punk . . . but as all bands do we were maturing, writing new stuff, checking new avenues, getting new ideas about songs and songwriting. 'Every song is a progression towards your musical pinnacle, until your eventual downfall.'

Formed in Bellshill, Thrum had inevitably been involved with Sean Dickson, Norman Blake and, of course, Douglas T. Stewart. They were another hugely talented band who deserved huge success.

Monica Queen (Vocals, Thrum): As a teenager my escape from industrial suburbia was the BJ Youth Theatre group. I met like-minded people there. Eugene Kelly was part of it. Another great musician and now owner of Mediaspec, Eric Joseph, knew Johnny and invited him along to one of our productions in Bellshill's Cardinal Newman Theatre. There were always parties afterwards where we met and clicked mainly over our shared interest in making music. We organised a date right away and it wasn't long before we had formed a group with Eric. It didn't last long and Eric went on to join a band that had a major record deal. It was the first time we had known someone personally with a record deal. That's when we first got the idea that it might be possible to do something.

Johnny Smillie (Guitar, Thrum): Monica and I had been getting a lot of attention as a duo, we had heavy management and record companies throwing money at us to demo as this 'pop' duo. Of course, not for the last time, just as we were being offered stardom and riches we took another direction. We were big on Neil and Crazy Horse but it wasn't till Teenage Fanclub came on the scene, all grunged up, that we had the confidence to pursue our love of guitars and so turned our back on all the attention to start a band making a whole lot of noise. It was like . . . what . . . you can actually sound like Crazy Horse now and people are gonna listen. Could not believe our luck. It was like maybe we can do this on our terms. Very quickly, Fire Records, who had Teenage Fanclub at the time (and The Pastels, Pulp, etc.), wanted to sign us without even seeing us. We were like . . . okay.

Johnny Smillie: Well, when we decided to form a band we needed a bass player and a drummer.

Dave Gormley (Drums, Thrum): I first met John and Monica after they answered an ad I had pinned up in several music stores in Glasgow. I had been turning down quite a few bands by the time they got in touch and to be honest they were the first folk that seemed like they had a bit of a clue and a bit more of a professional attitude. Not that I was particularly experienced but I knew what I was looking for. The ad I placed cited bands like the Mary Chain, Pixies, Sonic Youth, Ride, My Bloody Valentine, etc. Not really Thrum's main influences, like Teenage Fanclub, Neil Young, Lone Justice.

Johnny Smillie: Dave was only 16, he had long flowing hair and could already play a bit. We taught him the rest and he did all right. We were a gang after that, touring the world. In those early days I had to always drive him back to his parents safely and sober or they wouldn't let him out to play again.

Dave Gormley: I'm a Motherwell boy and liked Teenage Fanclub and respected a lot of Thrum's influences but not as passionately as Johnica [John and Monica]. Thrum actually turned me down at first, saying I was a bit too like Loz from Ride and not enough like Brendan from Teenage Fanclub. This huge backhanded compliment made me chuckle.

Thrum eventually signed instead to Fire Records and quickly became well known in Glasgow. I think a.c. acoustics knew John and Monica before I even joined Thrum so it wasn't long before Paul [Campion] introduced himself to me. I then realised I had actually seen them play, supporting Jesus Jones at the QM. I had quite liked them considering they used a drum machine at the time.

Monica Queen: [The *Thrum* EP] was our introduction the world. Recorded by Duncan Cameron at Riverside, except the crazy live version of the big Roy Orbison's 'Crying'. I think you can hear Neil [Young], Sonic Youth, bit of punk rock and some more ambitious elements. 'Does Anybody Know?' [was] written about the downside of Glasgow culture and other stories about love and parents. All three tracks could've been on our debut album but it was cool at the time to have 12-inch EPs. I think you could make another good album from EPs and B-sides.

Dave Gormley: I remember Paul [Campion] approached me after a Thrum gig at Tuts and gave me a speech on how they [a.c. acoustics] had been thinking of changing direction and wanting to try a real drummer out. He told me they'd tried out a few but never got the right vibe and he'd be honoured if I would do a session with them just to see what it was like to play with a 'great drummer'. The Campion charm had started. The flattery worked and I agreed to do a session to help them out with a view to them understanding what they wanted to look for in a drummer. One thing led to another and after seeing me play for the second time with the a.c.'s, Monica instructed Thrum's manager to give me an ultimatum of it's either them or us. This came as a shock and completely out of the blue to me. My answer came reasonably quickly and as quite a shock to Thrum, I think, as they were pretty sure I wouldn't leave a signed band for one who'd never even had a sniff of a deal. I loved playing in a.c. acoustics way too much by this point.

I also hate ultimatums.

Paul Campion: It was an incredible leap of faith on Dave's part to leave Thrum and join a.c. acoustics. Thrum were signed to Fire Records and doing really well. We still hadn't even had a play on local radio. It was an incredible transformation. We were perfect from the first rehearsal in an embryonic way. I absolutely knew we were special together. I couldn't bring myself to listen to any of our albums for over a decade. It was too upsetting. Like looking at photographs of someone you loved with all your heart and isn't there any more. More recently, I have been listening to them, almost as an outsider. I have absolutely no idea how we did it. I appreciate now, far more than I did then, what a truly exceptional band a.c. acoustics were. It is a blessing and privilege to be part of it. We were truly a democracy. Like all democracies there was an often terrifying level of conflict. I don't think it was a conflict of egos, though anyone outside looking in would no doubt have seen it that way. I think it was because it absolutely mattered so much to all of us.

Despite losing their drummer, Thrum became one of the first of the new generation bands to gain mainstream TV coverage with an appearance on Channel 4's The Word.

Monica Queen: We were offered *The Word* last minute. We had to fly to London. Johnny had never flown as he was afraid of flying but had to overcome his fear to make the show. It was very exciting. It was THE music platform at that time. Nirvana had been on not long before. The whole show goes out live so you only get that one shot. We could be quite ramshackle, as was popular at the time, but we really nailed it that night and went on to party with Penn and Teller and the full *Word* crew. It really took us to another level but we couldn't completely capitalise on it. No Spotify. You had to print up vinyl and that couldn't be done quickly enough by the label to get the sales. However, it did bring us to the attention of Mark and Lard on Radio 1, who asked us on to their show twice after seeing us on the C4 show. It also brought us to the attention of Andrew Loog Oldham, who started coming to the shows and offered us a 'half a million' pound contract to restart Immediate Records that we naively turned down because he only wanted Johnny and me.

Meanwhile, a.c. acoustics found a deal with Elemental and released their debut.

Paul Campion: It was the 'Sweatlodge' demo, which included 'MV', that finally got us signed. We recorded this mainly in the downstairs venue at the 13th Note when it was downstairs from Bennett's night club. 'MV' was in part recorded at an empty level 8 hall at the Strathclyde University student union. The drums were recorded with Dave playing the whole thing alone, from memory. This was the only way to achieve the acoustics we wanted for the song with limited resources. It was incredible on his part, no headphones, nothing. It's a very long song. We packaged it like a finished product. I know that that got it noticed by Nick Evans at Elemental, who were part of Alternative Tentacles at that time, the label set up by Jello Biafra from The Dead Kennedys.

Caz Riley: Great indie record label at the time, eclectic amazing bands, Trumans Water, Bivouac, Rocket from the Crypt. Subsidiary of Alternative Tentacles. Don't really remember, but out of the initial interest that was happening they were the coolest, and Nick was always in touch and interested. We got signed without leaving Glasgow. Never played London.

Paul Campion: Those same tracks, with a bit of remixing, became our first single.

Caz Riley: I'm sure 'Sweatlodge' was self-recorded and self-produced, mostly live at the Apollo studios, with overdubs and vocals done in Roger's flat. If you listen to the B-side 'MV' there's a telephone ringing in the background of the vocal track.

Dave Gormley: 'Sweatlodge' was really special for me as it really solidified that I had done the right thing leaving Thrum. I had. Never heard or since heard anything so unique, at least to my ears. I loved recording it. We had to record the drums on an eight-track in the middle of the hall in level 8 of Strathclyde Uni (the same hall where I got the ultimatum). Not an easy task as I had no guide track and had to just watch Roger visually play his unplugged guitar from thirty feet away. I still think it was the best drum sound I ever got, but sadly it had to be bounced down, reducing the quality in the eight-track. I still think the recording has a great feel though. Still sounds huge.

Paul Campion: We didn't play Glasgow very much at that time though we did from time to time and had the privilege of being supported by exceptional bands like Urusei Yatsura and Mogwai. We had the chance to play London a lot and supported really significant bands from The Jesus Lizard to Royal Trux and Pavement. A particular pleasure was to be asked to support Madder Rose at the Astoria.

Caz Riley: As any band, our hopes were for people to like the single and gather interest in the band. Luckily, we got far more than we could have expected, and were receiving great write-ups, with frequent plays on radio from John Peel.

Paul Campion: John played it. You don't need much else. He asked, 'Are this band truly great, or am I hallucinating?'

The other new band earmarked for success off the back of Teenage Fanclub's surprise US fame were Whiteout. While Whiteout are perhaps now remembered (unfairly) due to their links to Oasis, they did produce a couple of excellent singles. Their story intersects with an interesting period where UK indie labels restructured after the Cartel's collapse, and the first inklings of proto-Britpop in the press gave them the notion that what had happened with Nirvana in the US may be possible with alternative UK bands here. Everything was up for grabs in 1992 and 1993.

Whiteout's manager, Andrew McDermid, gives his account of potentially making Whiteout superstars.

Andrew McDermid (aka McD, Manager Whiteout): I was 16, 17; I complained to the owner of Rhythmic Records that there were all these gigs happening in Greenock and I couldn't go to them. He said, you should write a letter to Slow Dazzle and complain about it. So I did. That was my first encounter with Chris Davidson . . . Chris (with Paul Barr and Tafty) started a club night called Subterraneans, at which point I was doing a fanzine. That was great for me, because I could interview bands and I felt it sort of introduced me to the scene. I was only 17 when I was going to Subterraneans, but because I was taking the car and interviewing bands, nobody really asked me my age. I was cutting about as a young person, feeling involved. Some of my friends were going to Splash One at the time but I was too young, so when Subterraneans finished I said to Chris Davidson, what are you going to do next? And he said, well it's your turn now. It was as simple as that. I just went, right, okay.

The experience of putting on gigs extended to band management and eventually discovering Whiteout, a proto-Britpop group with huge sixties and seventies classic influences and an ear for a strong melody.

Andrew McDermid: On the back of working with Spirea X (Jim Beattie's follow-up band to Primal Scream) I encountered this wee mod band from Gourock. When Spirea X fell through, I started to manage them. I was determined to get them a record deal. Round about the start of '93, I just absolutely felt that they were the real deal. I totally believed in them, and maybe that was naivety on my part. There was a bit of, you know, I'm going to prove to the world that I'm a good manager, but I had the band to do it with. The first single ['The Next Big Thing'] came out in 1991 on Bob Stanley's label, he was the first person who backed Whiteout. Then because Bob was interested, a couple of guys called Philip and Martin Hall came along. They were Hall or Nothing PR and they had set up a label called Sacred Heart. They were managing The Manics and had done The Stone Roses' press so they had the pedigree . . . this was '92. They paid for some demos and they weren't great, they didn't match up to what they were looking for. Ironically it was just a blip – wrong song choice, engineer, studio, etc.

During that time I never had a phone so I when I called Hall or Nothing they used to refer to me as 'Call-box Andrew'. We were gutted when it never worked out, but the band were developing, they rehearsed every day in the Gourock Bay Hotel and new songs were coming all the time.

The band would reconvene with an altered line-up in 1993 and began to demo new songs.

Whiteout were a four-piece by that time, and they went into Park Lane Studio with an engineer called Kenny Paterson. Paul and Andrew had been writing together and had a whole new set including 'No Time', 'Jackie's Racing', 'Starrclub' – they all became singles. They recruited Eric Lindsay on guitar at that time and suddenly everything started to fall into place.

They recorded eight tracks. Kenny (Marshall) had worked with the band six months earlier and couldn't believe the transformation. He put a lot of effort into the sessions. What started as demos ended up as master recordings. I used to drive up at night to pick them up and everyone was buzzing.

I made up a three-track demo tape with 'No Time', 'Jackie's Racing' and another track called 'Everyday', and started sending them out to record companies. Getting a band a deal was totally different back then. You got the *Music Week Directory* and started by targeting ten companies you wanted to sign to, send the tape then follow up by bombarding them with calls and appearing at their offices. Then pick another ten and repeat the process, and so on. I just worked my way through it. I was networking like mad at the time. Again, this is the days before email; it was telephone calls and face to face. It seemed easy to create a buzz and we ended up with serious interest from several record companies. The buzz surrounding the band was huge, with most of London's indie labels taking a huge amount of interest.

We were really keen to sign to Heavenly . . . it boiled down to a choice between Silvertone and Heavenly. There was a couple of other companies and our logic was that Heavenly didn't have much money and they wanted to do a deal through Sony. I didn't think Sony were particularly interested but I figured that Heavenly knew how to work the situation. But in the end, it was a bit of a discussion with the band. We were conscious of the fact that Silvertone Records' Roddy McKenna was an old-school A&R guy and he really knew his stuff. Other companies were saying they were going to make us an offer. Roddy had flown me down to meet people at his company and was like, what do you need? I was like, what do you mean, what do you need, just make me an offer? He was like, no, what do you actually need to run your band for a year – wages, rehearsal costs, whatever, let's sit and work it all out. With hindsight, there were a few things that happened with Roddy that are worth mentioning.

NEW BLOOD AND OLD SUCCESS

Heavenly just wanted to do a couple of EPs. They wanted to use 'No Time' and 'Jackie's Racing' on the first EP, and I was conscious that the drummer had left the band and the new drummer wasn't really working the same way. There weren't new songs coming through of that standard, so I was panicking about that. By that time, I'd spent £15,000, which was a lot of money. I mean, that was more than I'd been earning in an accountant's office. There was an element of that, there was an element of Heavenly wanting to use both tracks – they were my concerns. In the end, I'd probably have gone to Heavenly and said we'll do an EP with you, but it has to be, maybe, 'No Time' but not 'Jackie's Racing', or whatever. I'm sure they'd have done a good job.

There was a bit of a split in the band about it as well. In the end, we went with Silvertone and I've got no regrets about that. Heavenly . . . were really angry about it. It all boiled down to Jeff Barrett shaking my hand and I'd said, we want to sign with you. Anyway, when I tried to contact him, he just basically said 'respect' isn't just a word. I'd tried to contact him to say, look, we had to go with Silvertone but do you want to co-manage the band? But I never got to say it to him. Which didn't really help us when the whole Oasis thing came along. I've never spoken to anyone about this before, so you can print it. I was in my early twenties, I'd invested every penny I had, I'd got the band to a certain stage and there was dissent in the band about signing to Heavenly. It would have been a smart move. But the band signed to Silvertone, and the eight songs that we signed, the recordings that we'd made, ended up being the bare bones of the album.

We should have gone in and made an album really quickly.

We could have had it out before Oasis came along. It might have been a better thing for us. Camden was fucking rocking at that point, that was a really good time. We were signed in October '93, before 'Britpop' – you didn't really see people writing about it until early '94.

We played at Manchester 'In the City' in October '93. One of the band was going out with a girl called Debbie. Her band shared a rehearsal room with Oasis so we had heard about them. We played as part of a Scottish showcase. Our slot was fairly early so as soon as we finished we headed over to try and catch Oasis supporting the BMX Bandits but by the time we got there both bands had finished. Sushil (the Bandits' bass player) raved about them.

After that we went to see Intastella playing at Manchester Hop and Grapes. Debbie pointed out a couple of members of Oasis to me. It was Liam and Paul McGuigan. I said, 'I'm McD, I manage Whiteout. We're about to sign a deal.' Liam replied, 'We're about to sign to Creation,' and I said, 'Let's do gigs together.' It was a two-minute conversation.

The next time we saw Oasis was the day that they signed a record deal. We were playing at the Camden Falcon. Bonehead came up and asked if they could go on stage and do a song before Whiteout played. That was fine. They went up and did 'Shakermaker' as a four-piece. Noel stayed at the bar.

We had taken on a booking agent called Russell Warby. He had an amazing roster including Nirvana and The Lemonheads, He phoned me and said, did you really agree to do a tour with Oasis? I told him there had been a brief conversation about it. He said, well I've had their agent on the phone wanting to discuss this co-headline tour that's happening. It's amazing the way things happen sometimes. So we ended up doing this tour with Oasis.

We did *The Word* in the January for the 'No Time' single and Liam turned up with his manager Marcus. We had a busload of mates who had travelled down for it and they had been given a room by *The Word* staff, which was decent of them. Liam sat in there chatting to everyone the whole night. He made a great impression on Whiteout's inner circle before they had even seen his band. Oasis were on *The Word* a month later so both bands got great exposure prior to the April tour.

When we went on tour with them – I say this with no hidden agenda – it was brilliant. Both bands were all excited about being on their first headline tour, and there was a real vibe. I loved every minute of it. You have to remember that six months earlier I was financing the band with money I earned from DJing and there was no guarantee it would pan out. The first night of the tour was in Bedford. Oasis misheard Eric calling me McD and thought I was called 'Mark Dee'.

I got pretty friendly with Oasis but Whiteout were a wee bit insular. With the exception of Eric none of the rest of them made much effort. Bands hang about with each other but they were a wee bit guilty of not actually enjoying the scene for what it was. That was what they were and whatever, and I get it, and didn't interfere with things like that. One of the roadies got really annoyed about it because he said it would annoy him to see them being a bit standoffish. But you know, so be it. We did the tour with Oasis. Obviously the history has been rewritten, saying that we said Oasis should headline every night. That wasn't the case. The dates in Scotland ended up, because it was Glasgow Sound City, we did the Monday night in Glasgow and they did the Tuesday night, so there was no Glasgow show together. We didn't do the gig on the Wednesday night because Oasis went to play a Sony conference in Gleneagles.

So, we ended up not doing do any Scottish dates with them. And ironically, Ben Winchester, the Oasis agent, then said, do you want a Greenock gig on this tour? And I said, ach no I'll just wait until the next tour. I never got a shot at it again. I've actually got drafts of an Oasis poster I made . . . but hats off to them, they went on and fucking did it. There was a wee bit of a hate campaign getting conducted in the background for Whiteout, we definitely suffered from being Scottish. We got 'Jock and Roll', 'Rather Poor Jockos', 'Scots Also', etc.

We did the tour with Oasis and then we did some of our own dates. We did the Japan thing, which was brilliant. We came back and there was the second album and the band started to write and we were still releasing singles off the first album but there was a writing session in Park Lane with some great stuff. But Silvertone didn't hear a 'No Time' or 'Jackie's Racing', and to be fair, the band didn't have those. They were kinda, there was a Led Zeppelin thing going on, there was a Nick Drake thing going on. It never even got to the stage of that being a problem because Andrew chucked it. Andrew didn't feel cut out to be a frontman, and he didn't have the clout. He lost all his confidence and that left us in the situation of being a band in a record contract without a singer.

By that time it was difficult to get press. We had a girl called Polly, who did a bit of press for us on the second album. She was part of Savage & Best. But sadly, I always thought at the end of the day, it's all about the music. I still think that to a certain extent, but it's not. It's about marketing, it's about getting plays on the radio. Very importantly, Whiteout didn't get playlisted by Radio 1 on any single.

We were going to Japan at that point. It wasn't a big 'they're that size and we're . . .' I've got no ill feeling; I am obviously a bit envious that they got huge, but it's more that I'm annoyed that we didn't, not that they did. Now that I've seen what goes on in bands, as a manager the hardest thing to do with a band is to keep them together long enough to actually get any success. I was told that by the guys that manage Texas, and they're absolutely fucking right. The real role of a manager, it's not all the other things, it's basically trying to keep your band together long enough, without getting sacked. Managers take the fall for a lot of things.

a.c. acoustics had by now released an album, Able Treasury, *for Elemental and had two acclaimed singles – 'Sweatlodge' and 'Hand Passes Plenty'. As they had started earlier, the band were slightly on the outside of the 13th Note scene (currently at the epicentre of indie youth culture) but very much a part of the wider Glasgow scene. Their early success had elevated them and meant they could offer support to many of the new upcoming bands who cited them as an inspiration, especially Urusei Yatsura. However, they would again temporarily pause operations and reassemble with a new line-up.*

Caz Riley: There was no split. Roger started becoming increasingly ill, unable to play guitar, write, tour or even function in daily life. I remember, and have photos of the first Reading Festival we did, Roger could hardly walk. But he played a blinder and after the gig he collapsed, totally spent all the energy he had. Turns out he had multiple sclerosis – took the doctors ten fuckin' years to diagnose him.

Paul Campion: There had been an interesting band around for a while called Big Burd. We had seen them quite a bit and they were enthusiastic fans of the band. Colin Hardie, who went on to have a very successful career in band management, and Mark Raine, an obviously really special guitarist. We asked him if he wanted to join the band. He did. He could play every one of our songs already. Couple of rehearsals, warm-up last-minute gig to a lot of hostile locals at a pub in Helensburgh, and on stage at T in the Park a couple of days later, being recorded live to be broadcast on Radio 1. We were familiar with this but it was new to Mark. He was absolutely fearless and faultless. We were the first band to play a note at the first T in the Park. More accurately, Mark was. We were touring and I think he, like Dave before him, took an enormous leap of faith and dropped out of university. I believe, with the blessing of his parents.

Mark Raine (Guitar, a.c. acoustics): a.c. acoustics were one of my favourite bands. I loved the *Hand Passes Plenty* EP and must've been one of the first to buy 'Able Treasury' on the day of release. I think I actually started to follow them before they were signed and couldn't believe they were an unsigned band. So being asked to join, albeit only initially for a short period until Roger got over his illness, was unbelievable, but also very nerve-wracking. Caz phoned me, and it was when you only had house phones. So I was in my living room in Cumbernauld at my mum and dad's house. My dad was watching football and my mum was reading, and Caz is on the phone asking if I'll stand in for Roger in one of my favourite bands, at three gigs, two warm-ups and then T in the Park! He then read out a set list I had to learn for the first rehearsal in three days.

Caz Riley: We thought Roger's illness was just a temporary thing and had other gigs lined up, T in the Park being the next one. We knew Mark (Raine) from Big Burd; he was a cool guy and played really well, was a fan of the band and knew the songs, so after a bit of discussion it was decided to see if he would stand in and cover Roger till he was better.

Mark Raine: I was very nervous in the first rehearsal. Although I kind of knew them a bit, Paul and Caz could be a bit intimidating, not intentionally, more through my perception of them at the time, but especially now I was entering into their territory to replace their fantastic guitarist, and friend. And I had Roger up there as one of the most creative guitarists I'd seen so it was also daunting trying to follow him who had a completely different virtuoso style of playing, that I didn't really have – I was shite-ing it. The rehearsals went okay: I found the band to be very professional and focused, the equipment and studio to be better and everything was overall up a level from what I was used to. We played a tiny warm-up gig in Largs and another one, maybe in Paisley, and then T in the Park! We were actually first on the line-up on the second stage, which I think means we actually opened TITP, but the gates hadn't been opened by the time we started. So we played the first song, at the first TITP, to absolutely nobody. By the time we finished the second song, there were five thousand people in the tent and the gig was fantastic. And that was supposed to be that. Roger was supposed to get better and I was supposed to be back to Big Burd. But for a number of reasons, that didn't happen and I was asked to join a.c. acoustics full time. I was able to finish my course at university and then move 'full time' to rehearse three times a week for six hours and go on tours, etc.

Paul Campion: Playing songs is one thing, but writing them is another. Mark just seamlessly fitted in. We always pretty much wrote by jamming. Someone would have a bit of a guitar part, bit of a bass line or a bit of a drum part and we would just develop these for hour after hour and put finished arrangements together. We would record them in rehearsals on two tracks of a four-track. I would develop vocal parts by singing gibberish (some would say the final outcome was also gibberish) and then work at home on the other two tracks on the cassette. This was the way we always did it and Mark was just a natural new part. The music was just an evolution again. He shared our laser-focused absolute confidence in the quality of what we did and how we did it.

Mark Raine: But we also had to write new songs, and this is where some problems started. I became very insecure about how anything I wrote would be good enough for this band, so I was reluctant to share any ideas I had, instead trying to jam along with something someone else started. But I wasn't very good at that, certainly not as good as Roger was. Roger was also integral to the songwriting process, more often than not initiating the jams with riffs or chord progressions he had come up with. So not only was I not contributing great creative 'virtuoso' guitar parts to the ideas others were bringing, I wasn't bringing any ideas of my own. And it became quite noticeable. There were conversations about bringing Roger back into the band, keeping me as well, as I had a more melodic/pop slant on things, but getting Roger back as the chemistry wasn't quite working. But it was this conversation that jolted me into action as I thought it was now at a point where there was now nothing to lose. I'd been coming up with lots of ideas and riffs but just not sharing them with the band, but it was now or never. So the first one I shared was the riff that eventually became 'Stuntgirl'. Dave picked up the punk/pop vibes straight away and Caz and Paul followed quickly afterwards. That gave me the confidence to share the rest of the ideas I had and we started on a slightly different way of working than the band had previously – we never looked back from that point onwards.

Paul Campion: Placebo released their first album at the same time. It was properly promoted by Hut. Full-page adverts in every magazine and music paper. Massive posters, when these things weren't treated like vandalism in the way they are today, in every town and city across the country. We got a few posters at Ladbroke Grove and adverts the size of a fag packet in the arse end of publications where people were selling off second-hand instruments. It was absolute madness. Brian wore our 'Stunt Girl' T-shirt when Placebo immediately and deservedly appeared for the first time on *Top of the Pops* with 'Nancy Boy'. Both bands had become the best of friends. Lu Hunt, who worked at our management company, came up with the idea. She thought it would make a brilliant skinny T-shirt. She was right. It continues to feature in Placebo's merchandise, which is continuing testament to Lu. Lu was the one person at our management company who genuinely had absolute faith in us. She supported us. She fought for us. I want to thank her and pay tribute to her. She died at a young age from breast cancer and we all miss her terribly.

We immediately had an affinity with and great friendship with Placebo. Brian has the soul of a Scotsman. They should have been a Glasgow band. We often toured together. One of the tours involved them, us, Linoleum and, I think, Minxus. We all got on brilliantly. All of the crews got on. We all shared the same dressing room. We all put our riders together. We were all really looking out for each other. One of my happiest memories of all was on that tour. It was the Wulfren Hall in Wolverhampton. Everyone had finished soundchecking and disappeared. I was alone on the stage fiddling about with something or other. Out of nowhere a young boy appeared from some hiding place he had found having managed to sneak in in the morning. He told me he was too young to get into the gig but was a fan and had hidden in there all day to get our autographs. I told him I wasn't Brian Molko. He told me he knew that and could I get him the rest of a.c. acoustics autographs as well. I did better than that. I got him into the dressing room and made sure he saw the gig that night. Who knows, maybe he started his own band and had the chance to enjoy the countless extraordinary experiences that we did and meet countless extraordinary people, like we did.

Alex Chilton and Glasgow

Teenage Fanclub became associated with Big Star, which has become an unfortunate millstone for them – unfairly as it was perhaps only Bandwagonesque *that contained those references.*

NEW BLOOD AND OLD SUCCESS

Aptly, however, both the band and Glasgow had a far more intense association with Big Star, in that Alex Chilton became a huge friend to them and that scene.

Gerard Love: I imagine equally in London and Brighton and Manchester and in Liverpool and Birmingham, I think people would be influenced by Big Star, but for some reason, maybe people in Glasgow started to talk about them in interviews. Definitely the first time we spoke about it in interviews, the journalist had never heard of Big Star, which was surprising for us.

Norman Blake: I think me and Duglas were listening to Alex Chilton records, probably before we really got into Big Star.

Francis Macdonald: Well, Norman reckons actually, Raymond McGinley was the guy that got hold of the Big Star LPs, got all three of them. And then Duglas and Norman were so tight, sharing music with each other. So Duglas, very early on would have been aware. So it was actually Duglas and Norman who played me 'September Gurls' and 'Thirteen' and showed me these records.

Gerard Love: The Big Star records were certainly under the radar but there's obviously always people with keen ears in Glasgow. And even probably from the seventies, there was the Stax versions of the Big Star records doing the rounds in Glasgow and probably your more discerning listeners were passing them around. Purely on the strength of the quality of the records, in spite of the lack of success, they made their way to Glasgow and inspired a whole raft of people.

Joe McAlinden: We all got into Big Star at the same time, you know, 'September Gurls', and then you hear that and you're like, 'I need to find out more about that.'

Norman Blake: When we were making the early Fanclub records, especially *Bandwagonesque*, we'd been listening to a lot of the first two Big Star records.

Francis Macdonald: Teenage Fanclub name-checked them a lot in interviews.

Gerard Love: People used that influence almost like a hammer to hit us with I think, as if we were completely ripping them off, which, I mean, I can definitely hear influences but it definitely was not a cynical move on our part.

Norman Blake: The album was released and someone who knew him in the US passed a copy of the record on to Alex. And, of course, we were thinking he would have hated it, because Alex could be contrary. But for some reason, he liked it and we were playing in New Orleans and we met him. He came along to the gig and we, we hit it off. He liked to say, 'What's your sign?' I said, 'I'm a Libra.' Okay, that was it. 'What's your birthdate?' You know, he was into astrology.

Gerard Love: Those astrological descriptions or card descriptions of character, there's the good side and a bad side, and you'd hear him tell some people the complimentary part of it, and then maybe some other people that he wanted to put in their place tell them the bad side or something.

NEW BLOOD AND OLD SUCCESS

Duglas T. Stewart: I think straight away, there was just something that made a connection with people in Glasgow. I don't know if it was some sort of sense of humour, and also a musical connection. And particularly Jason McPhail, a friend of ours, who led a band called V-Twin for a while.

Jason McPhail: I love Teenage Fanclub. I just love that band. They talked about Big Star so you listen to these records and you go, 'They're really great too,' and then suddenly I had the notion of 'I wonder if we got that guy and phoned them up and said, "Would you come to Glasgow and we'll get Teenage Fanclub to be your band?"' You're just, like, a wee kid just having fun, right? We can do this and it might happen and you get lucky, sometimes. Sometimes it happens.

Norman Blake: He came over, he met us. He played with us at Jason's club and he got to know people here. He had friends here. And he felt comfortable here. I mean, Alex was a guy that lived in New Orleans, a smaller US city. Glasgow was a small city so maybe he felt comfortable here. He certainly did. I think.

Joe McAlinden: I mean, we're all pretty nice guys. Friendship is a real important part of anything I've ever done. So you just get on with people so maybe he just felt welcome. For him, he's coming here and he's just getting absolutely adored everywhere he goes. It's like, guys, 'It's Alex Chilton!'

Gerard Love: He had a reputation as being quite a difficult artist or a difficult person. Even at the time, we knew there was still episodes where people would recount that Alex is really difficult, but whenever he came to Glasgow he was a sweetheart. I think he really responded to people because I don't remember many people asking him about Big Star records. I think everybody was respectful of giving him his space. I think people were very engaging and friendly without intruding.

Norman Blake: If he liked you then great; if he didn't then forget about it.

Gerard Love: He came back to Glasgow about three, four or five times. I mean, he was a regular visitor.

Francis Macdonald: Every time he was over and did a gig and then he'd stay in town for a few nights and there'd be a get-together at someone's house and a couple of acoustics and sing songs.

Norman Blake: He was a real fan of music. And he turned us on to lots of good music and I think we let him hear some things that he really liked.

Francis Macdonald: He made compilation tapes for two or three of us and I remember sending him music.

Norman Blake: Someone at the *NME* had an idea that we could make a record together. So Alex and Jody happened to be in London and we recorded. We both played on each side and we made a record. And then from there Alex played some shows with the Fanclub. We actually recorded some music which we haven't released. We did some with Alex singing some of our songs and us singing Alex's songs. He was a great guitar player. And a cool guy, you know, like the epitome of cool.

Joe McAlinden: He just said, you know, if you've ever done anything, give us a shout. So I did and he came up to the studio and he played on a few tracks. That was a real experience as well as seeing him in that environment, because we would spend hours tweaking guitar amps and stuff like that, trying to get the perfect sound. He turned up with his guitar, plugged it into my amp, didn't even tune it. And he's like, just roll the tape, man. And he just played in tune but it was like proper old school.

Francis Macdonald: He phoned up once at my mum's house, where I was, and he was phoning up to say how much he liked the song 'Hello Again', which was on the BMX Bandits album, *Getting Dirty*. And that was like, amazing. The song I wrote. My God, pinch me.

Joe McAlinden: I remember asking him . . . I was worried before going onto that album about singing because I think I was still finding my voice. I remember speaking to Alex about vocals in the studio and stuff and then a couple of weeks later I got a letter, he'd gone back to America and sent me a letter about how we should deal with my vocal in the studio, which I've still got actually. It's brilliant and beautifully written, a real personal letter.

Francis Macdonald: He was very fond of Glasgow and after he died, Laura Chilton, his wife, came over to meet some of the people he talked about.

Duglas T. Stewart: She just wanted to come over and almost meet this, almost family that Alex had in this far-off place and then there was a notion that it would seem appropriate if some of Alex's ashes were brought to Glasgow for Jason to put around the place and some were sprinkled near a flat where we had a great party one night with Alex and some ended up in a guitar.

Norman Blake: My guitar. Jason gave me some and I didn't really know what to do with them, so I'll stick them inside the guitar. I got gaffer tape and put them upside down and stuck him inside the guitar. I'm still waiting to be pulled by customs. So Alex travels with me and the guitar.

BMX Bandits: Creation

Creation's continued support for Glasgow was especially beneficial for BMX Bandits. After the critical success of 'Serious Drugs' and the first Creation album, Life Goes On, *the band went on to produce a run of some of their greatest material.*

Duglas T. Stewart: When we joined Creation it almost felt like a kind of rebirth, like kind of a phoenix rising out of the ashes, because . . . and kind of from '90, from 1985 to around about 1987, regularly I would go into Glasgow on the train and be wandering around shops and pretty much every time I'd be approached by groups of quite often people from high school or people that were students or whatever, wanting like autographs and wanting like photographs and . . . 'cause we were getting played quite a lot on the radio and stuff at that time and then, 1987, 53rd & 3rd ended and I actually recorded some new tracks and sent them off to something like, more than twenty labels and got one reply, even though we'd had things like an indie-pop number one and had daytime Radio 1 playing things. One reply saying no. So there wasn't that much encouragement out there for what we were doing but we were continuing on and then the Creation thing happened and suddenly again people were recognising us in the street, people were organising photoshoots for us and video shoots and our records were getting played on the radio and we were getting talked about and not just British music magazines but international music magazines.

And, yeah, it felt like our rebirth and we felt like we had a real champion on our side because Alan was so passionate about what we were doing and was also so willing to let us do what we wanted to do. You know, there would be tracks that we would maybe play him that he wasn't as sure of but first he would go, 'I don't know if I totally get this but I trust you' . . . Alan didn't just sign groups, he sort of signed people: people that he believed in, people he saw a sort of potential in. But although that was all really great and we were getting to play a lot more countries than we had and things, I don't think I totally felt a sort of 'I've arrived' because it sort of almost ended before. I sort of thought, 'Yeah, this could just be us getting swept up in another kind of wave of something that's happening right now and people are buying into.' And in another six months we suddenly might be written off again and not seen as one of the happening things. So yeah, I was always a little bit cynical about that side of things and also I'd gone through the experience of when Teenage Fanclub became very popular and I'd be out in the shops with Norman and I'd see people approaching me with a big smile and happy eyes and kinda 'Aahh' and he'd walk past me. I'd be invisible and they'd be 'Look, Norman, Teenage Fanclub are amazing.' So I was very ready for that to happen again and sort of thought it probably is going to happen, you know, unless we end up being able to deliver a hit, but we weren't . . . you know it wasn't that we didn't want to have hit records – we sort of did but we wanted to have them on our own agenda, we weren't going to change what we thought was right to have any hits or anything like that.

But Alan kind of got ill round about the time we were making our second album for Creation and that really changed our relationship with the label. Sony started to get a lot more involved and I think were kind of confused by us. You know, we got told by a marketing guy, right, you're really funny at the shows, you know when you go and see BMX Bandits you're really funny and entertaining but the records are really musical and not really that funny, they kinda sometimes even deal with quite serious things. You should either make really funny records or be really serious at the shows. And it was like 'Okay, forget it, we're not going to even listen to that.' And Alan continued to champion us but he just wasn't as physically able to be around and support what we're trying to do. And then we made a third record for Creation, which I think was even less likely to tick the boxes for what was happening currently because it was a really, really wide and strange record with little self-indulgent instrumentals and almost strange power-pop/rock tracks produced by Kim Fowley and went off at lots of different tangents and directions.

I think Creation were just like, 'This is not working. We want more of what Oasis have to offer and we don't really want BMX Bandits and Momus and The Jazz Butcher and bands like that.

What's that got to do with anything?' And I guess when Creation sort of started the ethos of bands like that, that was very much what Creation was about, but these Sony accountants made sure, you know, that at the end of it that definitely wasn't what it was about. And again, a bit like Splash One had been years earlier, on a much bigger scale, I guess Creation ended up being a victim of its success.

It's funny with BMX Bandits. I think a lot of bands, they have a time which is sort of like the golden time for them. And very often that golden time I think is just before they make it big, just before then, when people are beginning to get excited and there's a momentum and everything seems to be going in a certain direction. Very often when it gets to the point of being really big . . . it ceases being as much fun 'cause a whole bunch of other parties take over and other people's wages are suddenly jeopardised by the continued success or the failure of it, that's going to come up next. And there's a lot of different pressures . . . BMX Bandits never quite reached that point, that point where it really did start to happen, but we've had quite a few times where it was heading in that direction. And I think because of that we've actually managed to have a sort of sustained time where it's almost like we're still like the beginners, we're still like . . . we still have the kind of dreams of maybe one day it's going to happen and it's still fun because it's still sort of playtime and we don't have people breathing down our necks going 'So where's the hit?' or 'Where's the follow-up? You had that hit, you know, you had a big critical success, this next one better get as much coverage as that last one.' There was a little bit of that later on when we were on Creation where it started to get a little bit like 'Is this really what we're doing here?'

When Alan moved out of the picture a wee bit people were kind of going, 'You guys really need . . . we've given you three albums now, we really need a hit'. And that kinda . . . that wasn't that much fun. But apart from that very small time and maybe a year or two where we were feeling a little bit dejected and no one was interested in releasing any of our records, I mean we just couldn't get arrested . . . It's actually pretty much always felt like it did in the early days for BMX Bandits, it still feels like playtime, it still feels like kind of getting together as it did when we started off and it was Sean, Norman and me sitting in the house getting out the old tape recorder and coming up with things and laughing a lot and being moved to tears by what we heard when we played things back and we thought, 'Wow, that sounds amazing, that sounds so good.' And being so excited about it and that kind of continues with BMX Bandits, I mean it's like twenty years later and it still feels like a group of kind of like daft teenagers sometimes. We can maybe play our instruments a little bit better – I can't, but a lot of the other guys can – but, yeah, the kinda magic has never really gone away.

Teenage Fanclub: *Thirteen* to *Grand Prix*

The unexpected success of Bandwagonesque *had led Geffen to believe Teenage Fanclub were perhaps going to be as successful as Nirvana. Their US label seemed unaware that the band would steadfastly conduct everything on their own terms with accommodations to commerciality seemingly being of little importance to them.*

NEW BLOOD AND OLD SUCCESS

Teenage Fanclub did not reach the giddy heights of superstardom. Instead, they delivered a series of beautifully crafted, melodic and uncompromising pop-filled albums that are as fine as anything that has emerged from these shores.

Gerard Love: I think *Bandwagonesque* is more kind of bubblegum in a way, it's kind of easier taste, kind of . . . I think maybe *Thirteen* is a bit more, there's a bit more depth to it in some ways. But I think maybe our kind of, our thoughts towards *Thirteen* are to do with the process of making it. You know, we just come off . . . obviously before *Bandwagonesque* we'd played a few shows, *Bandwagonesque* did very well, we'd played a lot of, you know, a lot of shows in America and stuff and it took us to a certain level. We come off . . . it's kind of a classic thing, you know, the first record by a band, they've got their life to write the songs and then all of a sudden they're touring and they've got a month off and they've got to come up with the next LP in the next month before they get into the studio. And that was part of our, our kind of memories of making *Thirteen*, it was just a very protracted, frustrating session.

Raymond McGinley: From November '91 until the summer of '92, we went through, I suppose, a certain amount of madness that we hadn't quite previously experienced and I think maybe our brains had been gently fried in the process of it. But as ever, certainly, we're thinking, I just want to get away from this. Fucking madness, build shit and go back into the creative space, do our thing and then move on. Because when you've made a record, it's not like we're sitting back saying, oh, yeah, *Bandwagonesque* is brilliant, isn't it? We're like, 'Can we go and make another record?' I think we were in a rush to go into the studio and make another record. And I think, thinking back to the process, we went into the studio too quickly, from finishing touring. And we lost a certain amount of the tightness amongst ourselves. It wasn't like it was fractious between us. Probably just a bit tired and we went quiet. But we wanted to go and do this thing quickly. As soon as you get back into the studio as a band, you're back on your own terms.

Gerard Love: We started off at CaVa in Glasgow, sleeping in our own beds, you know, waking up whenever we wanted to wake up, it's just . . . we're too close to home and we spent a lot . . . we tried to, you know, we tried to take on too much, we tried to record like thirty or forty songs. There was just nobody there with an overview. I think we were kind of let wild and I think maybe we kind of trusted our own instincts too much and it just took us too long to make it.

Bandwagonesque probably took us three weeks to record and mix and *Thirteen* probably took us three months or more. And I think we were just very frustrated at the end of it. So when we did interviews on the back of finishing the record we were kind of . . . we were jaded already and I think we were too honest in terms of expressing ourselves, I think. You learn how to play the game a bit more, obviously . . . if you say to someone, 'Ah, it's not very good,' they write, 'It's not very good.' Whereas it's just sort of self-deprecation, it's a way of us disarming people that, you know, we're not really sure about it – please reassure us or something, you know. I think maybe, after that if we thought this record is not very good we didn't really say it as loudly as we did with *Thirteen*, so I think it was a live and learn.

But I think maybe just the cover . . . it was a kind of dark cover. I think the idea for the sleeve . . . for example, the Jeff Koons idea called equilibrium, of a basketball half in and half out of water, I think maybe Norman had spotted it and we decided to kind of re-do that.

I think if we'd done it with a clear background it would have been more stark and it would have been a stronger image but it was a kind of wedding photographer took it . . . it was a friend of a friend of a friend and it was like a wedding photographer or something and he had like some mottled blue background. And I just think there was something . . . it was a strong idea but I think maybe the execution wasn't, it wasn't graphic enough or something, but that's me thinking why it wasn't really as well received. But I think part of it was us presenting it as a bit of a downer for us. [Laughs] But you learn, you learn how to play the game a bit more as you go, you know.

Raymond McGinley: I think through all processes of making anything, you get a feeling of anti-climax at the end of it; you felt, you know, we could have done better with that. We'd spent quite a long time making *Thirteen*. So the longer you spend on something, the more the sense of anti-climax. And we've never been the kind of people that are going to come out and say, 'Oh yeah, this new record. What are you listening to? Well, we just listen to our own record because it's so good. You know, how could I listen to anything else?' You know? And I think there was one particular interview where certain frustrations were expressed and that was portrayed. And you could say that people were being too honest, but at the same time, maybe it's no bad thing. I think if we were a band that just came out and gave someone some line, then we wouldn't be being true to who we are.

Gerard Love: I think it's that classic one of they know when you're kind of on the up . . . I think maybe *Bandwagonesque* was a big chance with Geffen, you know. And I think maybe because it didn't happen there, I think all of a sudden it was like their attention goes to the next thing. I think they thought . . . I mean, they signed Nirvana on, I believe they signed Nirvana on the recommendation of Sonic Youth. And I don't think they expected anything of Nirvana. Apparently their first pressing of *Nevermind* was quite small and it just flew out the door. And I think it was a phenomenon that they didn't know was about to happen. And I think they probably looked at us and thought yeah, well, if it happened with them of course it could happen with these guys as well, although they like speak in a strange accent and blah blah blah, you know. And it didn't really happen. That's what major record companies do, you know, they just look to the next thing. Although they kept us on, on the contract, I think by the time we made a stronger record . . . I think our strongest records were *Grand Prix* and *Songs from Northern Britain*, but I think by that point in time the game was up.

I think we'd had our chance and although they were stronger records I don't think . . . if, for example, *Grand Prix* had followed *Bandwagonesque* I think that would have taken us maybe to another level, but . . . *Thirteen*'s a kind of reactionary record, a lot of the songs are slightly cynical towards our experiences and the music biz and the treatment of us by the press and I think we were just young and inexperienced and you think that stuff is valid to write songs about and it is, but you're not . . . the press aren't going to love it if you're singing songs that are maybe questioning their integrity or their reading of your work. So you just learn to play the game a bit, and I think *Thirteen* is a good document of where we were at the time but if, for example, we could have followed *Bandwagonesque* with *Grand Prix* I think that would have, that could have been the magic formula.

Norman Blake: I think *Thirteen*, after the kind of craziness around *Bandwagonesque*, we spent a long time making it, we spent months making it in the studio, probably spent too much money. And that whole experience wasn't great. But I think when we made our next album, *Grand Prix*, things had settled down a bit more by then. Geffen realised that we weren't going to sell millions of records and they sort of . . . they sort of got off our case.

Raymond McGinley: I think Teenage Fanclub are lucky and have never been seen as part of any movement, never been grouped together with anything. I don't think we were ever particularly in fashion . . . and consequently we didn't have much fashion to go off. Plus, we would never really pay any attention to that . . . We toured *Thirteen*, we ended up breaking up with Brendan. We started *Grand Prix* with Paul Quinn in the band and we became a different band, because Brendan was intrinsic to what had gone before. So to me, it feels like there was a different band from that point onwards. But with reference to what we've done previously.

In *Thirteen*, which was a protracted, non-rehearsed record, we wanted to do something which was more, we went into the studio and kind of banged it out, in a more focused kind of way. But I think some people, I remember at the time when *Grand Prix* came out, thought that we'd made some kind of west coast sounding record through some influence from the record label or Geffen or something. And that was really funny to us because, in reality, Geffen wanted us to make a punky record or something. You know, people in the outside world wouldn't really believe what people might try and tell people what to do. And making *Grand Prix*, we were just doing what we've always done . . . just do exactly what we felt like doing at the time.

Gerard Love: You know after *Thirteen* there was kind of movement in the group . . . we kind of parted company with Brendan, who was our drummer, and we started working with Paul. Paul Quinn . . . he'd followed Francis Macdonald in Boy Hairdressers so he'd had, you know, kind of history with Norman and Raymond. But by that point in time we'd kind of made our mistakes, we learned by our mistakes and I think we were quite resolute that we wanted to be strong with the next record. I think we prepared for it more and I think we . . . I just think our songs were, I think we were learning how to write songs better. When you're young you come up with great ideas . . . I think your best ideas are probably when you're young and if you're able you can make those ideas into good songs but I think as you learn your craft, you're more able to make something strong but the actual idea may be weaker, you know. I think that's the irony of life. I think when you're younger you've got all the . . . you're just coming up with lots of great ideas but you don't know what to do with things, but as you learn to do things through repetition, sometimes the quality of the ideas go south, you know.

But yeah, *Grand Prix*, I think for a long time we maybe straightened our backs and thought, 'Yeah, we're going to put the ball in the net this time,' you know. And I think we did, I think that's why . . . I think it's our strongest record simply because of the process of us recording it. It was a very strong time. It was a beautiful time of the year, lovely studio, it just . . . everything was just right. And at that time Norman met his future wife as well. It was just lots of magic in the air at the time and it was a really good time, it was probably the high point of the group, I think, in a lot of ways. Because we still didn't think the game was lost at that point in time. We still thought, 'Yeah, if we make a good record of course people will love us again' and stuff. But I think we all knew we'd lost some ground with *Thirteen*, but, you know, we're still here.

I think it was just the songs we were writing. I'm not saying that we made people think about the idea of . . . a lot of things we did were made, all through my life, my kind of influences have been sixties stuff. I mean, I still go back there, I'm still discovering new things from that time that I had no idea of and I'm still influenced by that time because I think it is a golden period. I think we all were. Even the fact that we would reference bands like Big Star or whatever. I'm not saying that that would encourage people like, for example, Blur maybe to discover the Kinks, I don't want to say . . . it's possible though, because at that point in time when Blur first turned up they were that kind of baggy beat and it was more in line with maybe Stone Roses and stuff. But it seems like maybe there was a change in thinking with a lot of people where all of a sudden they were thinking about maybe the lineage of great British pop songs and stuff. And I'm not saying there was any influence from us, but what they were doing was things that we had been doing for a long time anyway. So I don't think we were too incongruous at that, maybe Eugene's thing was maybe a bit grungier, I think maybe Eugene's thing was maybe more in keeping with Nirvana and Mudhoney.

But our thing was maybe, yeah I don't think we were so grungy, although, as I say, we tuned down to make our strings buzzy and it sounded grungy and we were definitely . . . influenced, but I think we were quite a flimsy set-up maybe. Maybe Eugene's [band] could rock more than we could, you know, 'cause Gordon's a good kind of rock guitarist and Raymond Boyle was a good rock bass player and their drummer, you know, maybe they could rock more than we could. We were more, kind of . . . we all saw ourselves as slightly more pop or something, so I think maybe because of the pop in Britpop, I think we kind of slotted into that a bit more but we didn't really . . . although [we were] all from the island of Britain, we were certainly not invited to the party, you know, because we were too far north.

Norman Blake: We ironically named one of our albums *Songs from Northern Britain* as a kind of reaction to the Britpop thing, we didn't really feel . . . we met lots of the bands and we played with them. We played shows with Pulp and Blur actually, way back, but probably those bands . . . I mean I know for a fact those bands didn't see themselves as being part of any scene. The scene was created by the British music press, but I mean the *NME* and *Melody Maker* were famous for creating genres, you know . . . because they had to sell something every week. We've now moved to like a model of monthly music press, actually, and it's now moved on to the internet and it's different again, but, you know, certainly at that time it was weekly press so they had to have something new every week and, you know, probably their sales were down, sales of British music were down in general so they created Britpop to help flagging sales. But really, when you look at it, that was just a disparate group of bands who were clumped together by the press to sell something that didn't really exist.

Gerard Love: We're not nationalist or proud Scots, we are Scottish obviously, and, you know, we'd never call Scotland 'Northern Britain' . . . I thought it was something funny to call it Northern Britain but also it was a wee . . . it was a, well we're actually in Britain as well, you know, as are people from Manchester, as are people from Orkney, it's not as if, you know, Britain stops at Watford or whatever. No, it wasn't . . . we were quite happy, we were quite contrary anyway . . . I think if we'd gone on the good ship Britpop, we'd have gone down with it. So it's something good to just avoid these things, although sometimes you imagine, 'What if?', you know. But I think *Grand Prix* wasn't so far from a lot of things that were happening at that time, it wasn't as if it was alien music or something. It was pop and it was influenced by roughly the same period that a lot of like Oasis or Blur or whatever was . . . I mean, Suede were doing something slightly different but, you know, a lot of those ones like Blur and Oasis were more about the past I think, in some ways.

Gerard Love: We made an EP called *Teenage Fanclub Have*

Lost It, we just did acoustic versions, more like soft versions of songs we had done before and I think we were quite inspired by the sound of it, you know, so I think it grew out of that, the idea that it was more kind of softer sounds and more folk influenced in a way, in terms of sonics or whatever, you know. But it's also maybe us getting older and stuff and realising that we're not rockers, and we couldn't do the grunge thing, although we could make a racket at times. But I think our strength was melody, or whatever, and texture, so I think maybe that's quite a textured record as a result. But I think it's just the fact that *Grand Prix*, you know, we felt it was quite a strong record but it . . . it certainly wasn't a flop, I mean I think people who liked the group were really kind of, we were quite inspired by *Grand Prix*, it was kind of a return to form.

But I think, as I say, at that point in time, the boat had left and I think we knew that the original surge of the group through *Bandwagonesque*, through *Thirteen*, that idea of us possibly being a big group was probably not going to happen. But we were quite comfortable with that, we were quite happy with what we were doing and yeah, with *Grand Prix*, you know, as a result of *Thirteen* . . . I mean *Thirteen*, we kind of made it in Glasgow and in Manchester, in the south of Manchester in Cheshire. It was a very urban kind of record. And with *Grand Prix* we decided to go to the Manor Studios, which was opened by Richard Branson in the seventies, I think maybe *Tubular Bells* was recorded there and I think it was a beautiful kind of manor in Oxfordshire and we found it was the kind of formula for us. It was close enough to Glasgow, but far enough away, you know, that we could concentrate on what we were doing, and we kind of liked it.

Although we're all from kind of, you know, industrial areas

or council estates, or something. Living the good life in the rolling hills of Oxfordshire, we thought, 'This is for us, this is great.' So I think we responded well to that, so the subsequent record, *Songs from Northern Britain*, we tried to, we went to a farmhouse in Sussex this time and tried to re-enact it, so we kind of found . . . you find what things you respond well to, and for us, being in that kind of isolated country setting really suits us. But it did influence, as I say, the sound of *Songs from Northern Britain* – it probably softened as a result, you know, and that was probably the pattern that we started to follow for the next, well, ever since really.

Gerard Love: I think maybe as you become more confident in what you do, you can strip away the layers of noise. It's like you know and present yourself as you are, so maybe kind of the idea that when you're younger you want to make a noise simply because of the energy you have and the frustration you have or whatever, but also maybe some of it's there just to mask who you are and maybe as you become more confident in yourself or your abilities you are more inclined to strip away the noise and say to people: 'Here I am.' And maybe it's some of that, maybe it's just getting older and slightly more comfortable in your own skin. And it's just really knowing what your strengths are, it's wise to follow what your strengths are. Sometimes it's good to take a chance but sometimes it's good to kind of bring it back home and just try and make something strong.

CHAPTER 16
1983-95

The sound of young Scotland: the beat goes on

Duglas T. Stewart: I think that the family of bands that was emerging here, I keep using this word which feels like it now represents something different: alternative . . . It seemed like genuine misfits and outsiders and the records had a much more human quality. Sometimes technically the ambition would be beyond the actual grasp of what the musicians could achieve but actually hearing that could be something that's quite special and also a bit like, 'Well, if these guys can do it with their limited skills and they sort of seem like they don't really fit in and they're not really playing the game, we might be on the other side of the Atlantic but we feel a connection with them in a way that we don't feel with what we are hearing on MOR American radio or what we're seeing on MTV.'

Thurston Moore has said that the Scottish underground had a desire to write classic pop songs with no regard to moneyed

THE SOUND OF YOUNG SCOTLAND: THE BEAT GOES ON

production. This spirit is at the heart of every band in this book. Punk allowed this to happen, not because of the mantra of 'anybody can play guitar' but because it had always been there; it was just finally allowed to flourish. New Zealand is perhaps the only other example of the same dynamic but, almost uniquely, DIY and punk rock were the vector that allowed Scotland to unleash its own pop songbook regardless of whether the recording budget was £1 or £100,000.

The sounds that emerged in the period 1983–95 were informed by the 1977 punk ethos but, importantly, they were also informed by what they saw happen to many of the acts from that generation. In 1984 came a moment when infiltrating the mainstream was re-centred from 'selling in' back to 'selling out'. Indie would no longer mean independent; it would become its own genre, a badge to wear, a lifestyle choice and an ideology. There was pride in being genuinely alternative and this led to a genuinely alternative music industry.

Of course, this could never last. As had happened with the earlier generation, the major label record industry sensed a threat to their supremacy – and they could also smell the potential of money to be made. All of the bands featured in this book have played a part, and some, such as The Vaselines, have played a major role in the rise of the US musical underground reaching the mainstream. And generating millions of dollars.

The mechanism for Nirvana, Sonic Youth, Ministry and others becoming overground was far different in the US. In the UK, the Cartel offered an alternative; in the US, indie labels had far less power. It was the friends of bands who were given small roles within major labels and gradually worked their way up the corporate ranks who saw that the youth were now primed for this music.

I'd suggest that Britpop did not happen as a reaction to the supremacy of grunge; it happened because smart independent UK labels, bands and press saw that what happened in America could also happen to the UK underground. A large degree of success had been achieved with the Cartel, allowing independent music to reach the top end of the mainstream charts; therefore it was now not inconceivable that, with a little help, UK indie acts could become a cultural phenomenon too. A restricted distribution network and some major label input would achieve just this with Oasis.

It is inconceivable that 'corporate indie' (i.e. EMI, Sony and Universal's backing of the traditional DIY indie as seen in the 1980s) would have happened without Scotland's huge contribution towards indie as a genre. The DNA from almost all of these acts is contained within Britpop. But there were other strands of that same DNA that meant that few of the bands from Scotland found success in the Britpop era. The uncompromising attitude of the majority of bands in this book is largely what prevented them from being successful. Teenage Fanclub could not be ignored due to their superb songwriting, but had they not marched to the beat of their own drum they would likely have become what Geffen had envisaged for them. It's also no surprise that the new generation emerging around Glasgow's 1990s 13th Note scene found little success with Britpop's audience. Since the days of Fast Product, there has been an uncompromising attitude and strong belief that independent really does mean independent.

Thanks to

Zoë Howe
Angela Slaven
Douglas MacIntyre
Grace Fairley
Wendy Griffin
Jack Oliver
Adam Sanderson
John Harley Weston
Ally Gemmell, Manager, The Media Whores
Iain Key
Roque Ruiz
Keith Cameron
John Robb
Neil Taylor
Tayba Mason
Ian Smith at Last Night from Glasgow
Lee Brackstone
Pete Selby
David Keenan
Raymond Boyle
Paul Quinn
Douglas Fairgrieve
Paul Hartmann
Garry Torrance
Sarah Kneale
Kevin Buckle
Jessie McPhee
Albert McPhee
Barry McPhee
Kaye Kennedy
Joan Whiteley
Graham Whiteley
Bob Last
Neil Cooper

Mike O'Connor Kenny Marshall
Douglas McBride Erik Sandberg
Jim Barr Olivia Gifford

I'd like to offer a special thanks to my wife, Helen, and daughter, Françoise, for their huge support. I'd also like to give huge thanks to all at Omnibus and the wonderful Zoë Howe for her continued support and advice, Angela Slaven for her excellent film editing in *Teenage Superstars* (this book would not exist without her), Grace Fairley for her editing here, Douglas MacIntyre for his continued support and inspiration, and especially all the musicians, promoters, label owners, fanzine makers, distributors, photographers and journalists who together made this wonderful scene so vibrant.

In memory of
Richard Scott (without whom most records in this book would not exist) Keith Martin
Alex Taylor Martin Duffy
Eddie Connelly Tommy Cherry
 Kim McLachlan

Bibliography and Sources

Film
Teenage Superstars and *Teenage Superstars* DVD extras, Grant McPhee
Fast Forward, Grant McPhee
Industrial Accident: The Story of Wax Trax!, 2018, Julia Nash, Wax Trax! Records

Books, magazines and sleeve notes
Gardyloo sleeve notes by Angus McPake
Personal Diary by Margarita Vazquez Ponte
Narodnik archive
NME, 8 December 1984, Jim Reid interview, Neil Taylor
The Face, 9 March 1985, Max Bell
NME, 16 February 1985, Biba Kopf
Jamming, September 1985, Bruce Dessau
NME, 3 August 1985, Neil Taylor
Smash Hits, 28 June 1986, Andy Kershaw
The Observer, 9 March 1986, Mary Harron

Melody Maker, 28 June 1986, Simon Reynolds
Sounds, 5 July 1986, Hugh Fielder
Roque Ruiz at Cloudberry Records, Tommy Cherry and Martin Cotter interviews
Sounds, 11 August 1990, John Robb
Sounds, 3 November, Keith Cameron
Melody Maker, June 1990, Bob Stanley
Sounds, October 1990, Keith Cameron

***Teenage Superstars* and DVD extras**
Eugene Kelly
Bernice Simpson
Martin Hayward
Brian Taylor
Jowe Head
Alan McGee
Frances McKee
Francis Macdonald
Sandy McLean
Joe Foster
Douglas Hart
Tam McGurk
John 'Joogs' Martin
Duglas T. Stewart
Sean Dickson
Sandy McLean
Norman Blake
Raymond McGinley
Ross Sinclair
Joe McAlinden

BIBLIOGRAPHY AND SOURCES

Grant MacDougall
Gerard Love

Fast Forward
Margarita Vazquez Ponte
Angus McPake
Lenny Helsing
Nick Haines
Chris Henman
Michael Kerr
Ian Hoey
Sandy McLean
Katy Lironi
Davie Miller
Richard Scott
David Keegan

New interviews for this book
Martin Hayward
Eugene Kelly
David Keegan
Mal Kergan
Ian Binns
Chris Henman
Marigold Tully c/o Andrew Tully
Jonathan Muir
Alan McLean
Charles Kelly
Margarita Vasquez-Ponte
Gerard McInulty

Angus McPake
Brian Guthrie
Andrew Tully
John McCorkindale
Jim Shepherd
Murray Dalglish
Paul McDermott
Michael Kerr
Stephen McLean
John 'Joogs' Martin
Laura McPhail
Ann Donald
Ian Hoey
Mark Allan
Duglas T. Stewart
Sean Dickson
Hugh McLachlan
Sushil Dade
Fran Schoppler
Ian Boffey
Jimmy Jamieson
David Barker
Martin Parry
George Miller
Chris Davidson
Derek Moir
Paul Livingston
John Douglas
John Niven
Grant McLean

BIBLIOGRAPHY AND SOURCES

Craig McAllister
Allan Carruthers
Andy Crone
Andrew O'Hagan
Stuart Cant
David Scott
Janie Nicoll
Graham MacDonald
Steve Mason
John Scally
Chris Quinn
James Hackett
David Douglas McArthur
Neville Street
Chris Connelly
John Vick
Davie Miller
James MacDonald
Ian White
Roy Lawrence
Gordon Keen
John Gibbs
Nick Kennedy
David Scott (The Motorcycle Boy)
David Scott (The Pearlfishers)
Douglas MacIntyre
Paul Campion
Caz Riley
Monica Queen
Johnny Smillie

Dave Gormley
Andrew McDermid
Mark Raine
Jason McPhail

Picture Credits

Page 22: *On Our Honeymoon* 7" by The Wake, courtesy of Gerard McInulty

Page 33: Green Telescopes, courtesy of Lenny Helsing

Page 41: Rote Kapelle Balerno Town Hall poster, courtesy of Andrew Tully

Page 45: Rote Kapelle in the Niddry Street Vaults, courtesy of Mal Kergan

Page 49: Waterloo Bar poster, courtesy of Andrew Tully

Page 50: The Jasmine Minks at Living Room, courtesy of Jim Shepherd

Page 99: Miners' Benefit poster, courtesy of Andrew Tully

Page 102: 'They Brought Shame on Scotland', *The Sunday Post* excerpts, 18 August 1985. *The Sunday Post* ©DC Thomson & Co Ltd.

Page 115: Splash One Happening poster, courtesy of Grant MacDougal

Page 143: Jesse Garon and the Desperadoes live at the Onion Cellar (1987), courtesy of Ross McIntyre

Page 154: Posters courtesy of Lenny Helsing and Stuart Cant
Page 156: Moray House poster, courtesy of Andrew Tully
Page 158: *Shop Assistants* album cover, 1986, courtesy of David Keegan
Page 177: *C86* inner track listing, courtesy of Cherry Red
Page 224: The Vaselines, courtesy of Mark Flunder
Page 234: Onion Cellar poster, courtesy of Stuart Cant
Page 238: The Motorcycle Boy, courtesy of Steve Speller
Page 239: Meat Whiplash with Alex Taylor on vocal, courtesy of Ross McIntyre
Page 251: The Vultures, courtesy of Lenny Helsing
Page 276: The Vaselines *Dying for It* EP, courtesy of Sandy McClean
Page 278: The Hardy Boys, courtesy of Graeme Givan
Page 297: The Pastels and The Vaselines with Finitribe's Davie Miller, courtesy of Bret Lunsford and Davie Miller
Page 309: McDonalds Fuck Off poster, courtesy of Davie Miller
Page 311: Ministry with Chris Connelly, courtesy of Paul Elledge and Chris Connelly
Page 326: The Wendys, Paris 1990, prior to playing La Locomotive, courtesy of Peter Walsh
Page 328: *NME* single of the week: The Wendys
Page 366: *NME* article on Captain America name change
Page 367: Excerpt from *The Daily Record*
Page 370: Nirvana Live with Eugene Kelly by David Markey, image still from *Teenage Superstars*, courtesy of the author
Page 371: Nirvana tour flyer with Captain America as support
Page 377: The Batfinx and Keith Douglas, courtesy of John Gibbs

Index

4AD Records 216, 221–2, 331
23 Skidoo 116
53rd & 3rd Records 125–9, 131, 146–7, 149, 169–70, 228, 336
1000 Violins 201, 235

a.c. acoustics 408–11, 413–14, 415–17, 425–30
Adam, Graham 256, 258
Adventures in Stereo 403, 404
Allan, Mark 100–3
Allen, Carolyn 23
Allen, Steven 12, 23
Altered Images 8, 12, 26, 27
Alway, Mike 79
Apartment Six 204
Apes In Control 257, 258

Appendix Out 403
Armstrong, Matt 383
Associates, The 8
Aztec Camera 7

Baby Lemonade 251–4
Bain, Willie 256
Bannister, Alan 279–80
Barker, David 170–1, 173, 243, 346–7, 348, 364
Barker, Paul 301, 302–3, 311–12
Barr, Jim 209, 210
Barr, Paul 208, 210, 418
Batchelor Pad, The 201, 253–7
Beards, Dave 37
Beattie, Jim 26, 27, 65–7, 87, 115, 318, 319, 320, 404, 418

Béchirian, Roger 198
Beeville Hive 5 33, 36, 38, 154, 156, 235, 251
Bell, Max 80, 88
Best, Simon 16, 18–19
Beveridge, Ian 276
Big Flame 116
Big Gun 179–88
Big Life label 150–1
Binns, Ian 36, 37, 39–40, 46, 252, 285
Black, Jeremy 287
Blake, Norman: Alex Chilton/Big Star 431–5; Bennets club 227; BMX Bandits 149, 341, 362; The Boy Hairdressers 167, 169, 344–5; Francis Macdonald collaboration 406; musical friendships 112; musical beginnings 105–6, 107; Nirvana gig 358–9; The Pretty Flowers 109; Sounds article 349–50; Teenage Fanclub 344–5, 384–5, 386–90, 391, 445, 448–9; The Vaselines 228
Blakeway, Ted 216, 217
Blakey, Colin 35
Blanco Y Negro label 79, 87–8

Bluebells, The 8
BMX Bandits: Bellshill town's influence 103–7; *C86* album 340–2; Creation Records/Sony deal 436–40; Eugene Kelly and *Star Wars* 360–2; formation 143–5; live album 340; membership changes 394, 395; promotions and releases 145–8, 149–50; 'Serious Drugs' release 393–4; Subterraneans (club) 209
Bofey, Ian 160–1, 162, 163–4, 203–4, 205–6
Bollen, Andy 364
Bonini, Michael 279
Boon, Richard 28
Boots For Dancing 7
Bored 4
Bourgie Bogey 8
Boy Hairdressers, The 167–9, 344–5
Boyle, Denis 38, 156
Boyle, Judith 404
Boyle, Raymond 368
Branston, Carole 12
Broudie, Ian 327, 329–30
Bruces's Records 4, 16

INDEX

Buba & the Shop Assistants 46–9, 72
Buchanan, Ronnie 211–12
Buckle, Kevin 286
Burn, Tam Dean 2
Burt, Calvin 156, 218
Buzzcocks 4

C86 compilation 177
Callis, Jo 5
Cameron, Duncan 413
Cameron, Keith 349–50, 355
Campion, Paul 409–10, 413–14, 415–17, 426, 428, 429–30
Cant, Stuart 234–7
Cantrell, Laura 407
Captain America/Eugenius 361–9, 370
Carmichael, Ian 373
Carruthers, Allan 180, 181–2, 184–6, 187–9
Cartel, The (record distribution) 16–17, 29–30, 331–4, 454
Cathexis label 293, 296
Chart Show, The 123–4
Cheap Gods, The 13, 14–15, 48
Chegwin, Jeff 214, 217
Cherry, Tommy 254–5
Chilton, Alex 406, 431–6
Clark, Stuart 136, 140
Clouds, The 209
Cobain, Kurt 356, 359, 369–70
Cocteau Twins 220–3
Connelly, Chris: Finitribe 290–1, 293–4, 295–6, 301–2, 303–4, 313–14; Ministry 311–13; Revolting Cocks 303–4, 309–10; Whiplash Boychild album 312–13
Connelly, Eddie: Meat Whiplash 63, 82–3; Motorcycle Boy 239, 240, 242; Narodnik Records 134, 141, 142, 232; The Vultures 252
Cotter, Martin 255, 256, 257–60
Cowell, Simon 220
Crawford, Moray 42, 48, 74–5, 100
Creation Records: BMX Bandits 393–4, 436–40; distribution choices 331; ethos 53–4; influences 24–5; The Jasmine Minks 56; Jesus and Mary Chain

59–62; The Pastels 55, 171–2; Primal Scream 66–7; Teenage Fanclub 387–9
Creeping Bent Records 403–5
Crispie Crunchies, The 41–2
Crone, Andy 179, 180–1, 184, 186, 188–9
Cropper, Steve 174
Cruickshank, Stewart 399
Cutler, Ivor 53

Dade, Sushil 111, 112, 119, 274–5, 352–3
Dalgleish, Murray 59–61
Davidson, Chris 204–10, 418
Davis, Elliot 66, 216, 217–18
De Vries, Marius 315–16
Dead Neighbours 211–13
Del Amitri 8
Delmontes, The 13–14, 15
Dessau, Bruce 89
Dickson, Sean: BMX Bandits 144–5, 147, 148; EP disaster 121–2; musical friendships 112; musical beginnings 104, 106, 109–10; Soup Dragons 111, 113–14, 119–20, 121–3, 271–4, 314–17, 350–5, 400–2

Dine, Simon 196
Distemper 278–9
Doe, John 38, 156
Donald, Ann 71, 74, 75–7, 94, 127–8, 230, 233
Donnelly, Joe 12, 23
Douglas, John 183, 195–6, 197–8
Dragsters, The 160–2, 203, 209
Drive 4
Duffy, Jeff 235–6

Ege Bam Yasi 299–301
Elemental label 416
Evans, Nick 416
Everest, Stuart 212, 220
Exile, The 4

Factory Records 23, 27–8, 327–31, 331–2
Fagan, Graham 183, 189
Famous Monsters, The 225, 226
fanzines: *Anytime Swing* 180, 189; *'Are You Scared to Get Happy?'* 254–5; *Baby Bites Back* 280; *Bum Note* 192–4; *Communication Blur* 54; *It Ticked and Exploded* 13;

INDEX

Juniper Berri Berri 46;
Maximum Rocknroll 279;
Pure Popcorn! 111, 119;
Slow Dazzle 204–8
Fast Forward distribution: 53rd & 3rd Records 125–7; Brian Gutherie's involvement 218–19; Fast Product links 16–19, 29–30; Finitribe 292; Rote Kapelle single 98; Sandy McLean's management 30–1, 131–3
Fast Product 5–7, 16–19, 29–30
Faulkner, Eric 220
Felt 53, 118, 209
Findlay, Bruce 4, 5, 398–9
Finitribe: Animal Farm EP 307–9; 'De Testimony.' 295–7; electronic music projects/productions 304–6, 314; formation and early recordings 291–4; musical influences 290–1, 294–5; support gigs 298–9; Wax Trax! Records releases 301–2
Fire Engines 6, 7, 34
Fizzbombs, The 229–33
Flame Up! 282–3

Fleming, Don 348, 385, 386–7
Flowers 6
Flunder, Mike 248
Forde, Paul 195, 196
Foster, Joe: Creation Records 52, 53–4; Jesus and Mary Chain 59; The Living Room Club 50–1, 52; North London Poly gig 1985 85; The Pastels 67; Whaam! Records 24, 25
Fraser, Liz 221–3
French Impressionists 8
Future Pilot AKA 403

Gallagher, Liam 422, 423
Gallanders, Ross 38, 156
Gang of Four 5
Garden, Stewart 191
Gash, Jim 398
Gedge, David 193, 236
Gibbs, John 377–8, 381–2, 383
Gillespie, Bobby: Jesus and Mary Chain 58–9, 89–90; local band promotion 113–14; press interview 89; Primal Scream origins 26, 27, 87; Primal Scream's evolution 65–7, 152, 318–20; Splash One Club

469

114, 117; The Wake membership 23, 27
Gladstone, Charlie 216–17
Glasgow City Council 5
Glass Records 170–4
Godard, Vic 404
Gordon, Douglas 162
Gormley, Dave 410, 412–14, 416–17
Green Telescope, The 32–6, 154–5, 235
Gretton, Rob 28
Groovy Little Numbers, The 168, 169–70, 209
Guthrie, Brian 29–30, 211–23, 334–5
Guthrie, Robin 212, 216, 220, 221–3

Hackett, James 268, 269–70, 372, 374, 376
Haigh, Peter 76, 98, 201, 202
Haines, Nick 29–30
Hall or Nothing PR 419
Hanson, Johnny 279–80
Hardy Boys, The 209, 278–82
Harris, David 256
Harron, Billy 209
Hart, Douglas: Baby Lemonade single 254; Jesse Garon and the Desperadoes production 141–3; Jesus and Mary Chain 57–8, 59–61; Meat Whiplash 63; Motorcycle Boy video 241; North London Poly gig 1985 80, 84
Harte, Paul 115
Haynes, Matt 255, 268–70
Hayward, Martin: Alan McGee & Creation 54; The Cheap Gods 13, 14–15; The Pastels 15, 20, 67–9, 171, 172–4, 244–7, 248–51, 321–5; Radio Sweethearts 406
Head, Jowe 25, 52, 53, 131
Heggie, Bill 212, 220, 223
Helsing, Lenny 33, 34–6, 37, 38, 154–5, 156–7
Henderson, Robert 399
Henman, Chris 40–2, 44–5, 71, 73, 77–8, 97–8, 99, 262, 285, 289
Hipsway 8
Hitsville Greaseguns 382, 383
Hoey, Ian 95, 128, 129, 160–1, 163, 164–5
Hogarty, John 326, 395
Horne, Alan 7, 8, 14

INDEX

Househunters 131
Hughes, Davy 183
Human League, The 5, 7
Hunt, Lu 429–30
Hynds, Pauline 374

Innes, Andrew 50
Irvine, Linda 235–6
Irvine Music Club 191–4

Jacobites 209–10
Jamieson, Jimmy 161–2
Jamieson, Peter 203–4
Jasmine Minks, The 52, 56, 83, 84, 86–7, 201
Jazz Butcher 50
Jazzateers, The 8
Jenkins, Matt 399
Jesse Garon and the Desperadoes: early releases 141–3; last recording and break-up 285–9; membership changes 135–40; shared membership 262; Shop Assistants tour 163, 164–5; showcase gig, London 263–6
Jesus and Mary Chain 57–62, 79, 80–5, 87, 88
Johnny & the Self Abusers 4, 5

Johnson, Calvin 356
Josef K 7
Joseph, Eric 411
Jourgensen, Al 301–2, 311–12
Joy Division 5
June Brides 52, 118

Kaisers, The 382, 383
Keegan, David: 53rd & 3rd Records 125, 126–7, 228; Buba & the Shop Assistants 46–9; Crispie Crunchies, The 41–2; Edinburgh music scene 43; Napier College connections 71–2, 74; The Pastels, guest musician 323; Rote Kapelle 44; The Shop Assistants 74–5, 93–6, 125, 127, 128, 159, 165–6; The Stayrcase 37; Union City label and The Dragsters 160–1; The Vaselines EP 276
Keen, Gordon 342, 361, 364, 365, 368
Kelly, Charles 12, 225, 276–7, 335–6, 337, 338, 356–7, 359
Kelly, Eugene: BJ Youth Theatre 411; BMX Bandits 360–2; Captain America/

Eugenius 361–2, 363, 364–6; The Famous Monsters 225, 226; musical influences 224–5; Nirvana, Vaselines support 356–7, 358–9; The Pastels, guest musician 321; Splash One Club 118; The Vaselines 226–7, 228, 276, 277, 336, 337, 339
Kennedy, Nick 378–80
Kergan, Mal 36, 37, 39–40
Kerr, Andy 181–2, 187, 190–1
Kerr, Michael 63, 80–5, 90–3, 134, 240–1, 242
Kershaw, Andy 124
Kimpton Howe, George 334
King, James 8
King, Robert 296
Kingfishers, The 405
Kneale, Sarah 72, 233
Kopf, Biba 88
Kostrzewa, Tony 30

Lambie, Jim 167, 227
Last, Bob 5–6, 7, 16, 17–18, 29, 30
Laughing Apple, The 50
Lawrence, Roy 366–9
Lawrence, Vince 310

Legend, The 54, 119
Leopards, The 403, 404
Liberators, The 212, 220–1
Lironi, Katy 71, 74, 230, 231, 232, 233, 404
Living Room Club, The 50–2, 59–60
Livingston, Paul 194–5, 196–7, 198–9
Loder, John 299
Loft, The 50, 52, 116
Long, Janice 148, 186, 214
Longalong, Hermie 399
Lorentson, Craig 211
Loudon, Derek 115, 116
Love, Gerard: Alex Chilton 433–4; Big Star influences 431, 432; Francis Macdonald collaboration 406; Teenage Fanclub 345–6, 347, 348, 385–6, 389–92, 441–5, 446–8, 449–51
Love, Lenny 4
Lowlife 211–12, 213–18

Maben, Johnny 382–3
MacDonald, Andy 196–7
Macdonald, Francis 385; Alex Chilton/Big Star 431,

434–5; BMX Bandits 150, 340, 362, 394; The Boy Hairdressers 167–8, 169; Captain America 364; musical friendships 112; Shoeshine label 405–7; Teenage Fanclub 345–7
MacDonald, Graham 253–4
MacDougall, Grant 115, 117
MacIntyre, Douglas 6, 403–5
Marc Riley & The Creepers 209
Marshall, Kenny 419
Martin, John 'Joogs' 65–7, 89, 115–17, 152–3, 319–20
Martin, Keith 181–2, 184
Mason, Steve 377–8, 380–1
Mathieson, Ewan 371
Matter Babies, The 213, 218
Maxwell, Louise 115
Mazda, Richard 322
McAlinden, Joe: Alex Chilton/Big Star 433, 435; Big Star fan 432; BMX Bandits 149, 150, 342, 393, 394, 395–7; The Boy Hairdressers 167–8, 169; Groovy Little Numbers 169–70; musical friendships 112–13; Superstar 395–6

McAlister, Craig 191–3
McAlpine, Brian 398
McArdle, Willie 145
McArthur, David Douglas 278–81, 282–3
McCarthy 201, 202–3
McConville, Bruce 'Lyall' 35, 380
McCorkindale, John 13, 47–8
McCulloch, Jim: BMX Bandits 145, 147, 148, 149; musical friendships 112; Soup Dragons 149, 271, 273–5, 315, 351, 354
McDaid, George 183
McDermid, Andrew 417–25
McDermott, Paul 63, 64, 83, 84–5, 91, 239, 240
McDonald, Finlay 405
McDowall, Grant 211
McFedries, Sean 192–3
McGee, Alan: Blanco Y Negro label 87; BMX Bandits 393–4, 437–8; Bobby Gillespie 26; Creation Records, inspirations 24–5; Creation Records origins 52–3; Francis Macdonald correspondence 406–7; Jesus and Mary Chain 59,

60; The Living Room Club 50–2; North London Poly gig 1985 84–5; The Pastels 55, 171–2; Superstar 395; Teenage Fanclub 387–9

McGinley, Raymond: Big Star fan 431; The Boy Hairdressers 167, 168; Teenage Fanclub 339, 344–5, 348, 385, 386, 388, 392, 441–4, 445–6

McGlynn, Simon 291, 294

McGregor, Andy 291, 293

McGurk, Tam 65, 66, 89–90, 152, 153, 318–19

McInulty, Gerald 11–12, 22–3, 27

McKee, Frances: Nirvana, Vaselines support 356, 357–8; The Pretty Flowers 107–8, 109, 110; Splash One Club 118; The Vaselines 226–8, 277, 336–7, 338

McKenna, Roddy 420–1

Mclachlan, Hugh 107, 108–9, 110

McLachlan, Ian 278, 279–80

McLean, Alan 35, 37, 155, 156

McLean, Grant 194

McLean, Sandy: 53rd & 3rd Records 125–7, 128, 228; BMX Bandits debut 147; The Cartel's and Fast Forward's demise 331–4; Fast Forward distribution 16–17, 18–19, 29–31; Narodnik Records 134; record label expansion 132–3; Rote Kapelle's debut 97–8

McLean, Stephen 63–4, 81–2, 84, 90, 92

McMahon, Kevin 136, 140

McNeil, Paul 115

McPake, Angus: Fast Forward productions 133; The Fizzbombs 229–30, 231–2; Green Telescope 155; Jesse Garon and the Desperadoes 138, 140–1, 286–8; musical influences 33, 36–7; Pastels influence 25–6; populist bands, view on 31–2; Rubber Dolfinarium 38; The Vultures 251; Wump Records 155

McPhail, Jason 433, 436

McPhail, Laura 71, 74, 76–7, 94–5, 128, 163

INDEX

McRobbie (Pastel), Stephen: 53rd & 3rd Records 126, 146; Buba & the Shop Assistants 47-8, 49; The Pastels 14, 21, 23-4, 54-5, 171-2, 174, 245, 246-7, 248-50, 325; The Vaselines, advisor to 227-8, 277, 356
Meat Whiplash 62-4, 80-5, 90-3
Mekons, The 5, 51
Melody Maker articles 130, 350
Memphis 8
Miller, Davie 291-3, 296-8, 302, 304-5
Miller, George 203-4, 382-3
Mindpipes, The 209
Ministry 311-12, 313
Mitchell, Keith 215-16
Moir, Derek 199-203
Monaghan, Steve 35
Moodie, Greg 383
Moore, Thurston 452-3
Morrison, Grant 255
Morrison, Hilary 3, 5-6
Motorcycle Boy 237-42
Mr Egg (aka James McDonald) 299-301

Muir, Jonathan 46, 71, 75, 98, 261-2, 285
Mullen, Derek 279-80, 281

Napalm Stars, The 175
Narodnik Records: Baby Lemonade 254; The Fizzbombs 232; formation and early signings 134-5; The Vultures 252
Nectarine No. 9, The 403, 404
Nevin, Pat 116
New Order 28, 331
Next Projected Sound 209
Nicoll, Janie 238, 251-2, 252-3
Nightingales, The 51, 52
Nirvana 229, 275, 355-9, 369-71, 384
Niven, John 182-4, 188, 189-90, 194
NME articles: Bobby Gillespie 114; C86 compilation 176-7; Jesus and Mary Chain 59, 61-2, 88; Soup Dragons 119-20, 124; The Wendys 328
No Bad Records 4
Nocturnal Vermin 100-3
NRG Records 4

Oakenfold, Paul 296–7
Oasis 422–4
Offhooks, The 218
O'Hagan, Andrew 180, 181–2, 185, 186–7, 188
O'Hare, Brendan 347, 363, 364, 385, 445, 446
Oldham, Andrew Loog 415
One Little Indian label 306, 308
Onion Cellar, The 200, 234–7
Orange Juice 7
Orchids, The 267–71, 372–6

Paperhouse Records 346–7, 364
Parker, Karen 49, 115
Parry, Martin 175
Parsons, Fred 300
Pastels, The: band collaborations 47–8; band reforms 326; band relations/tensions 248–51; band's attitudes/ambitions 20–1, 25–6; 'Crawl Babies' single 248–9; Creation Records releases 54–5, 67–9; debut release 23–4; Glass Records deal 170–5; member sackings 325; origins 13–15;

Sitting Pretty, recording of 321–4; Splash One Club 116; Subterraneans (club) 209; *Up for a Bit* recordings 243–8
Paterson, Kenny 419
Pearce, Kevin 86
Pearlfishers, The 397–400
Peel, John 120, 185–6, 187, 208, 403, 404
Peutherer, John 42, 48
Pieroni, Basil 182, 183
Pinksy, Philip 291
Pioneer Corps 213, 218
Placebo 429–30
Pop Will Eat Itself 163–4, 236
Pop:Aural 6–7
Port Sulphur 404–5
post-punk scene 5–9, 453–4
Postcard Records 7, 8
Powell, Richard 333–4
Pragnell, Sophie 277
Prescription, The 36
Pretty Flowers, The 107–11
Primal Scream: band evolution 65–7; debut release 89; Gillespie/Beattie origins 26, 27; 'Loaded' and *Screamadelica* 320; member departures

INDEX

318–20; press articles 88–9;
'Velocity Girl' release 152–3
Prince, Bill 190, 191
Pterodactyls 380
punk, arrival and influence
1–5, 453

Queen, Monica 411, 413, 415
Quinn, Chris 267, 268–9,
270–1, 372–3, 374–6
Quinn, Paul 8, 315, 445, 446

Radio Sweethearts 406
Raine, Mark 426–9
Rampling, Danny 296–7, 304
Raw TV label 150–1
Raymonde, Simon 212
Reader, Frank 183, 195–6,
197–8
Red Rhino 29, 30, 201, 333
Reid, Jim 59
Restricted Code 7
Revolting Cocks 302–3,
309–10
Reynolds, Eugene 382–3
Reynolds, Simon 7
Rezillos, The 4–5
Rieflin, Bill 301, 313
Riley, Caz 409–11, 416, 417,
425–6, 427

Rivers, John 171, 173–4,
243–4
Robb, John 339–40
Ross, Jim 12
Ross, Malcolm 6
Rossi, Marco 203, 204
Rote Kapelle: debut release
97–9; first gig 40–2; last
recording and break-up
285; membership changes
44–6, 70–1, 72–3; origins
38–44
Rough Trade 17–18, 54–5,
158–9, 218, 241, 331, 333–4
Roundabouts, The 209
Rubber Dolfinarium, The 38,
156

Safe Houses 279–80
Sager, Gareth 405
Sarah Records 268–70, 284
Saxe, Phil 327, 328
Scally, John 267, 269, 270,
373, 374, 376
Scan 45 22
Scars 6, 34
Schoppler, Fran 138–9
Scot, Jock 403, 404
Scott, David 238–40, 241–2,
397–400

477

Scott, Richard 17–18, 30, 331, 334
Scritti Politti 7
Scrivner, Claire 380
Secession 12
Second Generation, The 378–81
Secret Goldfish, The 403, 404
Seenan, James 277, 364
Sensible Records 5
Sexual Objects, The 405
Shamen, The 306–7
Shelley, Michael 407
Shepherd, Jim 52, 56, 83–4, 86–7
Sherbet Tambourines, The 209
Shoeshine label 405–7
Shop Assistants, The: 53rd & 3rd Records debut 126–8; Blue Guitar signing 158–9; debut release success 93–6; early rehearsals and gigs 74–7; EP disaster 121–2; exit and break-up 164–5; membership 71, 72, 74; promotional tour 163–5
Shoppler, Fran 138–9, 140, 141–2, 265, 286, 288–9
Sidelnyk, Steve 316
Simple Minds 5, 31–2
Simpson, Bernice: The Delmontes 13–14, 15; The Pastels 15, 20–1, 172–3, 174–5, 244, 245–7, 249–50, 325
Sinclair, Ross 111–12, 114, 119, 120–1, 150, 274
Skids, The 4
Smarties, Wilf 306
Smillie, Johnny 411–12, 415
Smiths, The 62
Smyth, Karen 300
Sonic Youth 116, 117
Sounds articles 88, 130–1, 148, 339–40, 349–50
Soup Dragons, The: EP disaster 121–2; first gig booked 113–14; flexi-disc and John Peel hit 119–21; 'I'm Free' success 350–5; indie-dance era 314–17, 350–1; origins 111–12; Radio 1 airplay 271–2; Raw TV and Big Life labels 150–1; Sire Records, signing and drop 272–5; Subterraneans (club) 209; US success 400–2; 'Whole Wide World' 122–3, 124

INDEX

Spark, Rod 379–80
Speedboat 405–6
Splash One Club 115–18
Stanley, Bob 350, 419
Stayrcase, The 37
Steel, David 211
Stella Five Records 281–2
Stewart, Duglas T.: Alex Chilton/Big Star 433, 436; Bellshill and musical influences 103–5, 106–7; BMX Bandits 144–6, 147–8, 167, 341–3, 360, 362, 393, 394, 436–40; musical friendships 112; The Pretty Flowers 108–11; Scottish indie music 452; Splash One Club 117–18; The Vaselines 228
Stout, Mike 185, 257
Stranded Records 175
Strasbourg Club 200–1
Strawberry Switchblade 8
Street, Neville 281–2
Stricevic, Mil 398
Styng Rites 203–4, 382
Subs, The 5
Subterraneans (club) 208–10, 418
Subway Organization 93–4, 121–2

Subway Sect 404
Sudden, Nikki 52, 209–10
Summers, Jazz 150
Sunday Drivers, The 191–4
Superstar 395–7
Swamplands 8

Taft, Thomas 208
Taylor, Alex 44, 49, 71, 72, 139, 165–6, 239
Taylor, Neil 59, 61–2, 114
Taylor (Pastel/Superstar), Brian 14–15, 21, 172–3, 174, 243–4, 247, 249, 406
Teenage Fanclub: American connections 384, 385–6, 391–2; *Bandwagonesque* 386–7, 388–91; Big Star fans 430–3; Britpop, reaction to 448–9; CBGBs gig 348; debut album, recording of 342, 347; formation 344–6; *Grand Prix* 445–7, 450; *The King* 387–8; music press articles 349–50; record deals 346–7, 348, 349, 392; *Songs From Northern Britain* 451; *Thirteen* 441–5, 450
Television Personalities 24, 33, 209, 235

479

Thanes, The 156–7, 380
This Poison! 199–203, 236
Thompson, Billy 115
Thompson, Peter 12
Thornton, Andy 399
Three Johns, The 51
Thrum 411–15
Toner, Michael 220
Tong, Pete 296–7
Townsend, Cenzo 330
Trashcan Sinatras, The 179, 183, 191, 194–9
Travis, Geoff 54–5, 79, 87, 158–9, 240, 264, 265–6
Treacy, Dan 23–5, 234–5
Tully, Andrew: Fast Forward productions 133; Jesse Garon and the Desperadoes 135–8, 139–40, 141, 163, 164–5, 232, 263–6; Nirvana 358, 371; Rote Kapelle 39–40, 42–3, 44, 73, 78, 262; Shop Assistants success 128–9, 132; triple band membership 261–3
Tully, Marigold 41
Turnball, Paul 404
Turner, John 215–16, 220
TV Personalities 51

Valves, The 4, 5
Vann, Alisdair 405
Vaselines, The: debut release 228–9; demise of 338–9; *Dum Dum* 336, 337–9; Dying For It EP 275–7; formation 226–8; musical influences 224–5; Nirvana support 355–9; touring 335–7
Vazquez Ponte, Margarita: The Fizzbombs 229, 230–1, 233; Jesse Garon and the Desperadoes 135, 136, 138, 139, 140–1, 142, 263–6; Rote Kapelle 71 3, 96, Shop Assistants success 74; triple band membership 261
Vick, John 291–3, 295–6, 298–9, 302, 304, 305, 306–9
Villines, Jessica 313
Visitors, The 34, 291–2
Vultures, The 251–3

Wadd, Clare 268–70
Wake, The 11–12, 22–3, 26, 27–8
Walker, Scott 405

INDEX

Warby, Russell 422
Ward, Roger 409, 425–6
Warrior 220
Watson, Jamie 252, 254, 286, 365, 380
Watson, John 380
Watts-Russell, Ivo 221–2
Wax Trax! Records 301–2
Weather Prophets, The 91, 116, 209, 210
Weatherall, Andy 304, 320
Wedding Present, The 193, 200, 201, 236
Wee Cherubs, The 257–60
Wells, Bill 399, 403
Wendys, The 326–31

Whaam! Records 23–5
White, Ian 327–31
White, John 279–80
White Riot tour, 1977 2–3
Whiteout 417–25
Wilson, Tony 28, 329, 331
Win 8
Wire 116
Wishing Stones 182, 189–91
Wright, Annabel (Aggi) 46, 48, 174, 228, 248, 250

Young, Robert 65, 66

Zachman, Stuart 313
Zoom! Records 4, 5